CREATION IN CRISIS

SCIENCE, ETHICS, THEOLOGY

JOSHTROM ISAAC KUREETHADAM

ORBIS BOOKS

Maryknoll, New York 10545

ORBIS ✪ BOOKS
Maryknoll, New York 10545

Fathers and Brothers
MARYKNOLL™

Founded in 1970, Orbis Books endeavors to publish works that enlighten the mind, nourish the spirit, and challenge the conscience. The publishing arm of the Maryknoll Fathers and Brothers, Orbis seeks to explore the global dimensions of the Christian faith and mission, to invite dialogue with diverse cultures and religious traditions, and to serve the cause of reconciliation and peace. The books published reflect the views of their authors and do not represent the official position of the Maryknoll Society. To learn more about Maryknoll and Orbis Books, please visit our website at www.maryknollsociety.org.

Library of Congress Cataloging-in-Publication Data

Kureethadam, Joshtrom Isaac.
    Creation in crisis : science, ethics, theology / Joshtrom Isaac Kureethadam.
        pages cm
    Includes bibliographical references and index.
    ISBN 978-1-62698-100-3 (pbk.)
    1. Human ecology—Religious aspects—Christianity.   2. Ecotheology.
3. Poverty—Religious aspects—Christianity.   4. Church work with the poor.
I. Title.
BT695.5.K87 2014
261.8'8—dc23

2014009963

In loving memory of my dad, Isaac Kureethadam,
and my mum, Annamma Isaac Kureethadam,
who initiated me
into the world of letters.

Contents

Part II
THE CRY OF THE EARTH

Preface

My interest in ecological concerns dates back nearly a quarter of a century. After completing my postgraduate degree in philosophy, I taught cosmology for the first time in the early 1990s. While exploring the profound mysteries of the physical universe, our infinitely vast cosmic home, I also began to take note of how things were beginning to go radically amiss with our immediate planetary home, Earth. Ever since then I have tried to pass on to my students not only a sense of awe and wonder before the grandeur and majesty of the universe, but also a deep sense of concern for the increasingly precarious state of our common earthly home.

I offered my first seminar in ecology at the Salesian University in Rome in 2002, and since 2005 I have regularly taught a course in ecology for our postgraduate students while continuing to lecture on cosmology for the undergraduates. A realization that has grown within me ever since I began to take classes in ecology has been about the need to develop a broader and holistic understanding of the contemporary ecological crisis. In our present day the ecological crisis gets mostly reduced, unfortunately, to a mere "environmental" problem, or even a host of them. We do not realize that it is our "common home" itself that is in peril. In fact, our home planet is unique in the vast universe for its capacity to host advanced forms of life, at least as far as our current knowledge goes. The ecological crisis poses a real and unprecedented threat to the very capacity of Earth to be a "home" for humans and the rest of the biotic community.

In this context it is important to widen our understanding of the ecological crisis. All too often it is seen as a mere physical problem and a largely scientific concern. However, the crisis is also profoundly ethical in nature, given that its victims are disproportionately the poor communities who have contributed least to causing the problem in the first place. At a still deeper level the ecological predicament is a profoundly spiritual crisis. From a theological perspective the crisis poses a grave challenge to the integrity of God's creation, as it interferes with the Creator's loving plan to let Earth teem with life.

From my acquaintance with the literature on ecological questions, I am aware that the physical aspects of the crisis are very well studied, thanks especially to the remarkable contribution from the scientific community in recent years. The moral dimension of the problem has also received increasing attention in the last couple of decades. There is much talk about eco-justice today, which is indeed a positive development. However, the spiritual and religious dimension of the problem appears to be neglected on the whole. The greatest lacuna, in my judgment, is that we are still to see the ecological crisis as a physical, moral, and spiritual problem, and in fact all these things at once. Our understanding of the crisis is still fragmented and rather sectorial. Only a holistic perception of the ecological crisis can awaken us to the true magnitude of the challenge facing our common planetary home.

It has been my desire for some time to write a book that provides a comprehensive understanding of the contemporary ecological crisis in response to the concerns expressed above. The present book is the humble result of a project that I began nearly five years ago. I managed to do most of the writing during a sabbatical period that I spent at Campion Hall at the University of Oxford from 2011 to 2012, and completed when I returned in the summer of 2013. I am grateful to the master of Campion Hall, Brendan Callaghan, and to all the members of Campion Hall for their kind hospitality. I thank particularly Gerard J. Hughes, the former master, who welcomed me first to Campion Hall in 2004–5 as a research scholar during my doctoral studies, and also Nicholas King and Joe Munitiz. A special word of thanks to Gerard W. Hughes, a prolific writer himself, who read through the manuscript of the first few chapters and gave very encouraging initial feedback.

I thank the Faculty of Philosophy of the Salesian University in Rome for having granted me the sabbatical period to work on this book project. A special word of thanks to my colleagues in the faculty who have been a great source of support, particularly Mauro Mantovani, Scaria Thuruthiyil, and Luis Rosón Galache.

I am deeply indebted to Gill Ness Collins, who meticulously proofread the entire manuscript and offered valuable corrections. I am also grateful to Annabel Clarkson, who corrected the first few chapters of the book and showed keen interest throughout. I also thank Banzelao Julio Teixeira, who read through an earlier draft of the manuscript.

I thank Robert Ellsberg, publisher of Orbis Books, for having accepted my proposal; James Keane, my editor; and the wonderful team at Orbis who skillfully guided me through the journey of getting the book ready for publication.

I would also like to thank all my friends, who have been a great source of support and encouragement over these years. They are too many to be mentioned individually here but are lovingly and gratefully remembered on this occasion.

A good number of the ideas of this book were developed and shared during classes, seminars, and workshops in the last few years in Italy, India, and the UK. I remember fondly in this regard all my former students and the participants of these courses. I remember especially the young people, who were usually the most attentive group to hear and discuss the situation of our common home that is increasingly imperilled by human activities. This book is dedicated to them, they who will have to bear most of the consequences of the mindless lifestyles of today's generations, and to future generations, with a word of apology.

In the end, I thank God—the one who puts into us the desire to work for his greater glory (cf. Phil 2:13)—for his infinite love and providential care that I have continued to experience also while working on this project. This book is the humble expression of the zeal to protect and preserve our common earthly home, which is ultimately God's own home where he pitched tent in the supreme event of the Incarnation. I pray that this book may in a small way contribute to inflaming "the zeal for your house" (Jn 2:17) in many hearts.

Introduction

The Crisis of Our Home

The contemporary ecological crisis is proving to be one of the most daunting challenges, and probably the most arduous one, that modern humans have faced since their evolution as Homo sapiens. The crisis is about our very home, the common home of the Planet Earth, where the survival and flourishing of the biotic community, including humanity, is increasingly under threat.

Right at the outset it needs to be clarified that the contemporary ecological crisis is not merely an environmental problem or even a host of environmental problems, as it is generally supposed. It is time to liberate the ecological discourse from the environmental straightjacket. For too long we have remained complacent, seeing more space allocated to environmental issues in newspaper columns, on television channels, on bookstore shelves, and increasingly even in school and university curricula. And for most people, *environment* has meant all this while merely something external and outside of themselves; as such, it has remained a peripheral and secondary concern.

Thus in the modern neoliberal economy—which is one of the major drivers of the mindless plundering of the planet through its paradigm of infinite growth, which necessitates ever increasing production of material goods and voracious consumption of them—ecological costs are considered as only "externalities." Accordingly, one does not realize that the economic growth that inflicts irreparable damages to entire ecosystems amounts to tearing down the pillars of our common home, or that capital accumulation through the depletion of natural resources means depriving other members of the family, present and future, of their rightful share of the common resources. Most of the promoters of green economy continue to advocate that a bit of recycling, use of fluorescent light bulbs, and similar efforts are all it takes to be environmentally friendly, without having to alter radically the present course of economic development or undergo drastic personal and community lifestyle changes. In this vein the dream of sustainable development has remained mostly a fashionable catch phrase; so far, it

1

does not appear to have gone beyond hollow promises, as was evident in the last Rio+20 Summit.[1]

The ecological crisis has remained a merely environmental problem even at some of the higher echelons of thinking and critical debates. Most schools of philosophical thinking that arose in the wake of public awareness about the ecological crisis, beginning from the 1970s, have meekly surrendered to being labeled environmental philosophy and have more or less restricted their speculative domains to environmental ethics, often cogitating on nuanced issues like the intrinsic worth of nonhuman species, the rights of animals, and so on. Few of them have dared to grapple with foundational questions like the metaphysical grounds underpinning humanity's distorted relationship with the natural world, as evident in the current ecological crisis. At a more practical level most of the Green movements that arose in recent decades in the Western hemisphere, spanning a wide spectrum from conservationists to animal liberation groups, have remained—with a few notable exceptions—on the peripheries of political and economic life, even after years of strident activism. In the meantime people have carried on with their routine lives, consuming material goods with increasingly rapacious appetites, enthralled by the glittering promises of the advertisement and lulled by the beliefs subtly driven home by the corporate industry and mainstream media that environmental concerns are, after all, only peripheral and marginal concerns.

The only notable exception in this regard has been the steady inflow of authoritative warnings from the scientific community—of which abundant use will be made in this book—building up into a crescendo during the last few decades. There has been no dearth of admonitions from the scientists urging the public to wake up from slumber because our common home is beginning to collapse around us. However, their warnings appear to have fallen on deaf ears. The political leadership, on the whole, appears unable to look beyond the daily dips and rises of the stock markets and their own winning prospects in the next round of elections. They have sadly lacked the foresight and wisdom to understand the dire implications of the threats facing our planetary home and our common household.

The gravity of the situation of our common home is often lost sight of even in well-intentioned approaches like those of the churches and religious traditions. For example, in the 2004 *Compendium of the*

---

[1] The Rio+20 Summit was the third of a series of Earth Summits organized by the United Nations to reflect on sustainable development. A summit is held once every ten years. The first Earth Summit took place in Rio de Janeiro in 1992, the second in Johannesburg in 2002, and the third in Rio de Janeiro in 2012.

Social Doctrine of the Church the question of the care of creation is taken up only in a late chapter, almost at the very end of the volume, and only after other weighty issues and challenges have been dealt with. The chapter is titled "Safeguarding the Environment." In this document, as in many others, the constant reference is to the environment, while forgetting that it is our very common home that is in danger. Even the recent 2012 synod of bishops on new evangelization appears to have forgotten that the fundamental command of the Lord is to "go into all the world and proclaim the good news to *the whole creation*" (Mk 16:15, emphasis added). In the "Final Propositions of the Synod" the question of the stewardship of creation is mentioned only in the last of the propositions (no. 56), coming just before the conclusion to the document.

The lack of urgency in dealing with the contemporary ecological crisis is paradigmatic of the approach of mainstream society in general—political and economic institutions, on the one hand, and religions and churches, on the other. While they appear to have awakened at last to the groaning of the planet, they continue, at the same time, to see them as mere environmental problems. The result is a surprising ignorance coupled with a lack of concern on the part of the otherwise literate general public on such an important question as the alarming situation of our common home and the plight of millions of its least fortunate inhabitants. This ignorance is matched only by a frightening lethargy when it comes to action.

We have, indeed, a paradoxical situation today. On the one hand, there has been an explosion of environmental activism in recent years: environmental groups have sprouted in many parts of the world; environmental literature has grown a thousandfold, not to speak of environmental websites; and most universities have begun to offer courses in environmental concerns. Even oil companies and automobile groups are jostling to appear green. At the same time, reports from the scientific community indicate in no uncertain terms that the state of our home planet is deteriorating year after year, that many of the natural processes that sustain life on Earth are on the verge of collapse and that our common home is in danger.

Today we stand in need of nothing short of a paradigm shift in understanding and dealing with the crisis facing our home planet. Here, like in any crisis, we need to return to the roots, to the essentials, to the basic truths. In fact, if we were to follow the etymological route, the crisis has to do with the discourse (*logos*) centered around our common home (*oikos*). To see things in this perspective we will need to rediscover Earth as home more than as the mere environment that surrounds us. Only when we see and love Earth as our home, our common home, our only home, and see ourselves as Earthlings, children of Earth, *imago mundi*—literally formed from the dust of the earth—will we begin to understand the gravity of the contemporary ecological crisis. As I shall be arguing in the opening chapter, Earth is not only our *common* home but our *only* home, the home that engendered us and sustains us. Earth is not merely an environment that we can swap for another one by migrating somewhere else when our home planet becomes degraded beyond redemption, as it is sometimes presented in popular science fiction and in the techno-savvy media. Only when we learn to see the earth as our only home will we be willing to act to save it. For in saving our common home, we will be saving ourselves.

The right approach here would be to return to the book of Genesis, whose first verses take us to the dawn of creation. The creation narrative, unfolding as a majestic cosmic drama that spans over six celestial days, is centered on the preparation of a home for all living beings, including humans. Within the vault of the heavens a formless Earth is lovingly fashioned by the Creator into a beautiful home: separating the dry land from the waters; adorning it with trees and vegetation, flowers and fruits; and hosting living things of every kind, including birds, fish, and animals. In fact, animals and human beings are created only on the very last day, only after a proper abode has been prepared for them—a home to dwell in. The sequence of events in the creation saga is not casual. It is only after a home has been prepared that life, including human life, can be hosted there. In the second chapter of Genesis—in the second creation narrative—human beings are called to be responsible stewards of this wonderful home teeming with life. Similar accounts of creation, in which the earth is hailed as a home and entrusted to human stewardship, can be found in the creation narratives of many religious and cultural groups both large and small.

In a very insightful way Pope Benedict XVI summed up this important truth in *The Human Family: A Community of Peace,* his message for the World Day of Peace in 2008: "For the human family, this home is the earth," and it is "essential to *sense* that the earth is *our common home*" (nos. 7, 8, emphasis added).

It is fundamental to be in a home and to feel at home. These are the primary conditions that make all the rest possible. Life, human life, civilization, religion, philosophy, art, music, literature, science and technology, and a thousand other artifacts of human culture have been possible because there is the common home of the earth to dwell in, not vice versa. What is primary is being in this home; the rest, however important, are only secondary, because without the former the latter do not and cannot exist. Without our common home we cannot exist and flourish. Earth can exist without modern humans, as it has done for over 99.9 percent of its history, but we cannot exist without the earth. It is this common home that we are in the process of despoiling and destroying.

This book is about the crisis facing our common home (*oikos*), about how the capacity of the earth to be truly a home for all of humanity and for all living beings is increasingly placed in jeopardy. Breaking free of the environmental jargon in referring to the ecological crisis as the possible collapse of our common home adds a deeply existential dimension to the whole discussion. Seen in this way, we are not speaking of questions external and marginal to us. We are not talking about one of the many challenges that humanity has to face—and we know that there is no dearth of them. Instead, we are grappling with the destiny of our common home, indeed, humanity's common destiny, along with that of the rest of the biotic community. In fact, in front of this unprecedented crisis all our other crises—economic, social, moral, and so on—pale in comparison. *Primum vivere*—first, life—as the wise ancient adage attributed to Seneca goes. Without our common home, we cannot live, much less live well. When we pollute and despoil our common home, we are endangering the quality of our own life and well-being and that of other living beings on Earth, as well as of future generations, our children and their children. We cannot remain indifferent but must become passionate about the crisis facing our home and household.

Against this background the first part of the book will explore how the earth came to be shaped as a home in the larger context of cosmic evolution, and how the building blocks of our home planet came to be marvelously formed in the galactic furnaces of the vast universe, in complex processes that lasted for billions of years. It is amazing that Earth appears to be the only home for life—at least in its advanced stages—in the whole universe. Life evolved gradually on our home planet through a marvelous process of evolution stretching over millions of years; human beings themselves appeared only very recently. However, in a very short time human activities have reached proportions to threaten the very capacity of Earth to be a home for the whole of humanity and for the rest of living beings. Authoritative warnings from the scientific community in recent years tell us that humanity is about to cross crucial tipping points with regard to some of the fundamental geo-chemical processes that sustain life on our home planet. This is our current situation, and such a global predicament is the starting point of this book.

The main scope of this book is to offer a wider and integrated view of the crisis facing our common home by describing the ecological crisis—symbolically as well as in reality—as a triple cry of the earth, of the poor, and of "the gods." These three cries are attempts to look at the ecological predicament from three different angles—physical, moral, and religious—with a view to gaining a more complete view of the crisis. These three cries are explored in detail in the remaining three sections of the book.

The cry of the earth is taken up in the second part of the book. In this section some of the main physical manifestations of the ecological crisis are analyzed. The phenomenon of global warming and associated climate change is the most evident and long-lasting manifestation of the ecological crisis today—with a wide range of impacts like droughts and floods, melting of glaciers and sea level rise, ocean acidification and coral bleaching, and a host of others. However, global warming and climate change do not exhaust the ecological crisis as the cry of the earth. We go on to examine how we are literally pulling out living rivets from the living organism of the earth, which shelters us within its biospheric womb, as evident in the phenomenon of species extinction and biodiversity loss. Further, we explore how we have polluted our common home: its atmosphere, its land, and its waters. Equally important is the fast depletion of natural resources of our common household. We shall see how, for example, in the case of fresh water, we are fast depleting the very source of life itself for humanity and for our fellow species. The cry of the earth includes the multiple groans of our home planet, the manifold ways in which our common home is imperiled. So in the physical understanding of the ecological crisis I try to offer a more complete understanding of the ecological predicament than that which is normally presented.

The ecological crisis is not merely a physical problem. It has a human face, as we see in the third section of the book. Herein we see how the crisis has huge implications in key areas of human welfare like food security, health, and shelter. We also look into how the ecological crisis has a disproportionate impact on groups that are already vulnerable—women, children, indigenous groups, minorities, and not least, future generations. As the impacts of the ecological crisis impinge on fundamental and basic human rights, questions of eco-justice are bound to emerge, brought into sharper relief by the fact that the victims are those who have contributed least to causing the crisis. The ecological crisis thus becomes a profound moral crisis.

In the fourth part of the book we go deeper in our understanding of the contemporary ecological crisis. The crisis, besides being a physical and moral question, is also a deeply religious and spiritual problem. For believers, the physical world is ultimately the creation—the very home that God intended as humanity's household. It is also God's common home as the "the spirit of the Lord has filled the world" (Wis 1:7) and the place God pitched his tent in the supreme event of the Incarnation (Jn 1:14). This common home where the whole of the human family along with the rest of the biotic community is called to dwell in God's peace (*shalom*) is entrusted to human stewardship. Thus, despoiling the common home that is God's own handiwork is sin. It is an affront to the Creator, while at the same time it ruptures the bonds of communion with one's own fellow creatures. The ecological crisis also reveals how we have ignored the ultimate destiny of all creation to enter into God's own Sabbath, as the whole universe will be recapitulated in Christ.

The present book is an attempt to frame our understanding of the contemporary ecological crisis by offering a broader and more holistic view of the problem. We do it by weaving together the different strands of the crisis of our common home—physical, moral, and religious—into a unified whole. The three cries, though taken up separately for the sake of exposition, merge into one deafening cry of agony. The complex nature and manifold layers of the contemporary ecological crisis expose the utter insufficiency of technological solutions like geo-engineering—piecemeal solutions that are themselves heirs of a reductive perception of the ecological crisis as merely an environmental problem that is in turn often reduced to the phenomenon of global warming alone. We need to widen our understanding of the ecological crisis as the crisis of our common home, if we are to respond to it effectively.

This book is basically concerned with understanding the ecological crisis. Understanding a malaise is the first step to facing the challenges thrown up by it. This insight is not new. It was admirably demonstrated by Gautama Buddha, the Enlightened One, in the sixth century BCE. Faced with the dilemma of universal suffering—*Dhukha*—Buddha went on to discover the "Four Noble Truths." Significantly, the first of the noble truths had to do with the nature and reality of suffering. Before he went on to uncover the successive truths about the causes, cessation, and means toward the cessation of suffering, the Enlightened One sought to understand, in the first place, what suffering really is.

Today, faced with the contemporary ecological crisis, we need first of all to understand the crisis,. The fact that the ecological crisis is only getting worse even after decades of study, diagnosis, and mitigation efforts means that we have not sufficiently understood the malaise in the first place. Hence the attempt here to understand the ecological crisis, to acknowledge its existence, and to comprehend its wide-ranging implications before proceeding to decipher its causes and propose concrete solutions.

The ecological crisis is about our common home in peril. So we begin with a basic question: are we tearing down our home?

PART I

ARE WE TEARING DOWN OUR HOME?

On Christmas Eve 1968 the three astronauts who formed the crew of *Apollo* 8, the first manned spacecraft to leave the earth's orbit and circle the moon, gifted humanity with one of the most extraordinary images of our home planet. On their fourth orbit, as they began to emerge from the far side of the moon, a spectacular sight appeared. They would later describe it as the most beautiful thing that there was to see in all the heavens. It was the sight of the earth, seeming to rise magnificently above the lunar horizon, the image of which was photographed and subsequently immortalized in the collective memory of humanity as "Earthrise." Looking back at the earth from outer space, the astronauts were struck by the sheer beauty of this living blue-green jewel floating freely, in eternal silence, against the backdrop of the stark and sterile lunar horizon and the dark, deep space.

The image of Earth from space changed forever humanity's perception of its own cosmic home. In *Earthrise: How Man First Saw the Earth*, Robert Poole describes this extraordinary experience, one of the most profound events of human history and culture.

On Christmas Eve 1968 three American astronauts were in orbit around the Moon: Frank Borman, James Lovell and Bill Anders. The crew of Apollo 8 had been declared by the United Nations to be the 'envoys of mankind in outer space'; they were also its eyes. They were already the first people to leave Earth orbit, the first to set eyes on the whole Earth, and the first to see the dark side of the Moon, but the most powerful experience still awaited them. For three orbits they gazed down on the lunar surface through their capsule's tiny windows as they carried out the checks and observations prescribed for almost every minute of this tightly planned mission.

On the fourth orbit, as they began to emerge from the far side of the moon, something happened. They were still out of radio contact with the earth, but the on-board voice recorder captured their excitement.

Borman: Oh my God! Look at that picture over there! Here's the earth coming up. Wow, that is pretty!
Anders: Hey, don't take that, it's not scheduled.
Borman: (Laughter). You got a colour film, Jim?
Anders: Hand me that roll of colour quick, will you—
Lovell: Oh man, that's great!
Anders: Hurry. Quick . . .
Lovell: Take several of them! Here, give it to me. . . .
Borman: Calm down, Lovell.

The crew of Apollo had seen the earth rise. The commander, Frank Borman, later recalled the moment.

I happened to glance out of one of the still-clear windows just at the moment the earth appeared over the lunar horizon. It was the most beautiful, heart-catching sight of my life, one that sent a torrent of nostalgia, of sheer home-sickness, surging through me. It was the only thing in space that had any colour to it. Everything else was either black or white, but not the Earth.
'Raging nationalistic interests, famines, wars, pestilences don't show from that distance,' he commented afterwards. 'We are one hunk of ground, water, air, clouds, floating around in space. From out there it really is "one world."' 'Up there, it's a black-and-white world,' explained James Lovell. 'There's no colour. In the whole universe, wherever we looked, the only bit of colour was back on Earth. . . . It was the most beautiful thing there was to see in all the heavens. People down here don't realize what they have.' Bill Anders recalled how the moment of Earthrise 'caught us hardened test pilots.'
'We'd spent all our time on Earth training about how to study the moon, how to go to the moon; it was very lunar orientated. And yet when I looked up and saw the earth coming up on this very stark, beat up lunar horizon, an Earth that was the only colour that we could see, a very fragile looking Earth, a very delicate looking Earth, I was immediately almost overcome by the thought that here we came all this way to the moon, and yet the most significant thing we're seeing is our home planet, the Earth.'[1]

---

[1] Robert Poole, *Earthrise: How Man First Saw the Earth* (New Haven, CT: Yale University Press, 2008), 1–2, available on www.earthrise.org.uk. See also Frank Borman, *Countdown: An Autobiography* (New York: Silver Arrow Books, 1988), 212; Frank Borman interview, JSC OHA, 1999; *Life* (January 17, 1969).

The *New York Times* reported, "The writer Norman Cousins told the 1975 Congressional hearings on the future of the space program: 'What was most significant about the lunar voyage was not that men set foot on the moon, but they set eye on the earth.'"[2]

"Earthrise" offered the image of our home planet as infinitely beautiful and yet infinitely fragile. The ecological crisis, as pointed out in the Introduction, is about the threat to our common home; it is not just an environmental problem or even a host of them. Part I, therefore, responds to the basic question: Are we tearing down our home?

Before answering this fundamental question, it is important to realize how the Planet Earth is unique as a home of life, a fact that does not appear to be sufficiently appreciated by most of us. In fact, Earth is the only place in the infinitely vast universe that we can literally call home. It is the only known abode for complex forms of life like ours—at least as far as our present-day knowledge goes. So we begin with a cosmic meditation on how the earth became a unique habitat for life. This will be the program of the first chapter. We shall see how our common home came to be molded spectacularly over a period of billions of years, letting life evolve from single cells to the extravagant complexity of today. In this cosmic saga human beings arrived rather late on the scene, an event relatively insignificant in the long geological history of the earth but momentous in terms of its implications for the destiny of the planet and for the future of the rest of the commonwealth of species. Modern humans, our immediate ancestors, originated nearly 200,000 years ago. A relatively small band of them migrated from Africa over 2,000 generations ago and over the course of millennia went on to occupy our planetary home. The creation of our common home and its occupation by modern humans is indeed a fascinating story.

The second chapter demonstrates, based on recent and authoritative evidence from the scientific community, how our common home is increasingly in peril. The capacity of the earth to be a home for humanity and for the rest of the biotic community is under threat. The chapter points out how the ecological crisis is fundamentally anthropogenic in origin; that is, it is basically caused by human activities. It is striking to realize that human activities risk disrupting—within the blink of an eye of geological time—fundamental and complex geochemical and biological processes of the earth that have taken millions and millions of years to evolve. In some areas like biodiversity loss,

---

[2] William Irwin Thompson, "The Deeper Meaning of Apollo 17," *New York Times* (January 1, 1973).

depletion of natural resources, and climate change, we have already crossed the tipping point or are precariously poised on the brink. The deliberate and wanton destruction of our common home is bound to have not only physical consequences but also profound moral implications for our fellow human beings, for future generations, and for our fellow species.

1

The Making of a Home

Today, thanks to developments in cosmology, we know more about the universe than any other era in human history. Extraordinary advances in ideas—from Einstein's general relativity to particle physics—and in instruments—from space telescopes to particle accelerators—have dramatically changed our conception of the physical world and the cosmos.[1] The Hubble Telescope, for example, orbiting the earth for more than two decades now, has been able to gaze farther and deeper into the cosmos, disclosing to us a universe immensely large and incredibly old. We remain in utter awe and wonder before the infinity of the universe, so inconceivably large that distances can be measured only in light years. It is believed that the observable universe has a diameter of 93 billion light years (the speed of light being a whopping 186,411.4 miles per second) and contains hundreds of billions of galaxies, with a recent German supercomputer animation plugging the number at approximately 500 billion galaxies.[2] A galaxy, like our own Milky Way, contains approximately 200 to 250 billion stars, with a medium star, like our sun, being a million times more massive than the earth. According to our current knowledge, the observable universe is said to contain 300 sextillion (3×10^{23}) stars.[3]

It is also humbling to realize that the observable universe in terms of normal matter accounts for less than 5 percent of the mass of the universe (the stars and planets constituting a mere 0.5 percent and the rest being gas) while the bulk of the universe consists of dark

---

[1] See Michael S. Turner, "Origin of the Universe," *Scientific American* (September 2009): 36.

[2] For an account of the largest simulation experiment of the universe, the "Millennium Run" carried out at the Max Planck Institute for Astrophysics, see V. Springel et al., "Simulations of the Formation, Evolution and Clustering of Galaxies and Quasars," *Nature* 435 (2005): 629–36.

[3] See Pieter G. van Dokkum and Charlie Conroy, "A Substantial Population of Low-Mass Stars in Luminous Elliptical Galaxies," *Nature* 468 (2010): 940–42. This study almost tripled the previous estimates with regard to the total number of stars in the universe.

energy (68.3 percent) and dark matter (26.8 percent).[4] The vastness of the universe and its amazing order have been a source of wonder for humans since ancient days and have inspired generations of poets, sages, and mystics down through the ages.

Equally marvelous and awe inspiring is the realization that in such an infinitely vast universe, stretching across billions of light years, our home planet is a unique place capable of harboring advanced and complex forms of life. We quiver at the thought that in an area to be measured in light years, if not in infinities of time and space, we are alone.[5] The quest for extraterrestrial life has enthralled humanity since time immemorial, and the scientific exploration in this regard is only in its initial stages, having coincided with the onset of the space era. It would certainly be preposterous to rule out the possibility of life, even relatively advanced forms of it, elsewhere in the universe; there could very well be such life, given the sheer immensity of the cosmos. But limiting ourselves to the earth within the solar system and to our immediate galactic neighborhood, we remain awestruck by the wonderful saga of how our single planet became a marvelous home where life evolved from single cells to conscious beings through complex processes that unfolded over millions and millions of years. The contemporary ecological crisis threatens precisely this capacity of the earth to be a home for living beings to flourish. Thus, it is important that we reflect on the stupendous miracle of the gradual fashioning of our home before dwelling at length on the crisis itself.

In the Beginning . . .

Recent discoveries in cosmology reveal how the saga of Earth becoming a home is intricately linked to the wider cosmic epic of the origin, formation, and evolution of the universe. The building blocks necessary for the construction of our common home were originally created and gradually molded in the cosmic furnace of the universe over billions of years. So, in order to fathom the significance of the shaping of the earth as a home for life, we need to place our geological history in the larger cosmic odyssey of nearly 14 billion years. The emergence of our planet, and ultimately our own existence, can

---

[4] See Mark Peplow, "Planck Telescope Peers into the Primordial Universe," *Nature News* (March 21, 2013).

[5] See Paul Davies, *The Eerie Silence: Are We Alone in the Universe?* (London: Allen Lane, 2010); John Gribbin, *Alone in the Universe: Why Our Planet Is Unique* (Hoboken, NJ: Wiley, 2011).

be understood only by returning to the very dawn of creation, to the origin of the universe attributed to a singular moment called the Big Bang, and to the succession of events thereafter.

The most widely accepted scientific explanation for the origin of the universe is the Big Bang theory.[6] It posits that the material universe originated from the violent explosion that occurred 13.82 billions of years ago[7] and has expanded and cooled ever since. It is mind-boggling to realize that the initial point from which the universe blazed forth in a great flash, with an intensity never to be equaled again, would have occupied a tiny sphere 10^{-33} centimeters in diameter (trillions and trillions of times smaller than the head of a pin). The original searing hot fireball of the Big Bang must have been a point of extremely high temperature, 10^{32} centigrade, which means inconceivable energy density, and the crucial early sequences of its evolution took place in mere billionths of a second.[8] The initial moment of the Big Bang is itself shrouded in mystery. Time and space did not exist, because these came into existence only thereafter, and the four fundamental forces of nature—gravity, the strong and weak nuclear forces, and electromagnetism—existed as a single unified cosmic force. Scientists seek to approximate this instance by referring to it as Planck's limit-time.

At the end of the Planck limit-time, 10^{-43} second after the Big Bang, the first cosmic phase transition took place: gravity broke away to become a distinct entity, and space and time became well defined. At 10^{-35} second, the universe underwent a sudden inflation—a super-rapid expansion of space—that prevented the embryonic universe from collapsing on itself. At this stage the strong nuclear force split away, leaving only electromagnetism and the weak nuclear force tied together. The expansion continued, while temperature and

---

[6] The theory was originally proposed by the Belgian astronomer-priest Georges Lemaître in 1927, corroborated experimentally by Edwin Hubble's observation of the constant expansion of the universe, recognized by renowned astronomers like Arthur Eddington, theoretically elaborated by George Gamow and others, and eventually accepted by prominent scientists of the day, including Albert Einstein. The Big Bang theory found acceptance in scientific circles because of two cornerstone astronomical observations: the abundance of light chemical elements and the discovery of cosmic microwave background radiation.

[7] Peplow, "Planck Telescope Peers into the Primordial Universe."

[8] See Robert M. Hazen, *The Story of Earth: The First 4.5 billion Years, from Stardust to Living Planet* (New York: Viking, 2012), 7–13; Brian Swimme and Thomas Berry, *The Universe Story: From the Primordial Flaring Forth to the Ecozoic Era: A Celebration of the Unfolding of the Cosmos* (London: Penguin Books, 1992), 7; Leonardo Boff, *Cry of the Earth, Cry of the Poor* (Maryknoll, NY: Orbis Books, 1997), 44; Turner, "Origin of the Universe," 36.

density gradually diminished. At 10^{-32} second, radiation and matter were created. The energy that drove inflation was transferred to the multitude of Higgs particles, which decayed, releasing the energy as radiation. Quantum processes caused the radiation to decay spontaneously into subatomic particles of matter and antimatter, which annihilated each other. However, in the process a small imbalance in the laws of physics produced slightly more matter than antimatter. For every billion particles of antimatter, there were a billion and one particles of matter, which ensured that at the end of the process a small excess of matter remained. All the material content of the universe—including us—derives from this slight excess of matter. At 10^{-10} second the electromagnetic and weak nuclear forces finally went their separate ways. At 10^{-5} seconds the quark particles, which formed shortly after inflation, bunched together to form protons and neutrons, the building blocks of atomic nuclei. At 100 seconds the temperature of the Big Bang fireball dropped enough to allow protons and neutrons to stick together, allowing the nuclei of the lightest chemical elements—hydrogen, helium, and a small amount of lithium—to be formed. It is only after 3,800,000 years, with the temperature having been lowered substantially to approximately 6000°C—about the same as the surface of the sun, that the atomic nuclei forged during the first 100 seconds were able to capture electrons and form the first whole atoms.[9] Radiation streamed freely through space, and the universe became transparent. This moment in the evolution of the early universe has left a remarkable fossil relic in the form of the cosmic microwave background radiation that is still observable today.[10] A phase of stability was reached as far as the particle interactions were concerned, and the four original interconnections of gravity, the electromagnetic force, and the strong and weak nuclear forces came into play throughout the universe.

A second phase began called the galactic phase. In the billion years that followed, the primordial gas of hydrogen and helium expanded and eventually cooled down, giving rise to the first condensations of matter—the proto-galaxies—which contracted under gravity's effect.

---

[9] Paul Parsons, *The Big Bang* (London: BBC, 2001), 42–44, 53; Turner, "Origin of the Universe," 39, 41.

[10] The cosmic microwave background radiation is a residual echo of the hypothetical primordial explosion that allows cosmologists to deduce the conditions present in the early stages of the Big Bang and, in particular, helps account for the chemistry of the universe. See Peter Coles, *Cosmology: A Very Short Introduction* (Oxford: Oxford University Press, 2001), 61; Parsons, *The Big Bang*, 52.

It was from these gas nebulas in the grip of gravitational collapse that the first galaxies and stars were formed, depending on the fluctuations of density of matter that existed within the proto-galactic clouds.[11] The stars lit up as the gravitational pressures within the gas nebulas increased the temperatures and ignited nuclear fires at their core. Within the stars, nuclear reactions created ever heavier atomic elements. Only the three lightest elements—hydrogen along with traces of helium and lithium—were created in the first few minutes after the Big Bang; all other elements were produced later in stars.[12] In first-generation stars heavier elements like carbon—the chemical basis for life—nitrogen and oxygen were forged. Aging first-generation stars expelled them into space, which went on to form new generations of stars, accruing and producing ever heavier elements in the process. A special role was played in this regard by the supernovas—massive stars that ran through the process of nucleosynthesis within relatively shorter periods—which spewed out into interstellar space heavier elements in violent and spectacular explosions. This process continued for billions of years during which generations of stars, especially supernovas, created in their internal nuclear furnaces heavier elements like phosphorus, sulphur, iron, gold, and the rest of the elements in the periodic table. The stars disgorged these elements into space to become part of interstellar clouds from which newer solar systems—and ultimately we—were formed. We are indeed stardust.

Nearly 5 billion years ago our solar system was formed in the periphery of the Milky Way at a distance of nearly 27,000 light years from its center. It formed from a giant rotating cloud of gas and dust composed mostly of the residue of the explosion of a supernova. To be precise, the sun and the accretionary disk was formed 4.567 billion years ago.[13] The sun, a medium-sized star, was formed at the center of this protoplanetary disk, having gathered to itself more than 99 percent of the original interstellar debris, while the remaining swirling portion went on to create the planetary bodies that spun around it: four terrestrial planets—Mercury, Venus, Earth, and Mars—and four gaseous

---

[11] Computer simulations reveal that stars and galaxies first emerged when the universe was about 100 million years old. See Turner, "Origin of the Universe," 38.

[12] See Michele Fumagalli et al., "Detection of Pristine Gas Two Billion Years After the Big Bang," *Science Express* (November 10, 2011): 1.

[13] Alex N. Halliday, "In the Beginning," *Nature* 409 (2001): 144; Matthias Gritschneder et al., "The Supernova Triggered Formation and Enrichment of Our Solar System," *Astrophysical Journal* 745 (January 20, 2012): 22.

ones—Jupiter, Saturn, Uranus, and Neptune.[14] Most of the planets have their own satellites, like Earth's moon, which was formed 4.53 billion years ago.[15] The solar system is our immediate cosmic family.

Within the solar system, as the third planet in order of distance from the mother star, our home Planet Earth came into existence. The accretion of the earth with a metal core and primitive atmosphere was completed between 4.51 billion to 4.45 billion years ago.[16] The formation of Earth marked the end of a long and stupendous voyage of cosmic evolution, a journey that began with the primordial flash of the Big Bang and took billions of years, while chemical elements necessary for life brewed in the cosmic furnaces of the supernovas. Earth was also destined to become the home for intelligent beings composed of the atoms of oxygen, hydrogen, and carbon that streamed out of stellar explosions of the distant past in the remote recesses of the universe, who would one day look back at the very cosmic process that brought them into being.

The vastness of the universe against which the drama of the formation of our small home planet was played out fills us with a sense of profound awe. But we need to remember that such immense cosmic spatial and temporal scales were necessary to create a home like the earth, containing the proper chemical elements required for life. As John Polkinghorne reminds us:

> Those trillions of stars have to be around if we are to be around also to think about them. In modern cosmology there is a direct correlation between how big a universe is and how long it has lasted. Only a universe as large as ours could have been around for the fifteen billion years it takes to evolve life—ten billion years for the first generation of stars to generate the elements that are the raw materials for life, and about a further five billion years to reap the benefit of that chemical harvest.[17]

---

[14] The International Congress of Astronomers, gathered in Prague in August 2006, decided to declassify Pluto as a "nano planet."

[15] According to the Giant Impact hypothesis, the moon formed as a result of a collision between Earth and a Mars-size body called Theia. The impact caused a portion of the combined mantle of Earth and Theia to be expelled into space, eventually forming the moon.

[16] Halliday, "In the Beginning," 144.

[17] John Polkinghorne, *Beyond Science: The Wider Human Context* (Cambridge: Cambridge University Press, 1996), 84. Along similar lines Royal Astronomer Martin Rees argues that nothing as complex as humankind could have emerged in a smaller universe: "The cosmos is so vast because there is one crucially important

Such a propitious outcome was indeed accompanied by what Thomas Berry calls the "cosmic moments of grace," for the fact that events so crucial to the development of a universe calibrated to supporting intelligent forms of life appear to have happened at almost zero probability.[18] There were indeed several cosmic moments of grace in the story of the universe's evolution from the simplicity of the quark soup to the complexity we see today in galaxies, stars, planets, and life. It is indeed startling to realize how the initial conditions of the universe were so very fine-tuned for the development of life, of which the Planet Earth was to become a privileged and unique oasis in the vast cosmic ocean.

Earth—The "Goldilocks" Planet

The earth has been rightly called the garden planet of the universe.[19] Our home planet is indeed a unique home for life, a rare oasis in the barren cosmic ocean, where life has flourished in extraordinary abundance and variety.

However, the closer we study the geology, the chemistry, and the biology of the earth, we realize that it is also a "Goldilocks" planet, the "just right" place for life to have evolved. We enumerate a few of its unique features below, before going on to discuss a couple of them at length.

One factor that makes the earth hospitable for life is its location in the solar system. The earth is 93 million miles distant from the sun, a distance suitable for maintaining an optimal temperature that allows water to remain liquid, a fundamental requirement for life to exist and flourish. Its present position also guarantees the right gravitational pull from the sun, from its own moon—which keeps the earth spinning

---

huge number N in nature, equal to 1,000,000,000,000,000,000,000,000,000,000, 000,000. This number measures the strength of the electrical forces that hold atoms together, divided by the force of gravity between them. If N had a few less zeros, only a short-lived miniature universe could exist: no creatures could grow larger than insects, and there would be no time for biological evolution" (Martin Rees, *Just Six Numbers: The Deep Forces that Shape the Universe* [London: Phoenix, 2000], 2).

[18] See Seán McDonagh, "The Story of the Universe: Our Story," *SEDOS Bulletin* 41 (2009): 151. See also Seán McDonagh, *To Care for the Earth: A Call to a New Theology* (London: Geoffrey Chapman, 1986), 83.

[19] Among the many who have done so, see *The Cry of the Earth: A Pastoral Reflection on Climate Change by the Irish Catholic Bishops" Conference* (2009), 7; McDonagh, *To Care for the Earth*, 84.

at the right speed and tilting at the right angle, factors that affect the present day-night cycle and the tides in the oceans—and even from a fellow planet like Jupiter, which curiously influences the stability of Earth's orbit. The 23.5 degree inclination of the earth to the sun creates the seasons and makes agriculture possible. The earth also has the right mass to possess the proper gravitational attraction, which in turn entitles it to have its own atmosphere, unlike the moon, which does not have one and where consequently life can never evolve as it did on Earth. Earth retains an atmosphere and water at its surface because of the protective magnetic field generated in its liquid iron/nickel core. The magnetic field also acts as a protective shield from dangerous ionizing radiations from the solar wind, while the ozone layer in the upper layers of the atmosphere blocks out the harmful ultraviolet rays. The atmosphere on Earth has the right composition of gases conducive to life: nitrogen, oxygen, carbon dioxide, and others. Our home planet also enjoys the right greenhouse effect, which warms up the atmosphere to the optimum temperature.

The point about the earth being a Goldilocks planet—the "just right" place for life to have evolved—is best driven home if we compare the earth to its immediate neighbors in the solar system, Mars and Venus.

There is only a limited range of distance around any star, such as the sun, at which a planet can have a "habitable" surface. If the planet is too close to the sun, any water will be evaporated into the atmosphere. If the planet is too far from the sun, any water will be frozen all the way to the equator.[20] Among all the planets in the solar system only the three terrestrial ones—Mars, Earth, and Venus—are said to lie within or near the habitable zone. Mercury is too near the sun, while the rest of the planets are too far from it, besides being only gaseous bodies—like most celestial bodies—with almost no scope for life. As Martin Rees remarks, even if there is life elsewhere within our solar system, nobody expects that it would be anything but primitive.[21]

Earth, Venus, and Mars began with a similar collection of atmospheric gases. However, slight differences in their size and distance from the sun and the cascade of events that followed from these factors made our immediate neighbors lose out in becoming a hospitable terrain for life.

---

[20] James Hansen, *Storms of My Grandchildren: The Truth About the Coming Climate Catastrophe and Our Last Chance to Save Humanity* (London: Bloomsbury, 2009), 228.

[21] Martin Rees, *Our Cosmic Habitat* (Princeton, NJ: Princeton University Press, 2001), 19.

Although the orbit of Mars is within the habitable zone, it remains cold and lifeless. Mars is smaller than Earth, and this allowed its interior to cool quickly, so that the period of venting of carbon dioxide from volcanic activity—important to maintain the greenhouse effect on the planet, especially in the early stage when the sun was less luminous—was much shorter than Earth's. Levels of atmospheric carbon dioxide and water vapor necessary to establish temperatures conducive to life existed on Mars during its first billion years only. Mars lost its global magnetic shield at some point, which allowed the solar wind to strip away the planet's atmosphere, leading to the loss also of its surface water. This change probably stifled any chance for life to establish itself on Mars. Today, Mars has so little gas in its atmosphere that its greenhouse effect is negligible and the surface temperature averages about -50°C, which can drop to -120°C at night. The more massive Earth took much longer to cool and consequently escaped the fate of Mars.[22]

Venus, on the other hand, is almost as big as the earth, with a diameter about 95 percent as large and a similar mass. Venus and Earth, having originated from the same interstellar gas and dust, must have begun with similar atmospheric compositions. But Venus orbits too close to the sun, almost outside the habitable zone. This, coupled with a strong greenhouse effect because of abundant water vapor, amplified the warming. Eventually a "runaway" greenhouse effect occurred, with the ocean evaporating into the atmosphere and carbon dioxide in the crust baked out into the atmosphere. In this way the atmosphere of Venus became predominantly carbon dioxide (97 percent) with surface temperatures of 460°C, hot enough to melt lead. In contrast to the earth the surface pressure on Venus is 90 bars—90 times greater than the surface pressure on Earth. That is about 1,300 pounds per square inch, which would crush any human visitors who were not cooked first.[23]

Earth, unlike Mars and Venus, became hospitable for life largely due to its position within the habitable zone of the solar system, its right mass, and other "just right" factors, making it a "Goldilocks" planet.

---

[22] Alan Beeby and Anne-Maria Brennan, *First Ecology: Ecological Principles and Enviornmental Issues* (London: Chapman and Hall, 1997), 3; Hansen, *Storms of My Grandchildren*, 224; Mark Maslin, *Global Warming: A Very Short Introduction* (Oxford: Oxford University Press, 2004), 6.

[23] Hansen, *Storms of My Grandchildren*, 225; Beeby and Brennan, *First Ecology*, 3; E. G. Nisbet and N. H. Sleep, "The Habitat and the Nature of Early Life," *Nature* 409 (2001): 1083.

Caught between the too hot Venus and too cold Mars, conditions on Earth were—like Goldilocks's porridge—"just right." Its size allowed volcanic activity to persist so carbon locked in carbonate rocks could be recycled back to the atmosphere through volcanic venting. The carbon dioxide in the atmosphere helped to maintain appropriate temperatures through a greenhouse effect. If the earth had orbited more than 5 percent closer to the sun, it would have succumbed to the hot and lifeless fate of Venus.[24]

Privileged to cruise through space in the right niche, at the right distance from its home star, our home planet, which was initially only a cauldron of gaseous material and dust of heavy elements, gradually evolved to become the home for life. It was a long and tortuous journey. For nearly a billion years after its formation, Earth was in a molten state. Its interior began to heat up under gravitational pressures, leading to the formation of a molten nickel and iron core, with a relatively thin skin of rock with lighter metals riding on the mantle below. The gradual cooling of the earth allowed for crust formation. The young Earth was also constantly bombarded by meteors and comets, while melting magma gushed from the volcanoes that ringed the planet's surface. As the lava cooled and hardened, the first land masses appeared. The early Earth's atmosphere was perhaps sixty times more massive than the present one, containing mostly carbon dioxide vented from volcanoes, along with a small percent of nitrogen, hydrogen, sulfur, and some water vapor, and very little ammonium and oxygen. As the atmospheric clouds condensed, torrential rains began that carried on continuously for ages, forming the oceans and other water bodies.[25] Carbon dioxide in the early atmosphere of the earth was almost 98 percent—similar to the roasting atmosphere of Venus today—and it was a good thing, after all. Lawrence M. Krauss explains why:

> After the sun settled down to its steady-state long-term hydrogen burning, after its turbulent T-Tauri stage, its early luminosity was only about 70 percent as great as it is today. At this level, had the earth been surrounded with its present atmosphere, the oceans would have eventually frozen over. Yet there is no evidence at all

---

[24] Beeby and Brennan, *First Ecology*, 4. See also Hansen, *Storms of My Grandchildren*, 225.

[25] Lawrence M. Krauss, *Atom: Odyssey from the Big Bang to Life on Earth and Beyond* (London: Little, Brown and Co., 2001), 164–65; McDonagh, *To Care for the Earth*, 84–85; Boff, *Cry of the Earth, Cry of the Poor*, 48.

for an early period of glaciation throughout the earth. In fact, all evidence is that it was much warmer than now.[26]

Thus in the early stages of geological history, in spite of the fact that the sun was 30 percent less luminous, the high level of carbon dioxide along with some amount of methane that was produced by the ancient methanogenic bacteria and accumulated in the atmosphere helped to maintain a high temperature on the earth, keeping the bulk of the water liquid.[27] The presence of liquid water was to be crucial for the emergence and survival of life.

Earth, the Womb of Life

Our planet was formed 4.6 billion years ago, a "Goldilocks" planet uniquely prepared to host life. Life appeared relatively early on the earth, within a short billion years after Earth's formation, nearly 3.8 billion years ago.[28]

With the arrival of life on Earth an important threshold was reached, and animate organic life emerged from inanimate matter. Somewhere in the primordial oceans of the earth—the prebiotic soup of simple organic compounds—emerged amino acids, which are essential to life. These amino acids, the building blocks of proteins, gave rise to microbes, the autotrophic archaeobacteria, the first single-celled life forms on Earth. From 3.5 billion years ago we find microscopic fossils resembling modern cyanobacteria.[29] It was from these self-replicating bacteria-like tiny organisms (the last universal common ancestor [LUCA]), stewing in a primordial soup, that all life on Earth, including complex life forms like humans, arose.

Life's origins are shrouded in mystery even today. Much of the various origin-of-life scenarios proposed is still hypothesis. Current assumptions regarding the origin of life cover a wide spectrum from spontaneous emergence from existing simpler chemical molecules present on the early Earth to extraterrestrial origin through comets

---

[26] Krauss, *Atom*, 165.

[27] Ibid., 166. See also Uwe H. Wiechert, "Earth's Early Atmosphere," *Science* 298 (2002): 2341–42; James F. Kasting and Janet L. Siefert, "Life and the Evolution of Earth's Atmosphere," *Science* 296 (2002): 1067.

[28] Nisbet and Sleep, "The Habitat and the Nature of Early Life," 1083ff.; Alonso Ricardo and Jack W. Szostak, "Life on Earth," *Scientific American* (September 2009): 54.

[29] Nick Lane, *Oxygen: The Molecule that Made the World* (New York: Oxford University Press, 2002), 52.

(panspermia). The science on the origin of life is, compared to the science of biological evolution, still considerably underdeveloped. As science writer Richard Robinson notes, beyond assuming that the first cell must have somehow come into existence, biologists are unable to explain its emergence from the prebiotic world four billion years ago.[30] As scientists in the field admit, "The actual nature of the first organisms and the exact circumstances of the origin of life may be forever lost to science."[31]

We shall be concerning ourselves here not so much with the origin and evolution of life as such, but rather with how life contributed to making our planet a home for life itself, in the wider context of the contemporary ecological crisis that appears to tear down the very foundations of this home. A surprising feature about the saga of life on Earth is the unique role played by life itself in making Earth "livable." The amenability of Planet Earth is believed to be a consequence of life creating the conditions for its own flourishing.[32] It is not only environment conditioning life, as happened in the later stages of evolution, but amazingly life itself was creating the right ambient for its own survival and flourishing. In this sense Earth was more than a home for life; it was the very womb of life. The earth, and the biosphere in particular, became—in ways strikingly similar to what a womb is for a fetus in development—the tender ambient of gestation where infinite forms of life came to be hosted and nurtured.

Three major contributions were made in the evolutionary journey to make the earth more amenable to life as part of the stupendous odyssey of how our home planet gradually became a home for life.

The first major contribution of life toward creating the favorable ambient for the blossoming of life was by way of regulation of the planet's atmosphere. The early atmosphere of the earth was extremely dense and constituted almost entirely of carbon dioxide, with very little oxygen. So the cyanobacteria, the first and only forms of life for nearly the first billion years of life on the planet, began the task of gradually transforming the atmosphere by sucking up and pumping down the excessive carbon dioxide in the air. They were extremely tiny beings that lived in the oceans, but they made up for their size by sheer numbers. Over a period of billions of years, working in concert, trillions and trillions of cyanobacteria eventually reshaped the atmosphere of the

---

[30] Richard Robinson, "Jump-starting a Cellular World: Investigating the Origin of Life, from Soup to Networks," *PLoS Biology* 3/11 (November 15, 2005): 1860.

[31] Ricardo and Szostak, "Life on Earth," 56.

[32] Alastair McIntosh, *Hell and High Water: Climate Change, Hope, and the Human Condition* (Edinburgh: Birlinn, 2009), 20.

earth.[33] These tiny microscopic bacteria made the earth habitable for advanced forms of life that would follow. Our planet could support advanced life because more simple forms created the preconditions, as Alastair McIntosh points out:

> Without life constantly pumping down excess carbon to become ocean sediments and eventually rocks, the earth would have had far too much atmospheric carbon and would therefore be a hot and inhospitable place. Early life forms—mainly microscopic ones—thereby tamed the earth for us. A wonderful self-regulating process is kept in place that maintains equitable temperatures.[34]

Thus even at its earliest stages life was beginning to change the earth's environment through the removal of carbon from the planet's early atmosphere. In fact, it is estimated that 20 percent of the available reservoir of carbon on Earth, including that bound up in the crust, has passed through living systems over the past 3.5 billion years.[35] In this context it is important to remember that with our current addiction to fossil fuels, we are returning carbon dioxide to the atmosphere approximately 1 million times faster than natural processes removed it.[36]

Equally important in the reduction of carbon dioxide in the early atmosphere was the contribution of geological processes. As the sun slowly heated up, the acid water attacked silicates in rocks, forming precipitates that yielded carbonate rocks such as limestone and dolomite, which sedimented out to the ocean floor, thus effectively removing carbon dioxide from the atmosphere. This mechanism, called chemical weathering, operating over billions of years, contributed significantly to lowering the carbon dioxide levels in the atmosphere, accounting for 80 percent of the carbon now stored underground. In this way nitrogen—a stable nonreactive gas—slowly became the dominant gas in the atmosphere.[37] This function was also at the service

---

[33] Krauss, *Atom*, 201.

[34] McIntosh, *Hell and High Water*, 20.

[35] Krauss, *Atom*, 197.

[36] Andrew Simms, *Ecological Debt: The Health of the Planet and the Wealth of the Nations* (London: Pluto Press, 2005), 3.

[37] Krauss, *Atom*, 166–67; Robert Henson, *The Rough Guide to Climate Change* (London: Rough Guides, 2006), 196–97; Andrew Y. Glikson, *Evolution of the Atmosphere: Fire and the Anthropocene Climate Event Horizon* (Dordrecht: Springer, 2014), ix.

of life, yet another example of how chemistry and geology were leading to biology. Nitrogen is essential for nourishing living organisms. These is only 3.5 percent on Venus and 2.7 percent on Mars, while on Earth it is around 79 percent. Again, it was as a result of life that other gases that are biological in origin, forming an oven favorable to life, are present in Earth's atmosphere, and in the right quantities for the flourishing of life.[38]

A second and undoubtedly the most important contribution of the primordial microorganisms to make our home planet more congenial for life was the production of oxygen through photosynthesis. The oxygen revolution transformed Earth.[39] It meant a great leap in the evolution of life, since oxygen is fundamental to life. As Nick Lane reminds us, the presence of oxygen in a planetary atmosphere is the very litmus test of life. Water may signal the potential for life, but oxygen is the sign of its fulfillment. Only life can produce free oxygen in the air in any abundance.[40]

The atmosphere of the early Earth, the Archean atmosphere, had, if anything, only traces of oxygen.[41] Four billion years ago the atmosphere contained about one part in a million of oxygen (0.0001 percent) compared to what it is today—an astonishing 208,500 parts per million, or about one-fifth (21 percent) of the atmosphere. The oxygen in the earth's atmosphere was built up gradually over billions of years thanks to the activity of photosynthesis of the cyanobacteria. The cyanobacteria were the first ones to learn photosynthesis, and all others—eukaryotes, algae, and plants, the entire green planet, inherited it from them. In photosynthesis, powered by the sun's energy, six molecules of water and six of carbon dioxide are converted into one molecule of sugar and six of oxygen. Here is a more graphic description of the process.

> [Photosynthesis is] the process in which plants, algae and cyanobacteria use the energy of sunlight captured by the green pigment chlorophyll to "split" water. The splitting of water releases oxygen, which is discharged into the atmosphere as a waste product, while the energy rich compounds derived from the split (by the

---

[38] Boff, *Cry of the Earth, Cry of the Poor*, 15–16. On the co-evolution of Earth and life, see Hazen, *The Story of Earth*, 6ff.

[39] On the importance of the oxygen revolution, see Tim Lenton and Andrew Watson, *Revolutions That Made the Earth* (Oxford: Oxford University Press, 2011).

[40] Lane, *Oxygen*, 2.

[41] See Wiechert, "Earth's Early Atmosphere," 2341.

absorption of light energy) are used to bind carbon dioxide from the air and package it into the sugars, fats, proteins and nucleic acids that make up organic matter. Photosynthesis therefore uses sunlight, water and carbon dioxide to produce organic matter. It gives off oxygen as a waste product.[42]

The photosynthetic microscopic cyanobacteria in the oceans kept pushing out oxygen, day in, day out, for years, centuries, millennia, eons, and transformed young Earth's poisonous atmosphere. The evolution of life from single-celled prokaryotes to cells with nuclei, the eukaryotes, around 2.7 billion years ago, sped up the production of oxygen by the early forms of life. Consequently, oxygen levels steadily rose in the atmosphere. By 2 billion years ago we have rock evidence of oxygen accumulating in the atmosphere, with levels going on to reach 5 to 18 percent of the present atmospheric concentration in the next billion years. The abundance of oxygen through photosynthesis led to a number of quiet developments in the history of life: the flourishing of the eukaryotes, genetic diversification, colonization of new habitats, and in the shape of the algae, the first tentative steps toward multicellular life.[43] As the quantity of oxygen increased in the atmosphere, newer and larger life forms were developing to take advantage of it. Oxygen became a source of energy to drive most of the biochemical reactions in living organisms. The specific paths followed by oxygen inside living species became more diverse, along with the growing diversity of life itself.[44] With the arrival of multicellular life (metazoa) about 600 million years ago, and land plants around 420 million years ago, atmospheric oxygen began to hover around 21 percent, the outcome of a sustainable natural balance. It was the optimum amount of oxygen needed for the survival and flourishing of life on Earth.

A third contribution in terms of life preparing the Planet Earth to be a home for life itself was the creation of the ozone layer. One important effect of the creation of the atmospheric oxygen was the production of a thin layer of ozone (a form of oxygen) in the upper atmosphere that blocks out the dangerous ultraviolet radiation from the sun. Not until oxygen was abundant enough in the atmosphere could the atmosphere make the ozone shield. And until the existence

---

[42] Lane, *Oxygen*, 23.
[43] Ibid., 53. See also Kasting and Siefert, "Life and the Evolution of Earth's Atmosphere," 1066.
[44] Krauss, *Atom*, 218.

of an ozone shield in the atmosphere, organisms could live only beneath the surface of the sea, whose waters protected them from the ultraviolet rays that otherwise would have spelled death for them.[45] Indeed, for the first 4 billion years of Earth's history, organisms were entirely aquatic. Nothing lived on the land. It was only after the ozone shield was in place, and the biologically harmful ultraviolet radiation began to be filtered out, that life could get a foothold on land.[46] It was the creation of the ozone shield that allowed organisms to invade the land and start the vast expansion of the biosphere.

The three factors mentioned above—the regulation of the atmosphere through the reduction of carbon dioxide along with the stabilization of nitrogen and other gases, the increase of oxygen in the atmosphere through the process of photosynthesis, and the creation of the ozone shield that filtered out the ultraviolet radiation harmful to living beings—were the principal ways, among others, in which life was preparing its own womb to nurture biological diversity on Planet Earth. The role of the microorganisms in the task of preparing this womb of life through the regulation of Earth's atmosphere was especially important. For most of the three billion years since the emergence of life on Earth, the planet was populated entirely by microscopic, single-celled bacteria and simple algae that swarmed in the oceans. These microorganisms prepared the planet for the flourishing of life, having determined the basic composition of Earth's atmosphere and keeping its temperature in a habitable state. The microorganisms created the breathable, oxygen-rich air that we enjoy today. They continue to play a critical role in maintaining the biogeochemical cycles on which all forms of life ultimately depend.

Earth was thus being prepared to host life in greater abundance. Scientists refer to this preparatory period as the Precambrian era. In its early phase the single-cellular organisms dominated the scene. Then a complexity revolution began around 2.7 billion years ago with the rapid rise of eukaryotic life—cells with nuclei containing their genetic material—whose emergence was a significant moment in the whole

---

[45] Ultraviolet radiation from the sun breaks down many molecules, such as DNA. This is why there has been a virtual ban on the production of human-produced chlorofluorocarbons (CFCs) that are implicated in stratospheric ozone depletion. See Stephen H. Schneider, *Laboratory Earth: A Brief History of Climate Change* (London: Phoenix, 1996), 35.

[46] Paul R. Ehrlich, *The Machinery of Nature* (London: Paladin Grafton Books, 1988), 171–72; Schneider, *Laboratory Earth*, 35–36.

history of life on Earth.[47] Without eukaryotic cells life would have consisted only of bacteria, very similar to those that existed more than 3 billion years ago. Eukaryotic cells began grouping in clusters of cells first, cooperating as autonomous cells; later, about 560 million years ago, they became proper multicellular organisms. It was this evolutionary leap that allowed the conquest of land and the advance of complex multicellular life forms.[48] The time was now ripe for a sudden and unprecedented explosion of life on Earth.

After over three billion years of quiet evolution, in a geological blink of an eye, beginning around 543 million years ago, the whole of creation as we know it exploded into being in a frenzy of evolutionary innovation.[49] The fossil record shows a sharp increase in the diversity and number of complex animals during a relatively short time span in Earth's history. Biologists call it the Cambrian explosion and have attributed this great flourishing of life to factors like the rise in oxygen, the evolution of shells and cuticles from marine life forms, and so on. The Cambrian explosion generated over 100 major animal groups; a very few of them survive to this day, including some insects, spiders, and mollusks.

Biologists divide this relatively short period of the flourishing of life on Earth into three eras: Paleozoic, Mesozoic, and Cenozoic; these are subdivided further into different periods. The evolution and flourishing of life on Earth was not linear and harmonious. It was halted dramatically by the five great mass extinctions, for example, which severely depleted biodiversity on Earth. But the odyssey of life on this planet was destined to continue, and life prevailed, until biological diversity reached its peak at the end of the Cenozoic period, prior to the arrival of humans on Earth.

The Paleozoic era, ranging from 545 to 245 million years of the geological history of the planet, was characterized by the origin of plants, the great diversity of marine invertebrates, and the emergence of the first vertebrates, including fish, amphibians, and reptiles. During the Siluarian period, nearly 430 million years ago, plants evolved

---

[47] See Robert J. P. Williams, "A System's View of the Evolution of Life," *Interface* 4 (2007): 1050; Ernst Mayr, *What Evolution Is* (London: Weidenfeld and Nicholson, 2001), 47.

[48] Wolfgang Lucht, "Shaped by Life," *Nature* 470 (2011): 460.

[49] Lane, *Oxygen*, 53. On the interval to the emergence of plants and animals, see also Martin A. Line, "The Enigma of the Origin of Life and Its Timing," *Microbiology* 148 (2002): 21.

from green algae and gradually came ashore. During the Devonian period, nearly 400 million years ago, the first land animals and the first forests appeared. The formation of plant communities on land, in turn, changed the amount of sunlight reflected from these surfaces and modified the carbon and hydrologic cycle—movements of water between oceans, atmosphere, and land, altering the earth's climate.[50] They also changed the physical surface of the land by helping to form soil.[51] Over hundreds of million years the swampy forests dominated by giant tree ferns, conifers, and mosses decomposed, storing their carbon in coal, gas, and oil deposits in sedimentary layers. The fossil fuels were thus formed from plants and small marine organisms that died and were buried and crushed beneath sediment over a time span of millions of years, especially in the Carboniferous period. The first fish in the oceans later gave rise to modern bony fish and also to amphibians, the first land-dwelling vertebrates. The reptiles arrived nearly 300 million years ago. The Paleozoic era came to an abrupt close with the greatest extinction of life on Earth, called the Permian Extinction, which occurred 245 million years ago.

The Mesozoic era, ranging from 245 to 65 million years ago, was characterized by the origin of flowering plants and the emergence of the dinosaurs, birds, and the first mammals. Around 200 million years ago geologists believe that Pangaea, the one land mass, began to break up into continents. This epoch also saw the evolution of flowering plants (angiosperms) nearly 130 million years ago with fertilization taking place through the pollen tube, an evolutionary feat that was destined to significantly alter life on Earth. The angiosperms fast diversified and radiated to the point of defining most of the earth's terrestrial ecosystems.[52] The Mesozoic dinosaurs ruled the land for nearly 150 million years until their sudden extinction, along with much of the rest of life, around 65 million years ago, in all probability due to a global catastrophe resulting from a massive asteroid colliding with the planet. This marked the close of the Mesozoic era.

The last of the eras in the flourishing of life on Earth is the Cenozoic era which began around 65 million years ago. At the beginning of this era, the individual continents had already taken shape. The evolution of life on separated land masses, on isolated islands in

---

[50] See Timothy M. Lenton et al., "First Plants Cooled the Ordovician," *Nature Geoscience* 5 (2012): 86–89.

[51] Ehrlich, *The Machinery of Nature*, 172.

[52] See Alan Graham, "The Age and Diversification of Terrestrial New World Ecosystems through Cretaceous and Cenozoic Time," *American Journal of Botany* 98 (2011): 336.

particular, took quite different paths in different parts of the world. In the Tertiary period the plant communities began to take on their modern form, with the flowering plants, the most prominent feature of the vast majority of the present-day habitats, having developed their modern diversity.[53] The Cenozoic era has rightly been called the age of the mammals. With the dinosaurs extinct, the mammals began their great diversification and became the dominant land animals. Within a span of 10 million years there were mammals of all kinds living on land, in the sea, and in the air. As warm-blooded animals, their ability to control their body temperature enabled them to adapt better to different climatic regions of the earth, while the females carried their fetuses within their bodies, which marked an advance in reproduction. During the Cenozoic era there was great diversification also in other groups, including birds, reptiles, amphibians, and fish. New survival skills, like stereoscopic vision, were evident especially in the emergence of primates, which evolved nearly 50 million years ago.[54] The Cenozoic era was also marked by a gradual lowering of global temperatures as well as the gradual establishment of different climatic zones of the earth: the tropics, the temperate zones, and the cool climates of the higher latitudes. In the Cenozoic era biological diversity reached a peak in the geological history of the planet. Life expanded with amazing rapidity on the earth, where it had found and built its own home.

Human beings, who had evolved through hominids from mammals, arrived on Earth, which had become the womb of life in such magnificent abundance. Seen against the long cosmic scale of the geological evolution of the planet and the biological evolution of life, the arrival of a new species is insignificant in itself. But not in the case of humanity. The arrival of humans on Earth was destined to alter the course of the evolution of life on this planet with profound implications for humankind and for the rest of the species.

Our Arrival at Home: The Peopling of the Planet

Humans arrived not on a lifeless and barren planet, like the bleak and desolate wastelands with which the Apollo images from the moon or the more recent Mars rover Curiosity images have made us familiar. Instead, human beings appeared on a planet that was verdant and

---

[53] Ehrlich, *The Machinery of Nature*, 172.

[54] See Richard Mackay, *The Atlas of Endangered Species* (London: Earthscan, 2005), 15; McDonagh, *To Care for the Earth*, 89.

lush, fertile and productive, with oceans and rivers teeming with fish; landscapes adorned with plants, trees, and flowers and inhabited by birds, animals, and all sorts of living beings. It is a description reminiscent of the "garden" in the Genesis account of creation—a garden fashioned by God in six days of cosmic labor and ready for the first humans. In ecological parlance the earth was a garden planet that was molded over millions of years for life to exist and flourish and where human beings finally arrived. On the earth human beings found a home—the planet's atmosphere was rich with oxygen, the carbon cycle was in place, the nitrogen cycle was regulating key ecosystem processes, liquid water was abundant, and the hydrological cycle powered by the sun's energy had brought climatic stability. These are but a few of the innumerable factors that rendered Earth a home for life. When human beings finally emerged on Planet Earth, at the end of a long process of evolution of life, they found themselves "at home."

The origin of human beings needs to be seen against the vaster panorama of the evolution of life on Earth. As it was with the evolution of life, the emergence of human beings was a complex and drawn-out process. From evolutionary evidence the origin of hominid (human-like) species is linked with the evolution of primates, one of the oldest of the surviving mammal groups that evolved in the Cenozoic era that began 65 million years ago. The first hominids appear to have diverged from the chimpanzees about 8 million to 5 million years ago; fossil records have been traced up to 4.5 million years ago.[55]

Africa is the place where the earliest episodes of the human evolutionary drama unfolded. It is suggested that drastic changes in climatic conditions associated with a burst of global cooling linked to the drying of the Mediterranean Sea that transformed the African landscape nearly 5 million years ago—turning the wet forests to open savannas—significantly influenced initial critical stages of human evolution. The new geographic conditions facilitated the development of crucial evolutionary traits like erect posture and bipedalism.[56] Ever since the split occurred between the line that led to chimpanzees and the line that led to modern humans in Africa, many hominid species have evolved, lasted for a while, and then died out. There is still uncertainty regarding the exact parentage among the various hominid species, with new fossil remains being discovered continually. It is believed that no fewer than six genera and fourteen species of the early

---

[55] Bernard Wood and Brian G. Richmond, "Human Evolution: Taxonomy and Paleobiology," *Journal of Anatomy* 196 (2000): 51.

[56] See Niles Eldredge, *Life in the Balance: Humanity and the Biodiversity Crisis* (Princeton, NJ: Princeton University Press, 1998), 26–29.

hominids existed between 7 million and 1.2 million years ago. The oldest known hominids are the genus Australopithecus, with remote descendants like Ardipithecus ramidus, Australopithecus anamensis, Australopithecus afarensis, Australopithecus africanus, Paranthropus robustus, and more. Our own genus, Homo, evolved in Africa approximately 2 million years ago.[57] It had a different body shape, slower growth, a more meat-based diet, and a larger brain than expected for body size (encephalization).[58] The Homo genus included, among others, Homo habilis, Homo rudolfensis, Homo ergaster, Homo erectus, Homo neanderthalensis, Homo floresiensis, and above all, Homo sapiens, our immediate ancestors, which appeared between 400,000 years and 250,000 years ago.[59]

The anatomically modern humans are at times referred in anthropological terms as the subspecies Homo sapiens sapiens, a denomination that serves to distinguish them from the rest of the hominid evolutionary shoots, all extinct now. The oldest fossil remains of anatomically modern humans are the Omo remains, uncovered on opposite sides of Ethiopia's Omo River in 1967. From the accurate dating of these fossils it can be surmised that modern humans—our direct ancestors—arose throughout Africa shortly before 195,000 years ago.[60]

Research over the past quarter of a century or so in archeology as well as in modern genetics has provided an increasingly clear picture of the way in which the human beings emerged and subsequently spread across the rest of the world. A conclusion that is widely shared among paleontologists is that Africa was not only the cradle of humanity but was also the launching pad for human migrations to the rest of the global home.[61]

---

[57] Ian Tattersall, "Human Origins: Out of Africa," *Proceedings of the National Academy of Sciences* 106 (2009): 16018; B. A. Wood and M. Collard, "The Human Genus," *Science* 284 (1999): 65–71.

[58] Marta Mirazón Lahr and Robert Foley, "Human Evolution Writ Small," *Nature* 431 (2004): 1043. See also Andrew Hill et al., "Earliest Homo," *Nature* 355 (February 20, 1992): 719–22.

[59] See Mackay, *The Atlas of Endangered Species*, 17.

[60] See Ian McDougall et al., "Stratigraphic Placement and Age of Modern Humans from Kibish, Ethiopia," *Nature* 433 (2005): 733–36. The fossils include two partial skulls as well as arm, leg, foot and pelvic bones.

[61] See Stephen Oppenheimer, "Out-of-Africa, the Peopling of Continents and Islands: Tracing Uniparental Gene Trees Across the Map," *Philosophical Transactions of the Royal Society B* 367 (2012): 770–84; Pedro Soares et al., "The Expansion of MtDNA Haplogroup L3 Within and out of Africa," *Molecular Biology and Evolution* 29 (2012): 915–27; Quentin D. Atkinson et al., "Bayesian Coalescent Inference of Major Human Mitochondrial DNA Haplogroup Expansions in Africa," *Proceedings of the Royal Society B* 276 (2009): 367–73;

The first hominid to move out of Africa was Homo ergaster, some 1.8 million years ago, resulting in the colonization of most of the warm and temperate zones of the world. Eventually their morphology became diversified through the process of genetic drift and natural selection as they lived in disparate geographical areas. Successively, Homo erectus evolved in Africa and gradually expanded to Eurasia beginning about 1.7 million years ago. These hominids evolved into Peking Man and Java Man in Eastern Asia, collectively referred to as Homo erectus. In Europe and Western Asia they evolved into the Neanderthals. In Europe, following a period of prolonged geographic isolation and independent isolation, the Neanderthals were so anatomically distinct that they are classified as a separate species, Homo Neanderthalensis. Homo sapiens, the species that finally gave rise to modern humans, emerged in Africa (in a geographical area including the Middle East), probably as a transition from Homo erectus. Eventually, Homo sapiens alone went on to evolve anatomically into the subspecies Homo sapiens sapiens, the modern humans that are our immediate predecessors. The anatomically modern humans that emerged nearly 195,000 years ago in East Africa eventually migrated and replaced the preexisting "archaic" populations elsewhere on the globe.[62]

For over 100,000 years since their emergence, the anatomically and genetically modern humans, the modern Homo sapiens, remained in Africa where they originated, while other hominid species continued to live in Asia and Europe. Current genetic and archeological evidence suggests that the anatomically modern humans left Africa sometime before 60,000 years ago.[63]

The exodus of modern humans out of Africa and their replacement of indigenous hominid counterparts elsewhere on the globe was indeed a momentous event that radically altered the human geography of the planet. The human populations all over the world today trace their origins anatomically, genetically, behaviorally, and culturally to these small bands of Homo sapiens sapiens. Surprisingly, they must have been an ancestral source population as small as 1,000 to 10,000 ef-

---

P. Forster and S. Matsumura, "Did Early Humans Go North or South?" *Science* 308 (2005): 965–66.

[62] See Paul Mellars, "Why Did Modern Human Populations Disperse from Africa ca. 60,000 Years Ago? A New Model," *Proceedings of the National Academy of Sciences* 103 (2006): 9381.

[63] See Hua Liu et al., "A Geographically Explicit Genetic Model of Worldwide Human-Settlement History," *The American Journal of Human Genetics* 79 (2006): 230.

fective individuals that migrated out of Africa.[64] How and why such a surge of migration took place still remains a mystery.

There is one climatic event that had a decisive effect on the hominization of the planet and against the backdrop of which the migration of the modern Homo sapiens out of Africa assumes special significance: the Mount Toba volcanic eruption that occurred in Sumatra approximately 73,000 BCE, considered the largest eruption of the last 2 million years. In its aftermath worldwide temperatures dropped significantly during a "volcanic winter." It is believed that the frigid climate and attendant drought that followed the Toba eruption wiped out many of Earth's hominids, leaving only small populations.[65] It was a moment of bottleneck for human evolution on the planet, as most existing populations were decimated by the volcanic winter. The populations that survived should have been found in the largest tropical refuge, equatorial Africa.[66] Relatively small bands of these anatomically modern humans were able to migrate out of their homeland in Africa to the rest of the world in the coming millennia. Eventually they became the billions of human beings that inhabit almost every part of the earth today.

It appears that East Africa was the homeland from which the ancestors of all living human populations today began their long exodus.[67] "Studies of both mitochondrial and Y-chromosome DNA patterns in modern world populations (inherited respectively through the female and male lineages) point to the genetic origins of all present-day populations within one limited area of Africa."[68] Archeological and genetic evidence points to a single successful dispersal event that took

---

[64] See A. R. Rogers and H. C. Harpending, "Population Growth Makes Waves in the Distribution of Pairwise Genetic Differences," *Molecular Biology and Evolution* 9 (1992): 552–69.

[65] See Stanley H. Ambrose, "Did the Super-Eruption of Toba Cause a Human Population Bottleneck? Reply to Gathorne-Hardy and Harcourt-Smith," *Journal of Human Evolution* 45 (2003): 231–37.

[66] Stanley H. Ambrose, "Late Pleistocene Human Population Bottlenecks, Volcanic Winter, and Differentiation of Modern Humans," *Journal of Human Evolution* 34 (1998): 623–61. For an opposing view see F. J. Gathorne-Hardy and W. E. H. Harcourt-Smith, "The Super-Eruption of Toba, Did It Cause a Human Bottleneck?" *Journal of Human Evolution* 45 (2003): 227–30.

[67] Toomas Kivisild et al., "Ethiopian Mitochondrial DNA Heritage: Tracking Gene Flow Across and Around the Gate of Tears," *American Journal of Human Genetics* 75 (2004): 752.

[68] Paul Mellars, "Neanderthals and the Modern Human Colonization of Europe," *Nature* 432 (2004): 461.

modern humans from the Horn of Africa fairly rapidly across southern and southeastern Asia into Australasia, with a later and secondary dispersal into Europe.[69] The exodus of modern humans out of Africa, spreading modern anatomy and behavior throughout the planet in its wake, would have taken place very late in the Pleistocene—as recently as 60,000 years ago. A small subset of the modern humans made the crossing from northeastern Africa, probably over the mouth of the Red Sea, and subsequently dispersed into Arabia,[70] and then onward into southern Asia and beyond. There are fossil indications that shoreline routes were used by early Homo sapiens to leave the African homeland; they might have taken a coastal route through the Red Sea, Southern Arabia, and into southern Asia. Continuing along the tropical coast of the Indian Ocean, they would have progressed into southeastern Asia, and Indonesia to arrive in both Malaysia and the Andaman Islands by at least 55,000 years ago. The subsequent southward dispersal of these populations into New Guinea and Australia (at that time connected as an extended landmass), crossing at least sixty-two miles of sea, happened by around 50,000 years ago.[71] While some pioneers crossed into Australia, another group may have continued eastward, eventually turning northeast to China and finally reaching Japan, leaving a trail of coastal settlements. It is believed that modern humans entered East Asia from the south and followed on with a northward migration coinciding with the receding glaciers in that area. Southeast Asia was home to scattered human populations as early as 40,000 years ago, and there is evidence that modern humans had reached the area of modern Beijing by around 25,000 years ago.[72]

It is amazing to realize that the spread of modern human populations eastward from their original African homeland along the so-called coastal express route into Australasia was rapid and occurred over a comparatively short period of 10,000 to 15,000 years.[73] Such a

[69] Paul Mellars, "Going East: New Genetic and Archeological Perspectives on the Modern Human Colonization of Eurasia," *Science* 313 (2006): 796.

[70] See Verónica Fernandes et al., "The Arabian Cradle: Mitochondrial Relics of the First Steps Along the Southern Route out of Africa," *The American Journal of Human Genetics* 90/2 (2012): 347–55.

[71] C. Stringer, "Coasting out of Africa," *Nature* 405 (2000): 24–27; Mellars, "Going East," 796–97.

[72] Li Jin and Bing Su, "Natives or Immigrants: Modern Human Origin in East Asia," *Nature Review Genetics* 1 (2000): 132; Cyril Aydon, *A Brief History of Mankind: 150,000 Years of Human History* (London: Constable and Robinson, 2009), 18–19.

[73] Mellars, "Going East," 797. See also Forster and Matsumura, "Did Early Humans Go North or South?," 965; Vincent Macaulay et al., "Single, Rapid

monumental journey was made possible largely due to lower sea levels because of the massive ice caps which trapped much of Earth's water, allowing humans and animals to migrate great distances on land. When the sea levels rose as the glaciers retreated, all Australian species, including humans, were left to evolve in isolation. The aborigines of Australia, along with Papuans and some other relict populations in southern India and southeast Asia, thus were descendants of the first wave of migration out of Africa.[74]

While there was only a single exodus of modern humans from Africa, there was an early offshoot, leading ultimately to the settlement of the Near East and Europe. In effect, there was a split of the migration routes of the first modern humans after they trekked out of the Horn of Africa across the Bab el Mandeb straits into southern Arabia. The principal route moved eastward toward India and Southeast Asia to reach Australasia. Another group remained and eventually settled in southwestern Asia. The evident delay in their migration toward the north, in contrast to the swift dispersal of the modern humans along the South Asia coastal routes, can be be attributed to climatic factors. Before 50,000 years ago it would have been impossible to migrate toward the north, because the desert extended from North Africa to Central Asia.[75] After a lengthy pause in Southwest Asia, the descendant populations of the modern humans that had originally left Africa dramatically expanded their range, colonizing lands as far removed from one another as northern Africa, temperate Europe, and Central Asia.

A change in climatic conditions, fragmenting and reducing the desert areas, allowed humans to enter the Levant and from there North Africa and on to Europe. They did not return to Africa along the southern coastal route of the out-of-Africa exit but from the Mediterranean area. The genetic and archeological records indicate that modern humans spread from the Levant into Mediterranean Africa by 40,000 years ago.[76] Shortly after modern humans entered Europe, the Neanderthals (Homo neanderthalensis)—stocky hominids widespread

---

Coastal Settlement of Asia Revealed by Analysis of Complete Mitochondrial Genomes," *Science* 308 (2005): 1036.

[74] Macaulay et al., "Single, Rapid Coastal Settlement of Asia," 1034.

[75] Ibid., 1034; Anna Olivieri et al., "The mtDNA Legacy of the Levantine Early Upper Palaeolithic in Africa," *Science* 314 (2006): 1767; Mellars, "Going East," 800.

[76] See Ted Goebel, "The Missing Years for Modern Humans," *Science* 315 (2007): 195; Olivieri et al., "The mtDNA Legacy of the Levantine Early Upper Palaeolithic in Africa," 1769; Macaulay et al., "Single, Rapid Coastal Settlement of Asia," 1036.

in Europe and parts of Central Asia who had successfully adapted to the glacial climates of northwestern Eurasia for at least 200,000 years—began a fairly rapid decline, culminating in their disappearance roughly 30,000 years ago. Though Neanderthals made tools and practiced community hunting techniques, they lacked the cognitive and communicative abilities of modern humans and were apparently no match for the technologically and culturally advanced modern humans.[77] Within Europe, the dispersal routes of the anatomically and behaviorally modern humans appear to have traced two different routes, as reflected in the archeological data. The first was a northern route, along the Danube, across a broad arc of western, central and southeastern Europe and extending into the immediately adjacent areas of the Near East. The second route of dispersal was along the Mediterranean coast of Europe, extending from at least northeastern Italy to the Atlantic coast of northern Spain. These migrations occurred between 35,000 and 45,000 years ago.[78]

From southwestern Asia modern humans moved also into Central Asia; they spread across Asia around 50,000 years ago.[79] Following the vast herds of antelope and bovids, they gradually dispersed along the steppes and populated much of Eurasia. As modern humans migrated farther north, into the Russian plain, they colonized southern Siberia and the Arctic Circle. It is believed that they reached southern Siberia by 45,000 years ago and artic Siberia by 30,000 years ago.[80] They also developed, over many generations, physiological features like stout trunks and short arms and legs, which helped them to survive the extremely cold environment. Finally, as the most recent Ice Age began to wane, around 15,000 years ago, one small clan of Arctic dwellers followed the reindeer herds over the Bering Strait land bridge into North America. Asia and North America were connected by a significant landmass called Beringia, which was mostly covered by ice, and the sea levels were significantly lower due to the Quaternary glaciation. Modern humans subsequently spread from Beringia to the rest of the Americas. After entering the Americas through

---

[77] See Mellars, "Neanderthals and the Modern Human Colonization of Europe," 461–65.

[78] Ibid., 462–63.

[79] Tim Appenzeller, "Eastern Odyssey," *Nature* 485 (2012): 24; R. Spencer Wells et al., "The Eurasian Heartland: A Continental Perspective on Y-chromosome Diversity," *Proceedings of the National Academy of Sciences* 98 (2001): 10247.

[80] Goebel, "The Missing Years for Modern Humans," 196.

modern Alaska, they dispersed following the ice-free corridors along the Pacific coast and Plains east of the Canadian Rockies. The current genetic, archeological, and environmental evidence indicates that humans colonized the Americas around 16,000 to 15,000 years ago, immediately after deglaciation of the Pacific coastal corridor.[81] Once humans reached the Pacific Northwest, they continued their spread southward along the coast to Chile and eastward along the southern margin of the continental ice sheets that still covered the interior areas of the continent.[82] The first migrants spread from Beringia to Tierra del Fuego at the tip of South America in a few millennia. The migration of modern humans out of Africa, radiating across Eurasia and Oceania, had reached the farthest point of the farthest continent.

Humans had arrived everywhere on the home planet.

Our examination of the peopling of the earth contains a profound truth; namely, we dwell in our common home as one, united family. It is amazing that all humans on the planet today have identical ancestors and are bewilderingly similar. Studies of contemporary DNA, especially mitochondrial DNA (mtDNA), which occurs only in the cellular organelles called mitochondria and which is of precious help in tracking evolutionary variations, reveal that humans are astonishingly homogeneous. There is only one humanity, in spite of the multitude of differences that appear to divide the humans on the planet and on the basis of which we have fought wars in the past and continue to erect walls of separation on the basis of race, caste, class, color, and a multitude of other differences. But the truth is that we all share a common humanity, having descended genetically from the same ancestors, nearly 2,000 generations ago, as we have seen above. The cultural, biological, and physiological differences among human beings today arose in response to geographical, environmental, and numerous other factors in the course of human evolution. Human physiological features marvelously adapted to diverse environmental contexts over millennia, creating various ethnic lineages among human populations. These physiological differences, along with other cultural diversities, are to be understood, however, within the encompassing unity of our common human family, itself encompassed within our common biological origin and cosmic fellowship. Humans dwell in the common home of Earth as a common family.

---

[81] See Andrew Curry, "Coming to America," *Nature* 485 (2012): 31.

[82] Ted Goebel et al., "The Late Pleistocene Dispersal of Modern Humans in the Americas," *Science* 319 (2008): 1501; Goebel, "The Missing Years for Modern Humans," 196.

The Transformation of Our Common Home:
From Agriculture to Industry and to the Era of Space Travel

The evolution of humans and the peopling of the earth took place in the Pleistocene epoch of the last 2.5 million years, which was characterized by repeated glacial cycles. The Pleistocene epoch ended nearly 12,000 years ago, marking the onset of a new interglacial warm period known as the Holocene epoch. By then modern humans had arrived everywhere on the globe. The global climate became fairly stable during the Holocene, aptly described as the "long summer" of human civilization.[83] As the ice retreated from northern Europe, Central Asia, and northern America, new feeding grounds opened up to the animals, and as the frozen rivers thawed, fishing grounds became more widespread. As grass and vegetation spread into new areas, so did fruit trees and wild cereals. As the climate warmed, there was increased rainfall in lands near the equator, with a consequent increase in the richness of plant and animal life.[84] The Holocene provided a sort of idyllic setting for humans to settle down and flourish. Bill McKibben sums up these ideal climate conditions, the sort of "Goldilocks" weather that eventually made human civilization possible.

> For the ten thousand years that constitute human civilization, we've existed in the sweetest of sweet spots. The temperature has barely budged; globally averaged, it's swung in the narrowest of ranges, between fifty-eight and sixty degrees Fahrenheit. That's warm enough that the ice sheets retreated from the centers of our continents so we could grow grain, but cold enough that mountain glaciers provided drinking and irrigation water to those plains and valleys year-round; it was the "correct" temperature for the marvelously diverse planet that seems right to us.[85]

As our ancestors spread across the globe and settled down, they also began to change the physical world around them. Beginning as early as 12,000 years ago most human populations transitioned from hunter-gatherers to agriculturalists and pastoralists. The stable climate that came along with the Holocene epoch made agriculture possible. People began to domesticate plants and animals, breeding them to

---

[83] See Brian Fagan, *The Long Summer: How Climate Changed Civilization* (New York: Basic Books, 2004).

[84] Aydon, *A Brief History of Mankind*, 21–22.

[85] Bill McKibben, *Eaarth: Making a Life on a Tough New Planet* (New York: Times Books/Henry Holt and Co., 2010), 1.

render them more productive. People manipulated once-wild plants and began to raise wheat, rice, corn, barley, millet, peas, beans, and many other crops. Concomitantly, they domesticated wild goats, sheep, pigs, horses, cattle, and other familiar farm animals. Grasslands were plowed, and rivers were diverted for irrigation.

The rise of agriculture was to alter dramatically the course of human history. Agriculture bound people to the land, leading to permanent settlements. Increased food availability allowed groups to remain in the same area and to increase in size. It is estimated that the development of agriculture facilitated a fivefold increase in population growth relative to more ancient expansions of hunter-gatherers.[86] Around this time sedentary communities arose in the Near East, Asia, in the Americas, and elsewhere. Human populations began to settle down, and Neolithic villages arose throughout the globe that survived on agriculture, pastoralism, pottery, weaving, and other occupations. These new societies eventually formed the basis of modern urban culture. One of the world's oldest cities is Jericho, founded more than 12,000 years ago, followed later by Çatal Hüyük, Hassuna, and others. In the Far East, Japan's Jomon people produced some of the world's earliest pottery around the same time. By approximately 8,000 years ago, people in the Levant—modern-day Syria, Lebanon, Jordan, Israel, the Palestine territories, and parts of southern Anatolia in Turkey—lived in settled villages and used Neolithic technologies.[87]

The greater abundance of food made possible by agriculture not only guaranteed human populations greater welfare and security but also provided them with more time and leisure to pursue activities that went beyond the arc of existence and survival. Eventually, a wide variety of languages and social, cultural, political, moral, and religious systems arose among human communities in various parts of the world.

As humans sought to observe and interpret the rhythms of nature more acutely, the study of natural phenomena became more common and better organized. A great step in this regard was the invention of calendars which sought to depict the movements of celestial bodies, especially of the sun and the moon and the alternation of seasons.

---

[86] Christopher R. Gignoux et al., "Rapid, Global Demographic Expansions After the Origins of Agriculture," *Proceedings of the National Academy of Sciences* 108 (2011): 6044. On the rise of agriculture see also B. D. Smith, *The Emergence of Agriculture* (New York: Scientific American Library, 1995).

[87] See David Robson, "Hunter, Gatherer . . . Architect? Civilization's True Dawn," *New Scientist* 2937 (October 3, 2013).

Besides being of practical help in farming, such timid beginnings eventually paved the way for the development of important disciplines like astronomy, mathematics, and cosmology. As the oral languages and traditions gave way to written languages and records, it became easier to codify, preserve, and transmit knowledge within and among generations.

The tribal peoples continued to maintain a primordial relationship with the cosmos. They sought a harmonious bond with the natural world around them, which they saw at the same time as imbued with supernatural spirits. The myths originally created by them went on to become the archetypal structures of human consciousness, guiding secular and religious life in later millennia.

On the banks of great rivers like the Tigris/Euphrates in Meso-potamia, the Nile in Africa, and the Indus, Ganges, and Yangtze in Asia, some of the great civilizations of antiquity arose: the Sumerian civilization in Mesopotamia with its extensive irrigation system; the Babylonians, who produced the Hammurabi law code; and the Indus Valley civilization with its well-laid-out and fortified cities. The introduction of agricultural technologies like irrigation and the development of trades like metallurgy and pottery led to the birth of great urban centers. In Meso-America the Olmec civilization rose and more recently the Mayan and Aztec civilizations.

The splendid civilizations of antiquity were followed by the great empires. They arose in succession, remaining in prominence for centuries before being replaced by newer and equally extensive ones. The Shang and Chou dynasties in China, the Assyrian Empire, the pharaohs of Egypt, the Greek Empire under Alexander the Great, the Empire of Ashoka in India, the Roman Empire under Augustus Caesar, the Byzantine Empire, the Islamic Caliphate, the Sung and Ming dynasties in China, the Carolingian Empire, the Mongolian Empire, the Aztec Empire—all arose and spread widely, only to be wiped away in the course of time.

The development of abstract thought can also be seen in this period. The Greeks pursued the idea of the Logos, and the idea of the Tao emerged in China, while a quest for the Ultimate Reality of Brahman engaged many thoughtful people in India. Their philosophical texts sought to encapsulate some of the most profound questions and yearnings of the human spirit. Around the same time we also find the first flowerings of science, with Euclidian geometry, Archimedean physics, and Ptolemaic astronomy, while later the notion of zero and decimals were invented in Indian arithmetic. Systems of medicine, political life, and administration were developed in the various parts of the world. As human populations settled and flourished, they also developed their own distinctive cultures, which found expression in unique aesthetic expressions like art, dance, and music; literary expressions such as poetry and drama; and splendid architectural and technological feats. The last few millennia of human history have witnessed an explosion of human creativity.

Since the dawn of human existence there has also always been the human search for the Ultimate Reality, the relentless quest for the Transcendent that has found fulfilment mainly in the various religious traditions of humanity. From ancient times the shrines, temples, and priestly castes played a significant role in the social, political, and economic life of the populations. Indigenous and tribal religious traditions with their repertoire of folklore and myths spread themselves out throughout the planet. In the course of millennia some of the major world religions were born: the great mystical religions of the East like Hinduism and Buddhism, and the great religions of revelation like Judaism, Christianity, and Islam in the Middle East, to cite the major ones. These religions, with their written scriptures, elaborate codes of faith, and structures of organization, soon spread to other parts of the world, profoundly shaping human moral and religious consciousness.

During the last few millennia there were also attempts among the various human societies to establish contacts among themselves. One concrete expression was worldwide commerce, which had existed from antiquity, for example, the long-distance Indian Ocean maritime trade, or the overland caravans that ran across the Sahara and along the Silk Road, which operated its full length from 100 BCE. Global commerce expanded especially beginning in the fifteenth century in America, Asia, and Africa, along with its subsequent and dark chapter of the slave trade.

However, the event that was destined radically to change humanity's relationship with the physical world was the birth of modern science in the seventeenth century, pioneered by thinkers like Bacon, Galileo, Descartes, and Newton, and the Industrial Revolution that followed in its wake. Modern science and technology brought improvements to human life and offered greater amenities in a way unparalleled in the history of humanity, ranging from nutrition to health and from transport to communication. Above all, they enabled humanity to harness the resources of nature in ways unimaginable in previous millennia. The process of industrialization, which saw enormous expansion in the use of fossil fuels and energy dependence, would leave a heavy imprint on Earth and its natural processes.[88]

The decades following the Second World War are described as the Great Acceleration period.[89] This period witnessed a tripling of the human population and a tenfold growth of the global economy, along with a three-quarters increase in atmospheric carbon dioxide. The current impact of human activities on the physical world and its ecosystems has been so great that scientists speak in terms of a new geological epoch called the Anthropocene—the age of humans.[90] We have begun to transform the natural world, to its detriment, as never in the past.

Earth Is Our Only Home

A pivotal moment in human history was when the first human beings, capsuled in a spacecraft, broke off from the gravitational pull of the home planet to reach outer space. Humans had for the first time stepped out of their planetary home.

The first images of Earth from space in the 1960s and 1970s changed once and for all humanity's perception of its proper home. As the astronauts looked back at this planet in the immensely vast universe, they realized that the survival of humanity depends on the proper stewarding of this one spot in the cosmos. In 1978, Sigmund Jähn, member of the spacecraft *Soyuz* 31, confided, "Only when I saw it from space, in all its ineffable beauty and fragility, did I realize that humankind's most urgent task is to cherish and preserve it for future generations."[91]

Earth is indeed a unique home for life in the infinitely vast universe. Today, after decades of space exploration, this awareness has only deepened. We are still to come across any planet in the galactic expanses that can rival the blue-green jewel Earth, the home of humanity along with millions of other life forms.

---

[88] For a comprehensive historical overview, see McDonagh, *To Care for the Earth*, 90–92; McDonagh, "The Story of the Universe: Our Story," 156–57; UNEP (United Nations Environment Programme), *Global Environment Outlook 5: Environment for the Future We Want* (Nairobi: UNEP, 2012), 22; Alex MacGillivray, *A Brief History of Globalization: The Untold Story of Our Incredible Shrinking Planet* (London: Robinson, 2006); Aydon, *A Brief History of Mankind*.

[89] See UNEP, *Global Environment Outlook 5*, 22.

[90] See Jan Zalasiewicz et al., "The Anthropocene: A New Epoch of Geological Time?" *Philosophical Transactions of the Royal Society A* 369 (2011): 835–41.

[91] Quoted in Beeby and Brennan, *First Ecology*, 2.

Such an awareness in the scientific community contrasts with a widely diffused mentality in public opinion, especially among the techno-savvy generations, that when Earth is rendered uninhabitable, we can easily swap it for another planet in our solar system or somewhere else in the universe. Such a way of thinking, which is well ingrained among the general public, is nurtured by the unconscious faith that technology will see humanity through any crisis whatsoever, including the crisis of our home, namely, the contemporary ecological crisis. The unscripted credo of such a faith is that we can carry on with our life as usual—exploiting our planet's natural resources, polluting its atmosphere, and running down its ecosystems—and if and when the ecological crisis spins out of control, we can pack up, leave the earth, and migrate elsewhere.

Such a way of thinking ultimately springs from a profound ignorance and a lack of appreciation for the uniqueness of Earth as a home for life, made possible by a series of intricate and complex mechanisms and processes that have evolved and been perfected over billions of years and that ultimately rendered this planet habitable. Within the solar system Earth is a "Goldilocks" planet—in the right position and with the right global temperature. Besides, there are many other planetary conditions that together make the earth hospitable for life, including the right composition of gases in its atmosphere. Life evolved through complex processes over millions and millions of years before humans eventually occupied the entire planetary home.[92] The sheer complexities, and the exorbitant costs of managing life conditions in human economic terms, even in a very tiny land area, were best evidenced in the famous and short-lived Biosphere 2 experiment in the Arizona desert, which has long been abandoned.[93]

Those who remain indifferent to the crisis facing our home planet, fancying an easy and quick escape to distant planets, appear to be naive also about primary facts like the immensity of the universe and the distances involved, on the one hand, and the rudimentary stage of space travel, on the other. Here one needs to distinguish between the realms of science fiction and reality. It is true that astronomers are continuously on the lookout for potentially habitable planets—called exoplanets—positioned the right distance from their stars and with an

---

[92] See also Edward O. Wilson, *The Creation: An Appeal to Save Life on Earth* (New York: W. W. Norton, 2006), 26ff.

[93] See A. Alling et al., *Life Under Glass: The Inside Story of Biosphere 2* (Tucson, AZ: Synergetic Press, 1993).

adequate mass to hold their own atmospheres.[94] It is part of the noble and insatiable human quest to know and explore the physical universe that has accompanied humanity from the dawn of civilization. However, given that the search for exoplanets is in very preliminary stages, it is important to avoid unnecessary hype. Two observations are in order here. First of all, with our present-day space technology, even to reach the most hypothetical "twin Earths"—in which the presence of clouds, land, and sea are purely speculative[95]—we would need thousands and thousands of years, in fact, light years in astronomical parlance. Apart from such immense distances, there is also the question of the enormous costs. Space stations and space travel today are possible only for trained astronauts as part of multi-million-dollar research projects or for the super millionaires who opt for a ride paying with their personal fortunes. In this sense the logic of continuing to despoil our common home with the hope of migration to hypothetic distant habitable planets or to future space colonies is also a direct affront to the multitudes of poor. "Almost half the world—over 3 billion people—live on less than $2.50 a day."[96] They are precisely the ones who are the most affected by the contemporary ecological crisis. We may one day in the distant future reach for the stars and migrate elsewhere in the universe. But the contemporary ecological crisis, imminent. In some aspects it has already caught up with us.

The fact that humanity has not really recognized its home planet as its proper home is the situation in which we find ourselves. We are willing to spend billions to search for traces of life, even life in its primordial forms like bacteria, elsewhere in the universe, while

---

[94] For a vivid account, see Michael Lemonick, *Mirror Earth: The Search for Our Planet's Twin* (New York: Walker, 2012). Some of the most recent discoveries in this regard are the planets orbiting a star designated Kepler-62, of which only Kepler-62f lies strictly within the hypothetically habitable zone. See Richard A. Kerr, "Kepler Snags Super-Earth-Size-Planet Squarely in a Habitable Zone," *Science* 340 (2013): 262. See also See Xavier Dumusque et al., "An Earth-Mass Planet Orbiting Alpha Centauri B," *Nature* 491 (2012): 207–10. The most recently discovered Kepler 78b lies at a distance of 400 light years and is expected to have a surface temperature of 2,800°C as it orbits very close to the parent star. See Andrew W. Howard et al., "A Rocky Composition for an Earth-Sized Exoplanet," *Nature* 503 (October 30, 2013).

[95] Kerr, "Kepler Snags Super-Earth-Size-Planet Squarely in a Habitable Zone," 262. The existence of an exoplanet is determined not directly but indirectly by analyzing the light from the parent star which is blocked by the planet as it passes in front.

[96] Anup Shah, "Poverty Facts and Stats," available on the globalissues.org website. The source for the statistics in the article is the World Bank Developmnet Indicators 2008.

trampling under our feet the already existing abundant forms of life on our home planet. As we shall see later, we are letting species disappear by hundreds and thousands every year, some of them even before being classified, while we are willing to traverse billions of miles in space to look for rudimentary forms of life elsewhere. We are pulling down the magnificent home of life with which we have been blessed while eagerly looking for possible ones elsewhere in the cosmos. It is certainly one of the great ironies of our present human civilization.

Perhaps we have not yet discovered and appreciated the truth of Earth as our home. Deeper philosophical reflection reveals that any dream to flee from Earth masks the fundamental lack of "at-homeness" of the contemporary human person. Val Plumwood perspicaciously remarks: "Space colonization is an extreme example of a rationalist project that misunderstands our nature as earth beings. . . . When we have learnt the true nature of our being as earth-dependent and have learnt both to cherish the earth and to go beyond it without damage, it may be time for us to try to leave for the stars—but not before."[97] We have not discovered ourselves as inhabitants of the common home of Earth, as truly Earthlings, *imago mundi*, formed from the dust of the earth.

Our lack of at-homeness on Earth probably has to do with our perception of our home planet as a mere environment—something that just happens to surround us—a fundamental misconception. Unconsciously, we continue to think that migrating from one planet to another, to somewhere else in space once Earth has been rendered inhabitable, is like shifting from one house to another, or from one country or continent to another. But the fact is that for Earthlings, our home is here and only here. We would not find tropical beaches and palm trees, not to speak of fundamental and indispensable requisites like oxygen to breathe and the right atmospheric pressure to survive, if we were to migrate to other planets. In the vast cosmic ocean, for human beings and for other forms of life that evolved before us on this planet, Earth is our home, and our only home. Other forms of life *may* exist on other planets, adapted to their homes. But we were born here as Earthlings, and we can exist and flourish only here. As biologist Edward O. Wilson reminds us, "Earth, and especially the razor-thin film of life enveloping it, is our home."[98] We belong here, to the biosphere of the earth. So *"alien planets are not in our genes.*

---

[97] Val Plumwood, *Environmental Culture: The Ecological Crisis of Reason* (London: Routledge, 2002), 240.

[98] Wilson, *The Creation*, 7.

If organisms exist on Mars, Europa, or Titanis, then these planets are in *their* genes, and those will surely differ radically from ours."[99] In the past, if we got things wrong and wrecked our surroundings, we could pack up sticks and move elsewhere. "Migration has always been one of our species'" great survival strategies. Now we have nowhere else to go. No new frontier. We have only one atmosphere; only one planet."[100] Like the inhabitants of the Easter Island isolated in the Pacific Ocean who had nowhere to flee after they had run down their only habitat, we too may find ourselves in an analogous situation in the vast cosmic ocean.[101]

---

[99]   Ibid., 27.

[100]   Fred Pearce, *The Last Generation: How Nature Will Take Her Revenge for Climate Change* (London: Eden Project Books, 2006), 296.

[101]   See Jared Diamond, *Collapse: How Societies Choose to Fail or Succeed* (London: Penguin Books, 2005), 119.

2

Our Common Home in Peril

In the 1960s, while the first images of the earth from space were being beamed across the globe, revealing the exquisite beauty of this blue-green jewel, earthbound scientists were already beginning to see signs of the increasing fragility of our planetary home. Some symptoms of the ecological crisis had already become evident. Industrial pollution, urban smog, and acid deposition were becoming common. Many ecosystems were under strain from the heavy use of pesticides and fertilizers that modern agriculture had introduced. Some species were already on the verge of extinction, and the planet's life arteries were beginning to choke. It was clear that not all was well with the common home of the earth, in which the common family of humanity dwells along with millions of other species.

The present chapter explores the extent to which our common home has been imperilled. We begin with a survey of authoritative warnings on the contemporary ecological crisis from the scientific community—especially from the major scientific academies of the world like the National Academy of Sciences and the Royal Society, among others. This is followed by a more detailed analysis of three studies in particular. The first explains that the planetary boundaries are about to be transgressed or have already been crossed, with regard to some of the fundamental geochemical and biological processes that sustain life on Earth. The second deals with the fast depletion of the natural resources of the planet, as calculated by the mechanism of the ecological footprint analysis. The third is about the disquieting predictions on future climate change by the Fourth Assessment of the Intergovernmental Panel on Climate Change (IPCC) in 2007 and updates thereafter. A constant preoccupation of the scientific community with regard to the contemporary ecological crisis, especially in recent years, has been about the danger of crossing crucial thresholds in tampering with the earth's climate and its natural processes. The concept of tipping points is analysed here. We then demonstrate the conspicuously anthropogenic character of the contemporary ecological crisis—how human activities have, in a relatively short period of time, caused irreparable damage to our common home. The impact of humanity on the planet appears to have reached such proportions that it may be justified to speak of the dawn of a new geological epoch, informally termed the Anthropocene (human) era, about which discussion has already begun among Earth scientists. The chapter concludes with a reflection on the ethical and religious implications of eco-cide, humanity's destruction of its common home.

The Gravity of the Contemporary Ecological Crisis: Warnings from the Scientific Community

It has been the singular merit of the scientific community to have perceived the signs of the impending ecological crisis and to have warned humanity of the serious threats to our common home. The scientific community has sought to present the crisis with remarkable objectivity, courage, and foresight, in spite of being met with derision and vilification at times, especially from some quarters of corporate industry, politics, and media guided by vested interests. From Rachel Carson to NASA's James Hansen, individuals and institutions of the scientific community have not shied away from their vocation to be prophets and seers, warning humanity of the serious threats to our common home.

One of the first scientists to alert humanity to the ecological crisis was Rachel Carson in her short but seminal 1962 *Silent Spring,* which dealt with pollution.[1] In this work Carson described the ecological consequences and health hazards involved in the introduction into the biosphere of thousands of toxic substances by industry and modern agriculture. She showed, for example, how a pesticide like DDT, which was widely used at that time, made its way into the food chain and eventually even into mothers' breast milk. Apart from such specific concerns, Carson was ultimately raising some fundamental questions about humankind's impact on the physical world and the rest of the biosphere.[2]

---

[1] Rachel Carson, *Silent Spring* (Boston: Houghton Mifflin, 1962).

[2] Significantly, as Mark Hamilton Lytle notes, *Silent Spring* actually went through a number of working titles, including *Man Against Nature, The Control of Nature,* and *How to Balance Nature,* none of which satisfied Carson or her literary agent, Marie Rodell. See Mark Hamilton Lytle, *The Gentle Subversive: Rachel Carson, Silent Spring, and the Rise of the Environmental Movement* (New York: Oxford University Press, 2007), 11.

The awareness regarding the crisis facing the earth and those dwelling in it was further deepened in a number of publications that followed in the successive decades, including *The Population Bomb, The Closing Circle, A Blueprint for Survival, Fundamentals of Ecology, The Limits to Growth, Only One Earth, The Global 2000 Report to the President,* and *Our Common Future.*[3]

These early warnings from the scientific community spearheaded the spread of public awareness about the ecological crisis and created campaign movements, especially in the West, for the stewardship of the planet. Earth Day was celebrated for the first time in 1970, and the United Nations organized an important conference on the theme of ecological stewardship that was held in Stockholm in 1972. The Preamble to its declaration stated: "A point has been reached in history when we must shape our actions throughout the world with a more prudent care for their environmental consequences. Through ignorance or indifference we can do massive and irreversible harm to the earthly environment on which our life and well-being depend."[4] A number of regional and international meetings have since been organized under the auspices of the United Nations, the most prominent among them the Earth Summits held every decade (1992 in Rio de Janeiro, 2002 in Johannesburg, and 2012 in Rio de Janeiro).

The United Nations also took the lead in establishing international bodies for the stewardship of the planet. In the field of climate change the IPCC was jointly established by the United Nations Environment Programme and the World Meteorological Organization in 1988,

---

[3] Paul Ehrlich, *The Population Bomb* (New York: Sierra Club/Ballentine Books, 1968); Barry Commoner, *The Closing Circle: Confronting the Environmental Crisis* (London: Jonathan Cape, 1971); Edward Goldsmith et al., *A Blueprint for Survival* (London: Penguin Books, 1972); Eugene P. Odum, *Fundamentals of Ecology* (Philadelphia: W. B. Saunders Company, 1971); Donella H. Meadows, Dennis L. Meadows, Jorgen Randers, and William W. Behrens III, *The Limits to Growth: A Report for the Club of Rome's Project on the Predicament of Mankind* (London: Earth Island Limited, 1972); Barbara Ward and René Dubos, *Only One Earth: The Care and Maintenance of a Small Planet* (Harmondsworth: Penguin Books, 1972); *The Global 2000 Report to the President: Entering the Twenty-First Century: A Report Prepared by the Council on Environmental Quality and the Department of State* (London: Penguin Book, 1982); The World Commission on Environment and Development, *Our Common Future* (Oxford: Oxford University Press, 1987). For an evaluation of the literature in this initial period see W. H. Baarschers, *Eco-facts and Eco-fiction: Understanding the Environmental Debate* (London: Routledge, 1996), 1–8; Peter Hay, *A Companion to Environmental Thought* (Edinburgh: Edinburgh University Press, 2002), 31–36.

[4] Preamble to the Declaration of the UN Conference on the Human Environment, Stockholm (June 5–16, 1972), item 6.

while the United Nations Framework Convention on Climate Change came into existence in 1994. In the area of biodiversity conservation, the Convention on Biological Diversity was set up in 1993. The most recent development in the field of biodiversity has been the setting up in 2011 of the Intergovernmental Science-Policy Platform on Biodiversity and Ecosystem Services, conceived on parallel lines to the IPCC. In other areas, there has been the United Nations Convention to Combat Desertification in 1996. In the meantime, several regional and national bodies and organizations have also been set up in various parts of the world for the protection of the home planet.

The scientific community has continued to alert humanity to the ecological crisis with greater urgency. In the last few decades a number of international scientific associations and institutions have issued direct warnings to humanity about the contemporary ecological crisis. One of the earliest admonitions came in 1992 and was titled *The World Scientists' Warning to Humanity*. It was signed by nearly seventeen hundred of Earth's leading scientists, including 104 Nobel laureates—more than half of the living recipients in the sciences. This declaration was not only a serious warning to humanity but also a clarion call for immediate action in order to avert disaster.

> Human beings and the natural world are on a collision course. Human activities inflict harsh and often irreversible damage on the environment and on critical resources. If not checked, many of our current practices put at serious risk the future that we wish for human society and the plant and animal kingdoms, and may so alter the living world that it will be unable to sustain life in the manner that we know. . . .
>
> We the undersigned, senior members of the world's scientific community, hereby warn all humanity of what lies ahead. A great change in our stewardship of the earth and the life on it is required if vast human misery is to be avoided and our global home on this planet is not to be irretrievably mutilated.[5]

More recently, the warnings from the scientific community have been centered around the threat of global warming and associated climate change, one of the most conspicuous facets of the contemporary

---

[5] "The World Scientists' Warning to Humanity," in Paul Ehrlich and Anne Ehrlich, *Betrayal of Science and Reason: How Anti-Environmental Rhetoric Threatens Our Future* (Washington, DC: Island Press, 1998), 242, 244. For the text of the declaration and for an abridged list of the signatories, see ibid., 241–50.

ecological crisis. An important document in this regard was the joint statement issued by the presidents of the National Science Academies of eleven major nations (the United States, Brazil, Canada, China, France, Germany, India, Italy, Japan, Russia, and the UK) on June 9, 2005. In this report the presidents acknowledge that "the scientific understanding of climate change is now sufficiently clear to justify nations taking prompt action" and warn that "action taken now to reduce significantly the build-up of greenhouse gases in the atmosphere will lessen the magnitude and rate of climate change."[6]

In the United States a group of 255 members of the US National Academy of Sciences in May 2010 took the unprecedented step of writing an open letter to the US Congress in which they cautioned their political leaders: "Society has two choices: We can ignore the science and hide our heads in the sand and hope we are lucky, or we can act in the public interest to reduce the threat of global climate change quickly and substantively."[7] Apart from climate change one may recall the statement of the Inter-Academy Panel on ocean acidification in June 2009, which was endorsed by as many as seventy of the world's leading national academies of science.[8]

Momentum has indeed been building in the scientific community, and scientists have continued to warn humanity about the risk of underestimating the challenges posed by the contemporary ecological crisis. Significantly, in recent years some of the most prestigious scientific institutions of the world, including major scientific academies and joint studies, have taken a clear and unambiguous stand on climate change and related ecological challenges.

In September 2010, the Royal Society, the oldest scientific academy in continuous existence, published an important document titled *Climate Change: A Summary of the Science*. The study aims to summarize the current scientific evidence on climate change and its drivers, aware that "changes in climate have significant implications for present lives, for future generations and for ecosystems on which humanity depends."[9] A month later the French Academy of Sciences

---

[6] "Joint Science Academies' Statement: Global Response to Climate Change," available at http://nationalacademies.org.

[7] P. H. Gleick et al., "Climate Change and the Integrity of Science," *Science* 328 (2010): 689–90.

[8] Inter-Academy Panel, "Statement on Ocean Acidification" (Trieste: The Academy of Sciences for the Developing World, 2009).

[9] The Royal Society, "Introduction," *Climate Change: A Summary of the Science* (September 30, 2010), para. 1.

published a similar document on the problem of climate change.[10] The most comprehensive document on climate change by any science academy to date was published by the US National Academies of Sciences, also in 2010, titled *Advancing the Science of Climate Change*. It states, "Climate change is occurring, is caused largely by human activities, and poses significant risks for—and in many cases is already affecting—a broad range of human and natural systems."[11] In May 2011, the Pontifical Academy of Sciences published a report on mountain glaciers. The Opening Declaration of this report states:

> We call on all people and nations to recognise the serious and potentially irreversible impacts of global warming caused by the anthropogenic emissions of greenhouse gases and other pollutants, and by changes in forests, wetlands, grasslands, and other land uses . . . aware that *we all live in the same home*. By acting now, in the spirit of common but differentiated responsibility, we accept our duty to one another and to *the stewardship of a planet blessed with the gift of life.* We are committed to ensuring that all inhabitants of this planet receive their daily bread, fresh air to breathe and clean water to drink as we are aware that, if we want justice and peace, *we must protect the habitat that sustains us.* (emphasis added)[12]

We may also mention in this regard the April 2012 report from the Royal Society titled *People and the Planet,* which states that "the 21st century is a critical period for people and the planet" and that "human impact on the earth raises serious concerns."[13]

The Alarming State of Our Common Home

From the avalanche of warnings from the scientific community regarding the disquieting state of our planetary home in recent years, we now pick up three recent and authoritative ones. All of these

---

[10] See Institut de France, Académie des sciences, *Le changement climatique* (October 26, 2010).

[11] The National Academy of Sciences, *Advancing the Science of Climate Change* (Washington, DC: The National Academies Press, 2010), 3.

[12] Pontificia Academia Scientiarum, *Fate of Mountain Glaciers in the Anthropocene: A Report by the Working Group Commissioned by the Pontifical Academy of Sciences* (May 5, 2011), 2, 15.

[13] The Royal Society, *People and the Planet* (April 2012), 7.

studies point to how the capacity of the earth to be a common home for humans and other living beings is increasingly jeopardized.

The first important study was carried out by twenty-eight scholars associated with the Stockholm Resilience Centre, among them prominent earth scientists like Nobel Prize winner Paul Crutzen and James Hansen of NASA.[14] The study seeks to identify and quantify the "planetary boundaries" that must not be transgressed in order to avoid irreversible ecological damage. In other words, the proposed planetary boundaries define the safe operating space for humanity with respect to the earth and its associated biophysical subsystems. The authors identify planetary boundaries in nine key areas: climate change, rate of biodiversity loss, interference with the nitrogen and phosphorus cycles, stratospheric ozone depletion, ocean acidification, global fresh-water use, change in land use, chemical pollution, and atmospheric aerosol loading.

According to the study humanity may soon be approaching the boundaries for global fresh-water use, change in land use, ocean acidification and interference with the global phosphorous cycle. The most alarming conclusion of the report is that with regard to the areas of climate change, rate of biodiversity loss, and interference with the nitrogen cycle, humanity has already transgressed the limits. With regard to climate change, some of Earth's subsystems appear to be moving outside their stable Holocene state, for example, the rapid retreat of the summer sea ice in the Arctic ocean, the retreat of mountain glaciers around the world, and the accelerating rise in sea levels during the past ten to fifteen years. As for the rate of biodiversity loss, where the transgression appears to be most flagrant, species are becoming extinct at a rate that has not been seen since the last global mass-extinction event. As for the nitrogen cycle, it appears that industrialized agriculture has already poured more chemicals into the land and oceans than the planet can process.[15]

---

[14] J. Rockström et al., "A Safe Operating Space for Humanity," *Nature* 461 (2009): 472–75. For a more detailed version of the same study, see idem, "Planetary Boundaries: Exploring the Safe Operating Space for Humanity," *Ecology and Society* 14/2 (2009): 32ff.

[15] Rockström et al., "A Safe Operating Space for Humanity," 472–73. See also O. M. Johannessen, "Decreasing Arctic Sea Ice Mirrors Increasing CO_2 on Decadal Time Scale," *Atmospheric and Oceanic Science Letters, Institute of Atmospheric Physics, Chinese Academy of Sciences* 1/1 (2008): 51–56; J. A. Church and N. J. White, "A 20th Century Acceleration in Global Sea Level Rise," *Geophysical Research Letters* 33 (2006): 1602; G. Mace et al., "Biodiversity," in *Ecosystems and Human Wellbeing: Current State and Trends*, ed. H. Hassan et al. (Washington, DC: Island Press, 2005), 79–115; J. N. Galloway and E. B. Cowling, "Reactive

The study on planetary boundaries conveys a very important message, namely, that it is the entire common home of humanity that is threatened. The contemporary ecological crisis is unique in the sense that it is not about a single environmental problem, like climate change, for example. Up to now, attempts at conceptualizing a global approach to managing humanity's relationship with the rest of the natural world have tended to focus on individual subsystems or processes in isolation, like climate, biodiversity, stratospheric ozone, or others. Such a simple cause-effect approach also guides many approaches to manipulate the earth system deliberately, as in geo-engineering proposals.[16] The concept of planetary boundaries instead demonstrates how the earth system is a single, integrated, complex system, with many interrelated and interdependent subsystems. The study also demonstrates that the current ecological crisis is not about a local or transitory phenomenon. It is the earth that is in peril. The contemporary ecological crisis in this regard is unparalleled in the geological history of the planet. It is the first time that humanity's own dwelling has been threatened.

A second authoritative indicator from the scientific community about the alarming state of our common home concerns the consumption of natural resources. A yardstick called ecological footprint anaylsis, pioneered by William Rees and Mathis Wackernagel, is being increasingly used to measure human impact on the planet.[17] It is widely considered to be the most comprehensive aggregate pointer of human pressure on ecosystems to date.

Authors Jason Venetoulis and John Talberth write:

Ecological footprints measure a population's demands on nature in a single metric: area of global biocapacity. By comparing humanity's ecological footprint with the Earth's available biological capacity, ecological footprint analysis (EFA) suggests whether or not our use of crop lands, forest lands, pasture lands, fisheries, built space, and energy lands can be sustained.[18]

Nitrogen and the World: Two Hundred Years of Change," *AMBIO: A Journal of the Human Environment* 31 (2002): 64–71.

[16] Will Steffen et al., "The Anthropocene: Conceptual and Historical Perspectives," *Philosophical Transactions of the Royal Society A* 369 (2011): 860.

[17] William Rees and Mathis Wackernagel, *Our Ecological Footprint: Reducing Human Impact on the Earth* (Philadelphia: New Society Publishers, 1996).

[18] Jason Venetoulis and John Talberth, "Ecological Footprint of Nations: 2005 Update," Sustainability Indicators Program (Oakland, CA: Redefining Progress,

Ecological footprint analysis can be used to determine the exact date that the global community begins to live beyond what the planet produces each year. Overall, humanity's ecological footprint has doubled since 1966. While economies, populations, and demands on resources grow, the size of the planet remains the same. There is a limit to the resources that the earth can produce and the waste it can absorb each year. The problem is precisely that human demands on the planet's services are exceeding what it can provide. Until very recently humanity's use of nature's services was within the means of what nature could regenerate. But sometime in the mid-1970s humanity appears to have crossed the critical threshold. Since then, humans have been in "ecological overshoot," using resources faster than they can be regenerated and putting carbon into the air more rapidly than it can be reabsorbed.

Ecological Debt Day or Earth Overshoot Day marks the precise day when humanity's demand for ecological resources and services in a given year exceeds what the earth can regenerate in that year.[19] According to the Global Footprint Network, in 2013 that day fell on August 20. In just eight months humanity had used up all the resources nature could provide for that year. From then until the end of the year, we dipped into our ecological reserves, borrowing from the future and depriving future generations as well as other nonhuman species of their rightful share of the earth's resources. Globally, human beings now demand the biological capacity of nearly one and one-half planets; that is, the rate of overshoot is up to 50 percent more than what the planet can renewably supply.[20] It is calculated that we will require the resources of two planets well before mid-century. The situation varies largely when it comes to individual nations, with the United States requiring five planets, the UK 3.4, Argentina 1.7, China 1.0, India 0.4. The situation is all the more alarming when it comes to the carbon footprint. According to "Human Development Report 2007/2008," if every person in the developing world left the same carbon footprint as the average North American or Canadian, we would need the atmospheres of

---

2005), 2. Available online.

[19] Global Footprint Network, "Earth Overshoot Day 2011," 1; WWF, "Living Planet Report 2010" (Gland, Switzerland: WWF, 2010), 8. Available online.

[20] WWF International—Institute of Zoology—Global Footprint Network, *Living Planet Report 2012: Biodiversity, Biocapacity and Better Choices* (Gland: WWF, 2012), 8.

nine planets to deal with the consequences.[21] But of course, we only have one planet.

Ecological overshoot is possible only for a limited time before ecosystems begin to degrade and possibly collapse. This can already be seen in global climate change, water shortages, reduced cropland productivity, erosion, overgrazing, deforestation, desertification, collapse of fisheries, and rapid extinction of species, to name a few. The multiple manifestations of the ecological crisis point to the truth that we are already using up more than our common habitat can provide. Living beyond our means is also returning to haunt us in the form of the contemporary ecological crisis.

The most authoritative pronouncements to date regarding the ecological threat facing our planetary home have been made by the IPCC—a co-recipient of the Nobel Peace Prize for 2007—which draws on the work of nearly twenty-five hundred scientists from nearly 130 nations. We quote here from the IPCC's Fifth Assessment Report:

> Warming of the climate system is unequivocal, and since the 1950s, many of the observed changes are unprecedented over decades to millennia. The atmosphere and ocean have warmed, the amounts of snow and ice have diminished, sea level has risen, and the concentrations of greenhouse gases have increased. . . . Each of the last three decades has been successively warmer at the earth's surface than any preceding decade since 1850.[22]

According to the report, almost the entire globe has experienced surface warming in recent decades; global average surface temperature increased by 0.85°C during the period 1880–2012.[23] The report predicts that the global temperatures are likely to rise by 0.3°C to 4.8°C, by the end of the century depending on possible carbon emission scenarios.[24] It is important to recall here that global average temperature

---

[21] See UNDP (United Nations Development Programme), "Human Development Report 2007/2008: Facing Climate Change: Human Solidarity in a Divided World" (New York: Macmillan, 2007), 3, 43, 48.

[22] IPCC, *Climate Change 2013: The Physical Science Basis: Contribution of Working Group I to the Fifth Assessment Report of the Intergovernmental Panel on Climate Change*, ed. T. F. Stocker et al. (Cambridge: Cambridge University Press, 2013), 4–5.

[23] Ibid., 5.

[24] Ibid., 20. The Arctic region will warm more rapidly than the global mean (ibid.).

variations have never exceeded 1°C since the beginning of the present human civilization! It may also be recalled that the 2007 IPCC report had warned that up to 30 percent of plant and animal species so far assessed are likely to be at increased risk of extinction if increases in global average temperatures exceed 1.5°C–2.5°C.[25]

The Danger of Crossing the Thresholds

While continuing to caution humanity about the precarious state of our home planet, a constant preoccupation of the scientific community in recent years has been the risk of crossing the thresholds in tampering with the earth's climate and its natural processes. Scientists fear that the current state of the planet could be destabilized if human activity causes critical thresholds to be passed. Such a concern is expressed through the concept of tipping points. When a small change leads to a large and abrupt change in the system, this represents a "tipping phenomenon," and the threshold at which an abrupt change occurs is the "tipping point."[26] A tipping point commonly refers to a critical threshold at which a tiny perturbation can have large, long-term consequences for the planet's natural systems. In fact, many subsystems of Earth react in a nonlinear and often abrupt way, and these subsystems are particularly sensitive around threshold levels of certain key variables. If these thresholds are crossed, then important subsystems could shift to a qualitatively new state, often with deleterious consequences for humans.[27] Both ecosystems and human communities are highly sensitive to abrupt shifts in climate because such alterations may exceed the tolerance of organisms and consequently have major effects on biotic diversity, human investments, and the stability of societies.[28] Many scientists now hold that "human activities may have the potential to push components of the earth system past

---

[25] IPCC, *Climate Change 2007: Synthesis Report. Contribution of Working Groups I, II and III to the Fourth Assessment Report of the Intergovernmental Panel on Climate Change*, ed. R. K. Pachauri and A. Reisinger (Geneva: IPCC, 2007), 48.

[26] National Research Council, *Understanding Earth's Deep Past: Lessons for Our Climate Future* (Washington, DC: The National Academies Press, 2011), 10.

[27] Rockström et al., "A Safe Operating Space for Humanity," 472. See also Marten Scheffer et al., "Catastrophic Shifts in Ecosystems," *Nature* 413 (2001): 591–96.

[28] National Research Council, *Understanding Earth's Deep Past*, 11.

critical states into qualitatively different modes of operation, implying large-scale impacts on human and ecological systems."[29]

The general impression among the public at large is that the threat to the common home of Planet Earth, as manifested in phenomena like climate change, is gradual and will fully manifest itself only in the distant future. The scientists instead warn that in some regions human pressure on the climate system can start abrupt and potentially irreversible changes. When Earth is operating near a tipping point, small changes in the driving factors are sufficient to tip the planet rapidly from one state to another, setting off cascading effects. In this sense the ecological changes occur not so much cumulatively but suddenly, after invisible thresholds have been reached. Tipping points occur because of amplifying feedbacks, also called positive feedback mechanisms, in which changes that are small in their own right can lead to hugely disproportionate consequences.[30] This new understanding has upset the common and comforting idea of a linear relationship between the amount of greenhouse gases emitted and the amount of global warming that will follow. Earlier, many people, including policymakers, believed that although we may be slow to respond to climate change, once we decide to get our act together, we will be able to redeem the situation.[31] Scientists warn that this may not be the case: "Society may be lulled into a false sense of security by smooth projections of global change. Our synthesis of present knowledge suggests that a variety of tipping elements could reach their critical point within this century under anthropogenic climate change."[32]

---

[29] Timothy M. Lenton et al., "Tipping Elements in the Earth's Climate System," *Proceedings of the National Academy of Sciences* 105 (2008): 1786. This paper drew on a workshop attended by thirty-six leading climate scientists in October 2005 at the British Embassy in Berlin, a further elicitation of fifty-two experts in the field, and a critical review of the pertinent literature. See also Tim Lenton and Andrew Watson, *Revolutions That Made the Earth* (Oxford: Oxford University Press, 2011), esp. part 4. See also Hans Joachim Schellnhuber, "Tipping Elements in the Earth System," *Proceedings of the National Academy of Sciences* 106 (2009): 20561–63.

[30] James Hansen explains the concept of amplifying feedbacks very clearly using an ordinary example: "as when a microphone is placed too close to a speaker, which amplifies any little sound picked up by the microphone, which then picks up the amplification, which is again picked up by the speaker, until very quickly the noise becomes unbearable." See James Hansen, *Storms of My Grandchildren: The Truth About the Coming Climate Catastrophe and Our Last Chance to Save Humanity* (London: Bloomsbury, 2009), ix.

[31] Clive Hamilton, *Requiem for a Species: Why We Resist the Truth about Climate Change* (London: Earthscan, 2010), 1.

[32] Lenton et al., "Tipping Elements in the Earth's Climate System," 1792.

Among the various tipping points identified, Arctic sea-ice and the Greenland ice sheet are regarded as the most sensitive tipping elements with the smallest uncertainty. With regard to the Arctic, the positive feedback mechanism appears to have a crucial role in causing the sea-ice cover to dwindle. As sea-ice melts, it exposes a much darker open surface, which absorbs more radiation than white sea-ice, so that the warming is amplified. This "ice-albedo" positive feedback causes more rapid melting in summer and decreases ice formation in winter. In September 2012, satellite data presented the lowest extent of sea-ice on record.[33] It is estimated that the critical threshold of global mean warming for the Arctic may be between 0.5°C and 2°C. It is feared that the tipping point has already been reached, and consequently there will be no arctic sea-ice during summer within a few decades. The worst consequence of the melting of the Arctic will be the thawing of permafrost covering almost one-quarter of the Northern Hemisphere. This contains seventeen hundred gigatonnes of carbon in the form of frozen organic matter, almost twice as much carbon as that currently in the atmosphere. As a recent UNEP report has warned, if this permafrost were to thaw, as expected with the warming of the Arctic, the organic matter will thaw and decay, potentially releasing large amounts of CO_2 and methane into the atmosphere and significantly amplifying global warming.

Thawing of permafrost could emit 43 to 135 Gt of CO_2 equivalent by 2100 and 246 to 415 Gt of CO_2 equivalent by 2200. Uncertainties are large, but emissions from thawing permafrost could start within the next few decades and continue for several centuries, influencing both short-term climate (before 2100) and long-term climate (after 2100).[34]

As for the Greenland ice sheet, the worst-case scenario of local warming of more than 3°C could cause the ice sheet to disappear within three hundred years, resulting in a rise of sea level of up to twenty-three feet. Other sensitive areas where global warming beyond a certain threshold could lead to tipping points with catastrophic outcomes include the Amazon rainforest, where a dieback of the forest could occur with the threshold of 3°C–4°Cdegrees global warming; the Boreal forest, which could suffer from large-scale dieback with a

---

[33] Hannah Hoag, "Arctic Snow Cover Shows Sharp Decline," *Nature News* (October 31, 2012).

[34] UNEP (United Nations Environment Programme), *Policy Implications of Warming Permafrost* (Nairobi: UNEP, 2012), i–iii.

threshold of 3°C–5°C; the West Antarctic ice sheet, which could lose mass with a threshold of local warming of 5°C–8°C in summer; and the Indian summer monsoon, which could become erratic from a combination of global warming and air pollution.[35]

The scientific community believes that crossing the thresholds can lead to abrupt and irreversible climatic shifts and other natural catastrophes. Tipping points are points of no return. Many scientists agree that if those boundaries are crossed, it would be difficult, perhaps impossible, to reverse the process, at least for thousands of years. This is so because once drastic changes in Earth's natural processes are brought about, it will take a long time, several millennia, to regain equilibrium. David Archer notes, for example, that the carbon cycle between the solid Earth and the atmosphere stabilizes the temperature of the earth by a mechanism called the weathering thermostat. However, the weathering thermostat takes half a million years or longer to adjust the temperature of the earth.[36] Other irreversible impacts to be expected are irreversible dry-season rainfall reduction in several regions and inexorable sea-level rise. The sea-level rise, for example, once started, will continue for thousands of years, even if all the greenhouse gas emissions were stopped abruptly. The scientists are forthright once again:

> It is sometimes imagined that slow processes such as climate changes pose small risks, on the basis of the assumption that a choice can always be made to quickly reduce emissions and thereby reverse any harm within a few years or decades. We have shown that this assumption is incorrect for carbon dioxide emissions, because of the longevity of the atmospheric CO_2 perturbation and ocean warming. Irreversible climate changes due to carbon dioxide emissions have already taken place, and future carbon dioxide emissions would imply further irreversible effects on the planet, with attendant long legacies for choices made by contemporary society.[37]

---

[35] See Lenton et al., "Tipping Elements in the Earth's Climate System," 1787–91; V. Ramanathan and Y. Feng, "On Avoiding Dangerous Anthropogenic Interference with the Climate System: Formidable Challenges Ahead," *Proceedings of the National Academy of Sciences* 105 (2008): 14245–50.

[36] David Archer, *The Long Thaw: How Humans Are Changing the Next 100,000 Years of Earth's Climate* (Princeton, NJ: Princeton University Press, 2009), 83.

[37] Susan Solomon et al., "Irreversible Climate Change Due to Carbon Dioxide Emissions," *Proceedings of the National Academy of Sciences* 106 (2009): 1708–9.

The warnings from the scientific community in the last few decades have revealed the precarious state of our home planet. With regard to some facets of the ecological crisis, like climate change, the timeframe is fast narrowing. It appears that we have just sufficient time to avert unimaginable disasters by keeping the temperature rise to below 2°C above pre-industrial levels—referred to as "the 2°C guard rail." Beyond this, climate change effects become more dangerous. "The scientific evidence strongly suggests that there is an upper limit for the concentration of greenhouse gases in the atmosphere, or a 'climate change boundary,' within which humanity should operate to reduce the risks of catastrophic outcomes."[38]

Earth, the Goldilocks planet, which was marvelously fashioned to become a home for life through the cosmic evolution of millions of years and peopled by the common family of humanity over thousands of years, has come under severe strain in hosting life and human civilization and in letting them flourish. Our planetary home is in a precarious state today. How was this situation created, and who has done it?

Humanity Fouling Its Own Nest:
The Anthropogenic Character of the
Contemporary Ecological Crisis

Life appeared on Earth nearly 3.8 billion years ago, and modern Homo sapiens, our direct ancestors, emerged nearly 200,000 years ago. This means that humans have existed in only 0.0054 percent of life's history on Earth. When we place humanity against the history of the planet, and realize how long it took to fashion this "home of life," we cannot but be appalled at how we have managed to despoil this home just in the blink of an eye of geological time. If we were to conceive the nearly 5 billion years of the geological history of the earth as recorded in ten volumes of five hundred pages each—as Richard H. Overman once proposed—so that each page records a million years, it will be only on page 499 of the tenth volume that humankind appears. The last two words on the last page would suffice to recount our story from the rise of civilization six thousand years ago until the

---

[38] K. Richardson et al., "Synthesis Report from Climate Change: Global Risks, Challenges, and Decisions," Copenhagen, March 10–12, 2009 (Copenhagen: University of Copenhagen, 2009), 36.

present.[39] It is only in the last letter of the last word on the last page of the last volume that humanity takes to tearing down its own home.

> Human life entered the scene on a planet that was biologically very rich indeed. To that organic richness we contributed little. Indeed, in certain localities over limited periods of time, our treatment of the environment was quite destructive. But only when we reach the last letter of the last word on the last page does humanity turn the tide against life; only then does the process of killing the planet begin. What is astonishing is that all that has been produced over a billion years is so vulnerable to destruction by this late-comer to the scene.[40]

It is even more startling when we move from the geological perspective to the cosmic scale with regard to human history. Carl Sagan, for example, speaks of a "cosmic clock" wherein the fifteen-billion-year lifetime of the cosmos is compressed into the span of a single cosmic year. On this scale, the Big Bang would occur on January 1, human beings would not emerge until late in the last day of the year, December 31, and the whole of recorded human history would fit into the last ten seconds of New Year's Eve.[41] The last two hundred years, since the Industrial Revolution, when humans have begun to have an unambiguously global impact on our common home, would occupy only the very last few milliseconds of the cosmic year. However, in this very short span of time humanity has come to dominate all of the complex ecosystems that have evolved over much longer periods of time, placing our common home on the verge of a collapse.[42]

Our home planet has already witnessed some of the manifestations of the ecological crisis like climate change, desertification, and mass extinction of species. For example, it is true that the earth has gone through periods of global warming. But the most recent one dates

---

[39] See Richard H. Overman, "A Christological View of Nature," *Religious Education* 66 (1971), 37; John B. Cobb, *Sustainability: Economics, Ecology, and Justice* (Maryknoll, NY: Orbis Books, 1992), 119–20.

[40] Cobb, *Sustainability*, 120.

[41] See Carl Sagan, *The Dragons of Eden: Speculations on the Evolution of Human Intelligence* (New York: Random House, 1977), 14–16; David Toolan, *At Home in the Cosmos* (Maryknoll, NY: Orbis Books, 2001), 140–42.

[42] See Jan Zalasiewicz, *The Earth After Us: What Legacy Will Humans Leave in the Rocks* (Oxford: Oxford University Press, 2008), 2; Grahame J. C. Smith, Henry J. Steck, and Gerald Surette, *Our Ecological Crisis: Its Biological, Economic, and Political Dimensions* (New York: Macmillan Publishing Co., 1974), 29–30.

back to the Palaeocene-Eocene Thermal Maximum (PETM) period, which occurred as far back as 55 million years ago, an epoch when humanity was nowhere around.[43] There have also been several mass extinctions of species in the past, but the last one was 65 million years ago. The contemporary ecological crisis is unique because it is caused by one species, human beings. The current crisis is anthropogenic, namely, caused by human activities.

The anthropogenic character of the contemporary ecological crisis is evident in almost all its manifestations, ranging from climate change to pollution, species extinction, deforestation, desertification, waste, and depletion of natural resources. Here we take up only climate change and species extinction, for the sake of brevity, and demonstrate how both of these perils in their present form are ultimately caused by human activities.

Today there exists a nearly unanimous consensus in the scientific community about the anthropogenic effect on climate change.[44] The periodical Assessment Reports from the IPCC reveal a progressive trend in this regard. The first definitive statement that humans are responsible for climate change is found in the Second Assessment Report published in 1995. The report concluded that the balance of evidence suggests "a discernible human influence" on the earth's climate. In the Third Assessment Report of 2001, the IPCC pointed to the human fingerprint of climate change, stating that there is strong evidence that most of the warming observed is attributable to human activities. According to the report, "Detection and attribution studies consistently find evidence for an anthropogenic signal in the climate record."[45] These positions also were in the Fourth Assessment Report of the IPCC in 2007, which provided multiple lines of evidence that human-induced climate change is indeed happening. The report showed a jump with regard to certitude that changes are due to human activities—from more than 66 percent in the 2001 report to more than

---

[43] See James C. Zachos et al., "Rapid Acidification of the Ocean During the Paleocene-Eocene Thermal Maximum," *Science* 308 (2005): 1611–14; Archer, *The Long Thaw*, 98.

[44] See John Cook et al., "Quantifying the Consensus on Anthropogenic Global Warming in the Scientific Literature," *Environmental Research Letters* 8 (2013): 024024; Naomi Oreskes, "Beyond the Ivory Tower: The Scientific Consensus on Climate Change," *Science* 306 (2004): 1686; National Academy of Sciences Committee on the Science of Climate Change, *Climate Change Science: An Analysis of Some Key Questions* (Washington, DC: National Academy Press, 2001), 3.

[45] IPCC, *Climate Change 2001: Synthesis Report* (Cambridge: Cambridge University Press, 2001), 5, see also 51.

90 percent.[46] According to this report human activities are responsible for about thirteen times as much of the warming as changes in the sun's output. The Fifth Assessment Report from the IPCC awards the highest margin of certainty to the human-induced factor of climate change, more than 95 percent:

> Human influence has been detected in warming of the atmosphere and the ocean, in changes in the global water cycle, in reductions of snow and ice, in global mean sea level rise, and in changes in some climate extremes. This evidence for human influence has grown since the Fourth Assessment Report. It is extremely likely that human influence has been the dominant cause of the observed warming since the mid-20th century.[47]

The anthropogenic character of climate change was reiterated in the statements of world's premier scientific academies in recent years. The Royal Society concluded its 2010 document *Climate Change: A Summary of the Science* by affirming that "there is strong evidence that changes in greenhouse gas concentrations due to human activity are the dominant cause of the global warming that has taken place over the last half century."[48] The document is explicit: "Various lines of evidence point strongly to human activity being the main reason for the recent increase [of CO_2 concentrations in the atmosphere], mainly due to the burning of fossil fuels (coal, oil, gas) with smaller contributions from land-use changes and cement manufacture."[49] The groundbreaking document of the US National Academies of Sciences in 2010, entitled *Advancing the Science of Climate Change*, states, "There is a strong, credible body of evidence, based on multiple lines of research, documenting that climate is changing and that these changes are in large part caused by human activities."[50]

Human responsibility for the current ecological crisis is equally evident when it comes to the problem of the mass extinction of species. Scientists believe that a sixth mass extinction is upon the earth[51] and

---

[46] Ibid., 38–41.

[47] IPCC, *Climate Change 2013: The Physical Science Basis*, 17.

[48] The Royal Society, *Climate Change*, para. 57.

[49] Ibid., para. 25.

[50] The National Academy of Sciences, *Advancing the Science of Climate Change*, 1, see also 3, 20ff.

[51] Chris D. Thomas et al., "Extinction Risk from Climate Change," *Nature* 427 (2004): 145–48; John C. Avise, Stephen P. Hubbell, and Francisco J. Ayala,

predict that between 15 percent and 37 percent of regional endemic species could face extinction as early as 2050.[52] The unique feature of the sixth mass extinction of species is that it is anthropogenic in origin. As the Millennium Ecosystem Assessment points out, although biodiversity and ecosystem services experience change due to natural causes, current change is dominated by anthropogenic drivers. "Over the past few hundred years, humans have increased species extinction rates by as much as 1,000 times background rates that were typical over Earth's history."[53] According to Harvard conservation biologist Edward O. Wilson, human-caused species extinction has accelerated from approximately one thousand species per year in the 1970s to more than ten thousand species per year at present and is bound to increase with the temperatures rising.[54]

The anthropogenic fingerprints behind the current mass extinction of species emerge with greater clarity when one examines the principal causes that are directly or indirectly triggering the decimation of species. According to the Millennium Ecosystem Assessment the most important direct drivers of biodiversity loss are habitat conversion (such as land use changes, physical modifications of rivers or water withdrawal from rivers, loss of coral reefs, and damage to sea floors due to trawling); climate change; overexploitation of natural resources; pollution of land, air, and water; and introduction of alien species and exotic organisms into native ecosystems.[55] Virtually all the factors leading to the accelerating loss of biodiversity have to do with human activities. Human activities are altering the geographic distributions of many biological groups around the world and are associated directly or indirectly with nearly every aspect of the current

---

"In the Light of Evolution II: Biodiversity and Extinction," *Proceedings of the National Academy of Sciences* 105 (2008): 11453; David B. Wake and Vance T. Vredenburg, "Are We in the Midst of the Sixth Mass Extinction? A View from the World of Amphibians," *Proceedings of the National Academy of Sciences* 105 (2008): 11466–67; UNEP, *Global Environment Outlook GEO4* (Malta: UNEP, 2007), 162. Available online.

[52] Thomas et al., "Extinction Risk from Climate Change," 145–48.

[53] Millennium Ecosystem Assessment, *Ecosystems and Human Well-being: Biodiversity Synthesis* (Washington, DC: World Resources Institute, 2005), 8, 3. See also Venetoulis and Talberth, "Ecological Footprint of Nations," 2.

[54] Edward O. Wilson, *The Diversity of Life* (London: Penguin Books, 1994), 268. See also Edward O. Wilson, *The Creation: An Appeal to Save Life on Earth* (New York: W. W. Norton, 2006), 79.

[55] Millennium Ecosystem Assessment, *Ecosystems and Human Well-being: Biodiversity Synthesis*, vi, 8.

spasms of extinction.[56] At the moment, much of the planet's total supply of energy is concentrated in one species (Homo sapiens) and its domesticates. We have begun to co-opt resources from, further displace, and cause extinctions of species with whom we have been coexisting for ten thousand years.[57]

> Indeed, most people still don't realize that humanity has become a truly global force, interfering in a very real and direct way in many of the planet's natural cycles. For example, human activity puts ten times as much oil into the oceans as comes from natural seeps, has multiplied the natural flow of cadmium into the atmosphere eightfold, has doubled the rate of nitrogen fixation, and is responsible for about half the concentration of methane (a potent greenhouse gas) and nearly a third of the carbon dioxide (also a greenhouse gas) in the atmosphere today—all added since the industrial revolution, most notably in the past half-century.[58]

According to Michael S. Northcott:

> There is not a stretch of ocean and very few areas of forest which do not show signs of the industrial and commercial transformation of the earth into a materials bank for human exploitation. The extent of human interference and disruption of natural systems can be measured three miles above the North Pole in the loss of protective ozone, and one mile deep in the rift valleys of the ocean floor in the polluted sediments which trickle down from the waste products of modern consumerism.[59]

As Lynn White noted in 1967, "Surely no creature other than man has ever managed to foul its nest in such short order."[60]

---

[56] Wake and Vredenburg, "Are We in the Midst of the Sixth Mass Extinction?," 11472; D. Jablonski, "Extinction and the Spatial Dynamics of Biodiversity," *Proceedings of the National Academy of Sciences* 105 (2008): 11528–35.

[57] Anthony Barnosky, "Megafauna Biomass Tradeoff as a Driver of Quaternary and Future Extinctions," *Proceedings of the National Academy of Sciences* 105 (2008): 11546.

[58] Ehrlich and Ehrlich, *Betrayal of Science and Reason*, 14.

[59] Michael S. Northcott, *The Environment and Christian Ethics* (Cambridge: Cambridge University Press, 1996), 32–33.

[60] Lynn White, "The Historical Roots of Our Ecologic Crisis," *Science* 155 (1967): 1204.

The Dawning of the Anthropocene Era

Anthropogenic changes to the earth's climate, land, oceans, and biosphere are now great and so rapid that some speak of this as a new geological epoch defined by the action of humans.[61] The human imprint on our planetary home has become so large that it rivals some of the great forces of nature in its impact on the functioning of the earth system. Climate change and other facets of the contemporary ecological crisis have brought into sharp focus the capacity of contemporary human civilization to affect adversely, and in many cases irrevocably alter, the broad range of ecosystem services that support human and other forms of life.[62] The dramatic transformation of the home planet by human activities in recent times has led many scientists to claim that the home planet is now being forcefully ushered into a new geological epoch altogether. The term proposed to evidence this quantitative shift in the relationship between humans and the rest of the natural world is *Anthropocene,* namely, "the age of humans." It was proposed by Paul J. Crutzen nearly a decade ago, though the concept that humans are capable of altering geological processes is more than a century old.[63]

The term *Anthropocene* suggests that the earth is now moving out of the current geological epoch of the Holocene, and that human activity is largely responsible for this exit, rendering humankind a global geological force in its own right.[64] As we have seen earlier, it was the Holocene epoch of the past twelve thousand years, along with its stable climate, that made human civilization possible. In the early part of the Holocene, as the planet moved out of the most recent Ice Age, the

---

[61] Jan Zalasiewicz et al., "The Anthropocene: A New Epoch of Geological Time?" *Philosophical Transactions of the Royal Society A* 369 (2011): 835–41. This is the opening article of a theme issue that the *Philosophical Transactions of the Royal Society A* dedicated to the discussion of the question of the new geological epoch of the Anthropocene. In 2008, the Stratigraphy Commission of the Geological Society of London decided by a large majority that there was merit in considering the possible formalization of this term.

[62] See Steffen et al., "The Anthropocene: Conceptual and Historical Perspectives," 842–43; P. J. Crutzen, "Geology of Mankind: The Anthropocene," *Nature* 415 (2002): 23.

[63] See P. J. Crutzen and E. F. Stoermer, "The Anthropocene," *Global Change Newsletter* 41 (2000): 17–18; Crutzen, "Geology of Mankind," 23. On the antecedents of the Anthropocene concept, see Steffen et al., "The Anthropocene: Conceptual and Historical Perspectives," 843–45.

[64] Steffen et al., "The Anthropocene: Conceptual and Historical Perspectives," 843.

global temperature rose and stabilized around eleven thousand years ago, and the sea level stabilized approximately eight thousand years ago. Global temperatures and sea level then reached a marked plateau where they have, until very recently, remained. This extraordinary period of climate stability (though modulated by a millennial-scale global temperature oscillation of around 1°C amplitude), the longest in at least the past 400,000 years, was a significant factor in the development of human civilization.[65] Human societies in the Holocene epoch, up to the era of modern industrialization, have had only local and transitory impacts on our home planet, well within the bounds of the natural variability of the earth's natural systems. It appears that the situation has changed radically since the 1800s, coinciding with the onset of the modern industrial era. The process of industrialization during the last two centuries has seen enormous expansion in the use of fossil fuels, first coal and then oil and gas, and the transition to a high-energy society, especially in the industrialized nations. It is significant that between 1800 and 2000 the human population grew more than sixfold, the global economy about fiftyfold, and energy use about fortyfold.[66]

The new geological epoch of the Anthropocene is stratigraphically evident in several physical, geochemical, biotic, and climatic imprints left on Earth's natural systems. Physically, humans have caused a dramatic increase in erosion and the denudation of the continents, both directly, through agriculture and construction, and indirectly, by damming most major rivers. Extensive deforestation and land conversion for cultivation and mechanized agriculture add to this process. Enhanced dissolution of increased atmospheric CO_2 in the oceans is increasing their acidity. Relative to pre–Industrial Revolution oceans, surface ocean waters are now 0.1 pH units more acidic due to anthropogenic carbon release. At the biological level the rate of biotic change in land and in the seas—the coral reefs in particular—because of human activities may also produce a major extinction event.

It is in the area of climate change caused by the rise of the concentration of greenhouse gases like CO_2 that find the most indisputable evidence that human activities are affecting the planet at the global scale. Carbon dioxide levels are currently a third higher than in pre-industrial times and at any time in the past 0.9 million years,

---

[65] Jan Zalasiewicz et al., "Are We Now Living in the Anthropocene?," *GSA Today* 18 (2008): 4–5.

[66] Will Steffen et al., "The Anthropocene: Are Humans Now Overwhelming the Great Forces of Nature?" *Ambio: A Journal of the Human Environment* 36 (2007): 616.

and methane concentrations in the atmosphere have already roughly doubled.[67]

Human activities are indeed affecting the structure and functioning of the earth system as a whole (as opposed to local and regional environmental issues), making it possible to speak of "a geological age of our own making."[68] We have entered into a distinctive phase of profound changes in our relationship with the rest of the physical world. The alleged transition of our home planet from the Holocene to the Antrhopocene is a clear statement that humankind has become a powerful force in the earth's evolution.[69] In fact, the new geological epoch of the Anthropocene represents a novel and unique phase in the history both of humankind and of the earth, when natural forces and human forces became intertwined, so that the fate of one determines the fate of the other.[70] It is not an exaggeration to say that the ultimate drivers of the Anthropocene, "if they continue unabated through this century, may well threaten the viability of contemporary civilization and perhaps even the future existence of *Homo sapiens*."[71]

The Moral and Religious Implications of Our "*Oikos*-cide"

The deliberate destruction of our common home—the current "*oikos*-cide" that has begun recently due to human activities, is bound to have not only physical consequences but also profound ethical implications for our fellow human beings, for future generations, and for our fellow species. Like every destructive act it raises several moral and spiritual questions.

---

[67] Zalasiewicz et al., "Are We Now Living in the Anthropocene?," 5–6; Jan Zalasiewicz et al., "The New World of the Anthropocene," *Environmental Science and Technology* 44 (2010): 2229; B. H. Wilkinson, "Humans as Geologic Agents: A Deep-Time Perspective," *Geology* 33 (2005): 161–64; Erle C. Ellis, "Anthropogenic Transformation of the Terrestrial Biosphere," *Philosophical Transactions of the Royal Society A* 369 (2011): 1010; F. S. Chapin et al., "Consequences of Changing Biotic Diversity," *Nature* 405 (2000): 234–42; K. Caldeira and M. E. Wickett, "Anthropogenic Carbon and Ocean pH," *Nature* 425 (2003): 365.

[68] A. Revkin, *Global Warming: Understanding the Forecast* (New York: American Museum of Natural History, Environmental Defense Fund, Abbeville Press, 1992), 55. See also Steffen et al., "The Anthropocene: Are Humans Now Overwhelming the Great Forces of Nature?" 618.

[69] Archer, *The Long Thaw*, 64.

[70] Zalasiewicz et al., "The New World of the Anthropocene," 2231.

[71] Steffen et al., "The Anthropocene: Conceptual and Historical Perspectives," 862.

Ethical Implications of the Ecological Crisis

Let us, first of all, highlight some of the ethical implications of the ecological crisis for two constituencies with little or no political voice: the world's poor and future generations.[72]

As the "Human Development Report 2007/2008" points out, it is the poor who are bearing the brunt of the ecological crisis, as "millions of the world's poorest people are already being forced to cope with the impacts of climate change."[73] The ecological crisis, then, becomes a moral issue. The core of the moral question is that actions of people in one part of the world can undermine the well-being of millions of their fellow citizens, especially the poor, with whom all share the home planet.

> While many features of the environmental crisis would appear to originate in the actions of the industrialised and economically developed nations which are mostly located in the Northern Hemisphere . . . the impact of the collapse of ecosystems and local climate regimes is experienced most dramatically by people who live in the South, in Africa, Asia and Latin America. It is on these continents that the consequences of desertification, deforestation, soil erosion or loss of biodiversity are experienced most sharply. For the peasant farmer or the landless rural labourer in drought-ridden Africa the state of the environment is a matter of basic survival.[74]

The contemporary ecological crisis will affect all inhabitants of the common home. But it will hit the poor hardest. Soaring temperatures could make agriculture unviable over huge areas of the world where people are already poor and hungry, while rising sea levels will destroy substantial coastal areas in low-lying countries such as Bangladesh or small island nations like Tuvalu, causing mass movements of climate-

---

[72] See UNDP, "Human Development Report 2007/2008," 2. On a similar note, in 2009 Pope Benedict XVI wrote: "The natural environment is given by God to everyone, and our use of it entails a personal responsibility towards humanity as a whole, and in particular towards the poor and towards future generations" (*Caritas in veritate*, no. 48).

[73] UNDP, "Human Development Report 2007/2008," 1.

[74] Aviji Gupta, *Ecology and Development in the Third World* (London: Routledge, 1988), 24.

change refugees.[75] As Richard W. Miller cautions us, "We are running the risk of condemning the poorest of the world, the 2.6 billion people who survive on less than $2 a day, to a desperate struggle for food and water and all the displacement, violence, and suffering that such a struggle could entail."[76]

In the same way the costs of the contemporary ecological crisis will have to be paid one day by the future generations. This raises profound ethical questions, as evidenced by the *Global Environment Outlook GEO4* of 2007, given that benefits are extracted from the environment by those who do not have to bear the burden for them.[77] The human-induced climate change, for example, will be a gross injustice to future generations, who have a fundamental right to a planetary home in which they can live.[78] The problem is that it will take thousands of years, even hundreds of thousands of years, for natural processes to absorb completely the human emissions of CO_2. Most of the excess CO_2 in the atmosphere is dissolved in the ocean in a few centuries, but the rest has to wait. In fact, about 10 percent of the CO_2 emitted today will still be affecting the climate in 100,000 years.[79] Thus, future generations will have to bear the heaviest burden for the present generation's irresponsibility.[80] It also means that "we are taking the greatest of gambles with our children's and our grandchildren's futures—indeed, the future of the next fifty generations."[81]

---

[75] Seren Boyd and Rachel Roach, *Feeling the Heat: Why Governments Must Act to Tackle the Impact of Climate Change on Global Water Supplies and Avert Mass Movements of Climate Change Refugees. A Report from Tearfund* (London: Tearfund, 2006), 5. There are already an estimated 25 million "environmental refugees"—more than half the number of political refugees, a figure that could soar to 200 million in less than fifty years (ibid., 6).

[76] Richard W. Miller, "Global Climate Disruption and Social Justice: The State of the Problem," in *God, Creation, and Climate Change: A Catholic Response to the Environmental Crisis*, ed. Richard W. Miller (Maryknoll, NY: Orbis Books, 2010), 18.

[77] United Nations Environment Programme, *The Global Environment Outlook GEO4*, 11, 33. See also UNDP, "Human Development Report 2007/2008," 2–16.

[78] Richardson et al., "Synthesis Report," 22.

[79] Archer, *The Long Thaw*, 1, 5.

[80] Mayer Hillman, Tina Fawcett, and Sudhir Chella Rajan, *How We Can Save the Planet: Preventing Global Climate Catastrophe* (New York: Thomas Dunne Books, 2008), 2.

[81] Miller, "Global Climate Disruption and Social Justice," 18.

Unless we are willing to understand the gravity of the situation and change course, we will be remembered as the "selfish generations," the ones who knew the damage their fossil fuel–driven and voracious lifestyles would do to the planet and to the future generations, but who carried on all the same regardless.[82] The testimony of climate scientist James Hansen is moving in this regard. Hansen confesses it was precisely the sense of moral responsibility toward his own grandchildren that changed his approach toward climate change—from a detached scientific observer to a sort of prophet who wanted to communicate the gravity and urgency of what he understood to the wider public. "But gradually, my perception of being a 'witness' changed, leading to a hard decision: I did not want my grandchildren, someday in the future, to look back and say 'Opa understood what was happening, but he did not make it clear.'"[83]

In fact, the heat-trapping gases sent into the atmosphere in 2014 will stay there until 2115 and beyond. We are therefore making choices today that will affect our own lives but even more the lives of our children and grandchildren.

> Future generations will pass a harsh judgement on a generation that looked at the evidence on climate change, understood the consequences and then continued on a path that consigned millions of the world's most vulnerable people to poverty and exposed future generations to the risk of ecological disaster.[84]

The contemporary ecological crisis raises some serious and disturbing questions about intergenerational and intra-generational equity and fairness. It is precisely these moral implications of justice and solidarity among human beings—members of the common family dwelling in the common home of the earth—that renders the global ecological challenge a deeply ethical issue. As Pope John Paul II prophetically pointed out to humanity in 1990, "The ecological crisis is a moral issue" and "the responsibility of everyone."[85] The future of our home planet, the one and only habitat we have, is certainly the most urgent moral issue of our time.

---

[82] See Dave Reay, *Climate Change Begins at Home: Life on the Two-Way Street of Global Warming* (London: Macmillan, 2006), 22–23.

[83] Hansen, *Storms of My Grandchildren*, xii, also 92.

[84] UNDP, "Human Development Report 2007/2008," 2.

[85] John Paul II, "Peace with God the Creator, Peace with All of Creation," Message for the Celebration of the World Day of Peace (January 1, 1990), no. 15.

Religious Implications of the Ecological Crisis

The contemporary ecological crisis also has profound religious implications, as the crisis is not only physical and moral but, at a still deeper level, is also a spiritual one. The home in crisis is not only of humanity but also of the Divine, who according to the various religious traditions of humanity has dwelt with humans. "God pitched his tent among us" is the beautiful expression employed by the evangelist John to communicate the profound truth of the Incarnation (Jn 1:14). Almost all religious traditions, in fact, speak of the world as permeated by God's presence. The Bhagavad Gita, for example, speaks of God's spirit as in-dwelling in the cosmos as its *antarayamin* ("indweller") (Bhagavad Gita 13:16). The abiding presence of the Divine in creation is also a common belief in indigenous religious traditions. In this vein, when we pull down our common home, we are despoiling the ground made sacred by God's presence; when we pollute the planet's streams, we are defiling the waters sanctified by the brooding of the Spirit of God at the dawn of creation; when we impoverish biodiversity, we are going against God's own creative project.

Most religious traditions perceive the natural world and every created reality as a symbol of God, as a sacrament of God's glory. In almost all traditions the natural world is perceived as the first book of revelation, the *vestigia Dei*, because the traces of God are clearly found in creation. According to Hugo of St. Victor, the whole of nature speaks of God *(omnis natura Deo loquitur)*.[86] When we ransack the planet's resources and drive its species into extinction, we are literally tearing away pages from God's natural book of revelation.

For many religious traditions the natural world is also an icon, a mirror of God's glory. The Qur'an says: "The seven heavens and the earth and all that they contain extol His limitless Glory; and there is not a single thing but extols His limitless Glory and Praise."[87] Every species driven into extinction impairs the ability of God's glory to shine through, just as the polluted atmosphere and skies speak less of the glory of God than they are meant to do (Ps 19:1). Significantly, in most religious traditions there also exists the concept of the common home of the earth as having been originally entrusted to human stewardship. The anthropogenic character of the contemporary

---

[86] Hugo of St. Victor, *Eruditio Didascalia* 6.5.

[87] Qur'an XVI, Banu Isra'il, 44, as cited in Seyyed Hossein Nasr, *Man and Nature: The Spiritual Crisis in Modern Man* (London: Mandala Unwin Paperbacks, 1968), 10.

ecological crisis—that it is caused precisely by human activities—is a stark reminder that humanity has fallen short of this command of responsible stewardship of the garden planet of the universe, our common home of the earth.

The moral and spiritual dimensions of the contemporary ecological crisis convey the profound truth that humanity cannot restore harmony with creation unless we live in harmony among ourselves and ultimately in harmony with the Creator, the Source of all being. We stand today in need of a wider and deeper understanding of the contemporary ecological crisis.

This is what we attempt to do in the next three sections of the book, wherein we look at the crisis of our common home as a physical, moral, and spiritual crisis from scientific, ethical, and faith perspectives, respectively. Such a multifaceted perspective provides us with a total view and can add depth to our perception of the crisis. Partial perspectives on the problem can only lead to piecemeal diagnoses and solutions, as in the case of geo-engineering, just to cite an example, while the ecological crisis itself only appears to get worse. Today, we need more than ever a comprehensive and unified view of the crisis facing our common home. This is the rationale for the choice to describe the contemporary ecological crisis as a triple cry—of the earth, of the poor, and of the gods.

PART II

THE CRY OF THE EARTH

The ecological crisis is above all the cry of the earth. O. N. V. Kurup, a contemporary poet, bemoans our disfiguration of Planet Earth in a requiem to a planet in the pangs of death.

Earth
not yet dead, but about to die, peace be on you.
Here is a song I scribble in my heart
for your funeral—and mine.

When in the shadow of death's poisonous flower,
    tomorrow
your body will be cold and numb,
there will be none left—not I, either, to pay you
    homage,
or let a tear drop on your ashen face.
So I scribble this for you, earth, about to die.

You gave birth to children innumerable, unsociable.
You watched them eat each other; you wept in
    secret.
Then they started eating you; and you, all-enduring
    one,
you made no move to protest or prevent.

They who had drunk at your breasts and grown
    plump
felt a new thirst—their last thirst—
to suck the blood of your sacred heart.
They stripped you of the green
in which the sun had clothed his beloved bride.
Into your flesh they sank their nails
and drank the blood that gushed from your
    wounds—

Raped, ostracized; with shaven head,
bent beneath the burden of your children's sin and
    shame,
you wander, alone, in space . . .
Earth, not yet dead, but about to die, peace be on
    you.[1]

In the overall context of our understanding of the ecological crisis as a triple cry of the earth, of the poor, and of the gods, we deal here with the groaning of the planet. Part II offers a physical understanding of the ecological crisis, looking at it mainly from a scientific perspective. The ethical and religious perceptions of the crisis are outlined in Part III and Part IV, respectively.

We are aware of the multiple facets of the ecological crisis already at the physical level. Thus, I pursue an approach that perceives the ecological crisis as encompassing more than just the problem of climate change alone. Climate change is, without doubt, the most important of the ecological challenges that human civilization has ever faced, and it is certainly the most conspicuous manifestation of the global crisis facing our common home. However, the ecological crisis has many facets that are interlinked but still distinct. Desertification, for example, is linked to climate change but is caused also by other factors like land degradation because of intensive agriculture, deforestation, and more.

Deforestation, while it contributes to global warming, also contributes to other significant ecological problems like species extinction. Species extinction is itself one of the impacts of climate change. But climate change is only one of the six main drivers linked to biodiversity loss. The current rate of species extinction, which exceeds by several times the natural background rate and threatens to tear down the very web of life, is a gross ecological threat in its own right. The case is equally evident when it comes to other manifestations of the ecological crisis like pollution and depletion of natural resources. Pollution of our common home—its land, water, and atmosphere—is by itself a major ecological preoccupation that has direct and serious impacts on human health and was, in fact, the launching pad for the birth of modern ecological consciousness. In the same way, the depletion of natural resources—the fact that we are consuming natural resources faster than ecosystems can regenerate them—is equally a matter of grave concern. It is feared that with the present rate of consumption

---

[1] O. N. V. Kurup, "Requiem for the Earth," in *Kavita* (Trivandrum: Kavita Samiti, 1985), 1160.

and waste, we will require "an extra planet" before the middle of the present century. Seen in this perspective, each of the various manifestations of the ecological crisis is in itself sufficient to set the alarm bells ringing about the precarious state of our home planet.

So the ecological crisis—the crisis of our common home—is much larger and more complex at the physical level. In this context the ecological predicament facing our planetary home is much larger than the issues of global warming and associated climate change alone. A tendency to reduce it to these two issues, which is widely prevalent in public media, often dominates political discussions and policy formulations regarding the stewardship of the planet. Such a perception of the ecological crisis may at times characterize those who propose geoengineering solutions as the panacea for problems facing the planet. In fact, piecemeal solutions to the ecological crisis, ranging from carbon sequestration to cap-and-trade proposals, have at their basis a perception of the crisis as limited to climate change alone. A limited view of the ecological crisis as an issue of global warming alone runs some apparent risks. It may encourage people to indulge in mechanisms of denial—it is easier to deny a single facet of the crisis than a whole host of them—or to postpone action while appealing to framework of a century or so when the more serious impacts of climate change are expected to hit hard. Exclusive attention on climate change may also distract public attention from other important ecological challenges like species extinction. Biodiversity is as crucial as a stable climate system to preserve the common web of life on our home planet, though it may not appear physically so evident. In fact, it is only when the various manifestations of the ecological crisis are seen together that we realize the magnitude of the situation of our common home. For this, it is important to have a total view of the crisis.

We need to see the different manifestations of the ecological predicament at the physical level as part of the total crisis that impairs the capacity of the earth to be a common home for the biotic community, including humanity. Part II groups them together under the title of the cry of the earth. This part is divided into four chapters that present some of the important and most evident physical manifestations of the contemporary ecological crisis. The choice of themes admittedly is far from exhaustive; rather, I limit it to the most conspicuous symptoms of the crisis facing our common home.

First, we deal with global warming and associated climate change. Climate change is the most important present threat to the capacity of the earth to be a home for the biotic community. Two chapters are dedicated to the question of climate change. In the first, Chapter

3, after a discussion of how the greenhouse effect renders the earth habitable for life and a short preview of Earth's climate history, we see how the current phase of climate change is caused by anthropogenic global warming due to the increase in the emission of greenhouse gases from human activities. In Chapter 4 we deal with the main impacts of climate change for human communities and ecosystems. The effects of anthropogenic climate change are manifold: extreme weather events, droughts and desertification, glacier melt, sea-level rise, ocean acidification, and biodiversity loss, to mention the most important ones.

Second, we examine in Chapter 5 the question of species extinction and biodiversity loss. According to the warnings of the scientific community, Earth is precariously poised on the verge of a sixth mass extinction of species. It is important to realize that by causing biodiversity loss we are threatening the very womb of life—the common biosphere—that sustains and protects the community of living beings on Earth. We explore the main causes of biodiversity loss as well as its implications for humanity and for the rest of the biotic community.

Third, we see in Chapter 6 how we have polluted our common home and depleted the natural resources of our common household. Human activities, modern industrial and agricultural activities in particular, appear to have polluted almost all areas of our common home: the land, the waters, and the atmosphere. Besides despoiling our common home, we are also fast draining the resources of our home planet, including the most precious of all, fresh water. Our current consumerist culture squanders Earth's finite resources, producing huge amounts of garbage, including toxic waste. The threats to our common home from human activities are indeed manifold.

We begin our journey of understanding the contemporary ecological crisis at the physical level with a study of the phenomenon of global warming and associated climate change.

3

Climate Change

Climate change is the defining issue of our time.[1] Some have described it as the world's greatest challenge and the greatest collective challenge to civilization.[2] Climate change is indeed an entry point into the whole of the ecological crisis.[3] It is the most important facet of the contemporary ecological crisis, which poses a real threat to the entire bio-system of the planet and raises serious questions regarding the present course of human civilization.

In this chapter we begin by analyzing the uniqueness of the greenhouse effect, which provides our planetary home with an ideal climate suitable for the existence and flourishing of life. We will also examine the long climatic history of our home planet in order to understand how the stable climatic conditions that we presently enjoy came to be. The crux of the chapter consists in the study of anthropogenic global warming, which is the cause of current climate change. We examine the main greenhouse gases that contribute to global warming, carbon dioxide in particular. We conclude by taking stock of the forecasts, with special emphasis on the danger of tipping points in the earth's climate system. The current phase of global warming and associated climate change is indeed totally unprecedented in human history and in the recent geological history of our home planet.

---

[1] The Geological Society, *Climate Change: Evidence from the Geological Record: A Statement from the Geological Society of London* (November 2010), 1.

[2] See Mayer Hillman, Tina Fawcett, and Sudhir Chella Rajan, *How We Can Save the Planet: Preventing Global Climate Catastrophe* (New York: Thomas Dunne Books, 2008), 1; Kirstin Dow and Thomas E. Downing, *The Atlas of Climate Change: Mapping the World's Greatest Challenge* (London: Earth scan, 2006); Thomas R. Karl and Kevin E. Trenberth, "Modern Global Climate Change," *Science* 302 (2003): 1722.

[3] Operation Noah, *Between the Flood and the Rainbow: Climate Change and the Church's Social Teaching—A Study Guide* (London: Operation Noah, 2008), 1.

The Greenhouse Effect as Rendering Earth a Home of Life

We earlier described Earth as the Goldilocks planet in our solar system, the place life originated and spectacularly evolved. Earth became a cradle of life because of innumerable factors, among them its location in the solar system. Unlike our immediate planetary neighbors, Venus, which has a surface temperature hot enough to melt lead, and Mars, which has a surface temperature cold enough to shatter steel in extreme winter, Earth, the Goldilocks planet, alone appears to be in the "just right" place. However, this does not present the whole picture. Going by our location alone, Earth, by rights, would be frozen over and rather inhospitable to life.[4]

It is the natural greenhouse effect that makes life as we know it possible on the earth. Without the greenhouse effect the average temperature at Earth's surface would be below the freezing point of water. Without the natural greenhouse effect, humans and most other life-forms would not have evolved on the earth. In short, the greenhouse effect is a natural phenomenon that is critical to life as we know it. It creates a climate system, unique in the whole universe, favorable for the flourishing of life.

When our solar system took shape nearly 4.6 billion years ago, the inner ring of terrestrial planets, Mercury, Venus, Earth, and Mars, all had thin, solid crusts hiding their large molten cores. The turbulent chemical processes that occurred in the depths of the planets' interiors released gases through the crusts. While Mercury was too small and its gravity too weak to capture these gases, the others held on to at least some of them, creating their own atmosphere. The evolution of the atmospheres followed different courses on Venus, Mars, and Earth. Venus ended up with an extremely dense and superheated atmosphere due to a runaway greenhouse effect that occurred on that planet; Venus currently has an atmosphere of 97 percent of carbon dioxide and a sizzling surface temperature of 460°C. Mars, on the other hand, appears to have lost most of its atmosphere; the present one is about a hundred times thinner than Earth's, and any remaining carbon dioxide lies frozen on its surface, with an average temperature of -50°C. The temperature drops to a bone-chilling -120°C when the sun goes down, as almost no warmth is retained.[5]

---

[4] Gabrielle Walker and David King, *The Hot Topic: How to Tackle Global Warming and Still Keep the Lights On* (London: Bloomsbury, 2008), 14.

[5] See Fred Pearce, *The Last Generation: How Nature Will Take Her Revenge for Climate Change* (London: Eden Project Books, 2006), 163–64; Mark Maslin,

Earth, on the other hand, has a balmy average surface temperature of 14.5°C (58.1°F), which is ideal for the flourishing of life. If it were below 0°C (32°F), Earth's entire surface would be an icy waste; if it were more than 100°C (212°F), all the water would have boiled off. While atmosphere is crucial for a planet to host life, it is the composition of gases in its atmosphere that enables a planet to maintain the right global surface temperature that is congenial to life. The temperature of the earth is controlled by the balance between the input from energy of the sun, which acts to warm the surface of the earth and the atmosphere, and the energy radiated back from the earth's surface and atmosphere, which acts to cool the earth. Certain atmospheric gases are critical to this temperature balance and are known as the greenhouse gases; they help to warm the earth through the greenhouse effect. Here is a physical description of the process:

> The Sun powers Earth's climate, radiating energy at very short wavelengths, predominately in the visible or near-visible (e.g., ultraviolet) part of the spectrum. Roughly one-third of the solar energy that reaches the top of Earth's atmosphere is reflected directly back to space. The remaining two-thirds is absorbed by the surface and, to a lesser extent, by the atmosphere. To balance the absorbed incoming energy, the Earth must, on average, radiate the same amount of energy back to space. Because the Earth is much colder than the Sun, it radiates at much longer wavelengths, primarily in the infrared part of the spectrum. . . . Much of this thermal radiation emitted by the land and ocean is absorbed by the atmosphere, including clouds, and reradiated back to Earth. This is called the greenhouse effect.[6]

The greenhouse effect warms Earth as the glass walls in a greenhouse trap heat. Like a greenhouse window, greenhouse gases allow sunlight to enter the atmosphere and then prevent heat from leaving. Analogously, but through a different process, the earth's greenhouse

---

Global Warming: A Very Short Introduction (Oxford: Oxford University Press, 2004), 6; Robert Henson, *The Rough Guide to Climate Change* (London: Rough Guides, 2006), 23; Michael S. Northcott, *A Moral Climate: The Ethics of Global Warming* (Maryknoll, NY: Orbis Books, 2007), 22–23.

[6] Hervé Le Treut et al., "Historical Overview of Climate Change Science," in *Climate Change 2007: The Physical Science Basis: Contribution of Working Group I to the Fourth Assessment Report of the Intergovernmental Panel on Climate Change*, ed. S. Solomon et al. (New York: Cambridge University Press, 2007), 115.

effect warms the surface of the planet. The atmosphere does not imprison the air the way a glass box does. Instead, it absorbs infrared radiation rising from the planet's sun-warmed surface. The two most abundant gases in the atmosphere, nitrogen (78 percent) and oxygen (21 percent), are both ill-suited for absorbing radiation from Earth, in part because of their simple linear, two-atom structure. Instead, the greenhouse effect comes from molecules that are more complex and much less common, which capture energy far out of proportion to their scant presence. These are the greenhouse gases that absorb the long wavelength infrared radiation emitted by Earth's surface (while some of Earth's outgoing radiation escapes through the atmosphere directly to space) and radiate it back, effectively trapping heat in the lower atmosphere. The warming that results from this infrared energy is known as the greenhouse effect and the gases that cause it are called greenhouse gases (GHGs). The greenhouse effect thus keeps the earth's surface much warmer—roughly 33°C warmer—than it would be otherwise. Without the greenhouse effect, our planet's average temperature would have been close to -18°C, which would have rendered Earth a frigid and inhospitable home for life.[7]

The understanding of how the earth is kept warm by the "greenhouse effect" is not altogether new. In fact, the discovery was made centuries ago, though it is only in recent decades that concern about global warming because of increase in greenhouse gases has reached public consciousness. In 1681, Edme Mariotte noted with great intuition that although the sun's light and heat easily pass through glass and other transparent materials, heat from other sources does not. In the 1760s, Horace Benedict de Saussure demonstrated with simple greenhouse experiments the possibility of an artificial warming of the earth's surface using a "helio-thermometer" (simple panes of glass covering a thermometer in a darkened box). The experiment provided an early analogy to the greenhouse effect. It was indeed a conceptual leap to recognize that the atmosphere could trap thermal radiation.[8]

In 1824, Jean Baptiste Joseph Fourier, a member of the French Academy of Sciences, was able to lay down the basic physics of the greenhouse effect. Fourier's insight was to add a layer of atmosphere to the planet, that absorbs and emits infrared radiation. Based on

---

[7] See Nick Spencer and Robert White, *Christianity, Climate Change, and Sustainable Living* (London: SPCK, 2007), 13–14; Maslin, *Global Warming*, 4; Dave Reay, *Climate Change Begins at Home: Life on the Two-Way Street of Global Warming* (New York: Macmillan, 2006), 16.

[8] Le Treut et al., "Historical Overview of Climate Change Science," 103.

de Saussure, Fourier showed that gases in the atmosphere that absorb infrared radiation could eventually warm the surface of the earth, as in the case of a greenhouse. Fourier realized that like the glass in a greenhouse, the greenhouse gases let sunlight through on its way from space but intercepted infrared light on its way back out. However, there was still no understanding of exactly what substance in the atmosphere was responsible for this interception.[9]

This missing ingredient was discovered in 1859 by John Tyndall, an Irish scientist who worked at London's Royal Institution. Tyndall was able to demonstrate through laboratory experiments how complex molecules of carbon dioxide, water, and methane in the atmosphere could absorb thermal radiation, as opposed to nitrogen and oxygen, the simple bimolecular gases that constitute nearly the whole of the atmosphere. Tyndall discovered that gases like carbon dioxide and methane and water vapor in the atmosphere were transparent to ultraviolet radiation from the sun, but they trapped the infrared heat that the earth's surface radiated. They actually absorbed the infrared radiation, as if they were bricks in an oven. Tyndall intuited that all the climate changes in the geological history of the earth were linked to changes in the amount of water vapor and carbon dioxide, which he correctly identified as the main greenhouse gas in the atmosphere.[10]

The scientific understanding of the greenhouse effect received a shot in the arm with the Nobel Prize-winning Swedish chemist Svante Arrhenius. Arrhenius was the first to argue that anthropogenic increases in the level of carbon dioxide in the atmosphere could significantly affect surface temperatures and global climate. Arrhenius, in fact, explicitly linked the massive burning of fossil fuels—mostly coal in his day—with global warming and potentially large changes in our home planet's climate system. "The slight percentage of carbonic acid in the atmosphere may, by the advances of industry, be changed to a noticeable degree in the course of a few centuries," he wrote in a paper that he presented to the Stockholm Physical Society in 1895.[11]

---

[9] David Archer, *The Long Thaw: How Humans Are Changing the Next 100,000 Years of Earth's Climate* (Princeton, NJ: Princeton University Press, 2009), 15; Le Treut et al., "Historical Overview of Climate Change Science," 103; Heidi Cullen, *The Weather of the Future: Heat Waves, Extreme Storms, and Other Scenes from a Climate-Changed Planet* (New York: HarperCollins, 2010), 18–19.

[10] See Andrew Simms, *Ecological Debt: The Health of the Planet and the Wealth of the Nations* (Ann Arbor, MI: Pluto Press, 2005), 17; Cullen, *The Weather of the Future*, 19–20; Pearce, *The Last Generation*, 20.

[11] Significantly, the title of the paper was "On the Influence of Carbonic Acid in the Air upon the Temperature of the Ground."

In 1938, Guy Stewart Callendar provided the first evidence of rising carbon dioxide levels in the atmosphere from fossil-fuel combustion, and he linked this increase to climate change through the rise in mean global temperature. He found that a doubling of atmospheric CO_2 concentration resulted in an increase in the mean global temperature of 2°C, with considerably more warming at the poles:

> As man is now changing the composition of the atmosphere at a rate which must be very exceptional on the geological time scale, it is natural to seek for the probable effects of such a change. From the best laboratory observations it appears that the principal result of increasing atmospheric carbon dioxide . . . would be a gradual increase in the mean temperature of the colder regions of the earth.[12]

These findings and others firmly established that carbon dioxide is an important constituent element among the greenhouse gases that contribute to climate change. In 1958, Charles David Keeling helped to set up, on Mauna Loa in Hawaii, a laboratory run by the US National Oceanic and Atmospheric Association for a continuous monitoring program of the rapidly rising carbon dioxide levels in the atmosphere. The high-accuracy measurements of atmospheric CO_2 concentration provided by Keeling and his team document the changing composition of our atmosphere. The graph depicting the slow rise in the concentration of carbon dioxide in the atmosphere, known as Keeling's curve, confirms earlier scientific predictions that human activities were contributing to the gradual increase of greenhouse gases in Earth's atmosphere, imperiling the planet's climate system in the process. Measurements at approximately 100 other sites have confirmed the long-term trend shown by the Keeling curve.[13]

Direct atmospheric measurements since 1970s led to the detection of other greenhouse gases like methane, nitrous oxide, and chlorofluorocarbons (CFCs), widely recognized today as important anthropogenic greenhouse gases. By the 1970s the role of aerosol-cloud effects in reflecting sunlight was also known. (Aerosols are small liquid or

---

[12] Cited by Le Treut et al., "Historical Overview of Climate Change Science," 105.

[13] See Charles David Keeling, "Rewards and Penalties of Monitoring the Earth," *Annual Review of Energy and the Environment* 23 (1998): 25–82; Le Treut et al., "Historical Overview of Climate Change Science," 100; Cullen, *The Weather of the Future*, 28. The Keeling curve graph and an explanation are widely available online.

solid particles suspended in the atmosphere.) The current picture of the greenhouse gases contributing to climate change offers a much more diverse mix of greenhouse gases.

The progressive understanding of the important phenomenon of greenhouse effect as essential to life on Earth and the composition of the various greenhouse gases—carbon dioxide in particular—enabled the scientific community to foresee that human activities were indeed beginning to affect the planet's climate system. Thanks to the remarkable advances in climate science in the recent decades, we are today able to study the past climate of the earth going back into millions of years of the earth's geological archives. Such a journey into the past is important to understand how what we do in the present can affect our common future in our planetary home.

A Walk Through Earth's Climate History

Earth's physical climate system, which includes the atmosphere, oceans, and land masses, has constantly evolved during the 4.6 billion years of our planet's geological history. Many factors interacting on a variety of timescales drive changes in our planet's climate system. These changes occur naturally over timescales ranging from decades to hundreds of thousands to millions of years. The changes are sometimes gradual and minor in nature and effect, but at other times they are abrupt and larger.[14] By the end of this century, without a significant reduction in greenhouse gas emissions, atmospheric CO_2 is projected to increase to levels that Earth has not experienced for more than 30 million years, leading to rapid changes in the planet's climate system and disastrous consequences for humanity and ecosystems.[15] In this context a proper understanding of our home planet's climatic past is crucial: it can provide us with critical insights to understanding the gravity of the rapid climate change that human activities are causing over a relatively short time. It is with an eye on the future of our planet that we look back into its deep past.

Earth is currently in an "icehouse" state, a climate state characterized by continental-based ice sheets at high latitudes and glaciated

[14] See The Geological Society, *Climate Change*, 1, 3. See also Thomas M. Cronin, *Paleoclimates: Understanding Climate Changes Past and Present* (New York: Columbia University Press, 2009).

[15] See The National Research Council, *Understanding Earth's Deep Past: Lessons for Our Climate Future* (Washington, DC: The National Academies Press, 2011), 5.

poles. Human evolution took place in this icehouse period, and civilizations arose within its most recent interglacial phase. But in the immense expanse of geological time, an icehouse Earth has not been the norm. For most of its geological history our home planet has been in a "hothouse" state—characterized by much warmer temperatures globally and only small or no ice sheets—punctuated by "icehouse" conditions, including several "snowball Earth" episodes. Earth has indeed gone through a wide array of climatic states in the past. Our planet's climate has lurched from periods warm enough that the poles were forested rather than icebound, when tropical forests grew at mid-latitudes and the tropics were much hotter and the sea levels were several meters higher than the present times, to full ice ages that caused ice sheets almost two miles thick to form over much of North America and Europe.[16]

Most paleoclimate studies have so far focused on the glacial-interglacial cycles that have prevailed during the past 2 million years of the current icehouse. The longest ice-core record so far extends back 800 millennia. However, to grasp better the climate changes that human activities are now driving, it is important to dig deeper into the geological records of Earth's climate states. The geological record contains abundant evidence of the ways in which Earth's climate has changed in the past. Such evidence includes a wide range of geological settings, including marine and lake sediments; ice sheets; sedimentary rocks; cave deposits; fossils of plants, animals, and insects; fossil corals and fossil tree rings; and pollen and other sources.[17]

The sun is the primary source of energy for the earth's climate. The greenhouse effect, as we have seen above, is fundamental in maintaining a life-supporting temperature on Earth. In the early part of the geological history of our home planet the enormous quantity of greenhouse gases in the Archaean atmosphere of the planet—the high level of carbon dioxide from intense volcanism—ensured that Earth was not frozen over, unlike our immediate planetary neighbor Mars. This happened in spite of "the faint young sun paradox," the fact that the radiation from the sun was 30 percent lower than the present level during about the first billion years of Earth's existence.[18] In the subsequent history of Earth, carbon dioxide levels in the atmosphere

---

[16] See ibid., 5, 18, 148; Maslin, *Global Warming*, 45.

[17] The Geological Society, *Climate Change*, 1; Archer, *The Long Thaw*, 57–59.

[18] See Pearce, *The Last Generation*, 165; Lawrence M. Krauss, *Atom: Odyssey from the Big Bang to Life on Earth and Beyond* (London: Little, Brown, and Co., 2001), 166; Uwe H. Wiechert, "Earth's Early Atmosphere," *Science* 298 (2002): 2341–42.

gradually decreased due to both biological (which also allowed for the steady increase of oxygen) and geological reasons.[19] Significant in this process was the mechanism of chemical weathering that occurs over million-year timescales. Robert Henson explains it succinctly:

Land masses reduce the amount of carbon dioxide in the air through a multimillion-year process known as *chemical weathering,* which occurs when rain or snow fall on rocks that contain silicate minerals. The moisture and silicates react with carbon dioxide, pulling the CO_2 out of the air. Carbon and water then flow seaward in various forms, and most of the carbon ends up stored in ocean sediments that gradually harden into rocks. Over billions of years, this process has been responsible for some 80 percent of the carbon now stored underground.[20]

As Heidi Cullen notes, "Ultimately, chemical weathering is the most likely explanation for Earth's habitability over most of the 4.6 billion years of its existence."[21] Chemical weathering is a mechanism that has negative and positive feedback built into it, as part of the larger carbon cycle that is important not only to the climatic stability of the planet but to the survival of life forms as well. Earth scientists speak of a crude thermostat of the carbon cycle that helps in this way to maintain equitable temperatures on Earth. The carbon cycle extends into the atmosphere, the oceans, and the solid parts of the earth. The large carbon reservoirs in the ocean, on land, and in the rocks all exchange carbon with the atmosphere. It is precisely the carbon cycle between the solid earth and the atmosphere that appears to stabilize the temperature of the earth by a mechanism called the weathering thermostat.[22]

Long-term climate changes on Earth—such as the 100 million year timescale drift between great ice ages and hothouse climates—are caused by gradual changes driven by the weathering thermostat.[23] The weathering thermostat determines the quantity of carbon dioxide, one of the principal greenhouse gases in the atmosphere, which in turn regulates Earth's surface temperatures. CO_2 degassing through

---

[19] See Krauss, *Atom,* 197ff.

[20] Henson, *The Rough Guide to Climate Change,* 196–97; Krauss, *Atom,* 166–67.

[21] Cullen, *The Weather of the Future,* 24.

[22] Archer, *The Long Thaw,* 83, 102. "The weathering thermostat takes half a million years or longer to adjust the temperature of the Earth" (83).

[23] Ibid., 84.

the continuous crunch of plate tectonics is an essential part of this complex mechanism. Plate tectonics have been rearranging Earth's continents ever since the plates on Earth became rigid approximately 2.5 billion years ago. Half of the CO_2 degassing from the earth to-day occurs at spreading centers, where new ocean crust is formed as plates pull apart. It is believed that major transitions between climatic icehouse and hothouse conditions are ultimately driven by the deep Earth processes of plate tectonics; as a function of the long-term balance between CO_2 degassing and the conversion of atmospheric CO_2 to mineral carbon through long-term silicate weathering; and oceanic carbonate formation.[24]

As opposed to the very long-term climate transitions discussed above, relatively shorter changes in climate cycles are brought about by factors linked to Earth's orbit around the sun that determine the glacial climate cycles on Earth. Climate changes due to slight shifts in the planet's orbit around the sun take place in the arc of only tens or hundreds of thousands of years. The link between changes in the earth's orbital variations and ice ages was originally proposed by James Croll in the eighteenth century. In the early 1900s, Milutin Milankovitch mathematically quantified the idea, producing the first numerical estimates of the impact of orbital variations on climate, called Milankovitch cycles.[25] Today, the role of variations in Earth's orbit to affect climate is recognized by the scientific community.[26] As our home planet revolves around its home star, the following astronomical factors have a direct effect on Earth's climate system: variations in Earth's elliptical orbit, its axial tilt, and its rotational wobble. All of these factors slightly alter the distribution of the solar radiation reaching the earth; the effects can be greatest in polar regions, where they can alter the amount of sunlight by as much as 10 percent.[27]

First of all, we need to consider Earth's movement around the sun along the supposed orbit. The evolution of ice sheets—their growth and decay through time—appears to be paced by variations in the earth's orbit around the sun, which is not precisely circular, but slightly

---

[24] See R. A. Berner, *The Phanerozoic Carbon Cycle: CO_2 and O_2* (Oxford: Oxford University Press, 2004); The National Research Council, *Understanding Earth's Deep Past*, 27; Archer, *The Long Thaw*, 84.

[25] For a synthetic description of how Milankovitch cycles drive the ice-age cycles, see S. Solomon et al., "Technical Summary," in *Climate Change 2007: The Physical Science Basis*, 56.

[26] See The Royal Society, *Climate Change: A Summary of the Science* (September 30, 2010), para. 11.

[27] See Pearce, *The Last Generation*, 170ff.

elliptical. The shape of this ellipse changes according to the gravitational pull on the earth of other orbiting planets like Jupiter and Saturn. These orbital variations affect climate by changing when and how much sunlight reaches Earth, controlling thereby the comings and goings of ice ages. The eccentricity of the orbit gives rise to two main cycles, one that averages about 100,000 years long superimposed on another cycle of about 400,000 years. The last eight ice ages have come and gone roughly in synchronization with the 100,000–year cycle.[28]

A second factor that determines glacial climate cycles on Earth is the angle of Earth's tilt. Sometimes the poles are tilted a bit more than at other times relative to the plane of the earth's orbit. Currently the tilt is 23.4 degrees relative to the plane of the earth's trajectory around the sun and is on the decrease. The interaction between the orbit around the sun and the tilt of the axis of the earth provides the seasons. When the axis is more tilted, the seasons are more intense. The tilt can vary over a period of approximately 41,000 years. Ice ages often set in as the tilt decreases because the progressively cooler summers can't melt the past winter's snow. At the other extreme, increasing tilt produces warmer summers that can help end an ice age.[29]

Third, there is a wobble in the imaginary axis around which the earth slowly rotates, as in a spinning top, which is called the precession. The axis of rotation of the earth, a line connecting the North and South poles, is tilted relative to the plane of the earth's orbit around the sun. It influences the time of year when the different hemispheres are furthest from or nearest to the sun. Currently the Northern Hemisphere has its summer and the southern hemisphere has its winter when the earth is farthest from the sun. But due to the wobble, in a cycle of 13,000 years, this situation will change inversely. This intensifies the seasonal changes in solar energy across the hemispheres, affecting the state of ice sheets and kicking in climatic changes like the bolstering or weakening of the African and Asian monsoons.[30]

The eccentricity of the earth's orbit around the sun is believed to condition the 100,000–year cycles of ice ages. The other two effects, especially the precession, seem to trigger the interglacial warm episodes that punctuate the ice ages.[31] An unusually large volcano

---

[28] Henson, *The Rough Guide to Climate Change*, 185–87; Archer, *The Long Thaw*, 72; Fred Pearce, *The Last Generation*, 171–72.

[29] Henson, *The Rough Guide to Climate Change*, 184–86; Archer, *The Long Thaw*, 73; Fred Pearce, *The Last Generation*, 172.

[30] Pearce, *The Last Generation*, 172; Henson, *The Rough Guide to Climate Change*, 187; Archer, *The Long Thaw*, 73.

[31] Pearce, *The Last Generation*, 172.

eruption also may cool the planet sharply, as with Mount Pinatubo in 1991, which spewed copious amounts of aerosols into the upper atmosphere and brought down global temperatures by nearly –0.6°C. This cooling lasted for only about two years.[32]

Earth has been in the warmer greenhouse state for most of the past 600 million years of geological time.[33] However, the most recent 1 percent of our atmosphere's history is mainly a story of cooling. Starting in the mid-Eocene, around 50–55 million years ago, sea levels began to drop, continents shifted ever closer to their current locations, and global temperatures began to fall. This cooling trend was closely linked to the reduction of CO_2 in the atmosphere, which went from several times its modern-day amounts in the mid-Eocene to barely half of its present-day concentration during the last few ice ages. The question of what brought down the carbon dioxide levels is far more challenging. Apart from the reduction of volcanism, the main factor is said to be the uplift of the Himalayas and Tibetan Plateau, an important geological event that began around 55 million years ago as the Indian subcontinent joined Asia, pushing the Himalayas and the plateau upward. The pace quickened about 30 million years ago. It is believed that these upheavals exposed large quantities of igneous rock to the chemical action of minute amounts of atmospheric carbon dioxide dissolved in the rain water that washed over them. Over millions of years the weathering of the rocks trapped vast quantities of carbon dioxide from the atmosphere. The intense chemical weathering produced by the Tibetan Plateau would have pulled enough carbon dioxide from the air to trigger the global temperature drop that led to the most recent ice ages. Other factors, like the opening of the Tasmanian-Antarctic gateway and the Drake passage, which isolated Antarctica from the rest of the world, and the closure of the Panama ocean gateway, are also believed to have contributed to the long-term cooling of the planet.[34]

The current icehouse began around 34 million years ago with increased glaciation in Antarctica. It has been called a *great ice age,* characterized by the presence of large and permanently frozen ice sheets holding significant amounts of water somewhere on Earth ever since. Within our current great ice age the ice sheets periodically grow and melt back, and global temperatures rise and fall in what

---

[32] Archer, *The Long Thaw*, 40.

[33] The National Research Council, *Understanding Earth's Deep Past*, 1.

[34] Henson, *The Rough Guide to Climate Change*, 204; Maslin, *Global Warming*, 43; R. A. Livermore et al., "Drake Passage and Cenozoic Climate: An Open and Shut Case?" *Geochemistry, Geophysics, Geosystems* 8 (2007): Q01005.

are called glacial cycles—the waxing and waning of the ice ages.[35] By around 24 million years ago, the CO_2 in Earth's atmosphere was below 500 parts per million (ppm), probably for the first time since the planet's early days. It was around then that an ice sheet spread across Antarctica—the first permanent ice to form on the planet for hundreds of millions of years. The cooling appears to have temporarily reversed around 15 million years ago (the middle Miocene climatic optimum),[36] and then resumed with gusto. Glaciers began to appear about 7 million years ago in the Andes, Alaska, and Greenland. And by about 3.2 million years ago another surge of cooling had begun, with ice-sheet formation in the Arctic ushering in the era of regular ice ages. Ice sheets began spreading across North America and Eurasia about 2.7 million years ago, repeatedly covering areas across much of present-day Canada, northern Europe, and northwest Russia. The glacial cycles were regularly punctuated by interglacial intervals of warmer and milder temperatures.[37] At first, between 2.5 and 0.9 million years ago, these interglacial periods occurred about every 41,000 years. This, in fact, corresponds remarkably well to the 41,000–year cycle in the tilt of Earth's axis. About a million years ago, however, the 41,000–year rhythm of ice ages ended. From then, the ice ages got stronger and began to last much longer—about 100,000 years each, with interglacial periods in the order of 10,000 to 15,000 years long.[38]

The most recent ice age, which started about 115,000 years ago, began a stuttering retreat 16,000 years ago. There's little debate about what brought the last ice age to an end. Two of the orbital cycles involving Earth's tilt and the rotation of its axis (precession) synchronized to produce a strong peak in the summertime input of solar energy across the Northern Hemisphere. The natural carbon cycle acted as a positive feedback, amplifying the response to the orbit.[39] Starting about 15,000 years ago ice sheets began to melt, influencing ocean circulation and triggering rapid climate shifts. Nearly 14,500

---

[35] See J. C. Zachos et al., "An Early Cenozoic Perspective on Greenhouse Warming and Carbon-Cycle Dynamics," *Nature* 451 (2008): 279–83; The National Research Council, *Understanding Earth's Deep Past*, 21; Archer, *The Long Thaw*, 78.

[36] See Alan Graham, "The Age and Diversification of Terrestrial New Word Ecosystems Through Cretaceous and Cenozoic Time," *American Journal of Botany* 98 (2011): 348.

[37] Henson, *The Rough Guide to Climate Change*, 203–6.

[38] Ibid., 206; The Geological Society, *Climate Change*, 2; Maslin, *Global Warming*, 45.

[39] Henson, *The Rough Guide to Climate Change*, 208; Archer, *The Long Thaw*, 6.

years ago sudden warming caused sea levels to rise 65.6 feet in 400 years. These dramatic climatic changes eventually ushered Earth (about 11,500 years ago) into an interglacial era of exceptionally stable climate, namely, the Holocene era.[40]

The present interglacial period of the Holocene is characterized by glaciated poles that have allowed a dynamic climate system. The double glaciated poles make the temperature difference between the poles and the equator extremely large, from an average of about +30°C at the equator to -35°C or colder at the poles. As Mark Maslin notes, it is precisely such an ideal situation that guarantees our home planet the dynamic climate system that it currently enjoys.

> This temperature gradient is one of the main reasons that we have a climate system, as excess heat from the tropics is exported both via the oceans and the atmosphere to the poles, which causes our weather. Geologically, we currently have one of the largest Equator-pole temperature gradients, which leads to a very dynamic climate system.[41]

The Holocene era of the last 12,000 years has been exceptionally stable globally, though with regional and local climatic variations in different parts of the globe. In this context one may remember the sudden drying of the Sahara 5,500 years ago, which pushed the region from savannah to desert. Around 4,200 years ago, another bout of aridification concentrated on the Middle East, leading to the widespread collapse of civilizations. More recently, from 950 to 1250, a medieval warm period in the Northern Hemisphere provided an optimal climate in Europe, with bountiful harvests, but led to droughts in North America that ravaged entire civilizations, including the Mayans. There must have been an estimated rise of roughly 0.2–0.5°C in global temperatures during the Medieval Warm Period.[42] After it faded, the Northern Hemisphere witnessed the resumption of long-term cooling, kicking in around 1300 and continuing into the mid-1800s, called the Little Ice Age, when it was at most 1°C (on average) colder than the natural climate, and during which plagues and famines ravaged Europe, where the cooling was particularly strong.[43] However, such

---

[40] See Henson, *The Rough Guide to Climate Change*, 208; The Geological Society, *Climate Change*, 2.

[41] Maslin, *Global Warming*, 45–46.

[42] National Research Council, *Understanding Earth's Deep Past*, 19.

[43] Michael E. Mann et al., "Global Signatures and Dynamical Origins of the Little Ice Age and Medieval Climate Anomaly," *Science* 326 (2009): 1258; Henson, *The Rough Guide to Climate Change*, 213; Archer, *The Long Thaw*, 61–62.

regional and local climatic variations need to be seen within the overall context of a relatively long and exceptionally stable climatic interval era during which the global average temperature has hardly varied 1 or 2 degrees, and with stable sea levels and other climatic constants.[44] Agriculture and civilization developed during the oasis of unusual climatic stability that characterized the Holocene epoch.[45]

After the mid-1800s Earth's climate took a decided turn for the warmer. During the recent ice ages—the entire timespan covering human evolution on Earth—the amount of carbon dioxide in our home planet's atmosphere had never gone beyond 300 ppm. It was the right amount to keep the planet at a temperature suited to the flourishing of a rich variety of life. However, since the onset of the Industrial Revolution around 1750, there appears to be a constant increase of carbon dioxide in the atmosphere, presently hovering close to 400 ppm, with the average global temperature closely following suit.[46]

If the past climate shifts in the geological archives of Earth were driven by natural factors, for the first time in the history of the planet and of humanity, climate forcing appears to be driven principally by human activities, precisely by the rapid increase of the greenhouse gases in our home planet's atmosphere. This, in turn, is inextricably linked to global average temperature and climate system, with disastrous consequences for humans and other ecosystems.

Anthropogenic Global Warming and Associated Climate Change

Against the backdrop of the long-term climate changes driven by the carbon cycle over a span of millions of years, and relatively short-term climate changes driven by orbital cycles over a span of tens of thousands of years—both of which are entirely normal climatic changes driven by natural factors—our home planet finds itself precariously poised on the verge of a totally unprecedented situation. We face the terrifying prospect of a sudden change in Earth's climate system, with

---

[44] As David Archer notes, "The Medieval Optimum was a real climate shift in Europe, but it was not clearly global" (Archer, *The Long Thaw*, 62).

[45] Ibid., 64, 93–94. See also the classical work of Brian Fagan, *The Long Summer: How Climate Changed Civilization* (New York: Basic Books, 2004).

[46] See World Meteorological Organization and Global Atmosphere Watch, *WMO Greenhouse Gas Bulletin: The State of Greenhouse Gases in the Atmosphere Based on Global Observations Through 2012* (November 6, 2013), 2; National Oceanic and Atmospheric Administration, "Carbon Dioxide at NOAA's Mauna Loa Observatory Reaches New Milestone: Tops 400 ppm" (May 10, 2013).

significant risks for a broad range of human and natural ecosystems. The alarming state of our common home in this regard is expressed in two incontrovertible conclusions of the scientific community in recent years. The first is that the earth is warming and that climate change is occurring. The second is that the current climate forcing is caused largely by human activities.

Warming of the earth is unequivocal, as stated by the Fifth Assessment Report of the Intergovernmental Panel on Climate Change (IPCC).[47] Global temperature is a popular and faithful metric that represents the state of global climate. Accurate measurements of the planet's average surface temperature are possible due to progress made in this regard over centuries of scientific research. It may be remembered that shortly after the invention of the thermometer in the early 1600s, efforts began to record weather. The first meteorological observation network was established in 1653 in northern Italy, and reports of temperature observations were published in the earliest scientific journals. By the mid-1800s, weather observations including temperatures were recorded throughout the inhabited world. The earliest reliable record of global average temperature dates to about 1860.[48] With the establishment of the International Meteorological Organization in 1873 and its successor, the World Meteorological Organization (WMO) in 1951, it has been possible to promote and exchange standardized and high-quality meteorological observations. Today, the vast majority of data that go into global surface-temperature calculations come from an impressive array of over 400 million individual readings of thermometers at land stations and over 140 million individual *in situ* sea-surface temperature observations, apart from satellites, weather balloons, and other sources.[49]

---

[47] IPCC, *Climate Change 2013: The Physical Science Basis: Contribution of Working Group I to the Fifth Assessment Report of the Intergovernmental Panel on Climate Change*, ed. T. F. Stocker et al. (Cambridge: Cambridge University Press, 2013), 4. See also IPCC, *Climate Change 2007: Synthesis Report: Contribution of Working Groups I, II, and III to the Fourth Assessment Report of the Intergovernmental Panel on Climate Change*, ed. R. K. Pachauri and A. Reisinger (Geneva: IPCC, 2007), 30.

[48] J. Kington, *The Weather of the 1780s over Europe* (Cambridge: Cambridge University Press, 1988); Archer, *The Long Thaw*, 58; Le Treut et al., "Historical Overview of Climate Change Science," 100–101; Henson, *The Rough Guide to Climate Change*, 161–62.

[49] Le Treut et al., "Historical Overview of Climate Change Science," 102; The National Academy of Sciences, *Advancing the Science of Climate Change* (Washington, DC: The National Academics Press, 2010), 30–32.

Based on the diverse, carefully examined, and well-understood body of evidence collected over both land and sea since the mid-1800s, scientists are virtually certain that the earth is warming. Today, there exists a strong, credible, and substantial body of evidence, based on multiple lines of research, documenting this reality. Furthermore, this widespread temperature increase is corroborated by a range of warming-related impacts like shrinking mountain glaciers, decreasing polar ice cover, increasing ocean temperatures, sea level rise, and a number of biospheric changes.[50] Measurements show a rise close to 0.8°C in the average surface air temperature of Earth since 1850, with greater increase in recent decades. Global surface temperature has increased approximately0.2°C per decade in the past 30 years. Each decade since the 1970s has been clearly warmer than the one preceding it.[51] According to the World Meteorological Organization, the period 2001–2010 was the world's warmest ten-year period on record. It was 0.21°C warmer than the warmest ten-year period of the twentieth century, 1991–2000. In turn, 1991–2000 was clearly warmer than previous decades, consistent with a long-term warming trend.[52] According to the World Meteorological Organization, the years 2001–2012 were all among the top thirteen warmest years on record,[53] while according to the latest report from the IPCC, 1983–2012 was likely the warmest 30–year period of the last 1,400 years.[54]

Observations thus show that the earth is gradually warming. Obviously, there must be a reason for these changes. This is the second unequivocal conclusion that the scientific community has been able to offer in recent decades; namely, the current warming is caused by human activities. The common conclusion of a wide range of studies conducted over the past years is that observed climate changes cannot

---

[50] The National Academy of Sciences, *Understanding and Responding to Climate Change: Highlights of National Academies* (Washington, DC: National Academies Press, 2008), 4; The National Academy of Sciences, *Advancing the Science of Climate Change*, 1, 32; Grant Foster and Stefan Rahmstorf, "Global Temperature Evolution," *Environmental Research Letters* 6 (2011): 044022.

[51] The Royal Society, *Climate Change*, paras. 21, 22; James Hansen et al., "Global Temperature Change," *Proceedings of the National Academy of Sciences* 103 (2006): 14288–93.

[52] World Meteorological Organization, WMO *Statement on the Status of the Global Climate 2011* (Geneva: World Meteorological Organization, 2012), 2.

[53] World Meteorological Organization, WMO *Statement on the Status of the Global Climate 2012* (Geneva: World Meteorological Organization, 2013), 6.

[54] IPCC, *Climate Change 2013*, 5.

be explained by natural factors alone. The perceived changes can be explained only by having recourse to a substantial anthropogenic influence in terms of human activities.[55]

Scientists refer to the change in the radiative balance of the earth as manifested in the increase in Earth's average surface temperature as a form of "climate forcing." There are three fundamental ways in which climate forcing can take place by changing the radiation balance of the earth:

> (1) by changing the incoming solar radiation (e.g., by changes in Earth's orbit or in the sun itself); (2) by changing the fraction of solar radiation that is reflected (called "albedo"; e.g., by changes in cloud cover, atmospheric particles or vegetation); and (3) by altering the longwave radiation from Earth back towards space (e.g., by changing greenhouse gas concentrations). Climate, in turn, responds directly to such changes, as well as indirectly, through a variety of feedback mechanisms.[56]

To explain the current phase of global warming, it is not credible to postulate a change in the quantity of energy reaching our planet from the sun. As James Hansen notes, "While our sun is an ordinary young star, still 'burning' hydrogen to make helium by nuclear fusion and slowly getting brighter, in 20,000 years the brightness increase was negligible—0.0001 percent, or about 0.0002 watt."[57] Satellite measurements also conclusively show that solar output has not increased over the past thirty years. So the warming during the past thirty years cannot be attributed to an increase in solar energy reaching the earth.[58] In the same way, the frequency of volcanic eruptions, which tend to cool the earth by reflecting sunlight back to space, also has not increased or decreased significantly. While past climatic changes can be related to geological events, it is not possible to relate the current warming of our home planet since 1970 to a geological cause (such as volcanic activity, continental displacement, or changes in the energy received from the sun). Thus, there are no

---

[55] Le Treut et al., "Historical Overview of Climate Change Science," 103.

[56] Ibid., 96. See also The Royal Society, *Climate Change*, para. 8.

[57] James Hansen, *Storms of My Grandchildren: The Truth About the Coming Climate Catastrophe and Our Last Chance to Save Humanity* (London: Bloomsbury, 2009), 45.

[58] The National Academy of Sciences, *Advancing the Science of Climate Change*, 38.

known natural factors that can explain the recent warming of the earth.[59]

Instead, it is becoming more evident that global warming and climate change are happening through the alteration of the composition of the greenhouse gases in the atmosphere—so fundamental for the stability of Earth's climate system and for the flourishing of life itself, as we have seen earlier. Humankind appears to have dramatically altered the chemical composition of the global atmosphere with substantial implications for climate.[60] In fact, "detailed simulations with state-of-the-art computer-based models of the climate system are only able to reproduce the observed warming trend and patterns when human-induced GHG emissions are included."[61]

Based on multiple lines of evidence, an overwhelming majority of climate scientists conclude that much of the observed warming since the start of the twentieth century, and most of the warming over the last several decades can be attributed to human activities that release carbon dioxide and other heat-trapping greenhouse gases into the atmosphere.[62]

Prior to the Industrial Revolution, the amount of carbon dioxide released into the atmosphere by natural processes was almost exactly in balance with the amount absorbed by plants and other natural sinks on the earth's surface, maintaining a natural climate equilibrium.[63] This situation changed drastically in the modern era. "Over the last 250 years or so human activity, such as the burning of fossil fuels, the removal of forests that would otherwise absorb carbon dioxide, and their replacement with intensive livestock ranching, has released a range of 'greenhouse gases' into the atmosphere."[64] The excess carbon dioxide in the atmosphere in the last few decades clearly bears

---

[59] The Geological Society, *Climate Change*, 6; The National Academy of Sciences, *Understanding and Responding to Climate Change*, 6.

[60] Michael D. Mastrandrea and Stephen H. Schneider, *Preparing for Climate Change* (Cambridge, MA: MIT Press, 2010), 20; Le Treut et al., "Historical Overview of Climate Change Science," 97.

[61] The National Academy of Sciences, *Advancing the Science of Climate Change*, 37–38; see also Mastrandrea and Schneider, *Preparing for Climate Change*, 28.

[62] The National Academy of Sciences, *Advancing the Science of Climate Change*, 4, 38; The Royal Society, *Climate Change*, para. 2; Pontificia Academia Scientiarum, *Fate of Mountain Glaciers in the Anthropocene: A Report by the Working Group Commissioned by the Pontifical Academy of Sciences* (May 5, 2011), 7.

[63] Walker and King, *The Hot Topic*, 18; The National Academy of Sciences, *Understanding and Responding to Climate Change*, 5.

[64] Dow and Downing, *The Atlas of Climate Change*, 30.

the fingerprint of human activities, as is evident from the chemical composition of their isotopes.[65]

Today, nearly two-thirds of CO_2 emissions, along with a significant amount of nitrous oxide and methane, derive from the burning of fossil fuels. Although fossil-fuel burning is the most significant human activity contributing to global warming, other activities also have a major influence. For example, tropical deforestation and land-use changes contribute 3 to 5 billion tons of CO_2 emissions and have a strong influence on both local and global climates.[66] Agriculture accounts for nearly one-third of global emissions of the greenhouse gases.

The human activities that contribute to greenhouse gas emissions are manifold. Carbon footprint analysis today pinpoints the specific contribution of various human activities to the emission of carbon dioxide and other greenhouse gases into the atmosphere. Human influences are now large enough to exceed the bounds of natural variability.

The Greenhouse Gases
Driving Anthropogenic Climate Change

The major greenhouse gases contributing to the current phase of global warming include water vapor, carbon dioxide, methane, nitrous oxide, and a host of industrial gases such as CFCs that do not appear naturally in the atmosphere. Despite the greenhouse gases often being depicted as one layer, they are in fact mixed throughout the atmosphere. The greenhouses gases constitute only 1 percent of the total volume of the atmosphere, but even relatively small increases in the amount of these gases in the atmosphere can amplify the natural greenhouse effect, warming the earth's surface.[67]

---

[65] "Measurements of the isotopic abundances of the CO_2 molecules in the atmosphere—a chemical property that varies depending on the source of the CO_2—indicate that most of the excess CO_2 in the atmosphere originated from sources that are millions of years old. The only source of such large amounts of fossil carbon are coal, oil, and natural gas." The National Academy of Sciences, *Advancing the Science of Climate Change*, 188. See also Le Treut et al., "Historical Overview of Climate Change Science," 100.

[66] The National Academy of Sciences, *Advancing the Science of Climate Change*, 34; The National Academy of Sciences, *Understanding and Responding to Climate Change*, 15.

[67] Mastrandrea and Schneider, *Preparing for Climate Change*, 23; The National Academy of Sciences, *Advancing the Science of Climate Change*, 184.

The two most important greenhouse gases are carbon dioxide and water vapor. Currently, carbon dioxide accounts for 0.03–0.04 percent of the atmosphere, while water vapor varies from 0 to 2 percent. Water vapor is technically the most abundant greenhouse gas in the atmosphere and has by far the biggest effect on the temperature of the air, given its relative abundance in the atmosphere. However, when it comes to the power to change the climate, carbon dioxide and methane, and to some extent the other trace gases, come into their own. Water vapor molecules typically remain in the lower atmosphere for only a few days before they are returned to the surface in the form of precipitation. Carbon dioxide molecules, on the other hand, are only exchanged slowly with the surface and may remain in the atmosphere for many centuries before being removed by natural processes.[68] Although carbon dioxide may make up less than 0.04 percent of the atmosphere, and methane even less than that, their impact on global warming is significant for two reasons:

First, there is already so much water vapour in the atmosphere that human activities make hardly any difference to the total, rather like adding a few bucketfuls of water to an ocean. But because there's relatively little carbon dioxide and methane, you don't have to add much to make a big proportional difference. It's like putting a few extra bucketfuls of water into a bath. Thus, humans have already almost managed to double the amount of greenhouse gases in the air.

And second, by trapping extra heat themselves, these greenhouse gases also have an indirect effect on the amount of water vapour in the air. Warmer air can soak up more water, and warmer lakes, rivers and seas can evaporate more easily into the atmosphere. The upshot of these two effects is that if you heat the air a little by adding extra carbon dioxide, it then takes up much more water vapour. This new water acts as a greenhouse gas in its own right and heats the air up even more, roughly doubling the effect the greenhouse gases would have had if they acted alone. Scientists call it a positive feedback.[69]

So when it comes to climate forcing, the long-lived greenhouse gases—carbon dioxide, methane, nitrous oxide, and others—matter

---

[68] The National Academy of Sciences, *Advancing the Science of Climate Change*, 185.

[69] Walker and King, *The Hot Topic*, 17–18.

directly much more than water vapor. These are the gases that have been increasingly added into the earth's atmosphere due to human activities, especially in the centuries since the beginning of the industrial era around 1750. They drive the current phase of global warming and associated climate change, and also have strong interactions with the biosphere and the oceans, leading to other consequences apart from global warming itself.

Carbon dioxide is the single most important anthropogenic greenhouse gas in the atmosphere. The role of carbon dioxide in warming the earth's surface by the natural greenhouse effect was first suggested by Swedish scientist Svante Arrhenius more than a century ago. Today in climate science, the causal link and the direct relationship between atmospheric carbon dioxide and global temperature is well established.[70] Carbon dioxide is a powerful modifier of the earth's climate even in small quantities. According to the latest estimates, carbon dioxide contributes to nearly 64 percent to the heating of all long-lived greenhouse gases and is responsible for 85 percent of the increase in global warming over the past decade.[71] The CO_2 emitted by human activities is the largest single climate-forcing agent, accounting for more than half of the total climate forcing since 1750.[72] From the point of view of human influence, carbon dioxide is therefore the most important of the anthropogenic greenhouse gases.

The volume of carbon dioxide in the atmosphere is calculated in terms of number of molecules of the gas per million molecules of dry air (ppm). Climate science is today able to trace back through its long geological past the atmospheric concentration of CO_2 that existed in the earth's atmosphere. This is done by measuring the CO_2 concentrations in "ancient air" trapped in bubbles in ice, deep below the surfaces of Antarctica and Greenland. Recent ice-core archives have revealed that during the past 800,000 years, the atmospheric CO_2 levels were less than 300 ppm. In fact, during the glacial and interglacial periods, CO_2 levels in the earth's atmosphere varied from 180 ppm to 300 ppm.[73] It is important to remember that carbon dioxide acted like

[70] See Damon Matthews et al., "The Proportionality of Global Warming to Cumulative Carbon Emissions," *Nature* 459 (2009): 829–33.

[71] World Meteorological Organization and Global Atmosphere Watch, *WMO Greenhouse Gas Bulletin: The State of Greenhouse Gases in the Atmosphere Based on Global Observations Through 2011* (November 19, 2012), 2.

[72] The National Academy of Sciences, *Advancing the Science of Climate Change*, 189.

[73] The Geological Society, *Climate Change*, 4; The Royal Society, *Climate Change*, para. 25.

a feedback rather than as an initial driver in climate change during the ice ages, reinforcing temperature changes initiated by natural variations in Earth's orbit. "Palaeoclimatologists think that initial warming driven by changes in the earth's orbit and axial tilt eventually caused CO_2 to be released from the warming ocean and thus, via positive feedback, to reinforce the temperature rise already in train."[74] While carbon dioxide acted as a feedback in the past, it is acting as a direct forcing agent in the current phase of climate change, intensifying the greenhouse effect which heats up the earth's surface and lower atmosphere.

For about 10,000 years before the Industrial Revolution—during the entire span of the Holocene era, during which modern humans settled down and civilizations arose in various parts of the globe—the atmospheric abundance of carbon dioxide was nearly constant at around 280 ppm. During this period of exceptionally stable climate the amount of carbon dioxide released to the atmosphere by natural processes was almost exactly in balance with the amount absorbed by vegetation and other "sinks" on the earth's surface. This ensured a sort of balance in the carbon cycle among the atmosphere, the oceans, and the biosphere.[75] However, with the onset of the Industrial Revolution in Europe around 1750, human activities began emitting large amounts of carbon dioxide into the atmosphere, amplifying natural greenhouse effect and tampering with the fundamental carbon cycle on Earth. The present level of atmospheric carbon dioxide is almost 40 percent higher than preindustrial conditions, usually taken as 280 ppm. The atmospheric concentrations of carbon dioxide in 2012 were 393.1 ppm,[76] and in May 2013 at the Mauna Loa Observatory in Hawaii, levels of this greenhouse gas surpassed 400 ppm for the first time since measurements began in 1958.[77] The current rapid rise in atmospheric CO_2 is as much as thirty times faster than natural rates in the geological past, and the present atmospheric levels of CO_2 are higher than at any time in at least the last 800,000 years and likely

---

[74] The Geological Society, *Climate Change*, 4.

[75] The National Academy of Sciences, *Understanding and Responding to Climate Change*, 5; World Meteorological Organization and Global Atmosphere Watch, *WMO Greenhouse Gas Bulletin 2010*, 2.

[76] World Meteorological Organization and Global Atmosphere Watch, *WMO Greenhouse Gas Bulletin: The State of Greenhouse Gases in the Atmosphere Based on Global Observations Through 2012*, 2.

[77] See the statement from the National Oceanic and Atmospheric Administration, "Carbon Dioxide at NOAA's Mauna Loa Observatory Reaches New Milestone: Tops 400 ppm" (May 10, 2013).

several million years.[78] Human activity is releasing stores of carbon dioxide into the atmosphere at a faster rate than it can be absorbed back into the natural carbon cycle. Stephen Schneider writes:

> The primordial CO_2 concentrations resulted from a combination of volcanic eruptions spewing the gas into the atmosphere, the formation and weathering of rocks, the synthesis and decay of organic matter, and the chemical transformation of undecayed organic matter into fossil fuels—all of which took place over the eons. We humans are digging up those fossil fuels and releasing them at a much faster rate than they were made.[79]

Once emitted, carbon dioxide added to the atmosphere and oceans remains for thousands of years. Almost half of the CO_2 emitted by human activity since the Industrial Revolution has remained in the atmosphere, with the other half absorbed by land and ocean sinks. "Models of the global carbon cycle and the geologic record both show that CO_2 produced from fossil fuels and other reservoirs will continue to impact global climate and atmospheric chemistry for tens to hundreds of thousands of years."[80] In fact, a quarter of the CO_2 emissions today will still be affecting the climate after 1,000 years, and around 10 percent will still affect the climate system after 100,000 years. David Archer points out that some of the effects of carbon dioxide we emit now will last longer than the effects of nuclear waste created today.[81]

There exists also the stark possibility that with all the fossil fuels still remaining in the belly of the planet, humanity could make the selfish and utterly foolish choice of using them up in a few centuries and overheating the planet; the impact would last for several millennia. The global economy is currently around 80 percent dependent on

---

[78] Scott C. Doney et al., "Ocean Acidification: A Critical Emerging Problem for the Ocean Sciences," *Oceanography* 22 (2009): 16; L. R. Kump et al., "Ocean Acidification in Deep Time," *Oceanography* 22 (2009): 94. See also Cullen, *The Weather of the Future*, 30; Eric W. Wolff, "Greenhouse Gases in the Earth System: A Palaeoclimate Perspective," *Philosophical Transactions of the Royal Society A* 369 (2011): 2133–47.

[79] Stephen H. Schneider, *Laboratory Earth: A Brief History of Climate Change* (London: Phoenix, 1996), 54–55.

[80] The National Academy of Sciences, *Advancing the Science of Climate Change*, 76.

[81] Archer, *The Long Thaw*, 1; Clive Hamilton, *Requiem for a Species: Why We Resist the Truth about Climate Change* (London: Washington, DC: Earthscan, 2010), 8–9.

fossil fuels.[82] Fossil fuels are nothing but CO_2 that once existed in the atmosphere and was converted by natural processes into fossil-fuel reserves over the course of 180 million years. Some seven trillion tons of old vegetable carbon have been stored for tens of millions of years beneath the earth's surface in the form of fossil fuels. That is a lot of warming stored away.[83] We will need to limit cumulative emissions of carbon dioxide today to avoid dangerous climate change in the future.

Human activities have also led to increases in the concentrations of a number of other greenhouse gases that contribute to global warming and climate change. "Many of these gases are much more potent warming agents, on a molecule-for-molecule basis, than CO_2, so even small changes in their concentrations can have a substantial influence."[84]

Methane contributes to nearly 18 percent of heating of Earth's surface and lower atmosphere by the long-lived greenhouse gases. Methane is produced from a wide range of human activities as well as natural sources. Anthropogenic sources include animal husbandry, rice cultivation, fossil-fuel exploitation, landfills, and biomass burning; these account for about 60 percent of the total emissions. Natural sources include wetlands, termites, and changes in land use. Globally averaged methane in the earth's atmosphere in 2012 was 1,819 ppb (parts per billion), which is more than two-and-a-half times its average preindustrial concentration.[85] This peak abundance of methane is much higher than the range of 400–700 ppb seen over the last half-million years of glacial-interglacial cycles, and the increase can be readily explained by anthropogenic emissions. While methane is 23 times more potent than carbon dioxide as a greenhouse warming gas, it is also relatively short-lived; molecules of CH_4 spend on average fewer than ten years in the atmosphere.[86] There are also concerns that warming temperatures could lead to melting permafrost across the Arctic or, less likely, the destabilization of methane hydrates on the seafloor.

---

[82] See Simms, *Ecological Debt*, 25–27.

[83] Pearce, *The Last Generation*, 167.

[84] The National Academy of Sciences, *Advancing the Science of Climate Change*, 189.

[85] World Meteorological Organization and Global Atmosphere Watch, *WMO Greenhouse Gas Bulletin: The State of Greenhouse Gases in the Atmosphere Based on Global Observations Through 2012*, 3.

[86] Ibid., 2–3; The National Academy of Sciences, *Advancing the Science of Climate Change*, 190–91; Le Treut et al., "Historical Overview of Climate Change Science," 100.

Nitrous oxide (N_2O) contributes to about 6 percent of the heating of the earth's surface and atmosphere by the greenhouse gases. Nitrous oxide is emitted into the atmosphere from natural as well as anthropogenic sources, the latter accounting for approximately 40 percent of the total N_2O emissions. Human activities contributing to nitrous oxide emissions include primarily agricultural activities (especially the application of chemical fertilizers), fossil-fuel burning, and various industrial processes. The volume of nitrous oxide in the atmosphere prior to industrialization was 270 ppb; in 2012 it averaged 325.1 ppb.[87] Nitrous oxide is an extremely potent warming agent—more than three hundred times as potent as CO_2—and its molecules remain in the atmosphere more than 100 years on average.[88] Apart from contributing to global warming, nitrous oxide is also now the most important stratospheric ozone-depleting substance being emitted by human activities.[89]

Current global warming is also caused by other gases, like halogenated gases and ozone. There are over a dozen halogenated gases, including ozone-depleting substances such as CFCs and hydrofluorocarbons (HFCs). These gases are rare, and their concentrations in the atmosphere are typically measured in parts per trillion. However, they also have very long residence times in the atmosphere and are extremely potent forcing agents. Ice-core research has shown that the compounds of halogenated gas did not exist in ancient air and thus confirms their industrial human origin. The ozone-depleting CFCs, together with other minor halogenated gases, contribute nearly 12 percent of the warming caused by the greenhouse gases. The Montreal Protocol[90] was successful in leading to the sharp decline in CFCs

[87] World Meteorological Organization and Global Atmosphere Watch, *WMO Greenhouse Gas Bulletin 2012*, 3.

[88] World Meteorological Organization and Global Atmosphere Watch, *WMO Greenhouse Gas Bulletin 2011*, 3; The National Academy of Sciences, *Advancing the Science of Climate Change*, 192.

[89] See A. R. Ravishankara et al., "Nitrous Oxide (N2O): The Dominant Ozone-Depleting Substance Emitted in the Twenty-first Century," *Science* 326 (2009): 123–25.

[90] The Montreal Protocol is an international treaty designed to protect the ozone layer by phasing out the production of numerous substances that deplete ozone in the atmosphere, namely, chlorofluorocarbons (CFSs), halons, carbon tetrachloride, and methyl chloroform. The treaty was signed in 1987 and has been ratified by 191 countries. Due to its widespread adoption and implementation, it has been hailed as one of the most successful international agreements to date.

over the past fifteen years or so, while the HFCs, which are also potent greenhouse gases, are increasing at rapid rates.[91]

Ozone (O_3) is also considered one of the greenhouse gases, besides the other function it has of blocking harmful ultraviolet radiation in the stratosphere. Ozone forms naturally in the upper atmosphere, where it creates a protective shield that intercepts damaging ultraviolet rays from the sun. However, ozone produced near the earth's surface through reactions involving carbon monoxide, hydrocarbons, nitrogen oxide, and other pollutants is harmful to both animals and plants and also has a warming effect. Today, the concentration of O_3 in the lower atmosphere is increasing as a result of human activities. It is calculated that changes in atmospheric ozone are responsible for a positive forcing that is comparable to that of halogenated gases. However, the exact radiative forcing caused by ozone is more uncertain than other well-mixed greenhouse gases.[92]

Many other pollutants, such as carbon monoxide, nitrogen oxides, and volatile organic compounds, although insignificant as greenhouse gases, have an indirect effect on the warming of the earth's surface through their impact on the tropospheric ozone abundance. Aerosols, which are short-lived substances that come from both natural sources and human activities, also influence the warming process. Most aerosols cool the planet by reflecting sunlight back to space. Some aerosols also cool the earth indirectly by increasing the amount of sunlight reflected by clouds. The net climate forcing associated with aerosols is estimated to offset roughly one-third of the total positive forcing associated with human emissions of GHGs. However, the forcing associated with aerosols is more uncertain than the forcing associated with GHGs, in part because the global distribution and composition of aerosols are not very well known and in part because of the diversity and complexity of aerosol radiative effects. Fossil-fuel burning, industrial activities, land-use change, and other human activities have generally increased the number of aerosol particles in the atmosphere,

---

[91] World Meteorological Organization and Global Atmosphere Watch, *WMO Greenhouse Gas Bulletin 2010*, 3; Le Treut et al., "Historical Overview of Climate Change Science," 100.

[92] The National Academy of Sciences, *Advancing the Science of Climate Change*, 195; The National Academy of Sciences, *Understanding and Responding to Climate Change*, 7; World Meteorological Organization and Global Atmosphere Watch, *WMO Greenhouse Gas Bulletin 2010*, 4.

especially over and downwind of industrialized countries.[93] In addition to their role in global climate forcing, aerosols also have other environmental effects, including acid rain, which has a major detrimental effect on certain ecosystems.

The greenhouse gases produced in human activities have the greatest influence on Earth's climate system today, driving the current phase of global warming and associated climate change with disastrous consequences for humanity and ecosystems. Spurred by the gravity of the present situation, the United Nations Framework Convention on Climate Change was set up in 1994. Its stated objective, laid out in Article 2, is precisely to achieve the stabilization of greenhouse gas concentrations in the atmosphere at a low enough level to prevent "dangerous anthropogenic interference with the climate system."

Projections of Future Climate Change and the Danger of Tipping Points

The constant rise in the concentration of greenhouse gases in the earth's atmosphere is bound to increase the rate of global warming and cause climate change. Over the last century Earth's average surface air temperature has increased by 0.8°C, and additional warming is already in the pipeline due to past and present emissions. In fact, the full warming effect of past emissions is yet to be realized, given the long lifespan of some of the greenhouse gases like carbon dioxide. As for the future, scientists have come up with a range of projections regarding the rise in global average surface temperatures, depending not only on past emissions of greenhouse gases, but also on the projected trajectory of emissions in the decades to come. The most authoritative prognostication in this regard remains the one offered by the IPCC in its Fifth Assessment Report in 2013. Based on available data, the IPCC estimates that global temperatures are likely to rise by 0.3C to 4.8C by the end of the century, depending on possible carbon-emission scenarios.[94] The full impact of the IPCC's projections regarding the rise in global temperatures in this century can be grasped only if we call to mind that average temperature variations have hardly exceeded 1–2°C since the beginning of the present human civilization.

---

[93] Ibid., 4; The National Academy of Sciences, *Advancing the Science of Climate Change*, 196; The National Academy of Sciences, *Understanding and Responding to Climate Change*, 7.

[94] IPCC, *Climate Change 2013*, 20.

As with all projections of the future, there is a range of uncertainty regarding the details of future climate change.[95] Such uncertainty is due to several factors, including the difficulty of predicting how human populations will grow and how human societies will decide to produce and use energy and other resources in the decades ahead; these will have a strong influence on future greenhouse gas emissions. Future emissions due to human activity will depend on social, technological, and population changes that cannot be predicted with confidence. Certain Earth system processes—such as ice sheet dynamics, cloud processes, and regional climate effects—are still incompletely understood in current climate models. For example, there is currently insufficient understanding of the enhanced melting and retreat of the ice sheets on Greenland and West Antarctica to predict exactly how much the rate of sea-level rise will increase above that observed in the past century. All these factors can lead to uncertainties in projecting the exact magnitude and rate of global climate change and its manifestations at local and regional scales. In general, global temperatures are easier to project than regional changes such as rainfall, storm patterns, and ecosystem impacts.[96] The previsions of future climate change made by the scientific community take into account these elements of uncertainty, which have often resulted in apparently too modest and too cautious forecasts of phenomena like sea-level rise. With the progress in climate science, however, better methods are being found to quantify the uncertainties regarding future climate change.[97]

While the projections of the IPCC and most other bodies speak in terms of climate change within a century-long framework—within the immediate and tangible lifespan of our grandchildren, the farthest our rational self-interest can stretch us—it is important to remember

---

[95] The scientific community is aware of this element of uncertainty and of the existence of some gaps in its research field, as in any other field, that characterize the current state of climate science. These gap areas include regional climate forecasts, precipitation forecasts, aerosols, and palaeoclimate data, on which increasing research is being carried out. See Quirin Schiermeier, "The Real Holes in Climate Science," *Nature* 463 (2010): 284–87. However, "such holes do not undermine the fundamental conclusion that humans are warming the climate, which is based on the extreme rate of the twentieth-century temperature changes and the inability of climate models to stimulate such warming without including the role of greenhouse-gas pollution" (ibid., 284).

[96] See The National Academy of Sciences, *Understanding and Responding to Climate Change*, 8–9; The Royal Society, *Climate Change*, paras. 40, 46ff.

[97] See Matthew Collins et al., "Quantifying Future Climate Change," *Nature Climate Change* 2 (2012): 403–8.

that climate change caused by anthropogenic emissions of greenhouse gases may persist for thousands of years, even after human-induced emissions have ended. This is a framework that has not received sufficient attention from the general public and policymakers. David Archer notes that "the first century is an impressive beginning, but the climate effects of global warming will persist for hundreds of thousands of years."[98]

The anthropogenic emissions of carbon dioxide into the atmosphere will have a predictable long-term impact on the carbon cycle and the future evolution of climate, as we know from the past climate history of the planet. This is precisely because of the extremely long lifespan of important greenhouse gases like carbon dioxide. As the Royal Society's document on climate change states:

> Once atmospheric CO_2 concentrations are increased, carbon cycle models (which simulate the exchange of carbon between the atmosphere, oceans, soils and plants) indicate that it would take a very long time for that increased CO_2 to disappear; this is mainly due to well-known chemical reactions in the ocean. Current understanding indicates that even if there was a complete cessation of emissions of CO_2 today from human activity, it would take several millennia for CO_2 concentrations to return to preindustrial concentrations.[99]

The carbon cycle that maintains Earth's climate system and ultimately life on Earth is extremely long and complex. Carbon-cycle models indicate that even after 100,000 years the anthropogenic perturbation to the carbon cycle—as with the current anthropogenic emission of greenhouse gases—will still be important, especially if the total amount of carbon emitted is large.[100] The natural carbon cycle is extremely slow when measured by human timescales. In fact, atmospheric CO_2's reaction with igneous rocks could take as long as 400,000 years.[101] So when the current centuries-long climate storm unleashed by the emission of greenhouse gases from human activities subsides, it is bound to leave behind—for future generations—a new, warmer climate state that will persist for thousands of years.

Confounding all projections of future climate is the possibility of abrupt changes in the climate system, the result of passing the tipping

---

[98] Archer, *The Long Thaw*, 54.
[99] The Royal Society, *Climate Change*, para. 31.
[100] National Research Council, *Understanding Earth's Deep Past*, 79.
[101] See Archer, *The Long Thaw*, 110.

points on which we reflected in Chapter 2. As the planet continues to warm, it may be approaching a critical climate threshold beyond which rapid and potentially catastrophic changes may occur. Studies of past climates show that Earth's climate system does not respond linearly to gradual CO_2 forcing but rather responds by abrupt change as it is driven across climatic thresholds. Earth's average surface temperature is now demonstrably higher than it has been for several hundred years, and the concentration of greenhouse gases in the atmosphere is higher than it has been in at least 800,000 years. "These sharp departures from historical climate regimes raise the possibility that 'tipping points' or thresholds for stability might be crossed as the climate system warms, leading to rapid or abrupt changes in climate."[102]

Among the various possible tipping points in the earth's climate system are two elements that scientists refer to as the climate "wild-cards." They concern the destabilization of methane and its release into the atmosphere in response to global warming— through either the melting of terrestrial permafrost reservoirs or the dissolution of sub-seafloor hydrate deposits. An initial warming from greenhouse gases released by burning fossil fuels could end up releasing even more greenhouse gases from natural sources, leading to global warming well beyond current projections.[103]

In the frozen waters of the Arctic lies a climate wildcard that stands out for its sheer horror-movie potential. From Alaska and northern Canada across northernmost parts of Europe and Siberia lie millions of square miles of frozen Earth. This is the Arctic permafrost, which contains a layer of soil that stays frozen through summer and winter. This soil is like a freezer, trapping organic carbon in the form of leaves, roots, dead mosses, and so on, which have been protected from degradation by their frozen condition. Trapped within the permafrost are billions of tons of methane hydrates (also known as methane clathrates), molecules in which water and the potent greenhouse gas methane are bonded under high pressure and/or low temperature.[104] Due to the rise in global temperatures, which are more pronounced in higher latitudes, the Arctic permafrost is thawing, giving off methane. Recent measurements show a 10–15 percent increase in the area of thawing lakes in northern and western Siberia. Methane emissions from Siberian lakes

---

[102] The National Academy of Sciences, *Advancing the Science of Climate Change*, 41.

[103] See National Research Council, *Understanding Earth's Deep Past*, 32–33.

[104] Walker and King, *The Hot Topic*, 80–81; Henson, *The Rough Guide to Climate Change*, 82; Archer, *The Long Thaw*, 128–29.

because of thawing permafrost in response to Arctic warming are estimated to have increased by 58 percent.[105] It is not fully clear what will happen to methane hydrates as the permafrost continues melting. With methane being a potent greenhouse gas—twenty-three times more powerful than CO_2—even a small percentage of the methane that might escape would dwarf the effect of greenhouse gases emitted by human activity so far. It is indeed a fearsome prospect.[106]

There is also a second climate wildcard. Besides their presence in permafrost, methane hydrates are even more extensive in seafloor sediments around the margins of continents across the globe. In fact, hundreds of billions of tons of carbon are believed to be locked in cold ocean seabeds in the form of methane hydrates—ice crystals that hold methane in their molecular structure, often in the form of clathrates. These exist in regions sufficiently cold and under enough high pressure to keep them stable. But a change in ocean temperature or circulation during a warm era could destabilize the methane and send it pouring into the atmosphere. This, of course, is a long-term concern for the future climate.[107] But projections of future climate change, and especially the specter of tipping points, are indeed a source of grave concern for the future of human civilization.

An Unprecedented Situation
in the Geological History of Earth

The alarming forecasts regarding changes in the global average surface temperatures by the end of the current century by the IPCC and other scientific bodies are at times met with a dismissive attitude, especially from the ranks of environmental skeptics. The skeptics claim that the earth has witnessed such temperature variations in the past in the long geological history of our home planet, which has swung from ice ages to warm periods. Accordingly, it is argued that such climate shifts are entirely natural, and that it is totally unwarranted to raise alarm bells about the current phase of global warming and associated climate change. A recent document from the Pontifical Academy of Sciences takes this argument head on:

---

[105] See K. M. Walter et al., "Methane Bubbling from Siberian Thaw Lakes as a Positive Feedback to Climate Warming," *Nature* 443 (2006): 71–75.

[106] See E. A. Kort et al., "Atmospheric Observations of Arctic Ocean Methane Emissions up to 82° North," *Nature Geoscience* 5 (2012): 318–21.

[107] Henson, *The Rough Guide to Climate Change*, 202.

In response to the argument that "since the earth has experienced alternating cold periods (ice ages or glacials) and warm periods (inter-glacials) during the past, today's climate and ice cover changes are entirely natural events," we state:

The primary triggers for ice ages and inter-glacials are well understood to be changes in the astronomical parameters related to the motion of our planet within the solar system and natural feedback processes in the climate system. The time scales between these triggers are in the range of 10,000 years or longer. By contrast, the observed human-induced changes in carbon dioxide, other greenhouse gases, and soot concentrations are taking place on 10–100 year timescales—at least a hundred times as fast. It is particularly worrying that this release of global warming agents is occurring during an interglacial period when the earth was already at a natural temperature maximum.[108]

With the rapid increase in the emission of greenhouse gases into the earth's atmospheres, well beyond the projections of scientists themselves, the fear is that the earth could eventually return—on a human timescale—to a greenhouse gas climate analogous to that of several million years ago. The latest study from the US National Academy of Sciences has issued a timely warning in this regard:

The atmosphere's concentration of carbon dioxide—a potent greenhouse gas—has been increasing in recent years faster than had been forecast by even the most extreme projections of a decade ago. At current carbon emission rates, Earth will experience atmospheric CO_2 levels within this century that have not occurred since the warm "greenhouse" climates of more than 34 million years ago. . . . As oceanographer Roger Revelle noted more than 50 years ago, humans are launching an uncontrolled "Great Geophysical Experiment" with the planet to observe how burning fossil fuels will affect all aspects of the climate, chemistry, and ecology of Earth.[109]

Earth's deep-time geological records provide several examples of Earth's rather sudden transition into a hothouse climate. The most dramatic of these—with potential parallels to the near future—is the

[108] Pontificia Academia Scientiarum, *Fate of Mountain Glaciers in the Anthropocene*, 4.

[109] National Research Council, *Understanding Earth's Deep Past*, 16.

Paleocene-Eocene Thermal Maximum (PETM) event, which occurred as far back as 55 million years ago. The event consisted in the repeated, rapid (millennial-scale), massive release of carbon in the form of methane—about 4.5 trillion tons—into the atmosphere, causing major disruption of the carbon cycle and driving a temperature rise of nearly 5°C in tropical areas and as much as 9°C at the poles.[110] The difference is that while the previous episode was caused by natural factors and stretched over a period of 10,000 years, today human activities are releasing greenhouse gases thirty times faster than the rate of emissions that triggered the PETM event, capable of achieving the same effect in just 300 years.[111] Besides, one needs to remember that it took 100,000 years after the PETM event for carbon dioxide levels in the air and water to return to normal, with disastrous consequences for the species then extant.[112] "The PETM serves as an important base level showing the effect on the biosphere of a rapid rate of addition of fossil carbon to the atmosphere . . . —yet dwarfed by the present rate of nearly 1 percent per year CO_2 increase in Earth's atmosphere."[113] The PETM event also serves as a warning that the natural climate may take hundreds of millennia to recover fully.

The current phase of climate change—caused by anthropogenic global warming—could take the planet to a climate unlike any in millions of years. Among the key dangers associated with projected climate trends for the end of the twenty-first century are the prospects that large portions of the earth's surface may experience climates not found at present, and that some twentieth-century climates may disappear.[114] It is clear that Earth's future climate will be unlike the climate that ecosystems and human societies have become accustomed to during the last 10,000 years, leading to significant challenges across a broad range of human endeavors. Modern human civilization took shape during the Holocene epoch, during which global temperatures were never more than a degree or two warmer than now. Thus warming exceeding two degrees is unprecedented in our entire historical

---

[110] Cf. James C. Zachos et al., "Rapid Acidification of the Ocean During the Paleocene-Eocene Thermal Maximum," *Science* 308 (2005): 1611–14; National Research Council, *Understanding Earth's Deep Past*, 7, 69ff.

[111] Zachos et al., "Rapid Acidification of the Ocean During the Paleocene-Eocene Thermal Maximum," 1614.

[112] Ibid., 1611; National Research Council, *Understanding Earth's Deep Past*, 69.

[113] National Research Council, *Understanding Earth's Deep Past*, 71.

[114] See John W. Williams et al., "Projected Distributions of Novel and Disappearing Climates by 2100 AD," *Proceedings of the National Academy of Sciences* 104 (2007): 5738.

experience. Indeed, some systems have already shown worrisome responses to the 0.8°C warming over the past century. Our societies, which are already plagued by other challenges and emergencies, can ill afford huge and drastic changes to the global climate system.

The current phase of global warming and associated climate change induced by human activities is totally unprecedented in the recent geological history of the earth and will have catastrophic consequences for human communities and ecosystems.

4

Impacts of Climate Change

John Houghton observes, "Talking in terms of changes in global average surface temperature . . . however, tells us little about the actual impacts of global warming on human communities."[1] What affects individuals and communities most are the day-to-day variations in climate in the specific regions where they live. The impacts of climate change, in fact, pose serious, wide-ranging threats to human societies and natural ecosystems around the world. The larger and faster the changes in climate are, the more difficult it will be for human and natural systems to adapt.[2]

In the present chapter we proceed from a physical explanation of climate change to its concrete consequences for human communities and ecosystems. We examine here the impacts of climate change that are already present as well as scenarios for the immediate future. Some of the major impacts of climate change discussed here are extreme weather events; droughts and desertification; reduction of snow cover, including the melting of glaciers; sea-level rise; ocean acidification with consequences for marine life; and the loss of biodiversity.

Extreme Weather Events

Extreme weather is probably the most tangible among the impacts of anthropogenic global warming and associated climate change. It appears that the exceptionally stable weather that characterized

---

[1] John Houghton, "Sustainable Climate and the Future of Energy," in *Creation in Crisis: Christian Perspectives on Sustainability*, ed. Robert S. White (London: SPCK, 2009), 15. See also National Research Council, *Monitoring Climate Change Impacts: Metrics at the Intersection of the Human and Earth Systems* (Washington, DC: The National Academies Press, 2010), 1.

[2] The National Academy of Sciences, *Understanding and Responding to Climate Change: Highlights of National Academies* (Washington, DC: National Academies Press, 2008), 16.

the Holocene epoch is under increasing threat from human-induced climate change. As we have seen earlier, it was the uniquely equable climate of the interglacial period of the Holocene that made agriculture possible and in its wake enabled the rise of various civilizations in different parts of the world. When stable weather patterns go awry, the very foundations of our present livelihoods and societies find themselves on a shaky ground, as communities and nations are discovering in many parts of the globe.

The link between climate change and extreme weather is immediately perceived, in a rather intuitive way, by the people who live closest to the Earth, attentive to the intricate rhythms of nature. These include subsistence farmers, forest dwellers, indigenous communities, fisher folk, and others. With every passing year those who live in intimate contact with the Earth—as opposed to those who live in the air-conditioned and artificially lit indoor spaces of corporate boardrooms—realize that nature's balance is tilting and that seasons and weather patterns are changing.

The scientific community has also been closely studying the phenomena of extreme weather patterns and its link to anthropogenic climate change during the last few decades. It had been cautious until very recently to attribute individual natural calamities or freak weather patterns directly to human-induced climate change for lack of sufficient and credible data. It is, in fact, difficult to attribute a natural calamity like hurricane Katrina, which struck New Orleans in 2005, to climate change, in spite of evidence showing that warming of the ocean surface can lead to more intense tropical storms.[3] The weather system is extremely complex; it is conditioned by so many factors and variables. So the scientists have been cautious to directly attribute extreme weather, unlike other impacts of climate change like desertification, melting of glaciers, sea-level rise, or biodiversity loss, to global warming and associated climate change.

Now it appears that the situation has changed. After decades of painstaking research and gathering data, the scientific community has begun to present its verdict on the link between anthropogenic global warming and extreme weather events. A high point in this process was the publication of a special report on the relationship between climate change and extreme weather events in 2012 by the scientists

---

[3] See Richard A. Anthens et al., "Hurricanes and Global Warming—Potential Linking Consequences," *Bulletin of the American Meteorological Society* 87 (2006): 623–28; Greg J. Holland and Peter J. Webster, "Heightened Tropical Cyclone Activity in the North Atlantic: Natural Variability or Climate Trend?," *Philosophical Transactions of the Royal Society* 365 (2007): 2695–716.

of the IPCC.[4] The document is an authoritative synthesis of scientific literature in the field during the last decade or so, and it sheds light on how human-induced climate change is leading to extreme weather events, a trend only destined to accelerate in the future. We shall rely on this important study as well as other pertinent sources in exploring the link between extreme weather and human-induced climate change.

Anthropogenic greenhouse gas emissions, as we saw in Chapter 3, are upsetting the atmosphere's balance and, with it, upsetting the balance of nature. Changes in global climate due to global warming can naturally lead to changes in extreme weather and climate events. In fact, raising the Earth's temperature is like turning up the heat under a saucepan. Global warming pumps more energy into weather systems, making them more turbulent and unpredictable.[5] As the IPCC's special report states: "A changing climate leads to changes in the frequency, intensity, spatial extent, duration, and timing of extreme weather and climate events, and can result in unprecedented extreme weather and climate events."[6] The scientists of the IPCC conclude from analysis of data of the past few years that "observed changes in climate extremes reflect the influence of anthropogenic climate change in addition to natural climate variability."[7] Thus, for the recent past scientists are able to infer that most of the observed weather extremes are linked to anthropogenic influences.[8]

However, when it comes to the link between human-induced climate change and extreme weather patterns in the future, the scientists are much more forthright. The reason is obvious: both greenhouse gas emissions and the global average surface temperature are destined to

---

[4] See IPCC, *Managing the Risks of Extreme Events and Disasters to Advance Climate Change Adaptation: Special Report of the IPCC*, ed. C. B. Field et al. (Cambridge: Cambridge University Press, 2012).

[5] Alastair McIntosh, *Hell and High Water: Climate Change, Hope and the Human Condition* (Edinburgh: Birlinn, 2009), 41. See also Kirstin Dow and Thomas E. Downing, *The Atlas of Climate Change: Mapping the World's Greatest Challenge* (London: Earthscan, 2006), 26–27.

[6] IPCC, *Managing the Risks of Extreme Events and Disasters to Advance Climate Change Adaptation*, 7.

[7] Ibid., 7. See also Dim Coumou and Stefan Rahmstorf, "A Decade of Weather Extremes," *Nature Climate Change* 2 (2012): 491.

[8] The Fifth Assessment Report of the IPCC of 2013 offers further confirmation in this regard. The report notes, for example, that since about 1950 the number of cold days and nights has decreased and the number of warm days and nights has increased on the global scale. See IPCC, *Climate Change 2013: The Physical Science Basis: Contribution of Working Group I to the Fifth Assessment Report of the Intergovernmental Panel on Climate Change*, ed. T. F. Stocker et al. (Cambridge: Cambridge University Press, 2013), 5.

rise steeply in the decades to come. From the analysis of past data and with the help of climate models scientists are able to make confident projections about the effects of human activities on weather patterns worldwide in the decades to come.

According to the scientists, it is virtually certain that increases in the frequency of warm daily temperature extremes and decreases in cold extremes will occur throughout the twenty-first century on a global scale. It is also very likely that heat waves will increase in length, frequency, and/or intensity of warm spells over most land areas. In fact, a "one in twenty years" hottest-day phenomenon is likely to become a "one in two years" event by the end of the twenty-first century in most regions except in the high latitudes of the Northern Hemisphere, where it is likely to become a "one in five years" occurrence.[9] The typical European summer of the 2040s will be even warmer than the extreme summer of 2003. As Robert Henson observes, a heat wave does not have to bring the warmest temperatures ever observed to have catastrophic effects. A long string of hot days combined with unusually steamy nights will suffice.[10] The 2013 Fifth Assessment of the IPCC states:

> It is *virtually certain* that there will be more frequent hot and fewer cold temperature extremes over most land areas on daily and seasonal timescales as global mean temperatures increase. It is *very likely* that heat waves will occur with a higher frequency and duration. Occasional cold winter extremes will continue to occur.[11]

The scientists are also able to predict with high confidence that changes in heat waves, glacial retreat, and permafrost degradation will affect high-mountain phenomena like landslides and outburst floods from glacial lakes. Landslides in some regions will also be driven by changes in rainfall patterns.[12]

There is growing evidence that human-induced climate change has begun to directly influence rainfall patterns and the planet's

---

[9] IPCC, *Managing the Risks of Extreme Events and Disasters to Advance Climate Change Adaptation,* 13. See also The National Academy of Sciences, *Ecological Impacts of Climate Change* (Washington, DC: The National Academies Press, 2009), 7.

[10] Robert Henson, *The Rough Guide to Climate Change* (London: Rough Guides Ltd., 2006), 43, 52.

[11] IPCC, *Climate Change 2013: The Physical Science Basis,* 20.

[12] IPCC, *Managing the Risks of Extreme Events and Disasters to Advance Climate Change Adaptation,* 15.

fundamental hydrological cycle. The physical basis underlying the link between global warming and precipitation changes is simple and direct. Rainfall patterns form part of the natural hydrological cycle of the Earth, sustained by the process of evaporation. "Heated by the sun's radiation, the ocean and land surface evaporate water, which then moves around with winds in the atmosphere, condenses to form clouds, and falls back to the Earth's surface as rain or snow, with the flow to the oceans via rivers completing the global hydrological (water) cycle."[13] One of the major impacts of present human-induced global warming and associated climate change is precisely an undue interference with the hydrological cycle of the planet, leading to drastic changes in precipitation patterns. Increased warming leads to greater evaporation of surface moisture, leading to extra water vapor in the atmosphere. It is estimated that the water-holding capacity of air increases by about 7 percent for every 1°C of warming.[14] This is a nonlinear relationship, meaning the effect gets stronger for each additional degree of warming. As the climate warms, water-holding capacity increases with higher temperatures, and consequently the water vapor amounts in the atmosphere rise as well. This moisture then gets carried around by atmospheric winds, and the convergence of increased water vapor leads to more intense precipitation and risk of heavy rain and snow events.[15]

In the context of current phase of human-induced global warming, climate models and empirical evidence point to an increase in rainfall. Warmer climates, owing to increased water vapor, can lead to more intense precipitation events, even when the total annual rainfall is

---

[13] K. E. Trenberth, "Changes in Precipitation with Climate Change," *Climate Research* 47 (2011): 123.

[14] The calculation is done based on the well-known Clausius-Clapeyron equation, according to which increased temperature causes increased atmospheric water vapor concentrations; hence, changes in water vapor transport and the hydrologic cycle can be expected. The typical values are about 7 percent change for 1°C change in temperature. See Trenberth, "Changes in Precipitation with Climate Change," 124; S. Solomon et al., "Irreversible Climate Change due to Carbon Dioxide Emissions," *Proceedings of the National Academy of Sciences* 106 (2009): 1706.

[15] Trenberth, "Changes in Precipitation with Climate Change," 123–25; K. E. Trenberth, "Precipitation in a Changing Climate: More Floods and Droughts in the Future," *GEWEX News* (May 19, 2009): 8; Henson, *The Rough Guide to Climate Change*, 57. The recent melting of the Arctic has led to more extreme winter weather in the Northern Hemisphere in recent years. See Nicola Jones, "Arctic Melt Leads to Extreme Weather Extremes," *Nature Climate Change* 2 (2012): 221.

reduced slightly, and with prospects for even stronger events when the overall rainfall amounts increase. It is also estimated that precipitation will generally increase in areas with already high amounts of precipitation and generally decrease in areas with low amounts of rainfall.[16] Apart from the general patterns the character of rainfall also appears to be changing. During the last three decades, increases in heavy rains are found to be occurring in most places, even when mean precipitation is not increasing. At the global level the number of very wet days has increased during the past fifty years, even in places where mean precipitation amounts are not increasing.[17] As for future prospects, it is projected that there will be more rain at high latitudes, less rain in the dry subtropics, and uncertain but probably substantial changes in tropical areas.[18] The 2013 IPCC report warns that "extreme precipitation events over most of the mid-latitude land masses and over wet tropical regions will *very likely* become more intense and more frequent by the end of this century, as global mean surface temperature increases."[19]

The changes in rainfall patterns due to global warming can lead to the risk of increased storms and floods, both of which have significant socioeconomic impacts. Floods are associated with extremes in rainfall that usually come with tropical storms, thunderstorms, orographic rainfall, and widespread extratropical cyclones. When it comes to floods, it is the character of the precipitation that really counts. Several areas around the globe in recent decades have seen rain concentrated in short, intense bursts that produce flash floods or in multi-day torrents that can cause near-biblical floods across entire regions.[20] Floods also have a huge human cost. Deaths as a result of flooding and cyclones are humankind's worst natural disasters, accounting for nearly two-thirds of lives lost from all forms of natural disasters. Moreover, the disease and famine that follow floods often cause even

---

[16] See The Royal Society, *Climate Change: A Summary of the Science* (September 2010), para. 44; Trenberth, "Changes in Precipitation with Climate Change," 131.

[17] Trenberth, "Changes in Precipitation with Climate Change," 128; Trenberth, "Precipitation in a Changing Climate," 8.

[18] The National Academy of Sciences, *Advancing the Science of Climate Change* (Washington, DC: The National Academies Press, 2010), 48; IPCC, *Managing the Risks of Extreme Events and Disasters to Advance Climate Change Adaptation,* 13; Nicholas Stern, *The Economics of Climate Change* (Cambridge: Cambridge University Press, 2007), 74.

[19] IPCC, *Climate Change 2013: The Physical Science Basis,* 23.

[20] Henson, *The Rough Guide to Climate Change,* 55–61.

more deaths than the floods themselves. Conservative estimates suggest that 80 million people worldwide will be at risk of flooding in the coming decades, 80 percent of them in the lower-income countries of Asia, like Bangladesh.[21]

In the context of climate change, scientists predict that it is likely that the average maximum wind speed of tropical cyclones (also known as typhoons or hurricanes) will increase throughout the coming century, although increases may not occur in all ocean basins. Significantly, "the observed increases in water vapor affect both the greenhouse effect, thus providing a positive feedback to climate change, and the hydrological cycle, by providing more atmospheric moisture for all storms to feed upon."[22] Heavy rainfalls associated with tropical cyclones are likely to increase with continued warming. However, it is also likely that overall there will be either a decrease or essentially no change in the number of tropical cyclones.[23]

Another impact of climate change, ironically the opposite of excessive precipitation, is drought, which exacerbates the phenomenon of desertification around the globe.

Droughts and Desertification

Drought may be defined as a recurring extreme climatic event over land characterized by below-normal rainfall over a period that can last from months to years.[24] Drought is probably the most conspicuous effect of anthropogenic global warming and associated climate change that could harm millions of people in the coming decades. The specter of extended or permanent drought over large parts of currently habitable or arable land, which may be irreversible over centuries, can also threaten food security and cause massive displacement of people.[25]

---

[21] Nick Spencer and Robert White, *Christianity, Climate Change, and Sustainable Living* (London: SPCK, 2007), 37; McIntosh, *Hell and High Water*, 41.

[22] Trenberth, "Changes in Precipitation with Climate Change," 126.

[23] See IPCC, *Managing the Risks of Extreme Events and Disasters to Advance Climate Change Adaptation*, 13; The National Academy of Sciences, *Advancing the Science of Climate Change*, 49–50.

[24] See Aiguo Dai, "Drought Under Global Warming: A Review," *Climate Change* 2 (2011): 45.

[25] See Millennium Ecosystem Assessment, *Ecosystems and Human Well-being: Desertification Synthesis* (Washington, DC: World Resources Institute, 2005), ii; Joseph Romm, "The Next Dust Bowl," *Nature* 478 (2011): 450–51.

In the current stage of climate science, attributing an increase in the severity of droughts to climate change is fraught with difficulties. This is so because drought is caused not only by climate change but also by other factors like ocean currents, urbanization, deforestation, changes in agriculture, and other climatic uncertainties. Recent studies of past climates through tree rings and other proxy data demonstrate that drought is itself a normal part of climatic variations. These studies have revealed that large-scale droughts have occurred several times during the past 500–1,000 years over many parts of the world, including North America, Mexico, Asia, Africa, and Australia. These historical droughts are linked to tropical sea-surface temperature variations, the La Niña and El Niño events in the Pacific, and other natural factors.[26] More recent events like the Dust Bowl drought of the 1930s over the Great Plains in North America, or the even more recent drought around Lake Chad in Africa, appear to be the result of a combination of many factors. The story of Lake Chad is a clear example of what can happen when climate change and land use intersect. Once the sixth largest fresh-water lake in the world, Lake Chad has shriveled by 95 percent over the last forty years, a victim of the 1970s and 1980s droughts as well as intensive irrigation.[27]

However, the intensity and frequency of droughts in recent decades appear to be linked with anthropogenic global warming. Climate scientists have noted marked global aridity changes since 1950, corresponding with the rapid increases in global surface temperatures and atmospheric CO_2 and other greenhouse gases:

> From 1950 to 2008, most land areas have warmed up by 1–3°C, with the largest warming over northern Asia and northern North America. During the same period, precipitation decreased over most of Africa, southern Europe, South and East Asia, eastern Australia, Central America, central Pacific coasts of North America and some parts of South America.[28]

A string of recent studies have clearly attributed the increasing aridity and decreasing rainfall in the Sahel region of Africa to anthropogenic climate change.[29] On the global scale some of the long-term records

---

[26] Dai, "Drought Under Global Warming," 48, 58. For an abundance of bibliographical information in this regard, see ibid., 62–63.

[27] Henson, *The Rough Guide to Climate Change*, 63.

[28] Dai, "Drought Under Global Warming," 50.

[29] See especially P. Gonzalez et al., "Tree Density and Species Decline in the African Sahel Attributable to Climate," *Journal of Arid Environments* 78 (2012):

like the Palmer Index from 1870 to 2002 show that very dry areas have more than doubled globally since the 1970s, and the expansion after the 1980s can be clearly associated with surface warming.[30] It is also alarming to note that since 1950 the global percentage of dry areas has increased by about 1.75 percent of global land area per decade.[31]

As for the future, climate models suggest that the area affected by drought globally and the number of dry days annually are likely to increase in the decades ahead. Global climate models predict increasing summer temperatures and decreasing summer precipitation in many continental areas, implying reductions in soil moisture.[32] The physics behind such future drought scenarios is simple and straightforward. Higher temperatures due to increased greenhouse gases in the atmosphere will cause a higher rate of evaporation and more drought. Higher temperatures not only allow more rain-producing moisture to enter the atmosphere, but they also suck more water out of the parched terrain where it hasn't been raining. In this way, in addition to triggering more rainfall, global warming can also increase the occurrence of drought.[33] Because the land surface heats up and cools down much more rapidly than ocean areas, the surface temperature just above the land is likely to experience 40 percent greater warming than ocean areas, leaving vast land areas arid.[34] Droughts also increase the risk of heat waves and wildfires; once the soil moisture is depleted, all of the heating goes toward raising temperatures and wilting plants.[35]

Apart from warming of the land areas, the warming of the ocean surfaces can also lead to droughts, and on a global scale too, as shown

---

55–64. See also I. M. Held et al., "Simulation of Sahel Drought in the Twentieth and Twenty-first Centuries," *Proceedings of the National Academy of Sciences* 102 (2005): 17891–96.

[30] Aiguo Dai et al., "A Global Dataset of Palmer Drought Severity Index for 1870–2002: Relationship with Soil Moisture and Effects of Surface Warming," *Journal of Hydrometeorology* 5 (2004): 1117–30.

[31] See Aiguo Dai, "Characteristics and Trends in Various Forms of the Palmer Drought Severity Index during 1900–2008," *Journal of Geophysical Research* 116 (2011): D 12115.

[32] See The National Academy of Sciences, *Advancing the Science of Climate Change*, 49; Romm, "The Next Dust Bowl," 450.

[33] See Henson, *The Rough Guide to Climate Change*, 56; Dai, "Drought Under Global Warming," 56.

[34] Spencer and White, *Christianity, Climate Change, and Sustainable Living*, 35; Henson, *The Rough Guide to Climate Change*, 68.

[35] Trenberth, "Precipitation in a Changing Climate," 8–9.

in the El Niño events in recent decades. A typical El Niño occurrence can increase the odds of drought across Indonesia, Australia, India, southeast Africa, and northern South America, and it can cause winter-long dryness across parts of Canada and the northern United States. In a similar way, should the Indian Ocean continue warming over the next century, as it does in some climate simulations, it may trigger persistent drought in some adjoining areas, particularly southern Africa.[36]

According to the latest report from the IPCC on extreme weather events, there is "medium confidence" evidence that droughts will intensify in the twenty-first century in some seasons and areas. This applies to regions including southern Europe and the Mediterranean region, central Europe, central North America, Central America and Mexico, northeast Brazil, and southern Africa. Regarding other areas there is less certainty because of inconsistent projections of drought changes.[37] The greenhouse climate of the future has the potential to produce mega-droughts, lasting for a decade or longer. Some other recent studies have projected "extreme drought" conditions after mid-century over some of the most populated areas on Earth—southern Europe, southeast Asia, Brazil, the US Southwest, and large parts of Australia and Africa.[38]

Closely associated with droughts caused by anthropogenic global warming is the phenomenon of desertification. Desertification occurs on all continents except Antarctica. It has local and global impacts, and it affects the livelihoods of millions of people. Desertification, however, is caused not only by climate change but also by factors like population pressure, agricultural practices, deforestation, loss of biodiversity, unsustainable use of scarce natural resources, among others. However, as with regard to droughts, climate change today appears to be exacerbating desertification in various parts of the globe, with enduring and large-scale impacts on human well-being and security. Droughts and desertification raise huge challenges for global food security.

The United Nations Convention to Combat Desertification defines *desertification* as "land degradation in arid, semi-arid and dry sub-humid areas resulting from various factors, including climatic variations

---

[36] Henson, *The Rough Guide to Climate Change*, 69.

[37] IPCC, *Managing the Risks of Extreme Events and Disasters to Advance Climate Change Adaptation*, 11.

[38] See Dai, "Drought Under Global Warming," 58. See also E. J. Burke et al., "Modelling the Recent Evolution of Global Drought Projections for the Twenty-First Century with the Hadley Centre Climate Model," *Journal of Hydrometeorology* 7 (2006): 1113–25.

and human activities" (art. 1(a)). The term *desertification* does not refer to the spread of existing deserts but to the creation of new ones through the degradation of dry lands. Desertification occurs world-wide in dry lands that occupy 41 percent of Earth's land area and are home to nearly one-third of the human population. Some 10–20 percent of dry lands are already degraded. The projected intensification of fresh-water scarcity as a result of global warming is expected to cause greater stresses in dry lands. These stresses further exacerbate desertification, with the most vulnerable areas being sub-Saharan and Central Asian dry lands. A particular area of concern will be sub-Saharan Africa—the Sahel, the Horn of Africa, and Southeast Africa.[39] Desertification is also a serious concern elsewhere. For example, it is estimated that one-fourth of India's geographical area, or over 200 million square miles, is undergoing a process of desertification.[40] Such a situation puts tremendous pressure on the country's natural resources, given that "India occupies only 2.4 percent of the world's geographical area, yet supports about 16.7 percent of the world's human population; it has only 0.5 percent of the world's grazing land but supports 18 percent of the world's cattle population."[41]

Desertification can also affect people living elsewhere on the globe, sometimes located thousands of miles away from the desert areas. These impacts vary from biophysical to socioeconomic ones. The biophysical impacts include dust storms, downstream flooding, impairment of global carbon-sequestration capacity, and regional and global climate change. The visibility in Beijing is often adversely affected by dust storms originating from the Gobi Desert in springtime. Dust storms emanating from China have been observed to affect the Korean peninsula and Japan. Dust emanating from the East Asian region and the Sahara has been implicated in respiratory problems as far away as North America and has affected coral reefs in the Caribbean. The societal impacts of desertification relate notably to human migration and economic refugees, leading to deepening poverty and political instability.[42]

Paradoxically, while desertification is caused mainly by climate change and the reduction of vegetation cover, desertification can, in its

---

[39] Millennium Ecosystem Assessment, *Ecosystems and Human Well-being: Desertification Synthesis,* 1, 20.

[40] A. S. Arya et al., "Desertification/Land Degradation Status Mapping of India," *Current Science* 97 (2009): 1478, 1483.

[41] Ibid., 1478.

[42] Millennium Ecosystem Assessment, *Ecosystems and Human Well-being: Desertification Synthesis,* 2, 8.

turn, exacerbate climate change and loss of biodiversity. Desertification contributes to global climate change particularly through the loss of carbon sequestration capacity of vegetation.

> Dryland soils contain over a quarter of all of the organic carbon stores in the world as well as nearly all the inorganic carbon. Unimpeded desertification may release a major fraction of this carbon to the global atmosphere, with significant feedback consequences to the global climate system. It is estimated that 300 million tons of carbon are lost to the atmosphere from drylands as a result of desertification each year (about 4% of the total global emissions from all sources combined).[43]

From an ecological perspective, the effects of climate change and desertification on the global carbon cycle are a matter of grave concern. Joseph Romm notes, "In the past six years, the Amazon has seen two droughts of the sort expected once in 100 years, each of which may have released as much carbon dioxide from vegetation die-off as the United States emits from fossil-fuel combustion in a year."[44] The realization that drought and desertification are not only caused by climate change but can also contribute to its exacerbation is a sober one indeed.

Melting of Glaciers

The melting of glaciers is both a conspicuous sign and a direct consequence of human-induced global warming. It has, like other major impacts of anthropogenic climate change, direct effects on ecosystems and human communities.

Worldwide, snow cover is decreasing, with substantial regional variability, especially in the Northern hemisphere, and with the highest rates observed at lower elevations.[45] The decrease in snow cover is a phenomenon that is closely associated with human-induced global warming. The 2013 report of the IPCC states clearly that over the last two decades, ice sheets have been losing mass and glaciers have

---

[43] Ibid., 17–8.

[44] Romm, "The Next Dust Bowl," 451.

[45] P. Lemke et al., "Observations: Changes in Snow, Ice and Frozen Ground," *Climate Change 2007: The Physical Science Basis: Contribution of Working Group I to the Fourth Assessment Report of the IPCC*, ed. S. Solomon et al. (Cambridge: Cambridge University Press, 2007), 337ff.; The National Academy of Sciences, *Advancing the Science of Climate Change*, 261.

continued to shrink almost worldwide.[46] We may cite in this regard also a recent document from the Pontifical Academy of Sciences, which sought to study mountain glaciers in particular. It states that "the widespread loss of glaciers, ice, and snow on the mountains of tropical, temperate, and polar regions is some of the clearest evidence we have for a change in the climate system, which is taking place on a global scale at a rapid rate."[47] According to the same study, robust scenario calculations clearly indicate that with increased warming many mountain ranges worldwide could lose major parts of their glaciers within the coming decades.

The reduction of snow cover is particularly evident in the Arctic, which appears to be responding more rapidly to global warming than most other areas on the planet.[48] For this reason the Arctic can be described as "the canary in the coal mine." If there is any place on the planet where global warming leaps from the abstract to the concretely tangible, it is in the frigid vastness of the Arctic. Here, the ice is increasingly melting, the ground is heaving, plant and animal species are moving, and indigenous communities are left bewildered by the drastic changes unfolding year by year. What is apparently so striking about climate change in the Arctic is the sheer pace of the rise in temperatures compared to the rest of the world. In fact, long-term residents of western Canada and Alaska have seen winter temperatures climb as much as 4°C since the 1950s, several times beyond the average global pace.[49]

Satellites have accurately monitored the extent of the Arctic sea-ice cover since 1979. The observational record shows a clear decline. During the past three decades there has been a reduction in ice extent, a decrease in ice thickness, and a shift from multiyear ice to first-year ice.[50] According to the World Meteorological Organization, September 2012 saw the lowest extent of Arctic sea ice in the satellite record. It was 49 percent below the 1979–2000 average minimum.[51]

---

[46] IPCC, *Climate Change 2013: The Physical Science Basis*, 9.

[47] Pontificia Academia Scientiarum, *Fate of Mountain Glaciers in the Anthropocene: A Report by the Working Group Commissioned by the Pontifical Academy of Sciences* (May 5, 2011), 3. See also N. P. Gillett et al., "Attribution of Polar Warming to Human Influence," *Nature Geoscience* 1 (2008): 750–54.

[48] See Robert F. Spielhagen et al., "Enhanced Modern Heat Transfer to the Arctic by Warm Atlantic Water," *Science* 331 (2011): 450.

[49] Henson, *The Rough Guide to Climate Change*, 71.

[50] D. K. Perovich, "The Changing Arctic Sea Ice Cover," *Oceanography* 24 (2011): 167.

[51] World Meteorological Organization, *WMO Statement on the Status of the Global Climate 2012* (Geneva: World Meteorological Organization, 2013), 10.

It is estimated that the Arctic will be entirely free of sea ice during the summer sometime between 2030 and 2080, much earlier than previously anticipated.[52] According to the 2013 IPCC report, a nearly ice-free Arctic ocean is likely before mid-century.[53] The Arctic's sea ice isn't just contracting horizontally; it's getting shallower as well. Because ice surface is highly reflective, while open water absorbs most of the incoming sunlight, an ice-free Arctic would accelerate global warming, serving as positive feedback. Of particular concern is the fact the Greenland ice sheet, the colossal ice sheet that covers about 85 percent of the island, is losing mass. Each summer parts of the Greenland ice sheet melt at the edges and on the surface.[54] It is a worrying phenomenon that can contribute to sea-level rise.

It has been observed that primary production by phytoplankton in the Arctic Ocean increased nearly 20 percent between 1998 and 2009, mainly as a result of increasing open-water extent and duration of the open-water season. There have been other biological and geographical changes that have affected typically native species like polar bears and walrus in terms of loss of habitat, disruption of their food chain, and more. With the continued warming of air temperatures, Arctic species that have adapted to the Arctic environments for millennia are expected to be displaced by the encroachment of more sub-Arctic species and ecosystems.[55]

The impact on human communities is felt especially as some permafrost that has undergirded the Arctic landscape for centuries has now begun to thaw. Permafrost covers nearly one-quarter of the Northern Hemisphere's land area, including half of Canada, most of Alaska, and much of northern Russia, as well as a small part of Scandinavia. Temperature at the top of the permafrost layer has increased by up to 3°C since the 1980s in the Arctic. Observations show a general increase in permafrost temperatures during the last several decades particularly in Alaska, northwest Canada, and Siberia. Permafrost degradation is leading to changes in land-surface characteristics,

---

[52] See J. A. Boé et al., "September Sea-Ice Cover in the Arctic Ocean Projected to Vanish by 2100," *Nature Geoscience* 2 (2009): 341–43; M. Wang and J. E. Overland, "A Sea Ice Free Summer Arctic Within 30 Years?" *Geophysical Research Letters* 36 (2009): L07502.

[53] IPCC, *Climate Change 2013: The Physical Science Basis*, 25.

[54] According to the 2013 IPCC report, the average rate of ice loss from the Greenland ice sheet has increased from 34 Gt/yr (gigatons per year) over the period 1992–2001 to 215 Gt/yr over the period 2002–11 (IPCC, *Climate Change 2013: The Physical Science Basis*, 9).

[55] *Artic Report Card 2011* and *Artic Report Card 2010*, ed. J. Richter-Menge and J. E. Overland. Available on the www.arctic.noaa website.

endangering vegetation, and creating subsidence that causes roads and buildings to collapse.[56] Trapped within permafrost are also billions of tons of methane hydrates, the leaking of even small fractions of which into the atmosphere can be a tipping point than can cause disastrous global warming, as pointed out in Chapter 3. In this regard the Arctic is of particular concern when considering future climate change.[57]

With the prospect of an ice-free Arctic in the present century, humanity is indeed taking a huge gamble with the planet's climate system. Our home planet has had glaciated bi-poles for millennia, which has a direct influence on our planet's current dynamic climate system. Empirical data shows that the Arctic region has not been free of major ice cover at any point in at least the last 800,000 years. If the Arctic proves to be the canary in the coal mine of global warming, human-induced climate change appears capable of ushering our home planet into a totally new state altogether.

As for Antarctica, where nearly two thirds of the planet's fresh water is locked, its ice sheets are not expected to start melting anytime soon. Antarctica has warmed more slowly than the Artic for various reasons: it is covered almost entirely by ice, which reflects sunlight back into space; it is surrounded entirely by oceans, which warm more slowly than land; and it lies under the stratospheric ozone hole, which has a regional cooling effect during late winter and spring. However, recent analysis indicates that west Antarctica has warmed at about the same rate as the rest of the globe over the past fifty years and that east Antarctica (and the continent as a whole) has also warmed slightly.[58] A dramatic example is the Antarctic Peninsula, which juts northward toward South America. Annual average temperatures there have soared by as much as 2.5°C since the 1950s. It is at this western edge that the Antarctic ice sheet appears to be fraying most rapidly. It was from there that the Larsen A Ice Shelf—an ice shelf is an extension of the land-based ice sheets into the ocean—broke in 1995, followed by the Larsen B in 2002. Fortunately, these events did not lead to a dramatic rise in sea level, since most of the ice was already in the water. However, there is concern that such breakups might open the

---

[56] Lemke et al., "Observations," 339; *Artic Report Card 2010*, 35–38; Henson, *The Rough Guide to Climate Change*, 79–82.

[57] See E. A. Kort et al., "Atmospheric Observations of Arctic Ocean Methane Emissions up to 82° North," *Nature Geoscience* 5 (2012): 318.

[58] Pew Centre on Global Climate Change, "Key Scientific Developments Since the IPCC Fourth Assessment Report," *Science Brief* 2 (June 2009): 3; E. J. Steig et al., "Warming of the Antarctic Ice-Sheet Surface Since the 1957 International Geophysical Year," *Nature* 457 (2009): 459–62.

door to a faster seaward flow of ice from glaciers upstream.[59] More recent data indicate that Antarctic ice shelves are collapsing more rapidly than expected. When these ice shelves collapse, the glaciers behind them begin to flow into the ocean more rapidly, accelerating sea-level rise.[60] The recent data are not very encouraging in this regard.

Another area of real concern in the context of the melting of glaciers driven by human-induced global warming is the Hindu-Kush Himalaya (HKH) region, including the vast Tibetan Plateau. This region is sometimes referred to as the Third Pole, as it is home to the largest set of ice caps and glaciers on Earth outside the two polar regions. From Afghanistan in the west, through Pakistan, India, Nepal, Bangladesh, and Bhutan to Myanmar and China in the east, the HKH region extends 2,175 miles over eight countries. The huge reservoirs of frozen fresh water in this region are the source of ten major Asian river systems, including the Ganges, Brahmaputra, Yangtze, Mekong, and Yellow rivers. For this reason the Third Pole region is often described as the water tower of Asia. The river and river basins provide water to 1.3 billion people. In total, around 3 billion people directly and indirectly benefit from the water, food, and energy provided by the river basins that originate in the HKH region.[61]

It appears that the HKH region is increasingly affected by global warming, though with regional variability. Some two-thirds of glaciers are retreating fast, while a smaller fraction appear to have advanced. Overall, the Himalayan glaciers have been retreating faster than many others around the world, thinning by up to 3.3 feet per year and retreating at rates ranging from 33–197 feet per year. Some small glaciers have already disappeared. The rate of glacier retreat has accelerated in recent times in comparison to the 1970s.[62] Because all the main rivers originating in the HKH region are fed to some degree by glacial-melt water, such a situation raises a real threat to local

---

[59] Henson, *The Rough Guide to Climate Change*, 87; Dow and Downing, *The Atlas of Climate Change*, 22.

[60] See E. G. Rignot et al., "Accelerated Ice Discharge from the Antarctic Peninsula Following the Collapse of Larsen B Ice Shelf," *Geophysical Research Letters* 31 (2004): L18401.

[61] See Humanitarian Futures Programme et al., *The Waters of the Third Pole: Sources of Threat, Sources of Survival* (London: King's College, 2010), 2, 7–9.

[62] Ibid., 10–11. See also S. R. Bajracharya et al., *Impact of Climate Change on Himalayan Glaciers and Glacial Lakes: Case Studies on GLOF and Associated Hazards in Nepal and Bhutan,* International Centre for Integrated Mountain Development in cooperation with the United Nations Environment Programme (2007); A. V. Kulkarni et al., "Glacial Retreat in Himalaya Using Indian Remote Sensing Satellite Data," *Current Science* 92 (2007): 69–74.

communities and the many more people farther away who depend on mountain water resources. The melt water is extremely important for river basins like the Indus, accounting for nearly 40 percent of the river flow, and also for the Brahmaputra basin, but it plays only a modest role for the Ganges, Yangtze, and Yellow rivers, making it difficult to generalize on its impacts.[63]

Apart from the Arctic, the Antarctic, and the Hindu-Kush Himalaya region, glaciers are found mainly in the European Alps, the South American Andes, and on peaks like the Kilimanjaro and Mount Kenya in Africa. The glaciers in these areas have also recorded signs of melting in the recent decades due to global warming. In fact, since these low-altitude glaciers are much smaller than their polar counterparts, they often respond more quickly to climate change.

Glacier decline is obvious to people who live in and near the Alps, whose ice has lost 30–40 percent of its surface area, with the pace of retreat faster since the 1980s. The Alpine glaciers have already lost more than 50 percent of their mass, though a few individual glaciers appear to have bucked the trend due to local variations in climate. Parts of the French Alps have been experiencing winters up to 3°C warmer than those of the 1960s. It is feared that 75 percent of Switzerland's glaciers could be gone by mid-century. Alpine warming has also increased the risk of avalanches in recent years, apart from other hazards to local communities. The melting of the glaciers also poses significant risks to the native plant and animal species of the alpine ecosystems.[64]

The Andes of South America, with their string of peaks and high valleys, many extending above 16,000 feet, hold more than 99 percent of the world's tropical ice. More than seven hundred glaciers dot Peru's Cordillera Blanca (White Mountains), including the Quelccaya ice cap, which sprawls across an area of 21 square miles. These glaciers are a veritable lifeline for the people living in their vicinities, but most of them have begun to shrink, if not disappear altogether. The Chacaltaya glacier in Bolivia has already disappeared, ahead of the forecasts. It began melting in the mid-1980s, and by March 2009 was completely gone, having thawed at thrice the expected rate. Peru's tropical glaciers provide 80 percent of the water supply for the perennially parched Pacific coast, which is now increasingly under risk. According to a 2005 study from researchers at the University of San

[63] See in this regard Walter W. Immerzeel et al., "Climate Change Will Affect the Asian Water Towers," *Science* 328 (2010): 1382, 1385.

[64] See Henson, *The Rough Guide to Climate Change*, 93–96; Pontificia Academia Scientiarum, *Fate of Mountain Glaciers in the Anthropocene*, 3.

Diego, glacier-covered areas in Peru have shrunk by 25 percent in the past three decades, and the glaciers may disappear in a few decades. As for Patagonia in the Southern Andes, about half of the glaciers surveyed in Chile show signs of retreat.[65]

The ice cap atop Africa's tallest mountain, Mount Kilimanjaro, is the most widely publicized of the tropics' disappearing glaciers. Its tallest peak, Kibo, the only one still retaining its glaciers, lost 80 percent of its vast ice cap in the twentieth century. Kilimanjaro's glaciers are projected to disappear completely by 2020.[66] The melting of glaciers appears to be driven mainly by human-induced climate change and wide-scale deforestation on the lower slopes.[67] Not far from Kilimanjaro, Mount Kenya lost seven of its eighteen glaciers over the last century, with the remaining ones occupying a paltry area less than .4 square mile. The situation is the same elsewhere on the peaks around the tropics. For example, the glacial area atop Mount Jaya in Indonesia shrank by 7.5 percent from 2000 to 2002, with its ice now covering only about 20 percent of the area it did in 1950.[68]

The melting of glaciers due to anthropogenic climate change has several consequences for human communities and local ecosystems. The most significant among them will be water scarcity. In regions like Central Asia or the South American Andes, mountains and their glaciers and winter snows are like water towers that store water for millions of people. "Disappearing glaciers are ultimately expected to lead to reductions in river flows during dry seasons and lost water resources for the hundreds of millions of people who rely upon glacier-fed rivers worldwide."[69] Mountain glaciers also serve another overlooked but critical function: they "preserve detailed information on past climate and the ability of glaciers to respond to different climate variables. This makes glaciers powerful tools for understanding

---

[65] Henson, *The Rough Guide to Climate Change*, 91; Michael D. Mastrandrea and Stephen H. Schneider, *Preparing for Climate Change* (Cambridge, MA: The MIT Press, 2010), 41; Stephen H. Schneider, *Science as a Contact Sport: Inside the Battle to Save Earth's Climate* (Washington, DC: National Geographic, 2009), 244–45; Dow and Downing, *The Atlas of Climate Change*, 24.

[66] See Georg Kaser et al., "Modern Glacier Retreat on Kilimanjaro As Evidence of Climate Change: Observations and Facts," *International Journal of Climatology* 24 (2004): 329–39.

[67] Michael S. Northcott, *A Moral Climate: The Ethics of Global Warming* (London: Darton, Longman, and Todd/Christian Aid, 2007), 45–46; Henson, *The Rough Guide to Climate Change*, 89–90.

[68] Henson, *The Rough Guide to Climate Change*, 89–90.

[69] The National Academy of Sciences, *Advancing the Science of Climate Change*, 262.

past and present climate dynamics. . . . It is time we pay more careful attention to mountain glaciers before their archives are lost forever."[70]

Sea-Level Rise

Another major impact of human-induced climate change, not altogether unrelated to the melting of glaciers, is the rising of sea levels all over. Our home planet is called the blue planet for its vast expanse of waters, which currently covers over 70 percent of its surface. Sea level on Earth has varied dramatically over the planet's history. For example, during the ice-age cycles of the past two to three million years—driven by periodic variations in Earth's orbit—there were fluctuations of several feet in sea level. During an ice age large amounts of water are stored in continent-sized glaciers. During interglacial periods much of this ice melts, raising global sea levels substantially as the water enters the oceans. In fact, during the most recent ice age, which began nearly 116,000 years ago and peaked between 25,000 and 20,000 years ago, global average sea level was almost 300 feet lower than it is today. Following the Last Glacial Maximum, sea level gradually increased overall to the present levels. The melting of the great ice sheets was largely complete by 6,000 years ago.[71] Stable sea levels enabled human communities to settle, mainly in the coastal and delta regions of the world, often the most fertile land for cultivation. This land presented other advantages like mild climates, easy and constant food availability, transportation, and more. However, after millennia of stable sea levels, small but significant changes have been measured shortly after the beginning of the industrial era, coinciding with the rise of greenhouse gas emissions into the atmosphere from human activities. Scientists today concur in attributing the current increase in sea levels all over the globe to human-induced climate change.[72]

Sea level can be considered both a powerful driver of and an indicator for global warming and climate change. As with other impacts of climate change, the rate of sea-level rise is proportionate to the amount of human-induced global warming. The warmer it gets, the

---

[70] Pontificia Academia Scientiarum, *Fate of Mountain Glaciers in the Anthropocene*, 9–10.

[71] See The National Academy of Sciences, *Advancing the Science of Climate Change*, 236; David Archer, *The Long Thaw: How Humans Are Changing the Next 100,000 Years of Earth's Climate* (Princeton, NJ: Princeton University Press, 2009), 138ff.

[72] See Anny Cazenave and William Llove, "Contemporary Sea Level Rise," *Annual Review of Marine Science* 2 (2010): 146.

higher the sea-level rises. Globally, it has been observed that sea-level rise has accelerated since the nineteenth century. In the late nineteeth century the rate of sea-level rise was about .02 inches per year. In the last half of the twentieth century this increased to approximately .07 inches per year. Satellite measurements reveal that sea levels have risen about recently 80 percent faster, at .13 inches per year.[73] Over the course of the twentieth century the rate of sea-level rise has roughly tripled in response to 0.8°C global warming. According to the 2013 IPCC report "the rate of sea level rise since the mid-19th century has been larger than the mean rate during the previous two millennia."[74] With more warming in the pipeline in the coming centuries, sea levels are expected to rise significantly in the future.

The two main causes of global mean sea-level change are thermal expansion of water in the world's ocean basins as it absorbs heat and the addition of fresh water from land-based sources—mainly ice sheets and glaciers, but also other smaller sources. Geological processes such as subsidence and uplift, ocean circulation changes, and other processes like salinity and density changes also determine local and regional rates of sea-level rise, but the total volume of the world's oceans—and in this way the global average sea level—is essentially controlled by thermal expansion and addition of water from land-based sources.[75] We shall examine each of these contributions below.

Ocean thermal expansion is a direct effect of global warming. The physical principle here is very simple. As heat is absorbed by the oceans, seawater warms up and the volume of the water expands, causing sea levels to rise.

The ocean is by far the most important heat reservoir in the climate system, with a heat storage capacity more than 1,000 times

---

[73] Stefan Rahmstorf, "A New View on Sea Level Rise," *Nature Climate Change* 4 (2010): 44; Cazenave and Llove, "Contemporary Sea Level Rise," 145–73; The National Academy of Sciences, *Advancing the Science of Climate Change*, 236–37. Instrumental records for sea level date back about 140 years, while satellite measurements currently offer precise sea-level maps across the entire globe. "For more than 15 years now, the global mean sea level has been routinely measured at 10–day intervals over the whole oceanic domain with high-precision satellite altimetry, and such observations show clear evidence of global mean sea level rise" (Cazenave and Llove, "Contemporary Sea Level Rise," 146).

[74] IPCC, *Climate Change 2013: The Physical Science Basis*, 11.

[75] The National Academy of Sciences, *Advancing the Science of Climate Change*, 238; Meehl et al., "Global Climate Projections," in IPCC, *Climate Change 2007*, 812ff.; Cazenave and Llove, "Contemporary Sea Level Rise," 152ff.

larger than that of the atmosphere. In fact, measurements of changes in ocean heat content show that 80 to 90 percent of the heating associated with human greenhouse gas (GHG) emissions over the past 50 years has gone into raising the temperatures of the oceans. . . . Approximately 50 percent of the observed sea-level rise since the late 19th century has been attributed to thermal expansion of the warming oceans.[76]

Ocean thermal expansion is not uniform throughout the globe. The warmer waters of the tropics and near the ocean surface expand more in response to a given temperature increase than the cold waters at high latitude and the deep waters. Climate models suggest that the eventual contribution to sea-level rise from thermal expansion of the ocean is expected to be 0.6–1.9 feet per degree Celsius of global warming.[77]

The addition of fresh water from the melting or flowing into the oceans of land ice contained in the world's glaciers and ice sheets is the second major factor that contributes directly to sea-level rise. It is estimated that if all of the water currently stored as ice on land surfaces around the world were to melt, sea levels would rise as much as to 230 feet. This, of course, is a rather unlikely scenario and would take place over hundreds to thousands of years.

The world's glaciers and ice caps, other than the ice sheets of Greenland and Antarctica, contain the water equivalent of up to 2.4 feet. Glaciers are very sensitive to global warming, and observations indicate that since the 1970s most of the world's glaciers are retreating and thinning. They have consistently been contributing about one-quarter of the total sea-level rise over the past fifty years. Mountain glaciers are expected to continue to be a significant contributor to sea-level rise during this century, though their overall contribution appears to be relatively small. The present losses of mountain glaciers cause almost .04 inches per year of sea-level rise.[78] It is from the melting of the major ice sheets of Greenland and Antarctic, which contain

---

[76] The National Academy of Sciences, *Advancing the Science of Climate Change*, 239. See also K. E. Trenberth and J. T. Fasullo, "Tracking Earth's Energy," *Science* 328 (2010): 316–17.

[77] See Meehl et al., "Global Climate Projections," 829; Solomon et al., "Irreversible Climate Change due to Carbon Dioxide Emissions," 1708.

[78] The National Academy of Sciences, *Advancing the Science of Climate Change*, 243; Pontificia Academia Scientiarum, *Fate of Mountain Glaciers in the Anthropocene*, 8; Cazenave and Llove, "Contemporary Sea Level Rise," 154.

about 99.5 percent of the Earth's glacier ice, that most of the future sea-level rise will come.[79]

Greenland and the West Antarctica ice sheets contain the equivalent of 23 and 11.5 feet of water, respectively. Even a small amount of ice-mass loss from these ice sheets could produce substantial sea-level rise. Recent observations, especially gravity measurements from satellites in space, reveal that ice sheets in Greenland and West Antarctica have been losing mass at an accelerating rate over the past two decades. In both Antarctica and Greenland many outlet glaciers are accelerating their seaward flow, hastening the delivery of ice to the surrounding seas. In Greenland there has been significant ice-mass loss in near coastal regions, and the melt appears to have increased 30 percent over the past thirty years, and especially since 2002/2003.[80]

If and when the entire Greenland ice sheet were to melt into the sea, it would trigger a truly catastrophic sea-level rise of more than 23 feet, swamping coastal cities around the world and, in some low-lying areas, closing the book on millennia of human history. However, many glaciologists are confident that total melting of the Greenland ice sheet would be a slow process, taking many hundreds of years to complete. At the same time, Greenland's peripheral glaciers appear to be losing ice at a faster rate than predicted by climate models. Even a small fraction of Greenland's ice entering the ocean in the present century can considerably raise sea levels. Greenland's ice is one of the biggest unknowns looming over our planet's coastlines.[81]

There is increasing concern about the overall stability of the West Antarctica Ice Sheet. Much of the ice rests on a soft, deformable bed of rock that lies below sea level. Satellite observations over West Antarctica during the past decade have found significant elevation decrease, especially in the Amundsen Sea sector.[82] "The disappearance of Antarctic ice shelves and the retreat of the ice sheet at the continent's margins could allow the surrounding sea water to flow into the ice-bedrock interface, eroding the ice further from underneath and

[79] J. L. Bamber and W. P. Aspinall, "An Expert Judgement Assessment of Future Sea Level Rise from the Ice Sheets," *Nature Climate Change* 3 (2013): 424.

[80] See W. Krabill et al., "Greenland Ice Sheet: Increased Coastal Thinning," *Geophysical Research Letters* 31 (2004): L24402.

[81] Henson, *The Rough Guide to Climate Change*, 83–85.

[82] Cazenave and Llove, "Contemporary Sea Level Rise," 153. See also Angelika Humbert, "Cryospheric Science: Vulnerable Ice in the Weddell Sea," *Nature Geoscience* 5 (2012): 370–71.

enhancing its discharge."[83] However, the timescales of these processes are not well known.

As for estimates of sea-level rise in the future, all recent studies have predicted higher rates than previous estimates. The IPCC's 2007 Assessment Report projected a global sea-level rise of anywhere between 7 and 23 inches by 2100.[84] Its 2013 report instead projects a higher sea-level rise—between 10 and 32 inches for 2081–2100.[85] Other recent studies foresee a rise in global sea levels that could be close to or even exceed 3 feet.[86] There is as yet no consensus in the scientific community on the exact rate and scale of future sea-level rise by the end of this century.[87]

The problem with sea-level rise is that, as with global warming, it will be irreversible for at least 1,000 years after the cessation of greenhouse gas emissions, given the longevity of some of the contributing gases. So we need to look beyond 2100. Persistent global warming will lead to substantial ice-sheet melting for centuries to come. As it will take centuries to millennia for the full ocean depth to adjust to surface warming, thermal expansion of the oceans also will carry on well into the future. For this reason, greenhouse gas emissions in this century might be enough to commit (and condemn) future generations to 13 or even 19 feet of sea-level rise, or even more, in the centuries to come, unless greenhouse gas emissions are reduced dramatically to keep the Earth from warming above 2°C.[88] It is clear that with anthropogenic

---

[83] The National Academy of Sciences, *Advancing the Science of Climate Change*, 241.

[84] Meehl et al., "Global Climate Projections," 350.

[85] IPCC, *Climate Change 2013: The Physical Science Basis*, 25.

[86] See Martin Vermeer and Stefan Rahmstorf, "Global Sea Level Linked to Global Temperature," *Proceedings of the National Academy of Sciences* 106 (2009): 21527–32; R. Horton et al., "Sea Level Rise Projections for Current Generation CGCMs Based on the Semi-Empirical Method," *Geophysical Research Letters* 35 (2008): L02715; A. Grinsted et al., "Reconstructing Sea Level from Paleo and Projected Temperatures 2000 to 2100 AD," *Climate Dynamics* 34 (2009): 461–72; S. Jevrejeva et al., "How Will Sea Level Respond to Changes in Natural and Anthropogenic Forcings by 2100?" *Geophysical Research Letters* 37 (2010): L07703.

[87] See IPCC, *Climate Change 2013: The Physical Science Basis*, 26. See also Mirko Orlic and Zoran Pasaric, "Semi-Empirical Versus Process-Based Sea-Level Projections for the Twenty-First Century," *Nature Climate Change* 3 (2013): 735–38.

[88] See Solomon et al., "Irreversible Climate Change due to Carbon Dioxide Emissions," 1704–09; Jonathan T. Overpeck and Jeremy L. Weiss, "Projections of Future Sea Level Becoming More Dire," *Proceedings of the National Academy of Sciences* 106 (2009): 21462.

global warming we are heading for inexorable sea-level rise that will continue into the future.

What are the consequences for human communities, especially for those living in coastal and delta regions and on small islands?

The large and growing concentration of human communities and assets in coastal areas means that the potential impacts of sea-level rise are high. While several regions are vulnerable to coastal flooding caused by sea-level rise, in absolute numbers, people living in South, Southeast, and East Asia appear to be most threatened. The net population expected to be displaced by sea-level rise in the current century is estimated to be between 72 and 187 million people, nearly two-thirds of whom are concentrated in the extensive and often subsiding coastal deltas of East, Southeast, and South Asia alone. The large populations in the low-lying deltaic plains of Bangladesh and Vietnam appear especially threatened in this regard, as well as some areas of Thailand, China, and India. Hot spots in Africa for impacts due to sea-level rise are the Nile Delta of Egypt—a 12.5 mile wide land strip along the coast that is less than 6.5 feet above sea level—and delta regions in Nigeria and Mozambique. Other vulnerable regions include Guyana, Suriname, and French Guiana in South America; Miami and New Orleans in North America; and most of the Netherlands, where one-quarter of the land (with 60 percent of the population) already lies below mean sea level.

Rising sea levels can also lead to entire small island nations being inundated. The small island regions in the Pacific and Indian Oceans and in the Caribbean are especially vulnerable to sea-level rise. On low-lying islands like the Maldives, Tuvalu, Kiribati, and others, communities will face the prospect of forced abandonment and eventual migration elsewhere. The average elevation of land is just a little over 3 feet in the Maldives—with 80 percent of the country's land mass lying under it—and around 6.5 feet in Tuvalu. The highest terrain in each nation is around 10 and 16.5 feet, respectively.[89]

Sea-level rise causes a range of impacts for coastal areas, including submergence, increased flooding, increased erosion, ecosystem changes, and increased salinization. Coastal areas are among the most densely populated and economically active land areas on Earth,

---

[89] See Josh Willis et al., "Sea Level: An Introduction to the Special Issue," *Oceanography* 24 (2011): 22; Robert J. Nicholls, "Planning for the Impacts of Sea Level Rise," *Oceanography* 24 (2011): 150–51; Nicholls et al., "Sea-Level Rise and Its Possible Impacts Given a 'beyond 4°C World' in the Twenty-First Century," 162, 172; Henson, *The Rough Guide to Climate Change*, 106–7.

including large conglomerations like Tokyo, Shanghai, Mumbai, Kolkata, Karachi, Hong Kong, London, New York, and Buenos Aires. The concentration of population and assets along the coasts make them risky places, exposed to multiple hazards associated with sea-level rise like storm-induced flooding. A region at particular risk is the Ganges Delta of eastern India and Bangladesh. In the case of Bangladesh—three-quarters of which is within the deltaic region formed by the confluence of the Ganges, Brahmaputra, and Meghna rivers, and half of which lies less than 16.5 feet above sea level—flooding is a common recurrence. In Bangladesh, about 10 million people live within the 3 foot contour.

The specter raised by the prospects of sea-level rise in the future—in the life span of our grandchildren and beyond—is worrying indeed. As the Geological Society of London's statement on climate change reads: "When the human population was small and nomadic, a rise in sea level of a few meters would have had very little effect on *Homo sapiens*. With the current and growing global population, much of which is concentrated in coastal cities, such a rise in sea level would have a drastic effect on our complex society."[90]

Ocean Acidification and Threats to Marine Life

Over a period of less than a decade or so, the problem of ocean acidification—the change in seawater chemistry due to rising atmospheric carbon dioxide levels, with subsequent impacts on marine life and ecosystems—has become a critical issue for the scientific community and for society at large.[91] The phenomenon of ocean acidification is linked to anthropogenic climate change—the problem is caused by the same process of human emissions of carbon dioxide into the atmosphere—but its consequences are so wide and far reaching as to merit

---

[90] The Geological Society, *Climate Change: Evidence from the Geological Record: A Statement from the Geological Society of London* (November 2010), 2.

[91] See Scott C. Doney et al., "Ocean Acidification: A Critical Emerging Problem for the Ocean Sciences," *Oceanography* 22 (2009): 16. See also important studies like The Royal Society, *Ocean Acidification due to Increasing Carbon Dioxide* (June 2005); Secretariat of the Convention on Biological Diversity, *Scientific Synthesis of the Impacts of Ocean Acidification on Marine Diversity*, Technical Series No. 46 (Montreal: 2009). See also the *Statement of the Inter-Academy Panel on Ocean Acidification* endorsed by seventy of the world's leading scientific academies in 2009. One may also recall important scientific events like the first, second, and third symposia on the ocean in a high-CO_2 world held in 2004, 2008, and 2012, respectively.

the term the "other CO_2 problem."[92] The acidification of the seawaters poses a major threat to the marine food chain and ecosystems, upon which a sizable portion of the world's population depends for its primary source of food.

Ocean acidification is directly linked to the emission of carbon dioxide from the combustion of fossil fuels, cement production, agriculture, deforestation, and other human activities. As we have seen earlier, the quantity of carbon released into the atmosphere by human activities is huge. The cumulative amount of human CO_2 emissions over the industrial era was measured in 2009 at around 560 billion tons. A little less than half of this anthropogenic CO_2 remains in the atmosphere, contributing directly to global warming. The remainder is removed in roughly equal parts into the ocean and by land vegetation. Approximately one-quarter to one-third of the human-generated CO_2 is currently absorbed by the ocean.[93] The physical process is direct and simple. As atmospheric CO_2 rises, some of the extra carbon dioxide is driven into ocean surface waters, which chemically reacts with seawater in the process (down to about 328 feet on average). Only some of the carbon dioxide absorbed by the oceans is taken up and used by marine plants; most of it combines with water to form carbonic acid, which is harmful to many kinds of ocean life. Carbon dioxide is a chemically inert, unreactive gas when it is present in the atmosphere. But when it is dissolved in seawater, it becomes more reactive and leads to several chemical reactions. An initial reaction between water (H_2O) and carbon dioxide (CO_2) forms carbonic acid (H_2CO_3). This results in a lowering of ocean pH, an increase in the concentration of hydrogen ions, and a decrease in the concentration of the carbonate ions, the basic building block of the shells and skeletons of many marine organisms. The aggregate of these chemical changes are called "ocean acidification."[94]

Over the past 250 years—coinciding roughly with the period of the Industrial Revolution—the oceans have absorbed over one-quarter

----

[92] See "Monaco Declaration"—Second International Symposium on the Ocean in a High-CO_2 World, Monaco, October 6–9, 2008, 3; S. C. Doney et al., "Ocean Acidification: The Other CO_2 Problem," *Annual Review of Marine Science* 1 (2009): 169–92.

[93] Doney et al., "Ocean Acidification," 16; James C. Orr et al., "Research Priorities for Understanding Ocean Acidification: Summary from the Second Symposium on the Ocean in a High-CO_2 World," *Oceanography* 22 (2009): 182.

[94] The Royal Society, *Ocean Acidification due to Increasing Carbon Dioxide*, 2, 6; Doney et al., "Ocean Acidification," 17; Orr et al., "Research Priorities for Understanding Ocean Acidification," 182.

of the CO_2 produced from human activities, causing the increasing acidification of seawaters. Ocean acidification directly follows the accelerating trend in world CO_2 emissions. In fact, observations collected over the last twenty-five years show consistent trends of increasing ocean carbon and decreasing pH in lockstep with increasing atmospheric CO_2. It has been found that surface ocean pH has dropped from 8.2 to 8.1 units since the beginning of the Industrial Revolution. This may not appear to be a big change. But, in reality, it means a 30 percent increase in hydrogen ion concentration or surface-ocean acidity.[95] It is a change that has not happened for the last 20 million years. It is predicted that at the current level of carbon dioxide emissions, ocean acidity will increase by 150 percent by 2050. "This significant increase is 100 times faster than any change in acidity experienced in the marine environment over the last 200 million years, giving little time for evolutionary adaptation within biological systems."[96] The ocean-acidification process of today differs radically from past events because it is human-induced, is occurring much more rapidly, and has no recent analogues in the geological history of our home planet. In fact, all previous natural acidification events go back to the major coral mass extinctions that are known to have occurred millions of years ago, like the end-Permian mass extinction (251 million years ago) and the PETM event (55 million years ago).[97]

The chemical changes brought about by ocean acidification, like the reduction of carbonate ions, will have serious biological consequences for many marine organisms and ecosystems. The most important of these consequences will be on the process of calcification, which is fundamental to marine life. An increase in ocean acidification will reduce the concentration and availability of carbonate ions, which leads to lower saturation levels for the carbonate minerals, aragonite and calcite, which are used by many marine organisms, such as corals and shellfish, to produce their skeletons, shells, and other hard structures. As the world's oceans become less saturated with carbonate minerals over time, marine organisms are expected to build weaker skeletons and shells and experience slower growth rates. Through its negative

---

[95] Orr et al., "Research Priorities for Understanding Ocean Acidification," 182–83; The Inter-Academy Panel, *Statement on Ocean Acidification* (June 2009), 1.

[96] Secretariat of the Convention on Biological Diversity, *Scientific Synthesis of the Impacts of Ocean Acidification on Marine Diversity*, 9.

[97] Orr et al., "Research Priorities for Understanding Ocean Acidification," 183; L. R. Kump et al., "Ocean Acidification in Deep Time," *Oceanography* 22 (2009): 94.

impact on the process of calcification, ocean acidification will endanger the survival of many marine organisms.

Carbonate ion concentrations are now lower than at any other time during the last 800,000 years. Ocean acidification impacts on marine life are already being observed in the polar region—where atmospheric carbon dioxide most readily dissolves—and the tropical regions. With current emission rates it is predicted that the surface waters of the highly productive Arctic Ocean will become under-saturated with respect to essential carbonate minerals by the 2030s, and the Antarctic Ocean by 2050, with disruptions to large components of the marine food web.[98]

A significant victim of decreased calcification due to ocean acidification will be coral reefs, which are present in an estimated 500,000 square miles of the world's tropical and subtropical oceans. Coral reefs provide manifold services. They provide fish habitat, generate billions of dollars annually in tourism, protect shorelines from erosion and flooding, offer buffer coastal zones from storm waves and tsunamis, and provide the foundation for rich biodiversity, equivalent to that found in tropical rainforests.[99] Healthy coral reef ecosystems develop only under a relatively narrow range of ocean temperatures and chemistry, and they are highly sensitive to even slight changes in this regard. For example, an increase in sea-surface temperature of 1°C for more than eight weeks can lead to severe coral bleaching of tropical corals. A rise in increasingly frequent and intense periods of warm sea temperatures since the 1980s led to the death of nearly 30 percent of warm-water corals through bleaching. Research suggests that global climate change has already caused steep declines in coral growth on reef systems around the world. A typical example is the Great Barrier Reef, by far the largest coral reef in the world, which is even more productive than tropical rainforests. However, over the last twenty years, living coral around the world has been destroyed five times more quickly than tropical rainforests. The corals in the waters of Galapagos and in the Caribbean have also suffered serious setbacks in recent decades.[100] The decrease in the calcification rates due to ocean acidification will damage the corals even further, as less calcium will be

---

[98] The Inter-Academy Panel, *Statement on Ocean Acidification* (June 2009), 1–2; Secretariat of the Convention on Biological Diversity, *Scientific Synthesis of the Impacts of Ocean Acidification on Marine Diversity*, 9.

[99] "Monaco Declaration," 2.

[100] See Alanna Mitchell, *Seasick: The Hidden Ecological Crisis of the Global Ocean* (Oxford: Oneworld Publications, 2009), 24, 28.

available to them to make bones and skeletal structures to survive. This means that corals are not able to make reefs as quickly, and that over time, as the ocean acidity increases, they will not be able to build their structures at all. Besides, once the ocean pH reaches a certain point, the water will become acidic enough to corrode the healthy reefs that remain. Naturally, ocean acidification also will affect the organisms that live in the corals. Once the corals are gone, the creatures that depend on them will be gone too, with the effects trickling through the entire reef ecosystem.[101] Coral reefs are the most widely recognized ecosystem threatened by ocean acidification, and the predictions for their future are not optimistic:

> It has been predicted that by 2100, 70% of cold-water corals, key refuges and feeding grounds for commercial fish species, will be exposed to corrosive waters. Tropical waters, such as those around the Great Barrier Reef, will also experience rapid declines in carbonate ions, reducing rates of net warm water coral reef accretion and leaving biologically diverse reefs outpaced by bioerosion and sea-level rise.[102]

It is estimated that if the atmospheric concentrations of CO_2 were to reach 560 ppm—double the preindustrial levels that they are expected to reach within the current century under the business-as-usual scenario—"all coral reefs will cease to grow and start to dissolve."[103] The synergistic interaction of elevated sea temperatures—about 80 percent of the extra heat created by global warming has been absorbed by the oceans, increasing ocean acidity, pollution from land, unsustainable fishing, and so on—is likely to place the world's coral reefs under great stress over the next few decades and centuries. "The coral reef crisis occurring in modern oceans may be the sixth such major reef crisis recorded in the past 500 million years of marine metazoan evolution."[104]

---

[101] Ibid., 35; The Royal Society, *Ocean Acidification due to Increasing Carbon Dioxide*, 25; Joan A. Kleypas and Kimberley K. Yates, "Coral Reefs and Ocean Acidification," *Oceanography* 22 (2009): 116.

[102] Secretariat of the Convention on Biological Diversity, *Scientific Synthesis of the Impacts of Ocean Acidification on Marine Diversity*, 9.

[103] J. Silverman et al., "Coral Reefs May Start Dissolving When Atmospheric CO_2 Doubles," *Geophysical Research Letters* 36 (2009): L05606.

[104] The National Research Council, *Understanding Earth's Deep Past: Lessons for Our Climate Future* (Washington, DC: The National Academies Press, 2011), 54.

Other calcifying organisms that will be affected by changes in the process of calcification due to increasing ocean acidification are components of the phytoplankton and the zooplankton, which are a major food source for fish and other animals. Regional variations in pH will mean that by 2100 the process of calcification will have become extremely difficult for these groups of organisms, particularly in the Southern Ocean. Without plankton, the food web of the ocean will collapse. It may be remembered that plankton produce half the oxygen we breathe or, put another way, every second breath we take. These microscopic creatures are indeed the lungs of the planet. The tiny plankton may be at the bottom of the marine food chain, but they are at the top of the biogeochemical system of the planet, since they help control its carbon and oxygen cycles. The plankton in the oceans will be increasingly threatened by ocean acidification in the future.[105]

The impacts of ocean acidification can also exacerbate the effects of climate change. Changes in the chemistry of the oceans will reduce their ability to absorb additional CO_2 from the atmosphere. A decrease in the amount of CO_2 absorbed by the oceans will mean that relatively more carbon dioxide will stay in the atmosphere, which will in turn affect the rate and scale of global warming.[106]

The socioeconomic effects of ocean acidification will be substantial. Ocean acidification could affect marine food webs and lead to substantial changes in commercial fish stocks, threatening protein supply and food security for millions of people. Since many calcifying species are located at the bottom or middle of global ocean food webs, the effects of the loss of shelled organisms to ocean acidification will be transmitted throughout the ecosystem.[107] The changes in marine food webs could significantly alter global marine harvests. Some of the countries most dependent on seafood for dietary protein include developing island nations with few agricultural alternatives. For nearly 1 billion people, seafood, especially calcifying species like mollusks, sponges, and so on, is the primary source of protein and income. For example, in countries such as Bangladesh, Cambodia, Equatorial

---

[105] Mitchell, *Seasick*, 14, 26; The Royal Society, *Ocean Acidification due to Increasing Carbon Dioxide*, vi.

[106] The Royal Society, *Ocean Acidification due to Increasing Carbon Dioxide*, vi, 1.

[107] "Monaco Declaration," 2; O. Hoegh-Guldberg et al., "Coral Reefs Under Rapid Climate Change and Ocean Acidification," *Science* 318 (2007): 1737; Secretariat of the Convention on Biological Diversity, *Scientific Synthesis of the Impacts of Ocean Acidification on Marine Diversity*, 49.

Guinea, French Guinea, Gambia, Ghana, Indonesia, and Sierra Leone, citizens get more than 50 percent of their protein from seafood, and it remains a significant source of dietary protein in most other developed nations and many costal developing nations.[108]

As with other effects of climate change resulting from greenhouse gas emissions, the most deleterious effects of ocean acidification lie mainly in the future (over decades and centuries), and their magnitudes are potentially large, though not entirely certain. Ocean acidification research is still in its infancy. But what we know already tells us that ocean acidification is going to be irreversible on timescales of at least tens of thousands of years. Even the current level of ocean acidification is essentially irreversible during our lifetimes and those of many generations to come. This is because the rate of anthropogenic carbon input to the atmosphere greatly exceeds the mixing time of the oceans (1,000–1,500 years). So, it will take tens of thousands of years for ocean chemistry to return to a condition similar to that occurring at pre-industrial times (about 200 years ago).[109] "If ocean acidification continues to worsen to the end of this century, as projected, thousands of years may be required for the Earth system to re-establish even roughly similar ocean chemistry; hundreds of thousands to millions of years will be needed for coral reefs to be re-established, based on past records of natural coral-reef extinction events."[110] Ocean acidification is yet another huge challenge that humanity is mounting for itself through the reckless emissions of greenhouse gases, unaware of the dire consequences, especially for the generations to come.

Climate Change and Biodiversity Loss

The last of the major impacts of human-induced global warming and associated climate change is the specter of biodiversity loss. One of the alarming conclusions of the Fourth Assessment Report of the IPCC in 2007 was that up to 30 percent of plant and animal species so far assessed are likely to be at increased risk of extinction if increases

---

[108] See Sarah R. Cooley, "Ocean Acidification's Potential to Alter Global Marine Ecosystem Services," *Oceanography* 22 (2009): 172, 175–77.

[109] Cooley, "Ocean Acidification's Potential to Alter Global Marine Ecosystem Services," 180; The Royal Society, *Ocean Acidification due to Increasing Carbon Dioxide*, vi, 10; National Research Council, *Understanding Earth's Deep Past*, 72.

[110] Orr et al., "Research Priorities for Understanding Ocean Acidification," 183. See also "Monaco Declaration," 2–3.

in global average temperatures exceed 1.5–2.5°C.[111] Climate change is itself, however, only one of the major drivers behind the current spasm of the extinction of species—a much larger problem in its own right within the overall context of the contemporary ecological crisis. We will, in fact, reserve an entire chapter to the discussion of it. In the present section we limit ourselves to dealing with some of the major impacts of climate change on biodiversity.

There is little doubt within the scientific community that anthropogenic climate change is having a large and sustained impact on Earth's ecosystems.[112] Although human land use remains the main driver of present-day species extinction and habitat loss, climate change is projected to become equally or a progressively more significant threat in the coming decades.[113] As the Millennium Ecosystem Assessment recognizes, "By the end of the twenty-first century, climate change and its impacts may be the dominant direct driver of biodiversity loss and changes in ecosystem services globally."[114] Some of the most vulnerable ecosystems will include coral reefs, mangroves, wetlands, dry and sub-humid lands, high-latitude ecosystems like boreal forests, mountain ecosystems, and Arctic and alpine-climate ecosystems. A few species might benefit from climate change, but the vast majority of them will suffer because the changes in ecosystems will be rapid and unprecedented, giving little time for adaptation.

Two major impacts of climate change on species and ecosystems deserve highlighting here: shifts in species' ranges (the locations in which they can survive and reproduce), and shifts in phenology (the timing of biological activities that take place seasonally).

As Earth warms, many plant and animal species on land have been observed to shift their geographical ranges. Climate change today is

---

[111] A. Fischlin et al., "Ecosystems, Their Properties, Goods, and Services," in *Climate Change: Impacts, Adaptation and Vulnerability: Contribution of Working Group II to the Fourth Assessment Report of the IPCC*, ed. M. L. Parry et al. (Cambridge: Cambridge University Press, 2007), 213.

[112] National Research Council, *Understanding Earth's Deep Past*, 51; Hannah Hoag, "Confronting the Biodiversity Crisis," *Nature Climate Change* 4 (2010): 51; C. Rosenzweig et al., "Attributing Physical and Biological Impacts to Anthropogenic Climate Change," *Nature* 453 (2008): 353–58.

[113] See Terence P. Dawson et al., "Beyond Predictions: Biodiversity Conservation in a Changing Climate," *Science* 332 (2011): 53. See also M. Hoffmann et al., "The Impact of Conservation on the Status of the World's Vertebrates," *Science* 330 (2010): 1503; H. M. Pereira et al., "Scenarios for Global Biodiversity in the Twenty-First Century," *Science* 330 (2010): 1496.

[114] Millennium Ecosystem Assessment, *Ecosystems and Human Well-being: Biodiversity Synthesis* (Washington, DC: World Resources Institute, 2005), 10.

driving the most massive relocation of species to occur without direct human assistance since the beginning of the current interglacial warm period. It is estimated that about 40 percent of wild plants and animals on land that have been followed over decades are relocating in order to remain within suitable climate conditions. Species' range boundaries have shifted an average of 3.7 miles per decade as well as moving upward in elevation. The range shifts observed during the past 30 years surpass changes that occurred during the current interglacial warm period of the past 10,000 years.[115] The geographical distribution of species and vegetation types is projected to shift even more radically in the future due to climate change, with ranges moving hundreds of miles toward the poles by the end of the twenty-first century. Such a phenomenon would have diverse and far-reaching consequences. Migration of marine species to cooler waters could make tropical oceans less diverse. Boreal and temperate forests could face widespread dieback at the southern end of their present ranges.[116] The species that cannot move fast enough will find their ranges shrinking. Some of these species will also become stressed as the climate around them becomes unsuitable. They will be at high risk of extinction if they cannot relocate. The problem will be particularly acute for those species already living at the edge of their habitats—like cold-adapted species located on mountain tops and at high latitudes—who will have nowhere to migrate to.

> Cold-adapted species living at the tops of mountains are also being stranded with nowhere to move as warmer temperatures—and formerly lower-elevation species—creep up to higher elevations. As these formerly lower-elevation species move into conditions suitable at higher elevations the available land area tends to get smaller as the elevation gets higher. Of course, an upward shift in each forest type means that the next higher type is either eliminated or pushed even higher. The tundra and subalpine plants and animals that grace the tops of the many high peaks and ridges may disappear completely as they are effectively pushed off the tops of the mountains.[117]

---

[115] The National Research Council, *Ecological Impacts of Climate Change* (Washington, DC: The National Academies Press, 2008), 17; C. Parmesan et al., "Overstretching Attribution," *Nature Climate Change* 1 (2011): 2.

[116] Secretariat of the Convention on Biological Diversity, *Global Biodiversity Outlook 3*, 10.

[117] The National Research Council, *Ecological Impacts of Climate Change*, 18.

The range of shifts due to climate change will acutely affect species mainly in the Arctic and Antarctic. The problem is that the temperatures are rising more rapidly near the poles—up to 3°C warming since 1850, compared with the average global average increase of 0.75°C. As the sea ice gets thinner and shrinks in area, so too the habitats of animals that live in this area, such as polar bears and seals in the Arctic and the Adelié penguin populations in the Antarctic, shrink.[118]

Climate change is also driving changes in phenology, that is, in the seasonal biological activities of species, like the timing of flowering, budding and breeding, and migration patterns. Various seasonal behaviors of numerous species, especially in the spring and autumn, now occur 15–20 days earlier than several decades ago. Spring events have been advancing by an average 2.8–3.2 days per decade. The types of changes include earlier flowering and budding of plants, earlier arrival of migrant birds, earlier appearance of butterflies, and so on.[119] These changes can alter food chains and create mismatches within ecosystems where different species have evolved in synchronized interdependence, for example, between nesting and food availability, pollinators and fertilization. In fact, the problem is precisely that not all of the species in an ecosystem shift their seasonal behavior in exactly the same way. These shifts can disrupt important ecological interactions, especially when a species depends upon another for survival, and only one changes its timing.

> For example, a small black-and-white bird called the European pied flycatcher has not changed the time it arrives on its breeding grounds even though the caterpillars it feeds its young are emerging earlier. Missing the peak of food availability means fewer chicks are surviving, in turn causing the flycatcher's population to decline.[120]

Other human activities can also compound the effects of climate change on biodiversity. These issues will be taken up for further discussion in the coming chapter dedicated exclusively to the theme of biodiversity loss.

---

[118] Ibid.

[119] The National Research Council, *Ecological Impacts of Climate Change*, 20.

[120] Ibid., 9.

A Reckless Gamble with Our Planetary Home

In light of the impacts of climate change, it is obvious that we are playing a huge and mindless gamble with the future of our common planetary home and of our fellow human beings—especially the future generations—and our fellow species, members of our common household.

The closing lines of the London Geological Society's 2010 statement are appropriate to remember here: "In the light of the evidence presented here it is reasonable to conclude that emitting further large amounts of CO_2 into the atmosphere over time is likely to be unwise, uncomfortable though that fact may be."[121] The same report warns, "Many climate change processes have long time lags, so future generations will have to deal with the consequences. Recovery of the Earth's climate in the absence of any mitigation measures could take 100,000 years or more, which is indeed a dreadful possibility."[122] However, in spite of such serious warnings from the scientific community, greenhouse gas emissions are constantly rising. Alas, they might—with the currently reigning myth of infinite growth around which our present civilization and economy are built—continue this rise till humanity has emptied into the atmosphere most of the carbon accumulated and preserved in Earth's geological reservoirs over millions of years.[123] In this context the choices that human societies make over the next several decades will have an enormous influence on the magnitude of future climate change and its impact on human communities around the world. We are indeed recklessly gambling with the future of our common home.

---

[121] The Geological Society, *Climate Change*, 7.

[122] Ibid.

[123] Some economic forecasts suggest that under the business-as-usual scenario, conventional fossil-fuel resources will be largely used up in the next 200–400 years, leading to atmospheric CO_2 levels that could reach even approximately 2,000 ppmv by AD 2300–2400, if humanity as a whole does not radically change course. See National Research Council, *Understanding Earth's Deep Past*, 76.

5

Species Extinction
and Biodiversity Loss

What distinguishes our home planet from the billions and billions of other celestial bodies in the infinitely vast universe is life. Life, as per our current knowledge, exists only on Earth. Only Earth has a biosphere that permeates the other spheres of air, land, and water. Other planets may have atmospheres, similar terrestrial and chemical compositions, or may even hold immense quantities of water as frozen ice. But those vast expanses are desolately barren. Only Earth is teeming with abundant life.

The origin of life on our home planet nearly 3.8 billion years ago and its magnificent evolution—nearly three-quarters of it in the primordial oceans, before arriving on land—has been a stupendous saga. As we have seen in our opening chapter, it was not that life happened to evolve on Earth; rather, it was life that molded our planet into the wonderful home for the millions of living beings that came into existence over millions of years. Life created its own womb where multifarious forms could exist and flourish, as an interconnected and interdependent web. All living beings on Earth, including human beings, can exist only as part of and as dependent on this common fabric of life. While the most unique feature of Earth is the existence of life, the most extraordinary feature of life itself is its magnificent diversity.[1] Biological diversity (commonly referred to as biodiversity) refers precisely to the rich abundance of life, from genes through species and to ecosystems.[2] The role of biological diversity in making our

---

[1] Bradley J. Cardinale et al., "Biodiversity Loss and Its Impact on Humanity," *Nature* 486 (2012): 59.

[2] As Harvard biologist Edward O. Wilson has pointed out, as many as 10 billion bacteria, belonging to as many as 6,000 species, live in only one gram of fertile soil. Edward O. Wilson, *The Creation: An Appeal to Save Life on Earth* (New York: W. W. Norton, 2006), 18, 118.

home planet into a home or womb of life is not only invaluable but also indispensable.

It now appears that this web of life is coming under serious stress from the actions of its dominant species, namely, humanity. There is consensus in the scientific community today that the earth is on the verge of a sixth mass extinction of species and consequent loss of biodiversity. Biodiversity loss is yet another important facet of the contemporary ecological crisis—the global crisis that humanity is causing to the earth. The problem of species extinction is often underrated; it is overshadowed by the mounting concern for global warming and associated climate change. But the loss of biodiversity is a no less urgent threat to life on Earth.[3] The exclusive attention to climate change can lead to the obfuscation of the multidimensional ecological crisis, of which climate change is certainly a part but not all of the problem.[4] The problem of biodiversity loss is so huge and its consequences so far-reaching that it deserves much more attention than what is presently accorded to it.

In this chapter we first reflect on the importance of biological diversity for the functioning of the biosphere in general and for human well-being in particular. Second, we review the current situation of biodiversity on Earth, taking stock of how our home planet is precariously poised on the verge of a sixth mass extinction of species. We will see evidence of the conspicuously anthropogenic character of this phenomenon. Third, we will examine the main drivers behind the current spasm of mass extinction of species: habitat loss and degradation, climate change, overexploitation, pollution, and invasion of alien species. Finally, we dwell on the consequences of the loss of biodiversity, moving from immediate consequences for human physical and economic well-being to ethical, aesthetic, and religious considerations.

Biodiversity and Its Importance

Virtually every part of our home planet—the continents, the oceans, and the atmosphere—teems with life, which is infinitely diverse and of which humanity forms an essential part.

---

[3] Bo Normander, "Biodiversity: Combating the Sixth Mass Extinction," in *State of the World 2012: Moving Towards Sustainable Prosperity* (Washington, DC: Worldwatch Institute, 2012), 169.

[4] See also Michael J. Novacek, "Engaging the Public in Biodiversity Issues," *Proceedings of the National Academy of Sciences* 105 (2008): 11571, 11577; T. E. Lovejoy and L. Hannah, eds., *Climate Change and Biodiversity* (New Haven, CT: Yale University Press, 2005), 387–95.

"Biodiversity" is that rich spectrum of life—all of the world's species ranging from the smallest bacteria to the giant redwoods; from the algae in the sea to the wild dogs of the African savannahs; from the worms in the soil to the falcons soaring overhead. Biodiversity embraces all the bacteria and other microbes, many of which perform vital chemical functions to keep ecosystems functioning. Biodiversity also includes the green plants that produce oxygen through photosynthesis, trapping solar energy and storing it in the form of sugars that are the base of energy resources for all other forms of life.

Biodiversity includes the fungi—mushrooms and their kin, responsible for decay, nutrient cycling, and chemical building blocks so vital to keep life going. And biodiversity also encompasses the animals—everything from sponges to birds and mammals, including our own species, *Homo sapiens*.[5]

Scientists use the term *biodiversity* to refer to all life—plants, animals, and micro-organisms—and interactions among living organisms. The term was used by the Harvard-based scientist Edward O. Wilson[6]—the doyen of living biologists—in the 1988 proceedings from a conference held in 1986 organized by W. J. Rosen, who coined the term.[7] The Millennium Ecosystem Assessment defines biodiversity as "the variability among living organisms from all sources, including terrestrial, marine, and other aquatic ecosystems and the ecological complexes of which they are part; this includes diversity within species, between species, and of ecosystems."[8] As the *Global Environment Outlook* 4 of 2007 succinctly states, "Biodiversity is the variety of life on Earth."[9]

It is a paradox that in spite of all advances in human knowledge, we do not yet have a precise idea of the size of the family of life on Earth, of which we are an integral part. Even after decades of

---

[5] Niles Eldredge, *Life in the Balance: Humanity and the Biodiversity Crisis* (Princeton, NJ: Princeton University Press, 1998), vii.

[6] See Edward O. Wilson, ed., *Biodiversity* (Washington, DC: National Academy Press, 1988).

[7] See Novacek, "Engaging the Public in Biodiversity Issues," 11571.

[8] Millennium Ecosystem Assessment, *Ecosystems and Human Well-being: Biodiversity Synthesis* (Washington, DC: World Resources Institute, 2005), 18. The Millennium Ecosystem Assessment was a monumental work carried out between 2001 and 2005, involving 1,360 scientists from ninety-five countries. It encompassed both a global assessment and thirty-three sub-global assessments.

[9] United Nations Environment Programme, *The Global Environment Outlook 4: Environment for Development* (Nairobi: UNEP, 2007), 160.

painstaking work, only a fraction of the total species on Earth have been formally identified, between 1.7 and 2 million species. Probably fewer than 10 percent of living species have been identified and classified. Estimates of the total number of species on Earth range from 5 million to 30 million (and conceivably even 100 million).[10] The great tragedy is that a sizable portion of these are likely to be destroyed by humans before they have even been identified.

Biodiversity is crucial to the functioning of the biosphere. The biosphere, the realm of life that is the extraordinary, singularly unique feature of Earth, functions through a delicate equilibrium of an infinity of interactions among millions of living species.

> This layer of living organisms—the biosphere—through the collective metabolic activities of its innumerable plants, animals, and microbes physically and chemically unites the atmosphere, geosphere, and hydrosphere into one environmental system within which millions of species, including humans, have thrived. Breathable air, potable water, fertile soils, productive lands, bountiful seas, the equitable climate of Earth's history, and other ecosystem services are manifestations of the workings of life.[11]

Biodiversity plays a critical role in underpinning ecosystem services that are vital to the functioning of the biosphere. Biodiversity ensures the regulation of climate, biogeochemical cycles, and hydrological functions. The carbon cycle and the water cycle, arguably the two most important large-scale processes for life on Earth, both depend on biodiversity at genetic, species, and ecosystem levels.[12] Without the recycling of carbon and many other elements, life would quickly come to an end. While biodiversity is by no means the only driver of ecosystem functioning, which is also influenced by other abiotic factors, it plays a significant role in assisting the ecosystems to maintain

---

[10] Millennium Ecosystem Assessment, *Ecosystems and Human Well-being: Biodiversity Synthesis,* 19; Paul R. Ehrlich and Edward O. Wilson, "Biodiversity Studies: Science and Policy," *Science* 16 (1991): 758–62; Robert M. May, "How Many Species Are There on Earth?" *Science* 241 (1988): 1441–49; Richard Mackay, *The Atlas of Endangered Species* (London: Earthscan, 2005), 7, 15; "Biodiversity on the Brink" (editorial), *Nature Climate Change* 1 (2011): 275.

[11] Millennium Ecosystem Assessment, *Ecosystems and Human Well-being: Biodiversity Synthesis,* 18.

[12] Convention on Biological Diversity, "Biodiversity, Gender, and Climate Change" (Copenhagen, 2010), 1. Available online.

multiple functions, such as carbon storage,[13] nitrogen and nutrient cycling, waste decomposition, seed dispersal, soil fertility, and so on. Biodiversity provides the biospheric medium for energy and material flows, which in turn provide ecosystems with their functional properties.[14] The more diverse an ecosystem is, the more ecological functions it performs. The loss of biodiversity can impair how natural ecosystems function by reducing the quantity and quality of services they provide.[15]

Biodiversity is critical to the equilibrium of the entire biosphere. It is even more vital to human well-being, because it is the foundation of ecosystems that play a central role in supporting vital Earth systems upon which humanity depends. These services are often unrecognized or grossly undervalued. "The bacteria and microbes that transform waste into usable products, insects that pollinate crops and flowers, coral reefs and mangroves that protect coastlines, and the biologically-rich landscapes and seascapes that provide enjoyment are only a few" of these services.[16] Biodiversity underpins a wide range of ecosystem services on which human societies have always depended for survival—from food and fresh water to medicine and protection from natural disasters—and to fulfill their cultural and spiritual needs.

Ecosystem services that are critical in supporting human well-being can be divided broadly into four categories:

1. *Provisioning services*, namely, the supply of goods directly consumed by people. This includes food from agricultural and forest ecosystems, fish from the oceans, rivers and lakes, medicines (from plants, animals and seaweeds) and cosmetic products, wood, fiber (including textiles), fuel, etc. Our supply and quality of fresh water also depends on ecosystems which play a critical role in circulating, cleaning, and replenishing water supplies.

---

[13] It is estimated that for the period 2000–2008, land ecosystems removed roughly one-third of the CO_2 emitted by human activities. See The National Academy of Sciences, *Advancing the Science of Climate Change* (Washington, DC: The National Academies Press, 2010), 56.

[14] Norman Myers, "Environmental Services of Biodiversity," *Proceedings of the National Academy of Sciences* 93 (1996): 2765.

[15] See Fernando T. Maestre, "Plant Species Richness and Ecosystem Multifunctionality in Global Drylands," *Science* 335 (2012): 214–15.

[16] United Nations Environment Programme, *Global Environment Outlook 4*, 158.

2. *Regulating services,* which include a range of vital functions carried out by ecosystems. They include regulation of climate through the storing of carbon and control of local rainfall, the removal of pollutants by filtering the air and water, disease and pest regulation, protection from disasters such as landslides, avalanches, and especially from coastal storms through mangroves, coral reefs, kelp forests, etc.

3. *Supporting services,* which are essential to the functioning of ecosystems and therefore indirectly responsible for all other services. Examples are photosynthesis—a process fundamental to life on Earth, soil formation, nutrient cycling, etc. In fact, without ecosystems there would be no soil to support plants, and agriculture would be impossible. Another example is algae in ocean ecosystems which produce much of the oxygen that we breathe.

4. *Cultural and spiritual services,* which respond to deeper needs and aspirations of people. They include the spiritual value attached to particular ecosystems such as sacred groves, and the aesthetic beauty of landscapes which have non-measurable value for art, recreation and tourism.[17]

The contributions of biodiversity in terms of ecosystem services to human well-being are invaluable. Biodiversity benefits people through more than just its contribution to material welfare and livelihoods; it also contributes to security, resiliency, social relations, health, and freedom of choices and actions. As the basis for all ecosystem services, critical to the functioning of the entire biosphere and upon which human beings are entirely dependent, biodiversity plays a fundamental role in maintaining and enhancing the well-being of the world's more than 7 billion people, rich and poor, rural and urban alike.[18] Biodiversity and human well-being are thus inextricably linked. The General Assembly of the United Nations, probably spurred by this awareness, declared the period 2011–20 the United Nations Decade on Biodiversity.

It appears that biodiversity, so crucial to the functioning of the biosphere and to human well-being, is now increasingly under threat

---

[17] See Secretariat of the Convention on Biological Diversity, *Global Biodiversity Outlook 3* (2010), 23; The National Research Council, *Ecological Impacts of Climate Change* (Washington, DC: The National Academies Press, 2008), 2.

[18] See United Nations Environment Programme, *Global Environment Outlook* 4, 160.

as our home planet is moving toward a sixth great mass extinction of species.

Earth on the Brink of a Massive Loss of Biodiversity

Many scientists think that Earth is heading for a period of loss of biodiversity at an unprecedented scale. The decline in global biodiversity continues unabated, despite concerted efforts towards prevention and conservation. According to the Fourth Assessment Report of the IPCC in 2007, up to 30 percent of plant and animal species so far assessed are likely to be at increased risk of extinction if increases in global average temperatures exceed 1.5–2.5°C.[19] If the temperatures rise further under the business-as-usual scenario, the loss of biodiversity will be even greater. At the same time, climate change is only one of the contributing factors to species extinction, and the synergistic effect of various human activities on Earth's biodiversity can be even more devastating. Rigorous analyses of current and future scenarios consistently indicate that biodiversity will continue to decline over the twenty-first century and well into the future.[20]

Extinction is not a novelty in the evolutionary history of life on our home planet. In the past the biosphere has been exposed to climate variability and extremes and other natural events that have put pressure on Earth's biodiversity. Fossil evidence abounds with testimonies of how the long march of the evolution of life has suffered innumerable setbacks in terms of mass extinctions of species and consequent loss of biodiversity. Among these, five are canonically referred to as the great mass extinctions because of the wholesale severe biotic changes that occurred during each. These extinctions are listed below in chronological order:

1. the mass extinction at the end of the Ordovician era (nearly 439 million years ago), during which approximately 25 percent of the families and nearly 60 percent of the genera of marine organism were lost;

---

[19] A. Fischlin et al., "Ecosystems: Their Properties, Goods, and Services," in *Climate Change: Impacts, Adaptation and Vulnerability: Contribution of Working Group II to the Fourth Assessment Report of the Intergovernmental Panel on Climate Change*, ed. M. L. Parry et al. (Cambridge: Cambridge University Press, 2007), 213.

[20] See Henrique M. Pereira et al., "Scenarios for Global Biodiversity in the Twenty-First Century," *Science* 330 (2010): 1496–1501.

2. the late Devonian extinction (nearly 364 Mys), when 22 percent of marine families and 57 percent of marine genera disappeared;

3. the Permian-Triassic extinction (nearly 251 Mys), the worst of the five mass extinctions, during which 95 percent of all species (marine as well as terrestrial) were lost;

4. the End Triassic extinction (nearly 199–214 Mys) during which marine organisms were most strongly affected (22 percent of marine families and 53 percent of marine genera were lost);

5. and the most recent mass extinction at the Cretaceous-Tertiary boundary (nearly 65 Mys) during which went extinct, among other species, the nonavian dinosaurs.[21]

Scientists now believe that a sixth mass extinction is imminent and predict that coming decades will see the loss of large numbers of species.[22] There are already multiple indications of continuing decline in biodiversity in all three of its main components—genes, species, and ecosystems.[23] We shall briefly discuss this three-tier loss of biodiversity at the genetic, species, and ecosystem levels.

Genetic diversity is in decline in natural ecosystems and in crop and livestock production. The decline in the population of species, combined with the fragmentation of landscapes, inland water bodies, and marine habitats, has necessarily led to an overall significant

---

[21] For a detailed account of the five mass extinctions, see D. Jablonski, "Extinctions in the Fossil Record," in *Extinction Rates*, ed. J. H. Lawton and R. M. May (Oxford: Oxford University Press, 1995), 25–44. For a synthetic summary of the five mass extinctions, see David B. Wake and Vance T. Vredenburg, "Are We in the Midst of the Sixth Mass Extinction? A View from the World of Amphibians," *Proceedings of the National Academy of Sciences* 105 (2008): 11466. See also D. H. Erwin, "Lessons from the Past: Biotic Recoveries from Mass Extinctions," *Proceedings of the National Academy of Sciences* 98 (2001): 1399–1403.

[22] See Chris D. Thomas et al., "Extinction Risk from Climate Change," *Nature* 427 (2004): 145–48; J. A. Pounds et al., "Widespread Amphibian Extinctions from Epidemic Disease Driven by Global Warming," *Nature* 439 (2006): 161–67; John C. Avise and Stephen P. Hubbell and Francisco J. Ayala, "In the Light of Evolution II: Biodiversity and Extinction," *Proceedings of the National Academy of Sciences* 105 (2008): 11453; Wake and Vredenburg, "Are We in the Midst of the Sixth Mass Extinction?" 11466–73; Ilya M. D. Maclean and Robert J. Wilson, "Recent Ecological Responses to Climate Change Support Predictions of High Extinction Risk," *Proceedings of the National Academy of Sciences* 108 (2011): 12337.

[23] See Secretariat of the Convention on Biological Diversity, *Global Biodiversity Outlook 3*, 9.

decline in the genetic diversity of life on Earth.[24] It is feared that we may have already eradicated three-quarters of the planet's agricultural crop genetic diversity.[25] Of particular concern is the general trend toward homogenization that is such a strong characteristic of modern agriculture.

> While this [genetic] decline is of concern for many reasons, there is particular anxiety about the loss of diversity in the varieties and breeds of plants and animals used to sustain human livelihoods. A general homogenization of landscapes and agricultural varieties can make rural populations vulnerable to future changes if genetic traits kept over thousands of years are allowed to disappear.[26]

Examples of the drastic reduction of genetic biodiversity are found all over the world. It is estimated that crop diversity has been greatly reduced in China, with the number of local rice varieties being cultivated having witnessed a decline from 46,000 in the 1950s to slightly more than 1,000 in 2006. Loss of genetic diversity is evident also in the case of livestock breeds. Approximately 21 percent of the world's 7,000 livestock breeds are classified as being at risk, and a further 36 percent are of unknown risk status. More than sixty breeds are reported to have become extinct in the first decade of this century alone.[27]

Biodiversity loss at the species level is better known. Species in all groups with known trends are, on average, being driven closer to extinction, with amphibians facing the greatest risk. Amphibians are on average most threatened due to a combination of habitat modification, climate change, and fungal diseases. Of nearly 6,300 extant species of frogs, salamanders, and caecilians, at least one-third are currently threatened with extinction, and many more are likely to become so in the near future. Species of birds and mammals used for food and medicine are on average facing a greater extinction risk than species as a whole.[28] There has been a decline of 27 percent in populations

---

[24] Ibid., 51.

[25] Global Footprint Network, *2010 and Beyond: Rising to the Biodiversity Challenge* (Gland, Switzerland: WWF—World Wide Fund for Nature, 2008), 10.

[26] Secretariat of the Convention on Biological Diversity, *Global Biodiversity Outlook 3*, 51.

[27] Ibid.

[28] Ibid., 26.

of terrestrial, marine, and fresh-water vertebrate species from 1970 to 2005.[29] The population of wild vertebrate species fell by an average of nearly one-third (31 percent) globally between 1970 and 2006. The decline was especially severe in the tropics (59 percent) and in fresh-water ecosystems (41 percent).[30]

The loss of biodiversity is evident also in the increasing degradation of ecosystems. Forests are estimated to contain more than half of terrestrial animal and plant species, the great majority of them in the tropics. Deforestation, although showing signs of slowing in several tropical countries, continues at an alarmingly high rate. Between 2000 and 2010 the global extent of primary forest declined by more than 154,500 thousand square miles, an area slightly smaller than California.[31] Among other ecosystems, rivers and their floodplains along with lakes and wetlands have particularly suffered due to a combination of human activities, including drainage for agriculture; drainage for irrigation, industrial, and domestic use; the input of nutrients and other pollutants; the damming of rivers, and more. It is known that shallow-water wetlands such as marshes, swamps, and shallow lakes have declined significantly in many parts of the world. To cite one example, the fertile Mesopotamian marshes of Iraq lost more than 90 percent of their original extent between the 1970s and 2002.[32]

The oceans that cover three-quarters of the earth's surface also manifest direct evidence of biodiversity loss as marine ecosystems have come under duress from human impacts. Coastal habitats such as mangroves, salt marshes, and shellfish reefs show signs of decline in extent, threatening highly valuable ecosystem services, including the removal of significant quantities of carbon dioxide from the atmosphere. Mangrove forests are highly productive ecosystems in the intertidal zones of many tropical coastlines. They provide wood for local communities, act as a nursery for a wide range of commercially valuable fish stocks, and serve as a natural protection against offshore storms. It is estimated that about one-fifth of the world's mangroves, covering almost 14,000 square miles, were lost between

---

[29] Global Footprint Network, *2010 and Beyond: Rising to the Biodiversity Challenge. The Living Planet Index 2008*, 2, 4ff.

[30] Secretariat of the Convention on Biological Diversity, *Global Biodiversity Outlook 3*, 24.

[31] Ibid., 32. "Since newly-planted forests often have low biodiversity value and may only include a single tree species, a slowing of net forest loss does not necessarily imply a slowing in the loss of global forest biodiversity" (ibid.).

[32] Ibid., 42.

1980 and 2005.[33] Salt marshes have lost 25 percent of the area they originally covered globally. Of particular concern is the situation of the world's tropical coral reefs—the most species-rich marine ecosystem on Earth—that have suffered a significant global decline in biodiversity since the 1970s. Coral reefs cover just 1.2 percent of the world's continental shelves, but they act as a food source for between 500 million and 1 billion people, with around 30 million people in the poorest and most vulnerable coastal and inland communities entirely dependent on resources derived from coral reefs for their well-being. Coral reefs also support 1–3 million species, including approximately 25 percent of all marine fish species.[34] Jeremy Jackson notes, "Today, the synergistic effects of human impacts are laying the groundwork for a comparably great Anthropocene mass extinction in the oceans with unknown ecological and evolutionary consequences."[35]

What is striking about the current spasm of extinction is that it is much faster than natural rates. As Michael J. Novacek notes, there is a persistent and widespread misperception on the part of a vast segment of the general public that what we are witnessing is merely a wave of extinctions that are part of the normal turnover in the history of life. The underlying argument here is that life on Earth has experienced myriad extinction events over billions of years, and it will continue to thrive, irrespective of the current extinction spasms, offering new opportunities for new, better-adapted species.[36] However, the truth is that the current rates of species extinction exceed those of the historical past by several orders of magnitude and are bound to accelerate. It is estimated that the normal background rate of extinction is roughly 0.1–1.0 extinctions per million species per year.[37] But, according to the Millennium Ecosystem Assessment, "over the past few hundred years, humans have increased species extinction rates by as much as 1,000 times the background rates that

---

[33] Ibid., 46.

[34] Ibid.

[35] Jeremy B. C. Jackson, "Ecological Extinction and Evolution in the Brave New Ocean," *Proceedings of the National Academy of Sciences* 105 (2008): 11458.

[36] Novacek, "Engaging the Public in Biodiversity Issues," 11752. Novacek refers to a survey conducted a few years ago by the American Museum of Natural History. See American Museum of Natural History, *Biodiversity and the Next Millennium: A Nationwide Survey* (Nichols Hills, OK: Harris, 1998).

[37] Millennium Ecosystem Assessment, *Ecosystems and Human Well-being: Biodiversity Synthesis*, 21.

were typical over Earth's history."[38] According to the same report the current extinction rate is up to 1,000 times higher than the fossil record when it comes to birds, mammals, and amphibians.[39] In fact, scientists fear that extinction rates will increase to 1,000 to 10,000 times background rates over the coming decades.[40] Our planetary home is on the verge of an unprecedented loss of biodiversity.

Current Spasm of Biodiversity Loss as Driven by Human Activities

A unique feature of the coming sixth mass extinction of species is that while the five previous mass extinctions were caused by physical or natural causes, the present one is being caused by one species alone—Homo sapiens. As the Millennium Ecosystem Assessment points out, although biodiversity and ecosystem services experience change due to natural causes, current change is dominated by anthropogenic drivers. Human actions are fundamentally, and to a significant extent irreversibly, changing the diversity of life on Earth, and often these changes represent a loss of biodiversity.[41]

The anthropogenic fingerprints of the current mass extinction of species are clearly evident when we examine the underlying causes of the current spasm of biodiversity loss. The most important anthropogenic drivers of biodiversity loss are habitat loss and degradation, climate change, overexploitation of natural resources, pollution, and introduction of alien species and exotic organisms into native ecosystems.[42] We briefly examine each of these in order to see how human activities are directly contributing to the loss of biodiversity.

---

[38] Ibid., 3.

[39] Ibid., 4.

[40] Ibid., 43. See also Pereira et al., "Scenarios for Global Biodiversity in the Twenty-First Century," 1497.

[41] Millennium Ecosystem Assessment, *Ecosystems and Human Well-being: Biodiversity Synthesis*, 2, 8. See also Eldredge, *Life in the Balance*, ix–x; Heffa Schücking and Patrick Anderson, "Voices Unheard and Unheeded," in *Biodiversity: Social and Ecological Perspectives*, ed. Vandana Shiva et al. (London: Zed Books, 1991), 16.

[42] Millennium Ecosystem Assessment, *Ecosystems and Human Well-being: Biodiversity Synthesis*, vi, 8; Secretariat of the Convention on Biological Diversity, *Global Biodiversity Outlook 3*, 55ff. For a synthetic presentation of these five principal causes for the loss of biodiversity see United Nations Environment Programme, *Global Environment Outlook 4*, 169.

Habitat Loss and Degradation

Habitat loss and degradation create the biggest single source of pressure on biodiversity worldwide today. Habitat loss driven by agriculture and unsustainable forest management is estimated to be the greatest cause of species moving closer to extinction.[43] Habitat conversion occurs particularly from conversion of land for agriculture, which affects terrestrial ecosystems. "Global market demand for high value commodities such as soya beans, coffee, cotton, oil palm, horticultural crops and biofuels, has resulted in substantial habitat conversion and ecosystem degradation."[44] Cultivated systems now cover more than one-quarter of Earth's terrestrial surface, a ratio that is only bound to shoot up with the burgeoning human population, which is predicted to exceed 9 billion by mid-century.

The conversion of forest land can lead directly to extinction of species. It is known from global mapping studies that nearly 50 percent of all temperate grasslands, tropical dry forests, and temperate broadleaf forests have been converted to human-dominated uses worldwide.[45] The threat of the loss of biodiversity is acute when the tropical forests—especially those considered "hot spots" of biodiversity—come under attack.[46] Michael S. Northcott notes:

> The biggest single cause of species extinction is the destruction of the rainforests of Amazonia, Central Africa and South East Asia. These areas are the richest in species diversity on the planet, and the ecosystem of the forest is fragile. Three or four hectares [7.5–10 acres] of rainforest in South East Asia or Central America contain more tree species than the whole of Europe or North America. These trees are in turn home to thousands of species of insects, birds, epiphytic plants and reptiles. Tropical

---

[43] Secretariat of the Convention on Biological Diversity, *Global Biodiversity Outlook 3*, 55; Millennium Ecosystem Assessment, *Ecosystems and Human Well-being: Biodiversity Synthesis*, 8; Fischlin et al., "Ecosystems," 216; Pereira et al., "Scenarios for Global Biodiversity in the Twenty-First Century," 1499.

[44] United Nations Environment Programme, *Global Environment Outlook 4*, 167.

[45] J. M. Hoekstra et al., "Confronting a Biome Crisis: Global Disparities of Habitat Loss and Protection," *Ecology Letters* 8 (2005): 23–29.

[46] See Xingli Giam et al., "Reservoirs of Richness: Least Disturbed Tropical Forests Are Centres of Undescribed Species Diversity," *Proceedings of the Royal Society B* (published online May 18, 2011): 1–10.

rainforests cover only 6 percent of the earth's surface and yet contain around 90 percent of its species.[47]

It is said that the island of Madagascar alone once contained around 12,000 plant species and possibly 190,000 animal species, 60 percent of which were unique to the island. With 93 percent of the original forest gone, scientists estimate that more than half of the original species have disappeared.[48] The recent demand for biofuels has also added to the pressure on cultivable land. It has been found that the conversion of forest to oil palm plantations, as is currently happening on a massive scale in Indonesia and elsewhere in Southeast Asia, can lead to the loss of 73–83 percent of the bird and butterfly species of the ecosystem.[49] The habitat losses in the tropics cannot be compensated by forest habitat gains in temperate regions, as the latter are notably species-poor in comparison.

Human activities have greatly reduced the amount of land area available to wild species. Infrastructure developments such as housing, industrial developments, mines, and transport networks contribute to conversion of terrestrial habitats. In the same way, the depletion of fresh water—increasingly used for irrigated agriculture and industry—and the construction of dams and flood levees on rivers can lead to the degradation of habitats and put pressures on biodiversity. Habitat loss also occurs in coastal and marine ecosystems, especially due to coastal developments for housing, recreation, industry, and transportation, and damage to sea floors due to trawling.[50] The impact of habitat transformation on biodiversity is complex. It affects not only species richness and diversity, but also the patterns of species interactions that link them in networks and the functions that species perform.[51] It is

---

[47] Michael S. Northcott, *A Moral Climate: The Ethics of Global Warming* (London: Darton, Longman, and Todd/Christian Aid, 2007), 21. See also World Commission on Environment and Development, *Our Common Future* (Oxford: Oxford University Press, 1987), 150; Norman Myers, *The Primary Source: Tropical Forests and Our Future* (New York: W. W. Norton, 1984), 106.

[48] World Commission on Environment and Development, *Our Common Future*, 149.

[49] Secretariat of the Convention on Biological Diversity, *Global Biodiversity Outlook 3*, 55.

[50] See Ibid., 55; The National Academy of Sciences, *Advancing the Science of Climate Change*, 275; Millennium Ecosystem Assessment, *Ecosystems and Human Well-being: Biodiversity Synthesis*, 8.

[51] Andrew Gonzalez et al., "The Disentangled Bank: How Loss of Habitat Fragments and Disassembles Ecological Networks," *American Journal of Botany* 98 (2011): 503.

obvious, then, why habitat loss and degradation take such a heavy toll on biodiversity on our home planet.

Climate Change

Climate change is already having an impact on biodiversity and is projected to become a progressively more significant threat in the coming decades—as we have already seen in the previous chapter with regard to the impacts of climate change. Global warming and its associated climate change may be the largest anthropogenic disturbances ever placed on natural systems.[52] Warmer temperatures are already having significant impacts on biodiversity and ecosystems. Ecosystems have already shown negative impacts, with an increase of 0.74°C in global mean surface temperature relative to pre-industrial levels. By the end of the twenty-first century, with a projected increase of 1.8–6.4°C, climate change and its impacts may be the dominant direct drivers of biodiversity loss and changes in ecosystem services globally.[53] As the 2007 report of the IPCC notes, during the course of this century the resilience of many ecosystems is likely to be exceeded by an unprecedented combination of change in climate and associated disturbances (for example, flooding, drought, wildfire, ocean acidification) if greenhouse gas emissions continue at or above current rates.[54] The report goes on to warn:

> By 2100, ecosystems will be exposed to atmospheric CO_2 levels substantially higher than in the past 650,000 years, and global temperatures at least among the highest of those experienced in the past 740,000 years. This will alter the structure, reduce biodiversity and perturb functioning of most ecosystems, and compromise the services they currently provide. ... With global average temperature changes of 2°C above pre-industrial levels, many terrestrial, freshwater and marine species (particularly endemics across the globe) are at a far greater risk of extinction than in the recent geological past. [55]

---

[52] See O. E. Sala et al., "Biodiversity: Global Biodiversity Scenarios for the Year 2100," *Science* 287 (2000): 1770–74. See also Maclean and Wilson, "Recent Ecological Responses to Climate Change Support Predictions of High Extinction Risk," 12337.

[53] Secretariat of the Convention on Biological Diversity, *Global Biodiversity Outlook 3*, 55; Millennium Ecosystem Assessment, *Ecosystems and Human Well-being: Biodiversity Synthesis*, 10, 56–57.

[54] Fischlin et al., "Ecosystems," 213.

[55] Ibid.

It is feared that 15–37 percent of regional endemic species could be committed to extinction as early as 2050 due to climate change.[56] A special area of concern is the Arctic, where the highest rates of warming have been observed. The prospect of ice-free summers in the Arctic Ocean within decades can mean the loss of entire ecosystems in the region. It can also affect biodiversity well beyond the region, as changes will reverberate on factors like ocean circulation, temperature, and salinity.[57] In a similar way, it is feared that strong drying over the Amazon, as predicted by several climate models, may result in dieback of forests with the highest biodiversity on the planet.[58] It should be remembered that climate change and biodiversity are interconnected. Biodiversity is affected by climate change, but conservation and promotion of biodiversity can also be powerful means to mitigate climate change.

Overexploitation of Natural Resources

The overexploitation of natural resources and their unsustainable use also drive species extinction and loss of biodiversity. Overexploitation and destructive harvesting practices lie at the heart of the threats being imposed on world's biodiversity and ecosystems. The most vivid example of the pressure being exerted on ecosystems by overexploitation is the case of world's fisheries. It is estimated that marine capture fisheries quadrupled in size globally from the early 1950s to the mid-1990s.[59] About three-quarters of the world's commercial marine fisheries are either fully exploited (50 percent) or overexploited (25 percent).[60] Many stocks appear to have been pushed beyond their capacity to replenish. Top piscivores suffer disproportionately in oceans as fleets fish down the food web.[61]

---

[56] Thomas et al., "Extinction Risk from Climate Change," 145–48.

[57] Secretariat of the Convention on Biological Diversity, *Global Biodiversity Outlook 3*, 56–57.

[58] Nicholas Stern, *The Economics of Climate Change* (Cambridge: Cambridge University Press, 2007), 93.

[59] Secretariat of the Convention on Biological Diversity, *Global Biodiversity Outlook 3*, 62; B. Groombridge and M. D. Jenkins, eds., *World Atlas of Biodiversity: Earth's Living Resources in the Twenty-First Century* (Los Angeles and Berkeley: University of California Press, 2002), 147.

[60] Millennium Ecosystem Assessment, *Ecosystems and Human Well-being: Biodiversity Synthesis*, 8; Secretariat of the Convention on Biological Diversity, *Biodiversity, Development, and Poverty Alleviation: Recognizing the Role of Biodiversity for Human Well-being* (2009), 7.

[61] D. Pauly et al., "Fishing down Marine Food Webs," *Science* 279 (1998): 860–63.

The various sources of energy for human activities—for which demand is projected to grow at least 53 percent by 2030—contribute directly or indirectly to biodiversity stress or loss.[62] In this process humankind has also appropriated for itself a disproportionate amount of Earth's resources, depriving the rest of the biotic community. According to Paul Ehrlich, "Human beings now use or co-opt some 40 percent of the food available to all land animals and about 45 percent of the available freshwater flows."[63]

Pollution

As for pollution, since 1950 nutrient loading—anthropogenic increases in nitrogen, phosphorus, sulphur, and other nutrient-associated pollutants—has emerged as one of the principal drivers of ecosystem change in terrestrial, fresh-water, and coastal ecosystems, a driver that is projected to increase substantially in the future.[64] Humans are increasingly polluting and toxifying the earth's ecosystems. A particular area of concern is the rapid changes being brought to the natural nitrogen cycle.

Nitrogen deposition has become a major driver of species change in a range of temperate ecosystems, especially grasslands across Europe and North America, while high levels of nitrogen have also been recorded in southern China and parts of South and Southeast Asia. Large parts of Latin America and Africa, as well as Asia, are projected to experience elevated levels of nitrogen deposition in the coming decades. The impacts of nitrogen buildup on species will be especially severe in biodiversity hotspots.[65] Pollution in terms of nutrient loading has a dire impact on inland and marine ecosystems as well. It has also led to the creation of literal "dead zones" in some areas of Earth's oceans.

In inland water and coastal ecosystems, the buildup of phosphorous and nitrogen, mainly through run-off from cropland and sewage pollution, stimulates the growth of algae and some forms

---

[62] For the impacts of various energy sources on biodiversity, see United Nations Environment Programme, *Global Environment Outlook 4*, 176, 179.

[63] Paul R. Ehrlich and Anne H. Ehrlich, *Betrayal of Science and Reason: How Anti-Environmental Rhetoric Threatens Our Future* (Washington, DC: Island Press, 1998), 14. See also Wilson, *The Creation*, 29.

[64] Millennium Ecosystem Assessment, *Ecosystems and Human Well-being: Biodiversity Synthesis* (Washington, DC: Island Press, 2005), 8, 53–54; Secretariat of the Convention on Biological Diversity, *Global Biodiversity Outlook 3*, 59–60.

[65] Secretariat of the Convention on Biological Diversity, *Global Biodiversity Outlook 3*, 59–60.

of bacteria, threatening valuable ecosystem services in systems such as lakes and coral reefs, and affecting water quality. It also creates "dead zones" in oceans, generally where major rivers reach the sea. In these zones, decomposing algae use up oxygen in the water and leave large areas virtually devoid of marine life. The number of reported dead zones has been roughly doubling every ten years since the 1960s, and by 2007 had reached around 500.[66]

Introduction of Alien Species and Exotic Organisms

The introduction of alien species and exotic organisms into native ecosystems have also wrought havoc on local biodiversity. It is a phenomenon still under study and scrutiny.[67] "Among the many threats to global biodiversity, the transport of species across historically distinct biogeographic boundaries remains one of the most enigmatic."[68] Invasive plant species are typically thought to pose a large threat to native biodiversity. The arrival of non-native species result in competition with and predation on native species, changes in ecosystem functions and genetic contamination, extinctions of some native species, and homogenization of the species with significant reduction in biodiversity. Trade patterns worldwide suggest that the size of the invasive alien species problem is increasing globally. Invasive species are the second leading cause of extinction for endemic species.[69]

Evidently, the synergistic effects or combined pressures of the various drivers of biodiversity loss acting together are greater than the sum of the single causes. In fact, the drivers do not act in isolation on biodiversity and ecosystems; frequently, one pressure exacerbates the impacts of another. For example, the fragmentation of habitats reduces the capacity of species to adapt to climate change by limiting the possibilities of migration to more suitable areas. In a similar way, pollution, overfishing, climate change, and ocean acidification all

---

[66] Ibid., 60.

[67] See Benjamin Gilbert and Jonathan M. Levine, "Plant Invasions and Extinction Debts," *Proceedings of the National Academy of Sciences* 110 (2013): 1744–49.

[68] Kristin I. Powell et al., "A Synthesis of Plant Invasion Effects on Biodiversity Across Spatial Scales," *American Journal of Botany* 98 (2011): 539. For a discussion in this regard see the whole article, 539–48.

[69] United Nations Environment Programme, *Global Environment Outlook 4*, 169; Secretariat of the Convention on Biological Diversity, *Global Biodiversity Outlook 3*, 64–65.

combine to weaken the resilience of coral reefs, which are rich in bio-diversity. It is the synergistic interactions of the various direct drivers that lead to the increased risk of irreversible extinctions.[70] It should be remembered that underlying the direct drivers of biodiversity loss are indirect drivers like demographic change, economic activity, con-sumption patterns, and so on.

> Indirect drivers primarily act on biodiversity by influencing the quantity of resources used by human societies. So for example population increase, combined with higher per capita consump-tion, will tend to increase demand for energy, water and food— each of which contribute to direct pressures such as habitat conversion, over-exploitation of resources, nutrient pollution and climate change. Increased world trade has been a key indirect driver of the introduction of invasive alien species.[71]

Finally, as with regard to other manifestations of the contemporary ecological crisis, there is the risk of tipping points in the case of bio-diversity loss. As the *Global Biodiversity Outlook* warns: "There is a high risk of dramatic biodiversity loss and accompanying degrada-tion of a broad range of ecosystem services if ecosystems are pushed beyond certain critical thresholds or tipping points."[72] A tipping point in this context would be a situation in which an ecosystem either collapses or experiences an abrupt shift to a new state as a result of human interference, with significant changes to biodiversity and the services to people it underpins at regional or global levels. It func-tions, as in the case of climate change, through positive feedbacks. For example, deforestation reduces regional rainfall, which increases fire risk, which in turn causes forest dieback and further drying. In the context of biodiversity loss, one such tipping point could be the Amazon forest, which on account of the synergistic interactions of the various drivers of biodiversity loss like climate change, deforestation, droughts, wild fires, and others could undergo a widespread dieback and eventually shift to savannah-like vegetation. Other biodiversity tipping point zones include the Sahel in Africa, island ecosystems, and the tropical coral reefs. It should also be remembered that once a threshold point has been crossed and an ecosystem switches to a

---

[70] See Fischlin et al., "Ecosystems," 213.

[71] Secretariat of the Convention on Biological Diversity, *Global Biodiversity Outlook 3*, 67.

[72] Ibid., 10.

new state, it can be very difficult if not impossible to return it to its former state.[73]

As is evident from the above analysis, virtually all the factors leading to the accelerating loss of biodiversity have to do with human activities. As the Millennium Ecosystem Assessment indicates, effectively all of Earth's ecosystems have now been dramatically transformed through human actions, which are fundamentally, and to a significant extent irreversibly, changing the diversity of life on Earth.[74] It can rightly be concluded that "there is no doubt that humans are the root cause of most ecosystem stresses and biotic extinctions in the modern world."[75]

Implications of the Loss of Biodiversity

The massive loss of biodiversity is bound to have important repercussions for human well-being at all levels. Let us consider the main consequences of the loss of biodiversity, moving from immediate consequences for human physical and economic well-being to ethical, aesthetic, and spiritual considerations.

A preliminary consideration is in order before going on to spell out the implications of the loss of biodiversity for human well-being. The approach of putting an "economic" cost on environmental services in order to assess the implications of species extinction—a trend that appears to be becoming increasingly popular today—is not the best one to adopt. While such an approach has some obvious merits,[76] the attempt to offer an economic view of environmental services proves insufficient in real terms. This is so because the importance of biodiversity and natural processes in producing ecosystem services that people depend on is not captured in the current financial market systems. As pointed out by the Millennium Ecosystem Assessment, "A country could cut its forests and deplete its fisheries which would show only as a positive gain to GDP, under the economic scenario, despite the

[73] Martin Scheffer et al., "Catastrophic Shifts in Ecosystems," *Nature* 413 (2001): 591; Secretariat of the Convention on Biological Diversity, *Global Biodiversity Outlook 3*, 10, 71–74; Fischlin et al., "Ecosystems," 219.

[74] Millennium Ecosystem Assessment, *Ecosystems and Human Well-being: Biodiversity Synthesis*, 2.

[75] Avise, Hubbell, and Ayala, "In the Light of Evolution II: Biodiversity and Extinction," 11453.

[76] See TEEB, "The Economics of Ecosystems and Biodiversity: Mainstreaming the Economics of Nature: A Synthesis of the Approach, Conclusions, and Recommendations of TEEB" (2010). Available online.

loss of the capital asset of biodiversity."[77] Unlike goods bought and sold in markets, many ecosystem services do not have markets or readily observable prices. In fact, biodiversity loss continues because the values of biodiversity are insufficiently recognized by political and market systems.[78] In addition, many people recognize that biodiversity has an intrinsic value that cannot be valued in conventional economic terms.[79] Besides, as will be made evident further ahead, the loss of biodiversity has enormous implications when it comes to cultural, aesthetic, ethical, and spiritual considerations, spheres that defy and transcend economic costs and calculations.

With the loss of biodiversity, nothing less is at stake than human physical well-being; humans depend on the intricate network of other species and biomass for their physical existence and survival. As we have seen earlier, biodiversity is the foundation for basic ecosystem services beginning with the oxygen humans breathe, the regulation of climate and of the bio-geochemical cycles, the pollination of crops and flowers by insects—a process fundamental to agriculture—soil protection, coral reefs and mangroves that protect coastlines, and a number of miscellaneous services. Biodiversity and the ecosystem services it provides sustain ecological functions on which all forms of life, especially human beings, depend.

At the immediate physical level the loss of biodiversity will have a strong impact on human livelihoods, especially in the areas of food security and health. A significant contribution of biodiversity is to human diet. It is estimated that about one-third of the human diet depends on insect-pollinated vegetables, legumes, and fruits.[80] According to the Millennium Ecosystem Assessment, "About 7,000 species of plants and several hundred species of animals have been used for human food consumption at one time or another. Some indigenous and traditional communities currently consume 200 or more species. Wild sources of food remain particularly important for the poor and landless to provide a somewhat balanced diet."[81] The current projected

---

[77] Millennium Ecosystem Assessment, *Ecosystems and Human Well-being: Biodiversity Synthesis*, 6.

[78] United Nations Environment Programme, *Global Environment Outlook 4*, 185.

[79] Millennium Ecosystem Assessment, *Ecosystems and Human Well-being: Biodiversity Synthesis*, 7; United Nations Environment Programme, *Global Environment Outlook 4*, 160.

[80] Myers, "Environmental Services of Biodiversity," 2766.

[81] Millennium Ecosystem Assessment, *Ecosystems and Human Well-being: Biodiversity Synthesis*, 31.

mass extinction of species has dire implications on food security for the masses.

Human health too depends largely on biodiversity and ecosystem services. Nature is a natural pharmacopoeia, with new drugs and medicines being discovered all the time. It is roughly estimated that 80 percent of people in developing countries rely on medicines based largely on plants and animals. More than half of all prescription medicines, including some of the most effective anti-cancer drugs, heart medicines, and antibiotics, were originally derived from living organisms.[82] At current extinction rates of plants and animals, Earth is said to be losing one major drug every two years. It is estimated that less than 1 percent of the world's 250,000 tropical plants has been screened for potential pharmaceutical applications. And among the 52,000 medicinal plants used today, about 8 percent are already threatened with extinction.[83] It should also be noted that the widespread anthropogenic changes to the ecosystems have altered patterns of human disease and increased pressures on human well-being. Some ecosystem changes create new habitat niches for disease vectors, for example, increasing the risk of malaria in Africa and the Amazon Basin.[84] According to the *Global Environmental Outlook*:

> Emerging diseases resulting from the destruction and fragmentation of tropical forests and other ecosystems, wildlife-human disease linkages (for example, Lyme disease, West Nile virus and avian influenza), the many known and as yet undiscovered pharmaceutical products found in nature, the contribution of ecosystem services to human health and the increasing recognition of the impacts of endocrine disrupters on both animal and

---

[82] Steven Kolmes, "Mental Cartography in a Time of Environmental Crisis," in *All Creation Is Groaning: An Interdisciplinary Vision for Life in a Sacred Universe*, ed. Carol J. Dempsey and Russell A. Butkus (Collegeville, MN: The Liturgical Press, 1999), 116. Childhood leukemia, once almost invariably fatal, is now one of the most curable cancers thanks to alkaloid compounds from the rosy periwinkle of Madagascar (ibid.).

[83] Secretariat of the Convention on Biological Diversity, *Biodiversity, Development, and Poverty Alleviation*, 7.

[84] United Nations Environment Programme, *Global Environment Outlook 4*, 167. See A. Y. Vittor et al., "The Effects of Deforestation on the Human-Biting Rate of Anopheles Darlingi, the Primary Vector of Falciparum Malaria in the Peruvian Amazon," *American Journal of Tropical Medicine and Hygiene* 74 (2006): 3–11.

human health, all underline the links between biodiversity and human health.[85]

It is important to note that the effects of species extinction and resultant biodiversity loss will be felt mostly by particularly vulnerable groups, as it strikes the poor most. Today, about 1 billion people live a subsistence lifestyle, and loss of ecosystem productivity (through loss of soil fertility, drought, or overfishing) can lead to malnutrition, stunted childhood growth and development, and increased susceptibility to other diseases. For those living in extreme poverty, maintaining ecosystem goods and services is critical for daily survival.[86]

Many aspects of biodiversity decline have a disproportionate impact on poor people. The decline in fish population, for example, has major implications for artisanal fishers and the communities that depend on fish as an important source of protein. As dryland resources are degraded, it is the poor and vulnerable who suffer the most.[87]

The loss of biodiversity, or changes in biodiversity patterns due to the mass extinction of species, will affect the rural poor most. It is estimated that 70 percent of the world's poor live in rural areas that depend directly on biodiversity for their survival and well-being. Rural men and women—among the world's most poor and vulnerable groups—are most directly dependent on ecosystem services at the local level for a particularly high proportion of their basic needs, and they are unable to pay for alternatives. The poor stand to suffer disproportionately from potentially catastrophic changes to ecosystems in coming decades.

The loss of biodiversity also has other implications. As the *Global Environmental Outlook* recognizes, "Human societies everywhere have depended on biodiversity for cultural identity, spirituality, inspiration, aesthetic enjoyment and recreation."[88] In fact, the importance

---

[85] United Nations Environment Programme, *Global Environment Outlook 4*, 180.

[86] Ibid., 180. See also Secretariat of the Convention on Biological Diversity, *Biodiversity, Development, and Poverty Alleviation*, 26.

[87] Millennium Ecosystem Assessment, *Ecosystems and Human Well-being: Biodiversity Synthesis*, 6.

[88] United Nations Environment Programme, *Global Environment Outlook 4*, 159.

of species in providing these services is inestimable. At the aesthetic level it is important to recognize how the wonder, beauty, and tranquility of nature provide human beings with solace and inspiration. Today, for example, biodiversity plays a vital part in the sector of ecotourism (nature-based tourism), one of the fastest growing segments of tourism worldwide.

At the social level many cultures attach spiritual and religious values to ecosystems or their components, such as a tree, hill, river, or grove. "Damage to ecosystems, highly valued for their aesthetic, recreational, or spiritual values can damage social relationships, both by reducing the bonding value of shared experience as well as by causing resentment toward groups that profit from their damage."[89]

At the spiritual level it is disheartening to realize that there has been a decline in the numbers of sacred groves and other such protected areas. "The loss of particular ecosystem values attributes (sacred species or sacred forests), combined with social and economic changes, can sometimes weaken the spiritual benefits people obtain from ecosystems."[90] Ecosystems serve for many cultural groups, especially indigenous and tribal communities, as a source of their cultural and spiritual identity. Thus, the loss of biodiversity on account of species extinction has implications that go beyond the immediate considerations about human physical or economic well-being. For these communities, cultural and biological diversity are closely intertwined, and the elements that bind them together are almost always spiritual considerations.

> For many people biodiversity and culture cannot be considered independently of one another. This is particularly true for the more than 400 million indigenous and local community members for whom the Earth's biodiversity is not only a source of wellbeing but also the foundation of their cultural and spiritual identities. The close association between biodiversity and culture is particularly apparent in sacred sites, those areas which are held to be of importance because of their religious or spiritual significance.[91]

---

[89] Millennium Ecosystem Assessment, *Ecosystems and Human Well-being: Biodiversity Synthesis*, 31.

[90] Ibid., 36.

[91] Secretariat of the Convention on Biological Diversity, *Global Biodiversity Outlook 3*, 40.

From a religious perspective, extinction of a species or the degradation of an ecosystem means that the integrity of creation is seriously compromised.[92] We return to this point in the fourth and final part of the book, where we look at the contemporary ecological crisis from a spiritual and theological perspective.

The loss of biodiversity is frequently linked to the loss of cultural identity, which in turn precedes the actual physical extinction of a people. Along with the disappearance of species and the resultant collapse of entire ecosystems, cultural traditions, identities, and memories of local communities become extinct once and for all. Testimonies abound in various parts of our globe of scores of tribal cultures and communities that have been driven to extinction following the devastation of their native habitats. Niles Eldredge notes, "All too often indigenous human groups—*especially* hunter-gatherers—are victims every bit as much as are the animals and plants of a ravaged ecosystem."[93] Unfortunately, this is a tragedy that is still unfolding in many parts of the world. Conversely, cultural changes such as the loss of indigenous languages can act as indirect drivers of biodiversity loss by affecting local practices of conservation and sustainable use of natural resources.[94]

The implications of the loss of biodiversity are thus far-reaching, moving from immediate consequences for human physical well-being to ethical, aesthetic, social, and spiritual repercussions.

The Death of Birth and the Rupture of the Web of Interdependence

Extinction is annihilation of life itself for the particular species driven out of existence, with dire implications for the entire web of life. The mass extinction of species is not just death for the individual species concerned but a death of birth itself. Once a species becomes extinct, we cannot get it back.

Here one might object that extinction is in nature's natural rhythm, that it has always been part of life on Earth, and that is the ultimate fate awaiting all species. This objection has been responded to earlier in this chapter. The key element to remember here is the

---

[92] Sean McDonagh, *The Greening of the Church* (Maryknoll, NY: Orbis Books, 1990), 88.

[93] Eldredge, *Life in the Balance*, 38.

[94] See Secretariat of the Convention on Biological Diversity, *Global Biodiversity Outlook 3*, 67.

vast difference between the current mass extinction of species and the natural background extinction rates. While the normal background rates of extinction were roughly 0.1–1.0 extinctions per million species per year, the current rates of extinction of species is nearly 10,000 times more than the background rates and is bound to accelerate.[95]

What takes place with the extinction of species is the loss of evolutionary history along with its biological legacy,[96] as no living traces of the extant species remain. Every extinction also represents the loss of irreplaceable genetic information. "Each living thing contains 1–10 billion bits of information in its genetic code, acquired by an astronomical number of mutations and episodes of natural selection over millions of years. It is this process that has enabled life to adapt to an incredible diversity of environmental circumstances."[97] It is a colossal loss for humanity too. "As biodiversity recedes, we also lose the stories that go with it and many ways of relating to the world in which we evolved."[98]

The effects of mass extinctions extend beyond the losses observed during the event itself. The loss of species threatens to impoverish future diversity.[99] The present mass extinction of species will alter not only biological diversity but also the evolutionary processes by which diversity is generated. In short, the current mass extinction of species will slice into both the legacy and future of evolution.

Public awareness about the specter of the sixth mass extinction of species is on the increase. However, "not so well known but probably more significant in the long term is that the crisis will surely disrupt and deplete certain basic processes of evolution, with consequences likely to persist for millions of years."[100] Recovery proceeds slowly in the wake of biotic disruption on a grand scale. From the geological records of past mass extinctions it can be calculated that the timespan

---

[95] See Millennium Ecosystem Assessment, *Ecosystems and Human Well-being: Biodiversity Synthesis*, 21, 43.

[96] See Douglas H. Erwin, "Extinction as the Loss of Evolutionary History," *Proceedings of the National Academy of Sciences* 105 (2008): 11520–27.

[97] David Toolan, *At Home in the Cosmos* (Maryknoll, NY: Orbis Books, 2001), 90.

[98] Paul Ehrlich and Robert M. Pringle, "Where Does Biodiversity Go from Here? A Grim Business-as-Usual Forecast and a Hopeful Portfolio of Partial Solutions," *Proceedings of the National Academy of Sciences* 105 (2008): 11580.

[99] See Michael L. Rosenzweig, "Loss of Speciation Rate Will Impoverish Future Diversity," *Proceedings of the National Academy of Sciences* 98 (2001): 5404–10.

[100] Norman Myers and Andrew H. Knoll, "The Biotic Crisis and the Future of Evolution," *Proceedings of the National Academy of Sciences* 98 (2001): 5389.

required for re-diversification and ecological reorganization is around 5 million years—a broadly representative recovery time.[101] The sober conclusion that one arrives at in the face of such a realization is that the ecological disruption of the current mass extinction of species is going to be permanent, as far the human chronological timescale is concerned.

The above reflection about the annihilation of life—and of birth— as it takes place in the current mass extinction of species raises several questions. One of them is about the responsibility of current generations, who are causing the extinction ripple in the first place, to future generations, who will be deprived of vast portions of the current biodiversity available on the planet.

To willfully cause extinction of species—as humanity is currently doing—is to rupture the common fabric of life that sustains all living beings on Earth. In the physical world the species are not only interrelated but are also interdependent. The biological interdependence of organisms is explicit in the case of the food chain composed of photosynthesizing plants, herbivores, carnivores, and decomposers (microbes and fungi). A species or biota cannot be seen in isolation from its support system. "A mammal species, a butterfly community, a wetland food web, or a forest ecosystem cannot exist except within the myriad ecological relationships and ecosystem processes (moisture supply, nutrient cycling, energy flow, and the like) of its environs.[102] The species are in themselves the fabric of ecosystems, which in turn provide essential services. The specter of the current mass extinction of species threatens precisely the complex interdependencies of the biotic community on which human life depends. Paul Ehrlich refers to species as rivets that hold together the airplane in which we circuit the sun. This analogy implies that the loss of species may threaten the continued existence of the biotic community. At some point so many rivets may be removed from the plane that it is bound to crash.[103] Such crashes can come even earlier when keystone species are driven

---

[101] Myers and Knoll, "The Biotic Crisis and the Future of Evolution," 5389. "When the dinosaurs became extinct 65 million years ago, it took 5 to 10 million years before biodiversity returned to the previous levels. Biodiversity—the available gene pool—is effectively irreplaceable. Once lost, for all practical purposes it cannot be regained" (Toolan, *At Home in the Cosmos*, 90).

[102] Myers, "Environmental Services of Biodiversity," 2765.

[103] Paul R. Ehrlich, *Extinction: The Implications of the Loss of Our Biological Heritage* (Murdoch, WA: Murdoch University Press, 1985). Cited in Michael S. Northcott, *The Environment and Christian Ethics* (Cambridge: Cambridge University Press, 1996), 22.

into extinction. When such species become extinct, the balance of the whole ecosystem can be threatened.[104]

A serious implication of the current mass extinction of species is that humans cannot survive unless they align themselves to the rhythm of the biospheric processes and become willing to acknowledge their dependency on them. In the case of the current spasm of anthropogenic biodiversity loss, human beings are tearing down our common home of life and decimating their fellow members of the common household. The challenge of preserving our common home can be realized only by preserving the manifold forms of life that render our planet habitable, a "habitat" for the entire biotic community. We are part of this living world. "We depend on the living world for our food and medicines, the oxygen that we breathe, and the elements that form our bodies. 'Earth is our home, and all Earth's species are our family, for we have evolved along with every other living thing.'"[105] For this reason, conserving biodiversity cannot be an afterthought, a concern only after other objectives have been met. It is the foundation on which the other objectives are built.[106]

A Unique Challenge and Opportunity

It is evident that the fate of biological diversity for the next 10 million years will almost certainly be determined during the next 50–100 years by the activities of a single species. Homo sapiens has unwittingly achieved the ability to directly affect its own fate and that of most of the other species on this planet.[107] The future of evolution and the destiny of the web of life on Planet Earth at this historical juncture depend on humankind. To this species falls the enormous and historical responsibility to steward global biodiversity through the crucial twenty-first century.

---

[104] See Mackay, *The Atlas of Endangered Species*, 7–8, 14; Eoin J. O'Gorman et al., "Loss of Functionally Unique Species May Gradually Undermine Ecosystems," *Proceedings of the Royal Society B* 278 (2011): 1886–93.

[105] Eldredge, *Life in the Balance*, vii.

[106] See Ban Ki-moon, the United Nations Secretary-General, "Foreword," in Secretariat of the Convention on Biological Diversity, *Global Biodiversity Outlook 3*, 5.

[107] See Ehrlich and Pringle, "Where Does Biodiversity Go from Here?," 11579; Wake and Vredenburg, "Are We in the Midst of the Sixth Mass Extinction?" 11472.

The gravity of the situation of the current mass extinction of species transforms it into a unique challenge and a unique opportunity. The warning from the scientific community is loud and clear:

> The current extinction crisis is of human making, and any favorable resolution of that biodiversity crisis—among the most dire in the 4–billion-year history of the Earth—will have to be initiated by mankind. Preserving biodiversity is undeniably in humanity's enlightened self-interest, but the tragic irony is that a majority of humanity is not yet enlightened to this fact. Little time remains for the public, corporations, and governments to awaken to the magnitude of what is at stake.[108]

The clarion call to humanity, in the wake of the current mass extinction of species, is to rediscover its vocation to be stewards and shepherds of the rest of creation rather than script the obituary of extant species. It is a choice that could determine the survival of humanity itself on Planet Earth.

---

[108] Avise, Hubbell, and Ayala, "In the Light of Evolution II: Biodiversity and Extinction," 11456.

6

Pollution, Waste, and Depletion of Resources

Astronauts say that Earth seen from space—a sparkling blue-green jewel that shimmers against the dark backdrop of immense celestial expanse—is a beautiful sight to behold. Moving closer, one sees the blue mantle of water in its oceans, lakes, and rivers that are so indispensable for life; the lush green canopy of the forests; the sprawling sweeps of grain fields and prairies; the gorgeous colors of flowers, leaves, and fruits; the occasional rainbows that lace the dark cloudy skies; the rich and diverse ecosystems teeming with infinite forms of life; and a thousand other marvels—all render our home planet incredibly delightful. Earth is a garden planet, a paradise in the barren expanses of our immensely large universe.

The contemporary ecological crisis reveals how we are despoiling our beautiful home and fouling our own nest. We are not only disrupting the stable climatic conditions of the last 10,000 years of the Holocene era that made possible human civilization and tearing asunder the precious and fragile womb of life which is the planet's biosphere, but we are also defiling our common home. Human activities, modern industrial and agricultural activities in particular, appear to have polluted almost all areas of our common home: the air, the land, and the waters. We are also wasting away and using up the finite resources of our common household, evident in humanity's voracious consumption patterns, measured in the unsustainable ecological footprints of societies and individuals. We not only squander Earth's resources, but we also create so much waste that defiles the land and has deleterious impacts on the health of humans and other forms of life. The fast depletion of natural resources raises some serious concerns for the future. In the case of depletion of fresh water—the very source of life and the most critical of all natural resources—it is estimated that we are fast approaching alarming thresholds. How we are polluting our common home and depleting and wasting away the finite resources of our common household are discussed in this final chapter of Part II, which deals with the physical description of the ecological crisis—the cry of the Earth.

We begin with the modern and ubiquitous phenomenon of pollution.

Pollution of the Air, Land, and Water

Among the various manifestations of the contemporary ecological crisis, the impacts of pollution are probably the ones to which people are most sensitive. The modern environmental movement had its origin precisely in public concerns about pollution. It was the work of young marine biologist Rachel Carson that drew the attention of the world to the health impacts of pollution.[1] Carson pointed out that the heavy dependence of modern industrial agriculture on chemical fertilizers and pesticides was beginning to take a toll on human lives:

> In the less than two decades of their use, the synthetic pesticides have been so thoroughly distributed throughout the animate and inanimate world that they occur virtually everywhere. They have been recovered from most of the major river systems and even from streams of ground-water flowing unseen through the earth. Residues of these chemicals linger in soil to which they have been applied a dozen years before. They have entered and lodged in the bodies of fish, birds, reptiles, and domestic and wild animals so universally that scientists carrying on animal experiments find it almost impossible to locate subjects free from such contamination. They have been found in fish in remote mountain lakes, in earthworms burrowing in soil, in the eggs of birds—and in man himself. For these chemicals are now stored in the bodies of the vast majority of human beings, regardless of age. They occur in the mother's milk, and probably in the tissues of the unborn child.[2]

Pollution reveals yet another alarming face of the contemporary ecological crisis, which cannot be reduced to climate change alone. Pollution is the poisoning of our home planet with the consequent

---

[1] Rachel Carson, *Silent Spring* (Boston, MA: Houghton Mifflin, 1962).
[2] Rachel Carson, *Silent Spring* (New York: Penguin Books, 1965), 31.

disruption of its natural processes, so vital for the well-being of various forms of life on Earth. Pollution is the impossibility of Earth's ecosystems and natural cycles to absorb and process the excess and noxious byproducts of human activities. It is not so much that nature has no capacity to cleanse itself of wastes produced by human activities: "It is just that the cleansing capacity of nature is finite, and the combination of human numbers and our demand for the production of an enormous variety of consumer goods has overwhelmed that regenerating capacity and produced a crisis of toxic accumulations within all that is breathed, drunk, and eaten."[3]

As with other forms of contemporary ecological crisis like climate change and the current spasm of mass extinction of species, pollution results mostly from human activities. Pollution is a distinctly modern phenomenon; it began with the onset of the Industrial Revolution and has peaked in the last few decades of economic expansion. In fact, the economic growth and industrial development of the modern era has a heavy bill attached to it, namely, the pollution of our planetary home: the atmosphere, the land, and the waters.

Atmospheric Pollution

Outdoor air pollution is steadily increasing in many parts of the world as a result of economic and industrial growth, especially in the urban areas of many developing countries. Along with emissions from industries and factories, which are usually located in urban areas, higher traffic volume in cities also contributes to deteriorating urban air quality, which is exacerbated with increasing temperatures. The main air pollutants are nitrogen dioxide, ozone, and particulate matter and its components including organic carbon and volatile organic compounds.[4] Some of the air pollutants that have a negative impact on public health like aerosols, including black carbon, organic carbon, and sulphates, play a significant role also in influencing climate. Aerosols are of particular concern for human health due to their impacts on lung function and on respiratory and cardiac disease. Air

---

[3] Steven Kolmes, "Mental Cartography in a Time of Environmental Crisis," in *All Creation Is Groaning: An Interdisciplinary Vision for Life in a Sacred Universe,* ed. Carol J. Dempsey and Russell A. Butkus (Collegeville, MN: The Liturgical Press, 1999), 109.

[4] Yoko Akachi et al., *Global Climate Change and Child Health: A Review of Pathways, Impacts, and Measures to Improve the Evidence Base,* Innocenti Discussion Paper (Florence: UNICEF, 2009), 6.

pollution is a major cause of respiratory and cardiovascular diseases globally.[5] It can have severe health effects, especially among the very young, the elderly, and people with heart and lung conditions, and it can eventually even cause death. An estimated 3.2 million people died prematurely in 2010 because of the poisonous effects of outdoor air pollution.[6] Two-thirds of those killed by air pollution lived in Asia, where air quality continues to worsen.

Urban air pollution is particularly significant in emerging economies like China and India. Air pollution has reached unacceptable levels in many urban areas in China, where rising energy consumption, based largely on coal and other solid fuels, and increasing vehicle pollution—the fastest-growing source of urban air pollution—have taken a toll on air quality with serious consequences to the health of the populations. "About 70 percent of the country's electricity is generated from coal, most of it high in sulphur. High sulphur dioxide emissions contribute to smog and acid rain, which affect more than half of China's cities."[7] Almost 20 percent of Chinese cities fail to meet government air-quality standards; far more would fail to reach World Health Organization (WHO) standards. In the spring of 2013 Beijing's air pollution soared past levels considered hazardous, nearly thirty-five times what the WHO considers safe. It is evident that the rapid drive toward industrialization is extracting a heavy price from countries like China. Outdoor air pollution is equally bad in India, where it has become the country's fifth-highest killer. According to WHO data, the Indian capital of New Delhi, with its burgeoning population, is the twelfth most polluted city in the world, worse than Beijing.[8]

Ozone pollution is another form of atmospheric pollution. Tropospheric ozone is not only a greenhouse gas, but it is also classified as an air pollutant. Ozone, which is the primary constituent of urban smog, is a secondary pollutant formed from the action of sunlight

---

[5] The National Academy of Sciences, *Advancing the Science of Climate Change* (Washington, DC: The National Academies Press, 2010), 314–15; United Nations Development Programme, "Human Development Report 2011: Sustainability and Equity: A Better Future for All" (New York: UNDP, 2011), 40.

[6] See Stephen S. Lim et al., "A Comparative Risk Assessment of Burden of Disease and Injury Attributable to Sixty-Seven Risk Factors and Risk Factor Clusters in Twenty-One Regions, 1990–2010: A Systematic Analysis for the Global Burden of Disease Study 2010," *Lancet* 380 (2012): 2224–60.

[7] UNDP, "Human Development Report 2011, 52.

[8] See the WHO 2012 data on air pollution with regard to the exposure of cities around the world to PM10 particles (particulate matter with diameter of 10 μm or less). According to the "2012 Urban Outdoor Air Database," Beijing had an exposure of 121, while New Delhi ranked higher on the table with 198.

with high temperatures on ozone precursors such as carbon monoxide, nitrogen oxides, and volatile organic compounds. The emissions of ozone precursors from human activities—transport vehicles being the key sources of nitrogen oxides and volatile organic compounds in urban areas—have led to large increases in tropospheric ozone over the past century in many regions.[9] It is estimated that climate change will increase concentrations of tropospheric ozone across many regions, increasing morbidity and mortality.[10] Pollutants from forest fires can also affect air quality for thousands of miles at times. The toxic gases and particulate air pollutants released into the atmosphere can significantly contribute to acute and chronic illnesses of the respiratory system, particularly in children.[11]

Indoor air pollution is also more widespread than commonly thought. As "Human Development Report 2011" notes, half the people in the world still use traditional biomass for heating and cooking, and in very poor countries the proportion goes up to 94 percent of the entire population.[12] It is estimated that the use of biomass amounts to almost 10 percent of today's energy demand, more than that supplied worldwide by nuclear and hydroelectric power combined.[13] Indoor smoke from fuelwood and other biomass fuels such as charcoal or dried cow dung contains health-damaging pollutants, such as small particles and carbon monoxide. Further, because more than 1.5 billion peope still lack electricity, many poor households continue to use kerosene-based lighting, which is costly, inefficient, and a safety and health hazard.[14] The health effects of indoor air pollution fall largely on rural women, who do most of the cooking and spend the most time

---

[9] The National Academy of Sciences, *Advancing the Science of Climate Change*, 315; U. Confalonieri et al., "Human Health," in *Climate Change: Impacts, Adaptation and Vulnerability. Contribution of Working Group II to the Fourth Assessment Report of the IPCC*, ed. M. L. Parry et al. (Cambridge: Cambridge University Press, 2007), 401.

[10] See K. L. Ebi and G. Mcgregor, "Climate Change, Tropospheric Ozone and Particulate Matter, and Health Impacts," *Environmental Health Perspectives* 116 (2008): 1449–55.

[11] Confalonieri et al., "Human Health," 402.

[12] UNDP, "Human Development Report 2011," 51. See also E. Rehfuess et al., "Assessing Household Solid Fuel Use: Multiple Implications for the Millennium Development Goals," *Environmental Health Perspectives* 114 (2006): 373–78.

[13] Paul R. Ehrlich and Anne H. Ehrlich, *The Dominant Animal: Human Evolution and the Environment* (Washington, DC: Island Press, 2008), 226.

[14] United Nations Environment Programme, *Towards a Green Economy: Pathways to Sustainable Development and Poverty Eradication* (Nairobi: UNEP, 2011), 12.

near the domestic hearth, and on their young children, who remain close to them.

Land Pollution

The main sources of soil contamination are mechanized agriculture and industrial discharge and waste. The rampant overuse of fertilizer and pesticides in cropland and the seeping of toxic and heavy metals—such as lead, arsenic, and cadmium—from factories, smelters, and mines into the ground have contaminated the land in many regions of the world.

Modern agriculture, in the quest to increase output at all costs, has made heavy use of chemicals and fertilizers. It is estimated that global use of nitrogen fertilizers increased roughly eightfold between 1961 and 2002, while use of phosphorus fertilizers increased by a factor of three between 1961 and the late 1980s before levelling off.[15] The remarkable growth in agricultural production in the decades after the Second World War caused some deleterious collateral effects in terms of land pollution, with attendant consequences for human health.

As pointed out by Rachel Carson and others, pesticides like DDT remain active in the soil for years. Crops grown in or near polluted soil absorb toxic chemicals and traces of heavy metals. They continue to pass their poison through the food chain, with serious health consequences. The constant use of chemicals in agriculture not only pollutes the land but also destroys the long-term natural fertility of soil. While killing organisms considered pests by farmers, they also destroy organisms that are beneficial to the soil and that naturally control pests. Pesticides, for example, kill earthworms, which play an important role in fertilizing and aerating the soil. Farmers in poorer countries are not well protected against pesticide poisoning. It is estimated that farmworkers in Central America carry about eleven times more DDT residue in their body tissues than their average North American counterparts.[16] The expanding production of high-volume chemicals is increasingly transferred to developing countries, with attendant ecological consequences and health hazards.[17]

---

[15] Diana Liverman and Kamal Kapadia, "Food Systems and the Global Environment: An Overview," in *Food Security and Global Environmental Change*, ed. John Ingram, Polly Ericksen, and Diana Liverman (London: Earthscan, 2010), 10.

[16] Seán McDonagh, *To Care for the Earth: A Call to a New Theology* (London: Geoffrey Chapman, 1986), 19–21.

[17] See Sara Mills-Knapp et al., *The World's Worst Pollution Problems: Assessing Health Risks at Hazardous Waste Sites* (New York: Blasksmith Institute; Zurich: Green Cross Switzerland, 2012), 7.

Industrial discharge is yet another source of land pollution. While the problem of soil contamination from chemical wastes was a problem mainly of developed countries in the past, it now appears that the crisis is shifting to developing nations. It is estimated that fifteen of China's thirty-three provinces and administrative zones have areas of severely contaminated soil, with the problem becoming severe especially in the southeastern industrial zones. According to a 2012 report that assesses the health risks of hazardous waste sites, the global burden of disease from toxic industrial pollution is on a par with better-known public health problems such as malaria and tuberculosis.[18] The health of 125 million people is at risk from toxic pollution globally.[19] According to the WHO, environmental exposures contribute to 19 percent of cancer incidence worldwide.[20]

Electronic waste (e-waste), which consists of obsolete electrical and electronic products, is the fastest-growing sector of global waste, estimated at 20–50 million tons per year. Only a small share of e-waste is recycled, less than 20 percent in the United States. The rest is usually exported from developed countries to developing countries, particularly in China, India, and Nigeria, to be disposed of in landfills. In these countries recovering and trading materials from discarded electronic devices has become a thriving economic sector that provides an important livelihood for poor people. But the lead, mercury, and cadmium in these products are highly toxic. The employment of crude processing methods such as open-air burning or acid leaching to recover valuable metals like copper and gold and other rare earth metals from discarded electronic equipment causes the toxic substances in the e-waste to contaminate the environment, particularly the soil. Such toxic elements evidently pose high risks to human health and ecosystems.[21]

Water Pollution

We have polluted not only the air and the land of our home planet but also its waters, rivers, lakes, and to some extent even the seas and oceans. Modern intensive agriculture is a major source of water pol-

---

[18] Ibid., 4.

[19] Ibid., 6.

[20] P. Vineis and W. Xun, "The Emerging Epidemic of Environmental Cancers in Developing Countries," *Annals of Oncology* 20 (2009): 205–12; Mills-Knapp et al., *The World's Worst Pollution Problems*, 8.

[21] UNDP, "Human Development Report 2011," 41; United Nations Environment Programme, *Global Environment Outlook 5: Environment for the Future We Want* (Nairobi: UNEP, 2012), 184.

lution. Many of the pollutants associated with intensive agriculture are chemicals that can leach into the soil and contaminate the waters. Chemical fertilizers (rich in phosphates and nitrates) and pesticides (insecticides and herbicides), when used indiscriminately in agriculture to achieve optimum yields, can severely pollute streams, lakes, and ponds adjacent to farmland.

The inputs of nitrogen and phosphorus in agriculture increased massively in the second half of the twentieth century, while varying enormously with geography. It is estimated that only around half of the nitrogen added in agriculture and only about 20–30 percent of phosphorus in fertilizer is taken up by crops, with a good portion of the remaining part ending up in aquatic systems. The increased amounts of nitrogen and phosphorus that enter Earth's nutrient cycles can threaten aquatic ecosystems with eutrophication—"the over-enrichment of waters with nutrients which can lead to over-fertilization and algal blooms, robbing the water of oxygen and suffocating many of the organisms in those ecosystems."[22] When the concentration of dissolved oxygen in the water falls below a critical level, many species of fish and other aquatic animals die. The consequences of eutrophication are being felt worldwide. A vivid example is the Gulf of Mexico, where excessive nutrient runoff, primarily from fertilizer use, has led to the world's largest dead zone.[23]

Rivers and lakes are polluted also from industrial activities and urban waste. In developing countries, 70 percent of industrial waste is dumped untreated into water, where it pollutes both underground and surface water.[24] Among the substances discharged by industry into the world's rivers, lakes, and aquifers (underground reserves) are organic pollutants; heavy metals such as lead, cadmium, and mercury; and some of the most dangerous chemicals ever created—persistent organic pollutants.[25] The lakes and rivers of poor and developing nations, where environmental regulations are less strict and often not strictly enforced, are particularly affected by industrial and urban pollution. Areas near New Delhi and Kathmandu suffer from severe river pollution.[26] The fabled Yamuna River is poisoned and clinically dead as it winds its way through New Delhi's teeming slums and industrial peripheries. Almost 65 percent of Bangladesh's groundwater

---

[22] Liverman and Kapadia, "Food Systems and the Global Environment," 10.

[23] Ibid.

[24] Robin Clarke and Janet King, *The Water Atlas* (New York: The New Press, 2004), 38.

[25] Ibid., 40.

[26] See UNDP, "Human Development Report 2011," 40.

is contaminated, with at least 1.2 million Bangladeshis exposed to arsenic poisoning.[27]

Even the seas and oceans are increasingly despoiled by human pollution. Decades ago it was thought that these water bodies are too large to be affected by human activities. Now it appears that this is not the case. Since 1945, the seas, particularly inland seas into which hundreds of rivers empty, carrying chemical and noxious waste, are poisoned by pollution. It is particularly evident in the case of the northern Baltic Sea, which is seriously under threat from eutrophication as excessive quantities of nutrients from the agricultural farms and chemical waste from factories of the adjoining countries have been washed into it in the last few decades. It has been found that toxic hydrogen sulphide has formed in the deeper regions of the Baltic, and nearly one-third of the bottom area is calculated to be dead in terms of aquatic life.

The oceans, which cover 71 percent of the Earth's surface, also bear clear marks of human pollution. Some 80 percent of marine pollution originates from land-based sources. Common manmade pollutants include pesticides, chemical fertilizers, heavy metals, detergents, oil, sewage, plastics, and other solids. Many of these pollutants accumulate in the deep oceans and sediments. These pollutants are a threat to marine life, fisheries, mangroves, coral reefs, and through small marine organisms may even be reintroduced in the global food chain.[28]

One of the most recent and conspicuous forms of marine pollution is caused by plastic garbage—the trademark of modern consumerism—which now extends thousands of miles across the world's oceans. Over the past five or six decades, consequent to the increased use of plastic, contamination and pollution of the world's enclosed seas, coastal waters, and open oceans by plastic has been an ever-increasing phenomenon.[29] Globally, we use in excess of 260 million tons of plastic a year, accounting for approximately 8 percent of world oil production. Plastic also accounts for approximately 10 percent of the waste we generate, some of which also ends up in the oceans.[30] It is estimated that more than 500 billion plastic bags are used every year,

---

[27] Maude Barlow, *Blue Covenant: The Global Water Crisis and the Coming Battle for the Right to Water* (New York: The New Press, 2007), 7.

[28] UNEP, *Global Environment Outlook 5*, 177–78.

[29] Murray R. Gregory, "Environmental Implications of Plastic Debris in Marine Settings—Entanglement, Ingestion, Smothering, Hangers-on, Hitch-hiking, and Alien Invasions," *Philosophical Transactions of the Royal Society B* 364 (2009): 2013.

[30] Richard C. Thompson et al., "Our Plastic Age," *Philosophical Transactions of the Royal Society B* 364 (2009): 1973–74.

and many are improperly disposed of, ending up as marine litter.[31] Today, plastic pollution is a major component of the anthropogenic debris ubiquitous throughout the marine environment, predominantly in the Southern Hemisphere.[32] One may recall in this regard the infamous floating plastic garbage islands in the Pacific. The ecological consequences resulting from the accumulation of plastic debris in the marine environment are many and varied; they can cause injury and even death to various forms of marine life, and can indirectly affect human health through the ingestion of such waste by marine organisms that are then consumed by humans.

Another important example of human impact on the oceans is oil pollution. Steven Kolmes provides some unsettling statistics in this regard:

> Almost a third of marine petroleum pollution is caused by open-sea bilge pumping and tank cleaning practiced by the shipping industry and the transportation via accident-prone oil tankers demanded by an increasingly oil-hungry world. A great amount of oil pollution also enters the oceans through rivers and direct dumping of wastes into the ocean by human activities inland. The numbers are sobering. The tens of millions of pleasure boats owned by people around the world are estimated to release 520,000 tons of oil and oil products into the atmosphere and another 260,000 tons leaked into the water.[33]

Pollution is indeed a ubiquitous phenomenon on Earth, stretching across land, waters, and atmosphere. It is truly global, as human activities today are increasingly defiling our common planetary home.

Waste and Depletion of Natural Resources

We are not only despoiling our common home but also wasting and fast depleting the finite resources of our common household. Our unsustainable levels of consumption are clearly evident in the

[31] UNEP, *Global Environment Outlook 5*, 183–84.

[32] Marcus Eriksen et al., "Plastic Pollution in the South Pacific Subtropical Gyre," *Marine Pollution Bulletin* 68 (2013): 71–76; Thompson et al., "Our Plastic Age," 1975. See also David K. A. Barnes et al., "Accumulation and Fragmentation of Plastic Debris in Global Environments," *Philosophical Transactions of the Royal Society* B 364 (2009): 1985–98.

[33] Kolmes, "Mental Cartography in a Time of Environmental Crisis," 110.

empirically measurable ecological footprints of societies and individuals. Our consumption of many important natural resources is clearly beyond their renewal rates. In the case of important natural sources like fisheries, forests, biodiversity, and especially fresh water, we are fast approaching crucial thresholds. The voracious consumption and consequent depletion of natural resources on the part of humanity— yet another manifestation of the contemporary ecological crisis—is the subject of this section.

In the epoch of the Holocene and during most of the last 6,000 years since civilization began, we have lived on the sustainable yield of the Earth's natural systems. But in recent decades it appears that we are overshooting the capacity of our home planet's natural resources that sustain us. This is evident in the popular and widely used mechanism of the Ecological Footprint Analysis (EFA), discussed in Chapter 2. Currently, humanity consumes 1.5 "planets" a year, and the situation will worsen in the future at current levels of consumption and waste.

The trend among economists and political commentators is to focus exclusively on the increase of wealth in the last century, especially the tenfold growth in the world economy since the 1950s and the associated gains in living standards.[34] "They either ignore or don't realize that this has been achieved by depleting humanity's natural capital—using up vital resources far more rapidly than they can be replaced—and mortgaging our future."[35] The mainstream economists do not regard the market system of production and consumption as a subsystem within the global or local ecosystem. They treat the economy as a self-contained arrangement separate from its external, natural surroundings, and they fail to ask how it depends on this larger context. They fail to see that there is a scale limit on the human economy that we ignore at our peril.[36] Our current development model, based on the economic paradigm of infinite growth, is indeed bumping against concrete limits of a finite home planet.

Today, our consumption patterns have reached frenzied levels beyond all levels of sustainability. At the same time we are coaxed to consume ever more by media advertising—the poster boy of modern consumerism. Global advertising expenditures hit $643 billion

[34] Lester Brown, *World on the Edge: How to Prevent Environmental and Economic Collapse* (London: Earthscan, 2011), 7.

[35] Ehrlich and Ehrlich, *The Dominant Animal*, 208.

[36] David Toolan, *At Home in the Cosmos* (Maryknoll, NY: Orbis Books, 2001), 93.

in 2008, and in countries like China and India they are growing at 10 percent or more per year.[37] Like a tsunami, consumerism is engulfing human cultures and Earth's ecosystems.

The modern consumerist lifestyle of the developed world, increasingly aspired to by the burgeoning upper- and middle-class populations in developing countries, is a profligately wasteful one. From the physical point of view, the furnishings of our modern consumer lifestyle—greenhouse gas–belching automobiles, throwaway goods and packaging, a high-fat diet, air conditioning, and a thousand other commodities—can only be provided at great cost to the ecosystems of our finite home planet. The sheer quantity of waste produced by modern economy and our consumerist lifestyle is striking.

Our modern wasteful consumption lifestyle is tragically evident with regard to food. Today, we produce about 4 billion metric tons of food a year. However, one-third of the food produced for human consumption is lost or wasted. Between 30 and 50 percent (or 1.2–2 billion tons) of all produced food never reaches a human stomach.[38] Food is lost or wasted throughout the supply chain, from initial agricultural production to final household preparation. In less-developed countries, such as those of sub-Saharan Africa and Southeast Asia, wastage tends to occur primarily on the farms and in storage. Inefficient harvesting, inadequate local transportation, and poor infrastructure mean that produce is frequently handled inappropriately and stored under unsuitable conditions.[39] Incongruously, however, it is the most "advanced" and affluent societies where the largest quantities of food are wasted by consumers.

> [In the developed countries] 30% of what is harvested from the field never actually reaches the market place (primarily the supermarket) due to trimming, quality selection and failure to conform to purely *cosmetic* criteria. This can include such reasons as the packaging is slightly dented, one piece of fruit is bad in an otherwise perfectly good bag of fruit, or it is thrown out in the warehouse because it had ripened too soon. In this way

---

[37] Erik Assadourian, "The Rise and Fall of Consumer Cultures," in The World-Watch Institute, *State of the World 2010: Transforming Cultures: From Consumerism to Sustainability* (New York: W. W. Norton, 2010), 11.

[38] Tim Fox, *Global Food: Waste Not, Want Not* (London: Institution of Mechanical Engineers, 2013), 2; Jenny Gustavsoon et al., *Global Food Losses and Food Waste* (Rome: Food and Agricultural Organization, 2011), v.

[39] Fox, *Global Food*, 2, 17; Gustavsoon et al., *Global Food Losses and Food Waste*, v.

the global food industry produces large amounts of food waste, with retailers generating 1.6 million tons of food waste per year.

Of the quantity that does reach the supermarket shelves, 30–50% is thrown away by the final purchaser in the home, often at the direction of conservative 'use by' labelling. . . . Many consumers have a poor understanding of 'best before' and 'use by' dates, and these dates are generally quite conservative, as they are driven by the retailer's desire to avoid legal action. Promotional offers and high-pressure advertising campaigns, including bulk discounts and 'buy one get one free' offers, encourage shoppers to buy large quantities in excess of their actual needs, which leads to substantial food wastage in the home. In the UK, for example, about seven million tons (worth about £10.2 billion) of food is [*sic*] thrown away from homes every year.[40]

It is estimated that the per capita food waste by consumers in Europe and North America is between 209 and 253 pounds a year, while this figure in sub-Saharan Africa and South and Southeast Asia is only between 13 and 24 pounds a year.[41] Industrialized countries throw away as much food as is produced in sub-Saharan Africa every year.[42]

Food wastage in our globalized world is tragic given that there are nearly 1 billion undernourished people in the world—all of whom could be fed with just a fraction of the food that rich countries currently throw away.[43] More food is produced than is needed to feed everyone adequately.[44] In fact, to meet the food deficit of the 13 percent of the population living with hunger, it would take around 1 percent of the current global food supply.[45] As Tristram Stuart writes in unambiguous terms: "If rich countries buy hundreds of millions of tons of food and end up throwing these into the bin, they are gratuitously removing food from the market which could have remained there for other people to buy."[46] By buying more food than can be eaten and

---

[40] Fox, *Global Food*, 23. See also H. Charles J. Godray et al., "Food Security: The Challenge of Feeding Nine Billion People," *Science* 327 (2010): 816.

[41] Gustavsoon et al., *Global Food Losses and Food Waste*, v.

[42] Gaia Vince, "Living in the Doughnut: Interview with Kate Raworth," *Nature Climate Change* 2 (2012): 225.

[43] Tristram Stuart, *Waste: Uncovering the Global Food Scandal* (London: Penguin Books, 2009), xvi.

[44] Erik Millstone and Tim Lang, *The Atlas of Food: Who Eats What, Where, and Why* (London: Earthscan, 2003), 8.

[45] Vince, "Living in the Doughnut," 225.

[46] Stuart, *Waste*, xvi–xvii.

by throwing food away, the industrialized world devours land and resources that could otherwise be used to feed the world's poor. The tragedy is that a sizable quantity of such wasted food is produced in developing countries and then imported by the rich countries.

Food wastage has huge ecological implications as well. Wasting food means also squandering precious natural resources, including limited agricultural land, precious water, costly energy, fertilizers, other inputs, and above all, human labor. In the case of water, for example, about 145 trillion gallons of water are wasted globally in growing crops that never reach the consumer. This water could be used for other human activity or to support natural ecosystems.[47] These losses are destined to be exacerbated by future population growth and dietary trends that are seeing a shift away from grain-based food and vegetarian dishes toward consumption of meat products. As nations become affluent, per capita calorific intake of meat consumption is predicted to soar 40 percent by mid-century. Meat products require many times more natural resources than grain to produce.[48]

Food wastage also contributes, apart from the depletion of precious natural resources, to other manifestations of the ecological crisis like species extinction, as in the case of deforestation for conversion to cropland and ranches, and especially climate change caused by emission of greenhouse gases through production and transportation of food. The wastage of nearly one-third of food produced for human consumption is equivalent to 6–10 percent of human-generated greenhouse gas emissions, which is indeed a large chunk of the total emissions from various human activities.[49] Food wastage inevitably means that huge amounts of the resources used in food production are used in vain, and that the greenhouse gas emissions caused by production of food that gets lost or wasted are also unnecessary emissions.

In a world with limited natural resources (land, water, energy, fertilizer) and the need to guarantee enough safe and nutritious food for all, reducing food wastage should be a priority and both an individual and collective responsibility.

The rapid depletion of our home planet's natural resources in blissful ignorance of the larger ecological context is a sure recipe for global disaster. As Seán McDonagh notes: "The Earth's ledger, which in the

---

[47] Fox, *Global Food*, 17.

[48] Ibid., 3.

[49] See S. J. Vermeulen et al., "Climate Change and Food Systems," *Annual Review of Environmental Resources* 37 (2012): 195–222.

final analysis is the only real one, tells us that the Earth is finite and vulnerable, and that natural systems will be seriously depleted and possibly collapse unless human beings begin to shape their lives in the light of this reality of ecological accounting."[50] No previous generation has survived the ongoing destruction of its natural supports. Nor will ours. Instead, we go on liquidating our home planet's finite natural assets to fuel our reckless consumption. The global picture in this regard is a matter of grave concern:

> Half of us live in countries where water tables are falling and wells are going dry. Soil erosion exceeds soil formation on one third of the world's cropland, draining the land of its fertility. The world's ever-growing herds of cattle, sheep, and goats are converting vast stretches of grassland to desert. Forests are shrinking by 13 million acres per year as we clear land for agriculture and cut trees for lumber and paper. Four fifths of oceanic fisheries are being fished out of capacity or over-fished and headed for collapse. In system after system, demand is overshooting supply.[51]

Many forms of natural capital are irreplaceable on a time scale of interest to humanity. Against this realization we briefly examine the depletion of three basic natural resources: forest cover, fisheries, and fresh water.

Forest Cover

A natural resource that is being depleted at unsustainable rates is forest cover. Earth's forest cover is only three-fifths of what it was in prehistoric times.[52] Latin America, the Caribbean, and sub-Saharan Africa, followed by the Arab States, have registered the greatest loss of forest cover, while other regions have seen minor gains.[53] However, most of the countries in the latter group have shifted deforestation to developing countries. For example, the European Union transfers 75 of every 100 cubic meters of reduced timber harvest to developing countries; the United States, 46 of every 100 cubic

---

[50] McDonagh, *To Care for the Earth*, 45.

[51] Brown, *World on the Edge*, 6.

[52] UNDP, "Human Development Report 2011," 38. See also J. B. Ball, "Global Forest Resources: History and Dynamics," in *The Forest Handbook*, vol. 1, ed. J. Evans (Oxford: Blackwell Science, 2001), 13–22.

[53] UNDP, "Human Development Report 2011," 38, esp. n59.

meters.[54] This pattern is being followed by emerging economies like China and India.

The worldwide retreat of forest cover is indeed an ominous signal for the flourishing of humanity. Today, a combination of forces—multinational companies seeking profits, governments desperate to pay off international debts, landowners and ranchers wanting farmland and grazing land, and peasants wanting firewood—conspires to eradicate tropical rainforests at an alarming pace. Deforestation is of grave consequence in that trees create and hold soil, control floods, maintain water tables, keep rivers and seacoasts free of silt, and recycle gases (especially carbon dioxide and oxygen) that maintain the chemical balance of the atmosphere.[55] History abounds in examples of civilizations that were wiped out due to the depletion of basic natural resources like agricultural soil and forest cover. The Mayan civilization, for example, went into extinction after flourishing for nine hundred years, mainly because of soil erosion resulting from uninterrupted cultivation of corn after the disappearance of the forest. The Carthaginians, Mesopotamians, and many others suffered a similar fate, with deforestation having been a significant factor in the demise of these civilizations.[56]

Fisheries

Another natural resource that is being fast depleted and will affect food security in the future is fish stocks. Besides farm production, fisheries are another source that guarantees food security to millions, especially to the poor, both in terms of nutrition and providing livelihoods. It is estimated that 1 billion people rely on fish as their main source of animal protein. Seafood provides about 15 percent of the calories and one-third of the protein that people worldwide consume. In addition, 500 million people in developing countries depend—directly or indirectly—on fisheries for their livelihoods.[57]

Today, the world's fish stocks are being rapidly depleted due to overfishing, local extinctions of certain commercially important fish species, rising sea levels, ocean acidification, water pollution, and

---

[54] See J. Gan and B. A. McCarl, "Measuring Transnational Leakage of Forest Conservation," *Ecological Economics* 64 (2007): 423–32; UNDP, "Human Development Report 2011," 38.

[55] Toolan, *At Home in the Cosmos*, 87.

[56] McDonagh, *To Care for the Earth*, 40.

[57] Oxfam, *Suffering the Science: Climate Change, People, and Poverty*, Oxfam Briefing Paper (July 6, 2009), 21.

more. The current rates of fishing are clearly beyond the natural rate of regeneration. The annual fish catch of 145 million tons far exceeds the maximum annual sustainable yield of 80–100 million tons.[58] Such unsustainable levels are mostly caused by developed-country fishers using capital-intensive methods such as technologically advanced fishing vessels with long-term storage facilities and mechanized trawls suitable for fishing in deep waters. There is considerable disparity when it comes to fish harvesting between the developed and the developing nations—where more than 95 percent of small-scale fishers live. Average annual production by a fish farmer is 172 tons in Norway, 72 tons in Chile, 6 tons in China, and 2 tons in India.[59] Large commercial fishing fleets not only catch more fish but also engage in damaging practices like high bycatch methods and bottom trawling.[60] The depletion of fish stock is a bad omen for global food security, especially for poor people who rely on fish for consumption and for their livelihoods.

The Problem of Water Scarcity

Water made life possible here on Earth, and the survival and flourishing of life on our home planet require the constant availability of water.

Unlike other resources such as forests and soil, which can be both destroyed and rejuvenated—though over long periods of time—the quantity of water on our home planet remains always the same. Every drop of water on Earth counts "because that drop never disappears or reproduces, even though it may change its state from liquid to gas to solid and back to liquid, and travel from the Antarctic to the Sahara and then on to the Russian steppes."[61] As climate and water

---

[58] UNDP, "Human Development Report 2011."

[59] Ibid.

[60] Bycatch refers to all the forms of marine life caught unintentionally while fishing for certain target species of fish, crabs, and so forth. Millions of tons of unwanted fish or other marine species thus collected are mostly thrown back into the sea dead or wounded. According to World WildLife Fund, bycatch represents nearly 40 percent of global marine catches. See Davies Rwd et al., "Defining and Estimating Global Marine Fisheries," *Marine Policy* (2009), available online. Bottom trawling is an equally harmful technique employed by industrial boats. The method consists in the use of enormous nets, weighed down with heavy ballast, which are dragged along the sea floor, raking up or crushing everything in their way, from fish to ancient coral. Many marine species, including those at risk of extinction, are accidentally caught and then discarded back into the sea, often already dead.

[61] Clarke and King, *The Water Atlas*, 11.

expert Pavel Kabat observes: "Water is much more valuable than oil; there are alternatives to oil, but there are no alternatives to water."[62] The depletion of fresh water in this regard becomes one of the most disquieting aspects of the contemporary ecological crisis, a concern that is yet to attract the due public attention it deserves.

We begin with some basic statistics about the quantity of water, especially fresh water available for human use, which is indeed only a very tiny fraction of the total amount, before we reflect on the unsustainable consumption of water for agriculture, industry, and domestic consumption. After that, we reflect on the scandalous disparity between the rich and the poor with regard to access to clean water and the challenges that water scarcity raises for human health in terms of sanitation and hygiene. We also reflect on how water scarcity can become a real challenge to social and regional security around the world.

Earth's surface is 71 percent covered in water. However, 97.47 percent of this water is salt water, contained in the oceans, seas, saltwater lakes, and salty aquifers. Fresh water amounts to just 2.53 percent of the total. Of this fresh water more than two-thirds (68.7 percent) is unavailable for human use because it is locked up in the great permanent glaciers: in Greenland (7.9 percent), and Antarctica (91.6 percent), and a tiny fraction concentrated in mountain glaciers (0.5 percent). Of the remaining one-third of fresh water that is technically available for people to use, most is stored in deep aquifers in the capillaries of porous rocks, so that it is very hard to extract. This groundwater represents the largest source of distributed fresh water on Earth. In fact, of the total volume of liquid fresh water, 99 percent exists as groundwater, with only the remaining 1 percent directly accessible at the surface—in lakes, rivers, wetlands, the soil, air humidity, and so on.[63]

In the final analysis, just 0.3 percent of the total amount of fresh water, equal to 0.01 percent of the total water present on Earth, is easily accessible and available for human use. Fresh water is thus a limited natural resource—and also a finite resource. The volume of fresh water on the Earth's surface is fixed: it can be neither increased nor decreased.[64] This tiny fraction of fresh water needs to sustain not only our growing population and our increasing needs but also millions of other species with whom we share our planetary home.

---

[62] Monica Contestabile, "Water at a Crossroads," *Nature Climate Change* 3 (2013): 11.

[63] See Marta Picciulin, *Water and Science* (Bologna: EMI, 2007), 41–42; Clarke and King, *The Water Atlas*, 20.

[64] Clarke and King, *The Water Atlas*, 19.

Fortunately, water is a renewable resource on our home planet, thanks to the marvelous water cycle. The hydrological cycle is "the global mechanism that transfers water from the oceans to the surface, or subsurface environments, and plants, to the atmosphere that surrounds our planet."[65] All of the water masses on Earth—in the oceans, in the rivers, in the subsoil, and in the atmosphere—are interconnected by the hydro-geological cycle. The engine moving the water cycle on our planet is the sun. Marta Picciulin explains this process:

> Every year, the Sun subtracts 577,000 km³ of liquid water, which evaporates, thus reaching the atmosphere. Most of the evaporation concerns the ocean's water (87.5%), but a significant amount comes from dry land (12.5%). 79.3% of this water goes back to the oceans in the form of rain, while the remaining 20.7% falls on the continents as rain or snow. Therefore, there is a net transfer of water from the oceans to the land, through the atmosphere. The cycle is closed when 47,000 km³ of water reach the oceans again, by washing away over land.[66]

The very existence of the hydro-geological cycle—key to our survival—is made possible by the unique capacity of water of existing in all the three states: solid, liquid, and gaseous. It also means that the various stages of the hydro-geological cycle move at very different speeds: "a water molecule remains in the atmosphere no more than 4 days on average. It can remain in the oceans for hundreds of years. Freezing can subtract a molecule from the cycle even for millennia."[67] As for groundwater in the deep aquifers, also called "fossil water," the cycle of complete renewal can be calculated only in thousands of years. The hydrological cycle has continuously renewed and replenished Earth's water flows since time immemorial. But the problem is that human consumption of fresh water far exceeds the natural rates of hydrological renewal through the water cycle.

It is against the sober realization that only a very tiny fraction of water present on Earth is really available for human consumption, and that water is a limited and finite resource that can be renewed only over long periods of time, that we need to consider the pressing problem of water scarcity around the globe.

---

[65] UNESCO, *World Water Development Report 2: Water: A Shared Responsibility* (Paris: UNESCO, 2006), 139.

[66] Picciulin, *Water and Science*, 42.

[67] Ibid.

The world is running out of fresh water. Throughout the world an unprecedented demand for water is recorded against limited availability. The steep rise in the consumption of water is due to a steep increase in human population, greater increased per capita consumption of water due to modern lifestyles, the phenomenal growth of industry, and especially the leap in irrigated agricultural production in the wake of the Green Revolution. An analysis of the main human activities that consume water—agriculture, industry, and domestic use—clearly evidences how our unsustainable patterns of water consumption is leading to global water scarcity.

Globally, the largest user of water is irrigated agriculture, representing 70 percent of fresh-water withdrawals. The increase in food production through modern agriculture in the last few decades has been possible largely due to large-scale irrigation, which is proving to be unsustainable in many parts of the world. Irrigated lands produce two to three times as much as rain-fed agriculture. However, irrigation is a voracious consumer of water. Further, more than half of it gets wasted, because 60–90 percent of irrigation water evaporates or is absorbed by the plants; only the remaining part goes back to the system.[68] Most of the groundwater pumped up is used to irrigate crops in arid and semi-arid areas. Here, waste is really high, with only a small percentage of the water that is used ever reaching the crop for which it was intended.[69] The demand for water for agricultural production is projected to double by 2050, when the world's population is expected to reach 9 billion people.[70] Along with rising standards of living and hunger for meat, our more crowded world is expected to require a 70 percent boost in food. Food means water: producing 2.2 pounds of rice requires about 925 gallons of water, while 2.2 pounds of beef sucks up a remarkable 4,000 gallons.[71]

Industry accounts for nearly 22 percent of the total consumption of water at the global level. In only a few highly industrialized countries, such as the United States, the Netherlands, and Germany, is more water consumed by industry than by agriculture. But although industrial demands are limited in terms of quantity, much of what industry withdraws is consumed; that is, it is so polluted that it cannot

---

[68] Ibid., 45.

[69] Clarke and King, *The Water Atlas*, 19.

[70] UNDP, "Human Development Report 2011."

[71] See Nicola Jones, "A Drop to Drink," *Nature Climate Change* 2 (2012): 222. For the relevant data, see UNESCO, *World Water Development Report 4: Managing Water Under Uncertainty and Risk: The United Nations World Water Development Report*, vol. I (Paris: UNESCO, 2012).

be easily reused. It is estimated that nearly 95 percent of the water returned to the hydro-geological cycle after industrial use, especially in developing countries, is polluted.[72] The amount of water used for domestic purposes, including municipal use in towns and cities, is relatively trivial—just 8 percent of the global water use. However, the proportions of water used in agriculture, industry, and domestic use can vary considerably by country. For example, in Europe water used for domestic, municipal, and service industries is a very high proportion of total demand.[73]

The global population tripled in the twentieth century, but water consumption went up sevenfold during the same period, mostly between 1950 and 2000, a relevant acceleration whose trend does not appear to be reversing.[74] Clean, fresh water, the lifeblood of the biosphere and the most critical resource for agriculture—and equally essential for industrial and household use—will be in short supply on a global basis in the near future.[75] Humans are presently using more than half of accessible run-off water, leaving little for the ecosystem or other species.[76]

It is thus evident that humanity is currently polluting, diverting, and above all, depleting the Earth's finite water resources at a dangerous and steadily increasing rate. The indicators regarding the impending fresh-water scarcity are manifold, beginning with dwindling rivers and streams and shrinking lakes and wetlands. Most of the rivers no longer reach the seas or remain dry for most part of the year. About half of the five hundred greatest rivers of the world are undergoing a process of gradual drying up. The Yellow River (Huangze) and the Blue River (Yangtze) in China, the Ganges and the Indus in Southern Asia, the Amu Dar'ya in Central Asia, the Chao Phraya in Thailand, the Nile in Northeastern Africa, the Colorado and Rio Grande in the United States and Mexico, all these no longer reach the sea all year long.[77] The main causes are the overexploitation of water for irrigation and industry as

---

[72] Clarke and King, *The Water Atlas*, 19; Picciulin, *Water and Science*, 49.

[73] Clarke and King, *The Water Atlas*, 19; Nicholas Stern, *The Economics of Climate Change* (Cambridge: Cambridge University Press, 2007), 79.

[74] See Barlow, *Blue Covenant*, 3; Maria Cristina Rulli et al., "Global Land and Water Grabbing," *Proceedings of the National Academy of Sciences* 110 (2013): 892.

[75] See Picciulin, *Water and Science*, 45; Toolan, *At Home in the Cosmos*, 86.

[76] Barlow, *Blue Covenant*, 6.

[77] See Alexander Bell, *Peak Water: Civilisation and the World's Water Crisis* (Edinburgh: Luath Press, 2009), 19; Marco Deriu, *Water and Conflicts* (Bologna: EMI, 2007), 11.

well as the diversion of rivers for other uses like hydro-electrical projects. Many of the forty-eight thousand large dams (higher than fifty feet) that have been built in the recent decades, at a whopping cost of around US$1 trillion, are currently threatening some of the largest and most important rivers. It is estimated that over 60 percent of the 227 main rivers of the world are broken up by dams.[78] The situation is equally alarming when it comes to the drying up of fresh-water lakes around the world. The tragic case of Lake Chad in Africa, which has lost more than 90 percent of its original size, is probably the most conspicuous example in this regard. Many of the wetlands that play an important role in the purification and storage of water are also disappearing. About half of them have disappeared in the past 100 years.[79]

The situation is most alarming when it comes to the depletion of groundwater contained in the aquifers, the most important source of liquid fresh water available for human use. About 2 billion people—one-third of the world's population—depend on groundwater supplies.[80] The aquifers (often referred to as fossil groundwater) were formed when rainwater seeped through the soil and collected in rocky chambers. Because rain has been falling for billions of years, these subterranean reserves can be huge. Some of the aquifers were formed during the ice ages, when large masses of ice covered land areas. Incredibly, the aquifers contain more than 100 times as much water as all the planet's surface water reserves put together.[81] Groundwater is also the origin of much surface water, feeding springs, wetlands, and streams. The vast reserves of groundwater are critical for the survival of human populations.

The problem is that in many places water is being withdrawn faster than it is being replaced. Today, we are quite literally robbing the aquifer bank, extracting water at rates that outpace the rate at which nature replaces it.[82] Overpumping of groundwater for irrigation and urban consumption in many parts of the world exceeds natural recharge rates by almost 62,000 square miles per year.[83] Farms, cities, and industries all over the world are increasingly turning to

---

[78] See Picciulin, *Water and Science*, 50; Barlow, *Blue Covenant*, 21.

[79] Clarke and King, *The Water Atlas*, 59.

[80] Barlow, *Blue Covenant*, 11.

[81] Clarke and King, *The Water Atlas*, 19.

[82] Clarke and King, *The Water Atlas*, 19; Bell, *Peak Water*, 20.

[83] See Joanne Green, "Let Justice Roll Down Like a Never-ending Stream," in *When Enough Is Enough: A Christian Framework for Environmental Sustainability*, ed. R. J. Berry (Nottingham: Inter-Varsity Press, 2007), 141; UNDP, "Human Development Report 2011," 38.

groundwater sources, using sophisticated technology to drill deep into the Earth and pull up ancient aquifer water for daily use. As Maude Barlow notes, the current practice of "water mining" is entirely different from the sustainable use of well water that has served farmers for generations.[84] Because of such unsustainable consumption, the rate of groundwater withdrawal has at least tripled over the past fifty years and continues to increase by 1–2 percent per year.[85] Water tables have declined in many parts of the world, most notably in all three of the world's most populous countries: China, India, and the United States. As water tables dip, water pumps have to worker harder and harder to extract water, and the process can lead to ground subsidence. Severe ground subsidence is a common feature of major cities, from Beijing to Mexico City, that depend largely on aquifers for their supplies.[86] Besides being overpumped, groundwater aquifers are also being polluted with chemical run off from industrial farming and mine tailings, as well as being invaded by saltwater from careless drilling practices.[87]

Some of the most worrying cases of unsustainable groundwater use involve the distinct minority of aquifers called fossil aquifers that hold water hundreds of thousands of years old and that receive little replenishment from rainfall today. Like oil reserves, these aquifers are essentially nonrenewable; pumping water from them depletes the supply in the same way that extractions from an oil well do. Since these aquifers do not recharge naturally, irrigation ends whenever they are pumped dry. Among the more prominent fossil aquifers are the Ogallala underlying the US Great Plains, those in Saudi Arabia, and the deep aquifer under the North China Plain.[88] In the United States the massive Ogallala Aquifer, the world's largest underground lake and the key resource for an area that runs from South Dakota to Texas and from Colorado to Missouri, may run dry within three decades.[89] The Middle East—where aquifers are rapidly becoming exhausted and the area under irrigation declining—offers a taste of what may be to come. The example of the depletion of the fossil aquifers in the arid kingdom of Saudi Arabia represents one of the most egregious cases of unsustainable water use in the world today. In some arid regions

---

[84] Barlow, *Blue Covenant*, 11.

[85] Jones, "A Drop to Drink," 222.

[86] Clarke and King, *The Water Atlas*, 19.

[87] Barlow, *Blue Covenant*, 11.

[88] Brown, *World on the Edge*, 23; Sandra Postel, *Last Oasis: Facing Water Scarcity* (London: W. W. Norton, 1997), 31.

[89] Paul Roberts, *The End of Food: The Coming Crisis in the World Food Industry* (London: Bloomsbury, 2009), xx.

of the world the rates of water extraction for irrigation are exceeding rates of replenishment of several major nonrenewable fossil aquifers, for example, in the Punjab, in arid North Africa, in the Arabian Peninsula, and in Australia.[90]

The problem of water scarcity will be further exacerbated in the coming decades by climate change, which will alter the patterns of water availability by intensifying the water cycle, leading to more severe droughts and floods in many areas. It is estimated that this will lead to more rain at high latitudes, less rain in the dry subtropics, and uncertain but probably substantial changes in tropical areas.[91] Those regions of the world where agriculture depends on water resources from glacial melt, including the Andean highlands, the Ganges plain, and portions of East Africa, are also at risk due to the worldwide reduction in snowpack and the retreat of glaciers.[92] Changing rainfall, rising temperatures, more frequent and more intense droughts and floods, and increasing groundwater salinity as a result of rising sea levels over the next decades are likely to make provision of clean water, good sanitation, and drainage even more complicated.[93]

Fresh water is not only becoming scarce all over the world, but there is also a scandalous disparity between communities and nations in the use of water. Access to water greatly varies geographically and at times within the same regions and countries. In today's world water has become yet another parameter of inequality. As with ecological and carbon footprints, the per capita consumption of water can be measured in terms of "water footprints," which show a marked geographical inequality. The average human needs 13 gallons of water a day for drinking, cooking, and sanitation. The average North American uses almost 160 gallons a day, with more than 210 gallons a day in Canada to 112 gallons in the United States. Europeans use approximately 45–66 gallons a day. The average inhabitant of Africa uses 1.5 gallons per day—less than that used in one flush of a modern

---

[90] The Government Office for Science, *Foresight: The Future of Food and Farming: Final Project Report* (London: The Government Office for Science, 2011), 58; UNESCO, *World Water Development Report 4*, 48.

[91] Stern, *The Economics of Climate Change*, 74.

[92] The National Academy of Sciences, *Advancing the Science of Climate Change*, 294.

[93] Anthony Costello et al., "Managing the Health Effects of Climate Change" (Lancet and University College London Institute for Global Health Commission), *Lancet* 373 (2009): 1705; Jamie Hosking et al., "Climate Change: The Implications for Child Health in Australasia," *Journal of Pediatrics and Child Health* 47 (2011): 493.

lavatory—with the average falling to just 0.26 gallons in some water-stressed areas in Ethiopia.[94]

The disparity between the rich and poor nations is evident also in the "virtual water trade" between countries. As Maude Barlow explains, if a country exports a water-intensive product to another country, it amounts to exporting water in a virtual form, although no water is technically being traded or sold.[95] Wealthy countries with low water supplies, such as Saudi Arabia, United Arab Emirates, Israel, and the Netherlands, import much of their water through food imports from countries that either have lots of water or that are so poor they have no choice but to exploit what is left of their water. Many poor countries are exporting huge amounts of water through virtual water trade because of a desperate need for income and because they have been strongly pushed by international institutions like the World Bank and the IMF to pay off their debts through monoculture crop exports—even if it means using their best, most arable land and their remaining water supplies to do so. In the Far East, Vietnam is destroying its water table to grow coffee for export and earn foreign exchange. Africa supplies much of Europe with out-of-season fruits and vegetables grown with scarce water resources, just as Latin America provides for North America. Kenya is destroying the waters of Lake Naivasha to grow roses for export to Europe, jeopardizing its own food security.[96]

Global water scarcity exists not only between rich and poor nations but often within the very poor countries themselves. Many of the mega-cities of the developing nations—like Cape Town, Johannesburg, Rio de Janeiro, New Delhi, Jakarta, Manila, and many others—evince a tragic contrast between shanty towns and urban slum areas with no or a limited water supply, and prosperous suburbs dotted with swimming pools and golf courses. The global water crisis has become a powerful symbol of the growing inequality in our world. While the wealthy enjoy boutique water at any time, millions of poor people have very little water or have access only to contaminated water from local rivers and wells. Water shortage is a major barrier to development around the world and an important reason why so many of the world's poor are still poor.

At the global level, about 1.1 billion people do not have access to a safe water supply, and 2.6 billion people do not have access to adequate

---

[94] Barlow, *Blue Covenant*, 5; Clarke and King, *The Water Atlas*, 30; Picciulin, *Water and Science*, 50.

[95] Barlow, *Blue Covenant*, 16.

[96] Ibid., 16–17.

sanitation facilities.[97] The tragic reality of many of our planet's inhabitants being denied access to drinking water and to adequate sanitation—common goods to which every human person is entitled—also exposes poor people to lack of hygiene and makes them more vulnerable to diseases. According to statistics, one ill person out of two in the world suffers from causes linked to lack of drinking water or use of contaminated water. It is estimated that 80 percent of the diseases and one third of the deaths in the developing countries are linked with the use of polluted water.[98] According to the WHO, an estimated 1.7 million deaths are caused annually by dirty water. Most of these deaths are of children under five years of age and are the result of dehydration from diarrhea caused by ingesting fecal bacteria. More children are killed by dirty water than by war, malaria, HIV/AIDS, and traffic accidents combined. Every eight seconds a child dies from drinking dirty water.[99]

In many regions of the world the problem of water scarcity risks becoming a challenge to social and regional security in the decades to come. In a water-short world, competition for increasingly scarce fresh water could trigger conflicts between regions and even nations. More than 260 international river basins are shared by two or more countries, crossing 145 international boundaries, with 13 of them shared by 5 or more countries.[100]

> In West Asia, nations scrap over the waters of the Yamak, the Euphrates and the Tigris, and there is serious conflict over water between Israel and Palestine; Mexico and the USA argue about the Colorado and the Rio Grande; Egypt, Ethiopia and the Sudan all want more of the Nile waters; and Bangladesh, Bhutan, India and Nepal have frequent disputes about the Brahmaputra and the Ganges.[101]

There is also the danger of some of these rows turning into military conflicts, as in the case of the Middle East region, where there have been long-running disputes over access to water between Turkey and Syria, Palestine, and Jordan. In fact, of more than eighteen hundred

---

[97] UNEP, *Global Environment Outlook 5*, 185.

[98] Picciulin, *Water and Science*, 50; Barlow, *Blue Covenant*, 3.

[99] Clarke and King, *The Water Atlas*, 12; Barlow, *Blue Covenant*, 1, 3.

[100] Clarke and King, *The Water Atlas*, 75; Norman Myers and Jennifer Kent, *The New Consumers: The Influence of Affluence on the Environment* (Washington, DC: Island Press, 2004), 46.

[101] Clarke and King, *The Water Atlas*, 12.

international water-related disputes during the last fifty years, fully one-quarter were outright hostile, with thirty-seven occasions when rival countries resorted to military violence.[102]

The question of water scarcity raises serious concerns for the welfare of human societies, especially for the weaker sections of humanity. Water is a fundamental human right. It is also the indispensable guarantee for other rights like nutrition, health, and ultimately the very right to life.

Humanity's Distorted Relationship with the Natural World

In the calm mirror of water, so fundamental for life but so depleted around the globe, the time has come for humanity to pause and look at the distorted image it has created of itself and of its relationship with its home planet. The challenges of pollution, waste, and depletion of natural resources that we have examined in this chapter, as well as the other major manifestations of the contemporary ecological crisis like climate change and biodiversity loss discussed in earlier chapters, are reflections of humanity's disharmonious relationship with our common home.

---

[102] Myers and Kent, *The New Consumers*, 46. See also A. T. Wolfe, *Water, Conflict, and Co-operation* (Washington, DC: International Food Policy Research Institute, 2001).

PART III

THE CRY OF THE POOR

On the banks of the Buriganga River in the centre of the capital, Dhaka, Masud Kalam and his family live in pitiful poverty, their home a small piece of ripped black tarpaulin held up by two bamboo canes. They arrived in the city a couple of months ago carrying only what they could save when the spit of land on which they had built their house broke in half and crumbled away, taking not only their home and possessions, but also their tiny daughter.

Through an interpreter, Mr Kalam explains that the family had lived in the mangrove forest region known as the Sunderbans, where they had made their living through shrimp fishing. "We had two goats, and a house we had built ourselves," he says. "We had only been there a few months because our last house began to sink into the mud."

One day, as floodwaters receded, a large part of the land fell into the sea, taking the goats with it, and a crack appeared under the house. Mr Kalam, his wife and their three older children had begun to collect their possessions, making a pile outside the house, a pile which included the youngest member of the family, only a few months old. They had less time than they thought. The house slumped suddenly into the crack and the entire piece of land was submerged under rushing water, which swept the pile of belongings, including the baby, into its muddy depths, leaving the rest of the family clinging to the wreckage of their home.

"We didn't know what to do, it happened so quickly," says Mr Kalam. "One moment the baby and the house were there and the next there was just water." The family had no alternative but to travel to Dhaka, in the hope of finding a new way to make a living. It is hard to imagine a more hellish destination for a bereaved family with no home and no money. Much of the city could be mistaken for a war zone and its slums have a medieval squalor about them, dirty, stinking and depressing. Overwhelmed by the pressure of the 13 million people it is required to support,

Dhaka's infrastructure appears to be on the verge of complete breakdown. Power blackouts are part of life, as are frequent interruptions to the water supply.

The most heartbreaking detail of all is that the average Bangladeshi has contributed little more to climate change than a butterfly. Forty percent of the population lives below the poverty line and many survive without access to electricity or running water. The most common form of transport is a bicycle rickshaw—few people have ever seen the inside of an aircraft—and there is almost no heavy industry. Nonetheless, global warming is causing ice caps that Mr Kalam and his wife have absolutely no idea about to drip steadily into oceans on the other side of the globe. Bangladesh has experienced none of the benefits of development but countries like this will bear the brunt of the resulting disaster.[1]

The sad story of the unfortunate family reveals another important facet of the contemporary ecological crisis. It is not only Mother Earth that is groaning under the burden of the ecological crisis, it is also the poor who are wailing with her. One argument often heard in the developed world against any concrete response to the ecological crisis is that such measures would threaten present lifestyles. However, the tragic truth about the ecological crisis is that problems like climate change are already becoming life threatening for millions of impoverished people in other parts of the world. It is not only the common home of Earth that is in peril, but also the real homes and lives of the poor who dwell therein. In this sense the ecological crisis is not only a physical problem, it is also a human tragedy of unimaginable proportions; it threatens security and livelihoods of people around the world.

---

[1] Isabel De Bertodano, "Rising Tide of Refugees," *The Tablet* (October 28, 2006). Bangladesh is one of the most vulnerable countries to climate change. It is also a crowded country of approximately 140 million people, more than 120 million of whom live and farm on lands located in the labyrinth of waterways and swamps that form the largest delta on Earth. Almost all the land is less than 20 feet above sea level; without effective protective barriers along the coast, even a moderate increase in sea level could cause flooding far inland. Estimates suggest that even a 3.2 foot rise could swallow 15 to 20 percent of the land area and render nearly 20 million people homeless. Bangladesh also faces other problems like dwindling water supplies, saltwater damage to crops, loss of biodiversity, and fiercer storms tearing through the region. See Mason Inman, "Where Warming Hits Hard," *Nature Reports Climate Change* 3 (2009): 18–21; Michael S. Northcott, *A Moral Climate: The Ethics of Global Warming* (London: Darton, Longman, and Todd, 2007), 18.

Then United Nations Secretary General Kofi Annan, while addressing the UN Climate Change Conference in Nairobi in November 2006, pointed out: "Climate change is not just an environmental issue, as too many people still believe. It is an all-encompassing threat."[2] So the ecological crisis "is not just about cyclones and floods, glaciers and forests. It is about people and the harm being done to their livelihoods and, ultimately, their chances of survival."[3] The ecological crisis will bring more suffering to the nearly 1 billion people who already go to bed hungry every night and the approximately 2 billion people exposed to insect-borne diseases and water scarcity. It will force millions of people living in drought-prone regions, deltas, and low-lying small island states to migrate. The ecological crisis is not only the cry of the Earth—the various manifestations of which were discussed at considerable length in Part II—it is also the cry of the poor.

It is the human face of the ecological crisis that we discuss in this part of the book. Behind charts and graphics depicting rising greenhouse emissions or trends in extreme weather events like droughts, storms, and floods, lie the real lives of individuals and communities, especially those who are already poor and most vulnerable. As the effects of the contemporary ecological crisis begin to manifest in various parts of the world, it is already becoming clear that their adverse effects on the lives of communities, especially in poor and developing nations, will be overwhelming and unprecedented. The impacts of the ecological crisis have the potential to threaten basic human welfare in key areas like food security, health, and shelter. With the ecological crisis looming on the horizon, there is a real danger that the developmental path of many communities and nations will come to a sudden halt or even take a turn for the worse. In fact, one of the main warnings of the "Human Development Report 2011" was precisely along these lines. The report cautions that progress in human welfare that was painstakingly achieved over the last few decades and will continue to be maintained in the coming years, but could be arrested or even reversed by mid-century when the effects of the contemporary ecological crisis, climate change in

---

[2] Kofi Annan, valedictory address, UN Climate Change Conference, November 15, 2006, Nairobi.

[3] Michael Holman, "The Amazon Changed Me," *The Tablet* (December 5, 2009).

particular, begin to hit home.[4] According to the same report, half of current malnutrition worldwide is attributable to ecological factors.[5] With ever-mounting pressures on the planet's biosphere and natural resources, it appears that several of the Millennium Development Goals—halving the number of hungry people and ensuring environmental sustainability in terms of guaranteeing access to safe drinking water and basic sanitation—will become increasingly more difficult to meet.

During the last few decades the perception of the ecological crisis as the cry of the poor became sharper as the scale of adverse impacts of the ecological crisis—from pollution to climate change—on human communities all over the globe began to rise drastically. It is becoming evident that the poor are turning out to be the early, disproportionate, and unjust victims of the crisis. Jürgen Moltmann notes that we will not be in a position to reach social justice without justice for the natural world and that we will not be able to obtain justice for nature without social justice.[6] In the 1990s such a realization became part of mainstream thinking on ecological issues, as evident in the title of Leonardo Boff's important work *Cry of the Earth, Cry of the Poor*, and other publications of the era.[7] The discussion on ecological questions today has certainly gone beyond concern for polar bears and pandas to include matters of equity, justice, solidarity with the poor and vulnerable, and responsibility toward future generations.

It is imperative, therefore, to look at the ecological crisis from a moral viewpoint, apart from the physical perspective, and discuss it within an ethical framework. It is toward an understanding of the

---

[4] See UNDP, "Human Development Report 2011: Sustainability and Equity: A Better Future for All" (New York: UNDP, 2011), iv and *passim*. According to the report, by 2050 the global Human Development Index will be 8 percent lower than the baseline for a modest "environmental challenge" scenario or even 15 percent lower in the case of extreme ecological degradation. See ibid., 2.

[5] Ibid., 53.

[6] See Jürgen Moltmann, *The Future of Creation* (Philadelphia: Fortress Press, 1979), 128.

[7] Leonardo Boff, *Cry of the Earth, Cry of the Poor* (Maryknoll, NY: Orbis Books, 1997). See also Peter S. Wenz, *Environmental Justice* (Albany: State University of New York Press, 1988); Wolfgang Sachs, Reinhard Loske, and Manfred Linz, *Greening the North: A Post-Industrial Blueprint for Ecology and Equity* (London: Zed Books, 1998); Barbara Rose Johnston, ed., *Who Pays the Price? The Sociocultural Context of Environmental Crisis* (Washington, DC: Island Press, 1994).

contemporary ecological crisis as a cry of the poor and as a moral crisis to which Part III is dedicated. We dwell on the human face of the contemporary ecological crisis, placing it in a much wider context and going beyond current approaches that see the crisis merely as a host of environmental problems, with the costs usually calculated in economic terms. But the human cost of the ecological crisis will not be measured in billions of dollars but in millions of lives. It is important to look at the contemporary ecological crisis as part of the wider human context, especially from the perspective of poor and vulnerable communities.

Our discussion of the ecological crisis as a cry of the poor comprises two chapters. In Chapter 7 we examine how the ecological crisis will have a pronounced impact on human welfare. It has the potential to threaten human welfare in the three vital and basic areas of human life: food security, health, and shelter. In Chapter 8 we see how the poor are the unjust and disproportionate victims of the ecological crisis. While the crisis is caused mostly by the rich world, its main victims will be those who have done least to cause it. As we all have the same right to equal ecological space, questions of justice and equity need to be addressed along with those of solidarity and fairness. All these considerations render discussions on the ecological crisis one of the greatest moral dilemmas of our age.

7

The Impacts of Ecological Crisis on Food, Health, and Shelter

The human face of the contemporary ecological crisis is most evident when we examine its impact on basic areas like food security, health, and shelter. Food and health security, along with safe shelter, are fundamental necessities for human survival. We now examine how the ecological crisis concretely affects food security, raises health concerns, and poses the specter of forced migration, as in the case of climate refugees.

We begin with the impacts of the ecological crisis in the key sector of food security. The current scenario with regard to global food security presents a stark challenge, with nearly 1 billion people already hungry and another 2 billion chronically undernourished. The impending ecological crisis, with its various manifestations ranging from land degradation to water scarcity and biodiversity loss, will further compound the precarious situation of food security at the global level. However, it is climate change that will have most pronounced impact on agriculture in the decades to come, with reverberating effects on food security. We also examine the disproportionate impact of food insecurity on human communities in the various parts of the globe, especially in the most vulnerable regions of sub-Saharan Africa and Southeast Asia. We explore the deleterious effects of the ecological crisis on human health, dealing with the health impacts of pollution, water contamination, poor sanitation, and above all, climate change. We explore the health impacts of anthropogenic climate change on two fronts: the effects from extreme weather events, and the changing patterns and transmission of diseases. Finally, we discuss how the contemporary ecological crisis, and climate change in particular, can lead to forced migration on a massive scale. We deal with the main drivers of ecological migration and offer a rapid overview of some of the hotspots of ecological migration in the future.

The Current Food-Security Scenario

The greatest scandal of our time, despite all our progress in science and technology and our remarkable economic growth—the world economy grew twentyfold in the twentieth century alone[1]—is the pernicious reality of nearly 1 billion hungry people in our common home. Today, there are more people going to bed with empty stomachs than in any other era in human history. In 2010, a total of 925 million people were estimated to be undernourished, representing almost 16 percent of the population in developing countries.[2] While the proportion of hungry population has declined in some parts of the world—with nations like China and regions like Latin America and the Caribbean having registered remarkable achievements on this front—this has not happened everywhere. As the "2011 Global Hunger Index" notes, "Although the world has made some progress in reducing hunger, the proportion of hungry people remains too high."[3] Paul Roberts notes, "Despite the fact that food costs are half what they were fifty years ago and despite a global food supply that now exceeds per capita calorific needs by about 20 percent, the world has nearly as many malnourished citizens as it does over nourished ones."[4] On a planet with sufficient food for all, nearly 1 billion people are hungry, while another 1 billion overconsume, with consequent diet-related chronic diseases. At the same time, another 1 billion are thought to suffer from "hidden hunger" (micronutrient malnutrition), in which important micronutrients (such as vitamins and minerals) are missing from their diet, with consequent risks of physical and mental impairment.[5] It is sobering to recall that about 6.5 million children

---

[1] See Angus Maddison, *The World Economy: Historical Statistics* (Paris: OECD, 2004); UNEP, *Global Environment Outlook 5: Environment for the Future of All* (Nairobi: UNEP, 2012), 5.

[2] FAO (Food and Agricultural Organization of the United Nations), *The State of Food Insecurity in the World: Assessing Food Insecurity in Protracted Crises* (Rome: FAO, 2010), 4. See also J. Beddington et al., *Achieving Food Security in the Face of Climate Change: Final Report from the Commission on Sustainable Agriculture and Climate Change* (Copenhagen: CCAFS, 2012), 9.

[3] International Food Policy Research Institute et al., "2011 Global Hunger Index: The Challenge of Hunger: Taming Price Spikes and Excessive Food Price Volatility," IFPRI Issue Brief 69 (Washington, DC: IFPRI, October 2011), 3.

[4] Paul Roberts, *The End of Food: The Coming Crisis in the World Food Industry* (London: Bloomsbury, 2009), xvii.

[5] See Government Office for Science, *Foresight: The Future of Food and Farming. Final Project Report* (London: The Government Office for Science, 2011), 9.

under age five die every year of malnutrition and hunger-related diseases—about 18,000 deaths a day.[6] Indeed, more than one-third of child deaths worldwide are related to inadequate nutrition.[7]

One of the great challenges of the twenty-first century will be to increase the global food supply to feed a population projected to reach 8 billion by 2030 and level off at just over 9 billion by mid-century.[8] Most of this century's population growth will occur in low-income countries, with Africa's population expected to double from just over 1 billion in 2010 to about 2 billion by 2050.[9] But the additional pressure on global food security will come not so much from population increase as from the increasing demand for "fat foods," as per capita consumption rates rise in keeping with the expected rise in people's income levels. The growth of income in the developing world, especially in Asia, will inevitably lead more people to catch up with the already unsustainable dietary patterns of the developed world. The structure of food demand has changed substantially in the last two decades in developing countries, where food consumption is shifting away from basic cereals to diets richer in meat, dairy products, and processed foods. This shift in dietary preferences will have far-reaching ramifications for the entire food chain.

The increase in population and the change in consumption patterns will certainly put greater pressure on food production. According to several authoritative estimates, the world will need 50–70 percent more food by 2050.[10] More food will need to be produced from less land, as increasingly less land is available for agricultural cultivation in most regions of the world, due to increasing urbanization, conversion of farmland for industrial use, and other factors. It appears

---

[6] Liliana Hisas, *The Food Gap: The Impacts of Climate Change on Food Production: A 2020 Perspective* (Alexandria, VA: Universal Ecological Fund, 2011), v. See also R. Black et al., "Maternal and Child Undernutrition: Global and Regional Exposures and Health Consequences," *Lancet* 371 (2008): 243–60.

[7] Brian Halweil and Danielle Nierenberg, "Charting a New Path to Eliminating Hunger," in The Worldwatch Institute, *State of the World 2011: Innovations That Nourish the Planet* (New York: W. W. Norton, 2011), 4.

[8] See United Nations Population Fund, *State of World Population 2011: People and Possibilities in a World of Seven Billion* (New York: UNFPA, 2011), 4; Government Office for Science, *Foresight*, 50; H. Charles et al., "Food Security: The Challenge of Feeding Nine Billion People," *Science* 327 (2010): 812.

[9] UNFPA, *State of World Population 2011*, 5.

[10] See Royal Society of London, *Reaping the Benefits: Science and the Sustainable Intensification of Global Agriculture* (London: Royal Society, 2009), 11; National Research Council, *A Sustainability Challenge: Food Security for All: Report of Two Workshops* (Washington, DC: National Academy of Sciences, 2012), vii.

impossible to increase food production dramatically using the modern agricultural practices heavily dependent on irrigation and widespread use of fertilizers and pesticides, with their attendant ecological consequences. The same constraints present also with regard to other non-agricultural sources of food. In the case of fisheries, for example, it appears certain that there are no major new fishing grounds and most are already overexploited.[11]

The prevailing situation with regard to global food security is grim. Harbingers of food insecurity include unacceptable levels of chronic hunger and malnutrition in many parts of the world, spiraling food prices, population increase, and higher levels of per capita consumption. Adding to the concern is the contemporary ecological crisis, climate change in particular.

Food security is intricately linked to the wider ecological context. Agriculture, more than any other human endeavor, relies on stable natural conditions like water availability, benign weather, robust ecosystems, natural cycles like that of nitrogen, soil fertility, crop diversity, and other biophysical influences. Now it appears that these stable conditions that guaranteed food security are being threatened by the contemporary ecological crisis. Tomorrow's farmers will have to feed more people, but they will need to do so without the benefit of some critical advantages their predecessors took for granted—a stable climate, abundant water, and cheap energy.[12]

The effects of the contemporary ecological crisis on food security are manifold. Climate change, in particular, will have the most severe and pronounced effects on agricultural production. However, the threats to food security go beyond climate change and include land degradation; transformation of the natural biogeochemical cycles, especially the nitrogen cycle, due to the increased use of fertilizers and pesticides in modern agriculture; decreasing water availability; changes in biodiversity due to extension of the agricultural frontier leading to deforestation in many regions of the world; and the fast depletion of natural resources. All of these will have a telling effect on food security.[13] The current global food system is consuming the world's natural resources at an unsustainable rate, placing in jeopardy

---

[11] See H. Charles J. Godray et al., "Food Security: The Challenge of Feeding Nine Billion People," *Science* 327 (2010): 813.

[12] Roberts, *The End of Food*, xix.

[13] See P. J. Gregory et al., "Climate Change and Food Security," *Philosophical Transactions of the Royal Society B* 360 (2005): 2146; Diana Liverman and Kamal Kapadia, "Food Systems and the Global Environment: An Overview," in *Food*

future global food security. Once we deplete the resources on which food production depends—primarily soil, water, and the natural stock of plants and animals—global food insecurity is sure to follow.

One of the first resources to run out will be fertile land. It will be a monumental challenge to find more agricultural land to produce enough food to meet rising demands for food supply. The total land currently used for agriculture stands at approximately 11.4 billion acres.[14] While it is true that global crop yields grew by 115 percent between 1967 and 2007, with an addition of only 8 percent of agricultural land, the outlook looks grim for the future. The conversion of croplands for biofuel production, cash crops, and non-food crops, as well as the increasing phenomenon of land grabbing in Africa and Latin America, will intensify squabbles for suitable land for food production. Agricultural land is currently being lost also to urbanization, desertification, salinization, and sea-level rise, and the loss will be even greater when the ecological crisis unfolds in full. At the same time, the amount of arable land per head is decreasing, having almost halved since 1960.[15]

Our home planet's rich biodiversity is also dwindling. The loss of biodiversity reduces crop diversity and affects agricultural output in the long run. Biodiversity losses can affect pollination, control of pest species, and soil nutrients. Biodiversity and crop diversity are important especially for poor communities and subsistence farmers. Wild animals and plants are crucial to many agricultural communities. Many vulnerable communities obtain a significant amount of food from the wild, which increases resilience to food shocks. It is estimated that about 1 billion people use wild foods in their diet.[16] Modern agricultural practices that privilege the spread of monocultures in the place of crop diversity, excessive use of pesticides and fertilizers, and widespread deforestation have led to the loss of biodiversity and erosion of the genetic resource base, with modern varieties displacing traditional ones. Modern agriculture concentrates on a "handful" of crops in the quest for the "right" seed to boost agricultural output

---

Security and Global Environmental Change, ed. John Ingram, Polly Ericksen, and Diana Liverman (London: Earthscan, 2010), 21.

[14] Government Office for Science, *Foresight*, 15.

[15] Robet Bailey et al., *Growing a Better Future: Food Justice in a Resource-Constrained World* (Oxford: Oxfam International, 2011), 17.

[16] Government Office for Science, *Foresight*, 10, 43; A. Aberoumand, "Nutritional Evaluation of Edible Portulaca Oleracia as Plant Food," *Food Analytical Methods* 2 (2009): 204–7.

and increase profits.[17] It appears that this search for just the right seed has led to the erosion of crop diversity in both rich and poor nations, with implications for food security.

The most important threat to global food security from the contemporary ecological crisis, however, is climate change.

Climate Change and Food Security

All the main elements of food production—land, water, and climate—will be affected by climate change, raising concerns for global food security. It is becoming increasingly clear that some of the most profound and direct impacts of climate change will be on agricultural and food systems. If global average temperature were to rise in the upper region of the estimated 1.8–4°C by the end of the century, as forecast in the Fourth Assessment of the IPCC in 2007, there could be shifts in crop zones by hundreds of miles, the abandonment of cropping in parts of Africa, and severe water shortages in many regions.[18] The challenge of ensuring global food security becomes even more daunting when one takes into account the various impacts of climate change (rising global temperatures, changing precipitation patterns, shifting seasons, more frequent and extreme weather events, flooding, and drought) on food production.[19] These effects will translate, especially for already vulnerable communities, into devastating consequences: crop failures, reduced cereal yields, and often hunger and undernutrition. Climate change will increase the number of people at risk of hunger.[20] According to the 2009 Oxfam report on the link between climate change and poverty:

> Hunger will be one of the major impacts of climate change. It may be the defining human tragedy of this century. Millions of people in countries that already have food security problems will

---

[17] Four firms—Dupont, Monsanto, Syngenta, and Limagrain—dominate over 50 percent of seed industry sales globally. See Bailey et al., *Growing a Better Future*, 34.

[18] Liverman and Kapadia, "Food Systems and the Global Environment," 18.

[19] Gerald C. Nelson et al., *Food Security, Farming, and Climate Change to 2050: Scenarios, Results, Policy Options* (Washington, DC: IFPRI, 2010), xi; Government Office for Science, *Foresight*, 55.

[20] W. E. Easterling et al., "Food, Fibre, and Forest Products," in *Climate Change 2007: Impacts, Adaptation, and Vulnerability: Contribution of Working Group II to the Fourth Assessment Report of the Intergovernmental Panel on Climate Change*, ed. M. L. Parry et al. (Cambridge: Cambridge University Press, 2007), 300.

have to give up traditional crops and agricultural methods as they experience changes in the seasons that they and their ancestors have depended upon. The social upheavals that result—such as migration and conflict—may mean that this change in the functioning of our planet affects more people than any other.[21]

Climate change alone is estimated to increase the number of undernourished people to between 40 million and 170 million.[22]

An analysis of the impact of climate change on agriculture in general, and on primary crop yields in particular, can help to explain why climate change will turn out to be the greatest threat to food security in the decades to come.

Climate change will affect the stable climatic conditions that are indispensable for agriculture. It was the stable climate of the Holocene era of the last 10,000 years that made agriculture possible. One of the effects of human-induced climate change will be the disruption of this stable climate essential for food production. Farmers in many parts of the word have begun to report that the natural climatic seasons that determine the sowing, growing, and reaping of crops have become unsteady. Farmers note also that seasons are becoming less distinct. In most regions of the world hitherto regular seasons appear to have shrunk. They are increasingly being replaced by seasons that are now simply either "hotter and dry" or "hotter and wet," with large temperature fluctuations. Seasonal rains are changing dramatically with rainfall becoming more erratic and at times more heavy and violent.

Added to the change in seasons is the increase in extreme weather events such as heat waves, intense rainfall, and drought, which can have severe impacts on agriculture and on food security. Intense rainfalls, for example, can delay planting, increase root diseases, damage crops, and cause flooding and erosion. Droughts can further exacerbate water availability in regions that already experience water stress.[23] The extreme weather events of the last few years appear to have been harbingers of how climate change can concretely affect food security. From the Russian heat wave in 2010, which triggered a major global wheat price hike, to one of the worst droughts in decades

---

[21] Oxfam, *Suffering the Science: Climate Change, People, and Poverty*, Oxfam Briefing Paper (July 6, 2009), 12. See also Angela Spivey, "More Lack in the World: The Complex Connection Between Undernutrition and Climate Change," *Environmental Health Perspectives* 119 (2011): 524.

[22] Easterling et al., "Food, Fibre, and Forest Products," 300.

[23] The National Academy of Sciences, *Advancing the Science of Climate Change* (Washington, DC: The National Academies Press, 2010), 294.

in the Horn of Africa in 2011, extreme weather has pushed millions into hunger. In a similar vein, heavy monsoon rainfall and multiple typhoons inundated large areas of productive rice lands in Southeast Asia—including Thailand, Cambodia, Vietnam, Laos, Myanmar, and the Philippines—and resulted in approximately eleven hundred deaths and affected nearly 10 million people across the region.

Crop Yields and Livestock Productivity

The impact of climate change on agriculture and food security will be even more pernicious when it comes to crop yields and livestock productivity. World food supply is very dependent on a few crops, especially cereals (wheat, rice, maize), oilseeds, sugar, and soybeans, all of which will be affected by climate change in different ways.

The productivity of important agricultural crops is drastically reduced when they experience even short episodes of high temperatures during the reproductive period. Peaks of high temperature, even when occurring for just a few hours, can drastically reduce the production of important food crops.[24] Even a 2°C increase in temperature could lead to a further 20–40 percent fall in cereal yields, mostly in Asia and Africa.[25] This is so because the crops have normal temperature thresholds. Most of today's crops have been carefully bred for traits that fit the present climate and will react negatively to even slight temperature fluctuations. Wheat that is exposed to 30°C (86°F) for more than eight hours produces less grain, and rice pollen become sterile after only an hour of 35°C (95°F) heat.[26] In southern Africa maize yields are predicted to fall by as much as 30 percent if temperatures rise 1°C. With a 2°C temperature rise, more than 80 percent of the land area over most African nations would become unsuitable for the crops now growing there.[27]

The severe impact of future climate change on crop yields is markedly evident in the case of cereals. For the majority of the world's population, especially those living in poverty, cereals are an extremely

---

[24] Edmar I. Teixeira et al., "Global Hot-spots of Heat Stress on Agricultural Crops due to Climate Change," *Agricultural and Forest Meteorology* 170 (2013): 206–7.

[25] Uma Lele, "Food Security for a Billion Poor" (editorial), *Science* 326 (2010): 1554.

[26] Robert Henson, *The Rough Guide to Climate Change: The Symptoms—The Science—The Solutions* (London: Rough Guides Ltd., 2006), 157.

[27] Hannah Hoag, "Confronting the Biodiversity Crisis," *Nature* 4 (2010): 51–52.

important source of calories: 90 percent of the world's calorific requirement is provided by only thirty crops, with wheat, rice, and maize
contributing roughly half of the calories currently consumed by the
world's poor.[28] These crops will be the ones most affected by climate
change in the coming decades.

Rice is the crop on which more people depend than any other. It
is Asia's major food staple, with the continent accounting for 90 percent of global production. East and Southeast Asia combined produce
56 percent of rice in the world. In the river delta coastal regions of
Southeast Asia, rice production has already suffered because of storms
that overwhelm sea defenses and salt-water intrusion into paddy fields.
Rice plants are also very sensitive to temperature change. Studies from
the International Rice Research Institute in the Philippines—a country
expected to suffer a sharp decline in rice production in the coming
decades—show that a 1°C rise in nighttime temperature can reduce
rice yields by 10 percent.[29] In Vietnam, rice yield in the south of the
country is forecast to drop about 6 percent by 2050, and by twice as
much in the north of the country.[30] Other countries in Asia that will
be negatively affected are India, which produces 22 percent of the
world's rice, and Bangladesh, the low-lying flood- and drought-prone
country that devotes 80 percent of its cultivated land area to rice.[31]

Wheat is the most widely grown crop in the world, harvested annually on more than 543 million acres of cropland. Wheat prefers
relatively cool temperatures, and so wheat is sown throughout much
of the world in late autumn or early winter and harvested before early
summer. Accordingly, the grains fill out toward the end of the season,
when hot conditions are experienced in many regions.[32] The most
pronounced effect of warming is to shorten the duration of grain filling, which negatively affects grain yields. For example, recent simulations of wheat yield in Australia indicate that average yields will be

---

[28] Liverman and Kapadia, "Food Systems and the Global Environment," 6;
David Lobell et al., "Prioritizing Climate Change Adaptation Needs for Food
Security in 2030," *Science* 319 (2008): 608.

[29] See S. Peng et al., "Rice Yields Decline with Higher Night Temperature and
Global Warming," *Proceedings of the National Academy of Sciences* 101 (2004):
9971–75; Asian Development Bank, *The Economics of Climate Change in Southeast Asia: A Regional Review* (April 2009), 19ff., 74.

[30] See Asian Development Bank, *The Economics of Climate Change in Southeast
Asia*, 41; Oxfam, *Suffering the Science*, 19.

[31] See Hisas, *The Food Gap*, 19–20; Oxfam, *Suffering the Science*, 18.

[32] David B. Lobell et al., "Extreme Heat Effects on Wheat Senescence in India,"
Nature Climate Change 2 (2012): 186.

50 percent less in a growing season that is 2°C warmer.[33] It has been calculated that for northern Indo-Gangetic plains—where 15 percent of the world's wheat is grown—crop models underestimate yield losses for +2°C by as much as 50 percent.[34]

Maize, known as corn in some countries, is among the world's most important food crops. It is the staple food for more than 250 million East Africans. It is also used as animal feed across the world. Maize is particularly vulnerable to temperature changes and water stress. Heat stress damages maize crops especially at the seedling stage, which can result in significant yield decreases or even in no crop at all. It is estimated that during the 2003 heat wave in western Europe, when temperatures rose to 6°C above average, maize production dropped by 36 percent in the Po Valley in Italy and 30 percent in France.[35] The maize crop is estimated to drop by 15 percent or more by 2020 in much of sub-Saharan Africa and in most of India. The viability of maize as a staple will become a serious challenge in a range of Southern African countries including Mozambique, Tanzania, and Zambia.[36]

Domesticated crops are not the only ones at risk. Other food crops on which many communities depend for livelihood and nutrition will be affected by climate change. According to one study, as many as 16–22 percent of the wild relatives of cowpeas, peanuts, and potatoes could go extinct by 2055.[37] Another important study has shown that in South Asia, seven out of nine non-primary food crops, important to large, food-insecure populations, would deteriorate in yield by as much as 14 percent by 2030 with just 1–2°C of warming. The same calculation made for Southern Africa forecasts the deterioration of six crops out of eight.[38] Due to climate change, crops—which employ millions of people and which are crucial to many equatorial countries as a source of income generation—are also likely to suffer. For example, coffee yields will not only change and quality deteriorate but also the climatic regions most suitable for coffee production will shift. Tea production is also highly sensitive to changes in heat and water. Tea

---

[33] See S. Asseng et al., "The Impact of Temperature Variability on Wheat Yields," *Global Change Biology* 17 (2011): 997–1012.

[34] Lobell et al., "Extreme Heat Effects on Wheat Senescence in India," 186–89.

[35] Easterling et al., "Food, Fibre, and Forest Products," 277.

[36] Oxfam, *Suffering the Science*, 18.

[37] A. Jarvis et al., "The Effect of Climate Change on Crop Wild Relatives," *Agriculture, Ecosystem, and Environment* 126 (2008): 13–23.

[38] Lobell et al., "Prioritizing Climate Change Adaptation Needs for Food Security in 2030," 319.

productivity in Sri Lanka, for example, is expected to drop by more than 20 percent during this century.[39]

The impacts of climate change on agriculture and food security will be even more severe in the long term, precisely beyond 2050. Up to 2050, the challenges from climate change to food security may be manageable, "in the sense that well-designed investments in land and water productivity enhancements might, conceivably, substantially offset the negative effects from climate change."[40] In the next two or three decades, a small amount of warming might even provide some benefits for food production for some countries situated in the moderate climatic zones. But after 2050 the situation will change, and the challenges to food security will become formidable. The delay in the three decades up to 2050 is provided by ocean thermal lag and other factors like aerosol particles in the atmosphere, which can temporarily hold back or partially offset the full impact of global warming and associated climate change resulting from greenhouse gas emissions from human activities.[41] By 2080, though, most cropping areas in the world are likely to be exposed to record average air temperatures.[42] Slowing greenhouse gas emissions today is critical if we are to avoid a calamitous post-2050 future.

Disproportionate Impacts

The food security impacts of the ecological crisis on people all over the world are hugely disproportionate. Those who are already poor and vulnerable will be hardest hit in this regard. As resource pressures mount and climate change gathers speed, poor and vulnerable people will suffer first—from extreme weather, from spiraling food prices, from the scramble for land and water. For the poorest, who spend up to 75 percent of their income on food, the food security impacts of the ecological crisis, and climate change in particular, will be catastrophic. Families will be forced into impossible trade-offs in a desperate bid to feed themselves. Between 3.3 and 5.5 billion people are expected to

---

[39] Oxfam, *Suffering the Science*, 20.

[40] Nelson et al., *Food Security, Farming, and Climate Change to 2050*, xxi.

[41] See also William R. Cline, *Global Warming and Agriculture: Impact Estimates by Country* (Washington, DC: Center for Global Development/Peterson Institute for International Economics, 2007), 2.

[42] See D. S. Battisti and R. L. Naylor, "Historical Warnings of Future Food Insecurity with Unprecedented Seasonal Heat," *Science* 323 (2008): 240–44; Teixeira et al., "Global Hot-spots of Heat Stress on Agricultural Crops due to Climate Change," 206.

be affected by losses in crop production if global temperatures rise by 3°C.[43] Climate change will also exacerbate the challenges in reducing the number of malnourished children. It is estimated that the number of malnourished children will increase between 8.5 and 10.3 percent by 2050 if adequate steps are not taken to mitigate climate change.[44]

The food security consequences of the contemporary ecological crisis are not evenly distributed around the globe. One may speak here of a double injustice: geographical and demographic.

First, the impacts of the ecological crisis on communities in the area of food security evidence a geographical imbalance. Essentially, those who live farther from the equator have better prospects of enjoying greater food security. The temperature rise associated with climate change will benefit crop production in the middle and high latitudes—the richer and less populated countries tend to lie in the higher latitudes of the Northern Hemisphere where precipitation will increase and winters will get warmer—while crop production will drastically decline in the low latitudes, which are also more thickly populated, mostly by people belonging to the developing nations. Temperate and subtropical agricultural areas are expected to bear substantial crop yield losses due to extreme temperature episodes.[45] The impact of climate change on crop yields will be felt most in poor countries. For a 2°C rise in global temperatures, the lowest-income countries will experience the sharpest yield losses, with drops ranging from 13 percent for spring wheat to 22 percent for soybeans and 27 percent for maize.[46] In contrast, crop yields will increase in most developed countries. For example, wheat production will rise, at least initially, in northern Europe and Canada. Meanwhile, on the Indo-Gangetic plain, wheat production could shrink by more than half by 2050, threatening the food security of 200 million people.

Second, apart from the so-called geographical injustice, food insecurity due to the ecological crisis will have particular impacts on specific groups like subsistence farmers, rural and indigenous com-

---

[43] See Bill Hare, "Relationship Between Increases in Global Mean Temperature and Impacts on Ecosystems, Food Production, Water, and Socio-Economic Systems," in *Avoiding Dangerous Climate Change*, ed. Hans Joachim Schellnhuber et al. (New York: Cambridge University Press, 2006), 179.

[44] Nelson et al., *Food Security, Farming, and Climate Change to 2050*, xviii.

[45] Oxfam, *Suffering the Science*, 17; Teixeira et al., "Global Hot-spots of Heat Stress on Agricultural Crops due to Climate Change," 207.

[46] Thomas W. Hertel and Stephanie D. Rosch, "Climate Change, Agriculture, and Poverty," *Applied Economic Perspectives and Policy* 32 (2010): 359.

munities, fisher folk, and such. Some of the most important effects of climate change will be felt among the populations, predominantly in developing countries, referred to as subsistence or smallholder farmers.[47] Rural communities that depend overwhelmingly on natural resources for their income and livelihood will be affected as resources are depleted and rising temperatures affect crop productivity. Fishing communities will also be particularly affected by the ecological crisis as fish are increasingly threatened by overfishing and climate change.

Among the regions that will be most affected by food insecurity because of the ecological crisis, two regions stand out. The ecological crisis, and climate change in particular, will increase the food insecurity of poor communities that live in the arid and semiarid tropics and in the large Asian and African deltas. An analysis of climate risks for crops in twelve food-insecure regions indicates that by 2030, "South Asia and Southern Africa as two regions that, without sufficient adaptation measures, will likely suffer negative impacts on several crops that are important to large food-insecure human populations."[48] Accordingly, the main battlegrounds for food security and poverty reduction are Africa and Asia, where 97 percent of the world's food-insecure populations reside.[49]

The agricultural landscape of sub-Saharan Africa is likely to undergo considerable change in the coming decades. For an already drought-prone continent, climate change will bring an even greater risk to food production in many areas. Food systems will also have to adapt to ensure food security for the extra billion people who will be populating the African continent by 2050.[50] Another hot spot for food insecurity will be South Asia, which is characterized by some of the highest levels of undernutrition in the world, including calorie deficits as well as deficiencies of essential micronutrients.[51] Bangladesh, beyond perhaps any other country in the region, will face the most acute threats to food security due to climate change. "Already half of

---

[47] John F. Morton, "The Impact of Climate Change on Smallholder and Subsistence Agriculture," *Proceedings of the National Academy of Sciences* 104 (2007): 19680.

[48] Lobell et al., "Prioritizing Climate Change Adaptation Needs for Food Security in 2030," 607.

[49] Lele, "Food Security for a Billion Poor," 1554.

[50] Philip Thornton et al., "Agriculture and Food Systems in Sub-Saharan Africa in a 4°C+ World," *Philosophical Transactions of the Royal Society A* 369 (2011): 131.

[51] IFPRI, *Nutrition and Gender in Asia: From Research to Action* (New Delhi: IFPRI, 2008), 1.

the population lives below the upper poverty line (2,122 kcal/day) and a third live below the lower poverty line (1,805 kcal/day)."[52]

In fact, there appears to be an overlapping of food insecurity hot spots over those regions of the world, which already experience higher levels of hunger and malnutrition.

Health Impacts of the Contemporary Ecological Crisis

The contemporary ecological crisis raises serious challenges to health too, as well as other basic areas like nutrition and shelter. Health hazards are on the rise with the worsening of the global situation of our planetary home. They are as varied as the multiple manifestations of the crisis. We limit ourselves here to examining the effects on human health of pollution, water contamination, poor sanitation, and above all, climate change.

Pollution

The consequences of our polluting of our common home are bound to fall on the members of our common household. Rachel Carson was one of the first scientists to alert the world to how human interference with the natural ecosystems, as in the case of chemical insecticides in agriculture or other pollutants in modern industry, could have serious and negative impacts on human health.[53] Today, our common home is much more polluted than in Carson's time, and the impacts of pollution on human health are graver.

Indoor air pollution—generated largely by inefficient and poorly ventilated stoves burning biomass fuels—continues to take a huge toll on the health of people, especially in poor households without access to modern cooking fuel. Because firewood is on the decrease due to widespread deforestation, the poor use dung and crop residues, which intensify the exposure to indoor air pollution. Their smoke is more toxic and often leads to irritation of the eyes; it can also cause acute respiratory infections, lung cancer, reduced lung function, carbon monoxide poisoning, and permanent harm to the immune system.[54] Indoor

---

[52] Stephan Baas and Selvaraju Ramasamy, *Community Based Adaptation in Action: A Case Study from Bangladesh* (Rome: Food and Agricultural Organization; Dhaka: Department of Agricultural Extension, 2008), 49. Available online.

[53] Rachel Carson, *Silent Spring* (Boston, MA: Houghton Mifflin, 1962).

[54] UNDP (United Nations Development Programme), "Human Development Report 2011: Sustainability and Equity: A Better Future for All" (New York: UNDP, 2011), 51–52.

air pollution is responsible for the deaths of nearly 2 million people a year, especially among the rural poor. Unfortunately, more than half of these deaths occur among children under age five.[55] As with other impacts of the contemporary ecological crisis, the poor are the disproportionate victims, especially women and children who live in rural areas. Indoor air pollution kills nearly twenty times more people in the least developed countries than the highly developed ones.[56]

Outdoor air pollution is a major cause of respiratory and cardiovascular diseases globally. Long-term exposure to air pollution can cause respiratory disorders, damage to immune systems, and other deleterious effects. Exposure to increased levels of ambient air pollutants and pollens can exacerbate asthma and respiratory allergies. Allergic respiratory diseases and bronchial asthma are increasing worldwide, especially in urban areas. Cases of asthma have been increasing all over the world, including developed countries like the United States, especially among children.[57] Urban air pollution is particularly significant in emerging economies like China and India. Air pollution is leading to serious health consequences in many urban areas in China, where rising energy consumption, based largely on coal and other solid fuels, and increasing vehicle pollution have taken a heavy toll on air quality.

Water

Poor sanitation associated with water contamination and water scarcity also has important consequences for human health. Water is a basic necessity for sustaining life on our home planet. Clean and adequate water, however, goes undelivered to many of the world's poor. Over 884 million people lack access to clean drinking water; 2.6 billion do not have access to adequate sanitation services; and 1.4 million children under the age of five die every year as a result of lack of access to clean water and adequate sanitation services.[58] Unsafe water, inadequate sanitation, and poor hygiene are among the

---

[55] Ibid., 51; Yoko Akachi et al., *Global Climate Change and Child Health: A Review of Pathways, Impacts, and Measures to Improve the Evidence Base*, Innocenti Discussion Paper (Florence: UNICEF, 2009), 7.

[56] UNDP, "Human Development Report 2011," 51–52.

[57] Ibid., 52; Akachi et al., *Global Climate Change and Child Health*, 6.

[58] WHO and UNICEF, *Progress on Sanitation and Drinking Water: 2010 Update*, WHO/UNICEF Joint Monitoring Programme for Water Supply and Sanitation (2010), 7, 22; UNICEF, *The State of the World's Children 2005: Childhood Under Threat* (2006), ii; UNEP, *Towards a Green Economy: Pathways to Sustainable Development and Poverty Eradication* (Nairobi: UNEP, 2011), 11.

top ten causes of disease worldwide. In poor countries 65 percent of the population lacks access to sanitation, and 38 percent lacks access to clean water. Nearly four in ten people worldwide lack sanitary toilets; the figures increase to as many as eight in ten when it comes to the least economically developed countries.[59]

The impacts of both poor sanitation and fresh-water scarcity take a high toll on human health. Water-related diseases can be classified by route of transmission, thus distinguishing between water-borne (ingested) and water-washed diseases (caused by lack of hygiene). Access to safe water remains an extremely important global health issue. Half of all malnutrition is attributable to ecological factors, particularly poor water, sanitation and hygiene. Poor sanitation affects children most. Almost 2 million deaths a year, mostly in young children, are caused by diarrheal diseases and other conditions that are attributable to unsafe water and lack of basic sanitation. It is estimated that improved sanitation and drinking water could save 2.2 million children a year, or some 5,500 a day.[60]

Climate Change

The most important source of concern for human health in the context of the contemporary ecological crisis, however, is climate change. Changes in our home planet's climate system, to which humans have contributed substantially, could prove to be the greatest challenge to human health in the twenty-first century.

Climate change has multiple direct and indirect consequences for human health—all of which are important. Human beings are exposed to climate change directly through altering weather patterns (rising temperatures, changes in precipitation, sea-level rise, and more frequent extreme events) and indirectly through changes in water, air, and food quality and changes in ecosystems, agriculture, industry, and settlements and the economy. Climate change, in fact, threatens to disrupt the basic life-support systems that ultimately underlie human health and well-being. After all, health and well-being depend on the health of crop systems, forests, other animals, and marine life. Nearly all of the other adverse impacts of climate change (food yields, water flows, sea-level rise, infrastructural damage, and so on) converge on human biological well-being. Thus, the threats that climate change holds for societies and for ecosystems—coral

---

[59] UNDP, "Human Development Report 2011," 51–53.
[60] See ibid., 53.

reefs, forests, and agriculture—ultimately turn out to be the greatest long-term threats to health, nutrition, and well-being.[61]

Most health impacts of climate changes are likely to be adverse, with a few notable exceptions like reduced mortality from cold exposure. Thus, the overall effects of climate change on health are predicted to be negative, with significant threats to many basic human needs for health and survival.[62]

Climate change can affect human health through a range of mechanisms. We limit the dicussion here to exploring the health impacts of anthropogenic climate change on two fronts: the impacts from extreme weather events, and the changing patterns and transmission of diseases.

Extreme weather events are one of the most conspicuous manifestations of the current anthropogenic climate change. Weather extremes can lead to hazard events such as heat waves, droughts, wildfires, floods, hurricanes, cyclones, and windstorms, which in turn pose serious threats to human health. In recent years it is estimated that more than 2 billion people were affected by natural disasters, many of which were directly or indirectly related to extreme meteorological phenomena.[63] In fact, of the 238 great natural catastrophes that occurred between 1950 and 2007, two-thirds resulted from extreme weather or climate-related events, mainly floods and windstorms.[64] Most susceptible among the victims of extreme weather events are those populations living in developing nations that occupy coastal tropical regions.

Extreme weather events, especially heavy downpours and floods, can create conditions conducive to clusters of diseases carried by mosquitoes, rodents, and water.[65] As the 2007 IPCC report notes, floods are the most frequent natural weather disaster and they take a heavy toll on human health and life. Floods result from the interaction of rainfall,

---

[61] Juan Almendares and Paul R. Epstein, "Climate Change and Health Vulnerabilities," in Worldwatch Institute, *2009 State of the World: Into a Warming World* (Washington, DC: Worldwatch Institute, 2009), 78; A. J. McMichael and E. Lindgren, "Climate Change: Present and Future Risks to Health, and Necessary Responses," *Journal of Internal Medicine* 270 (2011): 411.

[62] Jamie Hosking et al., "Climate Change: The Implications for Child Health in Australasia," *Journal of Pediatrics and Child Health* 47 (2011): 493.

[63] Anthony Costello et al., "Managing the Health Effects of Climate Change," *Lancet* 373 (2009): 1706.

[64] See Munich Re, *Natural Catastrophes 2007: Analyses, Assessments, Positions* (Munich, 2008).

[65] Almendares and Epstein, "Climate Change and Health Vulnerabilities," 78.

surface runoff, evaporation, wind, sea level, and local topography. Floods are low-probability, high-impact events that can overwhelm not only physical infrastructure but also human resilience and social organization. The last decades have witnessed increased occurrence of major storm and flood disasters. Health impacts range from deaths, injuries, infectious diseases, and toxic contamination to mental-health problems. Drowning by storm surge is the major killer in coastal storms in countries like Bangladesh. After a flood, rates of diarrheal disease, including cholera, are likely to increase, especially in areas where sanitation facilities are poor.[66]

Extreme weather events like hurricanes and floods can cause severe damage even in rich countries, as was made evident in the wake of hurricanes Katrina and Sandy in the United States. However, in terms of deaths and populations affected, floods and tropical cyclones have the greatest impact in South Asia and Latin America. Flooding can also lead to contamination of water with dangerous chemicals, pesticides, heavy metals, or other hazardous substances, which can lead to long-term contamination of soil and water sources.[67]

Extreme meteorological events of an opposite nature, like droughts and heat waves, can also have substantial impacts on the lives of individuals and communities. Droughts are predicted to become more frequent and severe in many areas of the world, especially in subtropical regions as the effects of anthropogenic climate change begin to unfold. The effects of droughts on human health and well-being are manifold, ranging from malnutrition and hunger to displacement and misery. As the 2007 Fourth Assessment of the IPCC points out:

> The effects of drought on health include deaths, malnutrition (undernutrition, protein-energy malnutrition and/or micronutrient deficiencies), infectious diseases and respiratory diseases. . . . Drought diminishes dietary diversity and reduces overall food consumption, and may therefore lead to micronutrient deficiencies. . . . Malnutrition increases the risk both of acquiring and of dying from an infectious disease. . . . Drought and the consequent loss of livelihoods is also a major trigger for population movements, particularly rural to urban migration. Population

---

[66] See M. Ahern et al., "Global Health Impacts of Floods: Epidemiological Evidence," *Epidemiology Review* 27 (2005): 36–46; Nerlander, *Climate Change and Health*, 3.

[67] U. Confalonieri et al., "Human Health," in Parry et al., *Climate Change 2007*, 399.

displacement can lead to increases in communicable diseases and poor nutritional status resulting from overcrowding, and a lack of safe water, food and shelter.[68]

At hotter temperatures it becomes difficult for people to work for longer hours, and if they do, their health may suffer. Once core body temperature passes 38°C (100.4°F)—the maximum safe heat for outdoor work—heat stress sets in, which can take a heavy toll in terms of working hours lost and even lead to casualties. The physiological coping capacity for temperature thresholds varies depending on the climatic acclimatization of the people as well as other factors like humidity, wind movement, and heat radiation. Exposure to extreme heat stress can cause dehydration, heat cramps, heat exhaustion, heat strokes, respiratory failure, myocardial infarction, organ damage, fatigue, and risk-prone behavior, and it increases the rate of short-term mortality.[69] Mortality rates rise when temperature maximums rise a few degrees higher than the normal and optimum temperature that a population is accustomed to. One may recall in this context the devastating effects of the 2003 European heat wave—the continent's hottest summer in over five hundred years—when temperatures rose 3.5°C above normal. This was linked to the premature deaths of some forty thousand to fifty thousand people, especially older persons and people in any age group with lung disorders and cardiovascular diseases.[70]

The increased frequency and intensity of heat waves put small children, the elderly, and people with heart and lung problems at higher risk. The heat waves in South Asia, a region particularly vulnerable to heat stress, are associated with high mortality in rural populations and among the elderly and laborers who work outdoors.

Both outdoor and indoor workers are at risk of heatstroke, but the occupations most at risk include construction, agriculture, fishing, and so on. Working in hot environments increases the risk of diminished ability to carry out physical tasks, diminishes mental-task ability,

---

[68] Ibid. See also McMichael and Lindgren, "Climate Change," 407; Nerlander, *Climate Change and Health*, 4.

[69] See McMichael and Lindgren, "Climate Change," 406; T. Kjellstrom et al., "The Direct Impact of Climate Change on Regional Labour Productivity," *Archives of Environmental and Occupational Health* 64 (2009): 217–27; Costello et al., "Managing the Health Effects of Climate Change," 1702.

[70] See A. Fouillet et al., "Excess Mortality Related to the August 2003 Heat Wave in France," *International Archives of Occupational and Environmental Health* 80 (2006): 16–24.

increases accident risk, and if prolonged, may lead to heat exhaustion and even death.[71]

Extreme weather events can affect mental health. There is increasing evidence of the mental and psychological hazards caused by extreme events associated with climate change that may result in geographic displacement of populations, damage to property, loss of loved ones, and chronic stress.[72] The psychological effects of extreme weather events tend to be much longer lasting and at times may be worse than the direct physical effects. The mental-health impacts include posttraumatic stress disorder, fear, anxiety, depression, lethargy, sleeplessness, feelings of helplessness, and in extreme cases, even suicide. These impacts are certainly important but currently difficult to assess because of the dearth of studies in this field.[73]

Climate change can also lead to changing patterns and migration of diseases. Diseases appear to be shifting geographically and seasonally in the wake of climate change.

Climate change in terms of rising temperatures and changing patterns of rainfall are expected to alter the geographical distribution of vector-borne infectious diseases. Many microorganisms multiply more rapidly in food and in nutrient-loaded water in warmer conditions, and many of the infectious disease agents (such as protozoa, bacteria, and viruses) and the vectors or organisms that carry them (such as mosquitoes, ticks, and rodents) are highly sensitive to climatic conditions like temperature and rainfall.[74] Infectious agents and their associated vector organisms are devoid of thermostatic mechanisms, and so reproduction and survival rates are strongly affected by fluctuations in temperature.[75] Thus, climate change can make certain environments more hospitable for some infectious diseases, thereby reintroducing some diseases into areas where they had been previously eradicated and worsening their already significant global burden.

---

[71] Confalonieri et al., "Human Health," 396–97, 405.

[72] National Institute of Environmental Health Sciences et al., *A Human Health Perspective on Climate Change: A Report Outlining the Research Needs on the Human Health Effects of Climate Change* (Washington, DC: Environmental Health Perspectives—National Institute Environmental Health Sciences, 2010), vi.

[73] A. Haines and J. A. Patz, "Health Effects of Climate Change," *Journal of the American Medical Association* 291 (2004): 99–103; The National Academy of Sciences, *Advancing the Science of Climate Change*, 313; Confalonieri et al., "Human Health," 399; Oxfam, *Suffering the Science*, 30.

[74] McMichael and Lindgren, "Climate Change," 408; Jonathan A. Patz, "Impact of Regional Climate Change on Human Health," *Nature* 438 (2005): 310–17.

[75] Patz, "Impact of Regional Climate Change on Human Health," 311.

Vector-borne diseases like malaria, tick-borne encephalitis, and dengue fever will become increasingly widespread within the context of climate change. Malaria, a common disease that currently accounts for more than 80 percent of the climate-related deaths globally and causes 1 million child deaths annually, will have a greater geographical range due to climate change.[76] This is so because malaria is strongly influenced by temperature variations.[77] Malaria is synonymous with poverty in poor countries prone to the disease, as it takes a heavy toll on people's health and their productive output. Climate change and other ecological factors are facilitating the migration of malaria to countries where it was previously unknown. According to Oxfam:

> Driven by local practices such as deforestation, and exacerbated by the changing climate, malaria is now affecting people who have previously had little experience of it, for example in the East African highlands and in the Andean foothills. Large average temperature increases in the uplands of Tanzania since the 1960s have brought the *Anopheles* mosquito and the parasite *P. falciparum* (which cannot survive below 16°C) to a new population. . . . Malaria is on the move, with incidence rising fastest in southern Europe and in African cities. In Colombia, it is estimated that 18–24 million people are now at risk of the disease.[78]

Dengue fever, the world's most important vector-borne viral disease, is also sensitive to climate. Other infectious diseases have seen the rate of their transmission and migration altered due to climatic variables.

The spread of allergies and asthma can also be influenced by climate change. Numerous plant species—like ragweed, poison ivy, and stinging nettle—and pollens can increase growth and toxicity at higher temperatures and with higher concentrations of CO_2, causing a prolonged allergy season. Global warming appears to cause an earlier onset of the spring pollen season in the Northern Hemisphere and consequently increased production of allergens.[79] It is estimated that

---

[76] Confalonieri et al., "Human Health," 394; Laura Anderko et al., *Climate Change and Health: Is There a Role for the Health Care Sector?* (Washington, DC: Catholic Health Association of the United States, 2012), 8.

[77] K. Paaijmans et al., "Influence of Climate on Malaria Transmission Depends on Daily Temperature Variation," *Proceedings of the National Academy of Sciences* 107 (2010): 15135–39.

[78] Oxfam, *Suffering the Science*, 27.

[79] The National Academy of Sciences, *Advancing the Science of Climate Change*, 317; Anderko et al., *Climate Change and Health*, 9.

respiratory allergies and asthma will become more common and severe because of increased exposure to pollen, molds, and air pollution as a result of climate change.[80]

It is evident that climate change will affect human health in multiple and interrelated ways. As Anthony Costello and others warn:

> The epidemiological outcome of climate change on disease patterns worldwide will be profound, especially in developing countries where existing vulnerabilities to poor health remain. The added pressure of climate change to the environment will worsen this burden and pose challenging questions for public and global health.[81]

According to the estimates of the World Health Organization, the warming and precipitation trends due to anthropogenic climate change from 1970 to 2000 have already claimed over fifteen thousand lives annually.[82] However, the threats of climate change in the future are going to be even more overwhelming.[83] The threats to human well-being, health, and survival from climate change is a real "bottom line" issue. Society's increasing understanding of the current and future risks to human health from human-induced climate change should be a real motivator to initiate serious and urgent measures for mitigation of the ecological crisis, and of climate change in particular.

Ecological Crisis and the Specter of Forced Migration

As we have seen so far, the contemporary ecological crisis will have concrete and lasting effects on human welfare in basic areas like food security and health. A third and equally worrisome consequence of the crisis will be the specter of forced migration. It is not only Earth, the "common home" of humanity and other nonhuman species, that will be jeopardized by the ecological crisis, but also the homes of some of our fellow human beings. In the decades to come, our brothers and sisters, especially in poorer nations, will face the threat of forced displacement

---

[80] See G. D'Amato et al., "Urban Air Pollution and Climate Change as Environmental Risk Factors of Respiratory Allergy: An Update," *Journal of Investigational Allergology and Clinical Immunology* 20 (2010): 95–102.

[81] Costello et al., "Managing the Health Effects of Climate Change," 1702.

[82] The World Health Organization, *The World Health Report 2002* (Geneva: WHO, 2002); Patz, "Impact of Regional Climate Change on Human Health," 310, 313.

[83] See McMichael and Lindgren, "Climate Change," 401.

in the wake of the ecological crisis, and climate change in particular. Herein we deal with the main drivers of ecological migration and map out some of the "hotspots" of ecological migration in the future.

Ecological factors appear to have played a decisive role on human mobility in the past. Millions migrated out of Europe into the Americas from the early seventeenth century onward, following the prolonged nadir of the Little Ice Age, which brought in its wake dramatic spikes in food shortages, hunger, epidemics, and wars, the Irish migration caused by the 1840s potato famine. In the United States thousands left their homelands and migrated to escape the nightmare of the Dust Bowl during the 1930s. However, while past episodes of migrations were largely localized and were spurred often by isolated natural calamities that affected selected groups and regions, the current challenge of ecological migration threatens to be unprecedented both in terms of its drivers and the number of people affected. The Oxford Refugee Studies Centre notes: "The global scale of environmental change and thus the potential impacts it will have, such as forced migration, are new phenomena. No longer will these impacts be episodic or localized."[84] The various manifestations of the contemporary ecological crisis, and climate change in particular, hold the potential to displace millions of people from their native lands. In its 1990 report the IPCC warned that "forced migration and resettlement would be the most severe effects of climate change."[85]

The element of multi-causality with regard to the drivers of migration make it difficult to estimate the precise number of people who will be displaced on account of ecological factors. Currently, it appears that only approximate predictions can be made with regard to numbers of ecological migrants. Currently, the most accepted estimates seem to suggest that the various manifestations of the contemporary ecological crisis could displace nearly 200 million people from their homes and homelands, in the second half of the twenty-first century.[86] This number is appalling in itself for the sheer size of people who will be

---

[84] Camillo Boano et al., *Environmentally Displaced People: Understanding the Linkages Between Environmental Change, Livelihoods, and Forced Migration* (Oxford: Refugee Studies Centre, University of Oxford, 2008), 5.

[85] IPCC, *Climate Change 1990: Report Prepared for Intergovernmental Panel on Climate Change by Working Group II*, ed. W. J. McG. Tegart et al. (Canberra: Australian Government Publishing Service, 1990), 188.

[86] See Norman Myers, "Environmental Refugees: An Emergent Security Issue," Organisation for Security and Co-operation in Europe (May 25, 2005), 1; Nicholas Stern, *The Economics of Climate Change* (Cambridge: Cambridge University Press, 2007), 65.

displaced. We may cite Oli Brown of the International Organization for Migration in this regard:

> This is a daunting figure: representing a ten-fold increase over today's entire documented refugee and internally displaced populations. To put the number in perspective it would mean that by 2050 *one in every 45 people* in the world will have been displaced by climate change. It would also exceed the current global migrant population.[87]

Despite lack of precise figures, the hard truth is that the contemporary ecological crisis can displace millions in the decades to come.

Two groups of ecological factors can act as drivers of forced displacement of individuals and communities: rapid-onset triggers, mainly extreme weather phenomena like floods, storms, and droughts; and slow-onset processes, like land and ecosystem degradation, depletion of natural resources, and sea-level rise. In the case of natural hazards like extreme weather events, a return of the displaced victims might be possible. Migration will be permanent for most in the case of long-term processes like sea-level rise.

Extreme weather events, one of the direct consequences of climate change, can drive population displacement.[88] Major natural disasters have doubled over the last two decades (from about two hundred to more than four hundred a year).[89] In a typical year between 1998 and 2007, nearly 98 percent of victims of natural disasters suffered from climate-related disasters such as droughts and floods rather than, for example, devastating but relatively rare events such as earthquakes.[90]

---

[87] Oli Brown, *Migration and Climate Change*, IOM Migration Research Series 31 (Geneva: International Organization for Migration, 2008), 11–12. Currently over 70 million people are forced migrants—more than 1 percent of the world's citizens—displaced by conflict, political upheaval, violence, and disasters, as well as by climate change and other ecological factors. International Federation of Red Cross and Red Crescent Societies, *World Disasters Report: Focus on Forced Migration and Displacement* (Geneva: International Federation of Red Cross and Red Crescent Societies, 2012), 9, 15.

[88] See IPCC, *Managing the Risks of Extreme Events and Disasters to Advance Climate Change Adaptation: Special Report of the Intergovernmental Panel on Climate Change*, ed. C. B. Field et al. (Cambridge: Cambridge University Press, 2012), 80.

[89] International Federation of Red Cross and Red Crescent Societies, *World Disasters Report*, 16.

[90] Tanja Schuemer-Cross and Hen Heaven Taylor, *The Right to Survive: The Humanitarian Challenge for the Twenty-First Century* (Oxford: Oxfam International, 2009), 2.

The increase in extreme weather events—in particular, heavy rainfall and resulting flash or river floods in tropical regions—can make it difficult for people to survive where they are or can exacerbate already existing vulnerabilities, setting in motion population movements.[91] Climate- and weather-related natural disasters have indeed become the main sudden-onset triggers for displacement. At least 36 million people were displaced by natural disasters in 2008, and a record high of 43 million in 2010—substantially surpassing conflict-induced internal displacement.[92] It is estimated that Hurricane Katrina resulted in the displacement of over half a million people in the United States, while the Cyclone Nargis uprooted 800,000 people in Myanmar and South Asia. Pakistan's 2010 floods left an estimated 6 million people in need of shelter.[93] For most people affected by natural disasters, subsequent displacement and resettlement often constitute a second disaster in their lives, and the impact is greater for those who are already poor and vulnerable.

While the rapid-onset triggers of forced migration like the extreme weather events tend to capture media headlines, it is the less dramatic slow-onset processes like land and ecosystem degradation (including desertification; depletion of natural resources, especially water; and inexorable sea-level rise) that will have a greater impact on forced displacement of populations in the future. Their real impact on human lives and livelihoods already outweighs natural hazards. For example, during the period 1979–2008, 718 million people were affected by storms, but 1.6 billion were affected by droughts.[94] Slow-onset events unfold over months or years, and it may take time for exposed populations to realize their full severity. As their impacts increase, households grow more vulnerable and have less capacity to adapt; migration, often driven by hunger, may be the only option left for many people.

Land and ecosystem degradation can directly affect the livelihoods of people and thus act as a trigger for migration. It is estimated that currently more than one-third of drylands are affected by land

---

[91] Frank Laczko and Christine Aghazarm, eds., *Migration, Environment, and Climate Change: Assessing the Evidence* (Geneva: IOM, 2009); WHO, *Gender, Climate Change, and Health* (Geneva: Public Health and Environment Department—WHO, 2011), 16.

[92] IPCC, *Managing the Risks of Extreme Events and Disasters to Advance Climate Change Adaptation*, 300; International Federation of Red Cross and Red Crescent Societies, *World Disasters Report*, 16.

[93] IPCC, *Managing the Risks of Extreme Events and Disasters to Advance Climate Change Adaptation*, 457.

[94] Laczko and Aghazarm, *Migration, Environment, and Climate Change*, 15.

degradation.[95] The Millennium Ecosystem Assessment points out that "droughts and loss of land productivity are predominant factors in movement of people from drylands to other areas."[96] Land degradation is reinforced by desertification, erosion, soil salinization, and water scarcity. When secure water and food supplies cannot be guaranteed, people frequently migrate to areas where they believe they can find them. According to the UN Convention to Combat Desertification, land degradation has already forced between 17 million and 24 million people to leave their homes.[97] Human adaptation to prolonged, extreme drought is difficult or impossible. So, faced with the specter of drought or increasing desertification, most people must migrate. The very word *desert* comes from the Latin *desertum,* meaning "an abandoned place."[98]

Land and ecosystem degradation and the competition for natural resources in the context of their fast depletion, evident especially in the case of water, may lead to conflict in the context of migration.

Globally, resource-related conflicts appear to be on the rise. Over the past sixty years an estimated 40 percent of civil wars and intrastate conflicts were associated with disputes over natural resources.[99] Recent episodes appear to underline the influence of ecological factors in driving migration and fueling conflicts. The most discussed is the Darfur (Sudan) conflict, in which water scarcity, land degradation, and desertification were major influential factors.[100] Sahel—a region that already faces severe drought and desertification—is another volatile zone where conflicts over land and water resources appear to have risen in the context of migration, between pastoral communities and sedentary farmers. At the July 2011 debate on climate change and

---

[95] See J. Clarke and D. Noin, "Introduction," in *Population and Environment in Arid Regions*, ed. J. Clarke and D. Noin (Paris: UNESCO/Parthenon, 1998), 1–18; Koko Warner et al., *In Search of Shelter: Mapping the Effects of Climate Change on Human Migration and Displacement* (Geneva: Care International et al., 2009), 9.

[96] Millennium Ecosystem Assessment, *Ecosystems and Human Well-being: Desertification Synthesis* (Washington, DC: World Resources Institute, 2005), 8.

[97] See UN Convention to Combat Desertification, "World Day to Combat Desertification 17 June 2009—Background Note."

[98] Joseph Romm, "The Next Dust Bowl," *Nature* 478 (2011): 451.

[99] See United Nations Environment Programme, *From Conflict to Peacebuilding: The Role of Natural Resources and the Environment* (Nairobi: UNEP, 2009). See also Oxfam, *Suffering the Science*, 49; UNDP, "Human Development Report 2011," 59.

[100] See UNEP, *Sudan Post-Conflict Environmental Assessment* (Nairobi: UNEP, 2007).

security in the UN Security Council, Secretary-General Ban Ki-moon stated:

> Competition between communities and countries for scarce resources, especially water, is increasing, exacerbating old security dilemmas and creating new ones, while environmental refugees are reshaping the human geography of the planet, a trend that will only increase as deserts advance, forests are felled and sea levels rise.[101]

It is important to remember, however, that natural resources are rarely, if ever, the sole driver of violent conflicts. They often interact with other risks and vulnerabilities, becoming threat multipliers for instability in the more volatile regions of the world. More substantial research is warranted to determine if there is a direct causal linkage between ecological factors and conflicts.[102]

Another slow-onset process that can significantly contribute to forced displacement of populations in future is the projected sea-level rise. The phenomenon of sea-level rise is essentially controlled by thermal expansion of water in the oceans (because of higher temperatures) and the addition of fresh water from land-based sources, mainly ice sheets and glaciers. The Fourth Assessment of the IPCC projected a global sea-level rise of anywhere between 7 and 23 inches by 2100 under various scenarios—excluding changes in large ice sheets covering Greenland and West Antarctica[103]—while more recent studies project a rise in global sea levels of nearly 40 inches or more in the same period.[104]

Rising sea levels will make migration inevitable in many regions. Sea-level rises can render uninhabitable extensive and highly productive

---

[101] Quoted in UNEP, *Livelihood Security: Climate Change, Migration, and Conflict in the Sahel* (Nairobi: UNEP, 2011), 7.

[102] See Boano et al., *Environmentally Displaced People*, 20–23.

[103] G. A. Meehl et al., "Global Climate Projections," in *Climate Change 2007: The Physical Science Basis: Contribution of Working Group I to the Fourth Assessment Report of the Intergovernmental Panel on Climate Change*, eds S. Solomon et al. (Cambridge: Cambridge University Press, 2007), 350.

[104] See Martin Vermeer and Stefan Rahmstorf, "Global Sea Level Linked to Global Temperature," *Proceedings of the National Academy of Sciences* 106 (2009): 21527–32; A. Grinsted et al., "Reconstructing Sea Level from Paleo and Projected Temperatures 2000 to 2100 AD," *Climate Dynamics* 34 (2009): 461–72; S. Jevrejeva et al., "How Will Sea Level Respond to Changes in Natural and Anthropogenic Forcings by 2100?" *Geophysical Research Letters* 37 (2010), L07703.

low-lying coastal areas and low-lying islands that are currently home to millions of people. No other form of ecological migration is likely to be as permanent as that caused by climate-induced sea-level rise. "As the average sea level continues to rise, coastal inundation, saltwater intrusion, and storm surges will become more intense and people will find it increasingly difficult to stay in their homes and will look for ways to migrate inland."[105] It is estimated that 145 million people are presently at risk from a sea-level rise of approximately 40 inches, three-quarters of whom live in East and South Asia.[106] Sea-level rise will affect mainly the populations living in deltaic regions of the world and in the low-lying island states, triggering forced displacement of many of them.

In the densely populated deltaic regions of the Ganges, Mekong, and Nile—considered the world's top three "hotspots" in terms of potential displacement due to rising sea levels[107]—millions of people will be affected. The nation that will be most affected in the Ganges Delta will be Bangladesh, one of the most densely populated countries in the world, three-quarters of whom live within the deltaic region formed by the confluence of the Ganges, Brahmaputra, and Meghna rivers. As half of the country lies less than 16.4 feet above sea level, and about 17 million people live within the 40–inch contour, it is estimated that millions of Bangladeshis will be exposed to the impacts of increased flooding, severe cyclones, and rise in the sea level.[108]

Another hotspot in this regard will be the Mekong Delta of Vietnam, a low-lying plain only 10 feet above sea level at its highest point. The Mekong Delta supported a population of 28.5 million in 2000, 14 million of whom lived in areas that would be inundated by a 6.5–foot sea-level rise. The delta covers 40 percent of Vietnam's cultivated land surface, producing half of the country's rice output, 60 percent of the fish and shrimp harvest, and 80 percent of Vietnam's fruit crop.

---

[105] Sujatha Byravan and Sudhir Chella Rajan, "The Ethical Implications of Sea-level Rise due to Climate Change," *Ethics and International Affairs* 24 (2010): 240.

[106] UNDP, "Human Development Report 2009: Overcoming Barriers: Human Mobility and Development" (New York: UNDP, 2009), 45.

[107] International Federation of Red Cross and Red Crescent Societies, *World Disasters Report*, 235.

[108] G. McGranahan, D. Balk, and B. Anderson, "The Rising Tide: Assessing the Risks of Climate Change and Human Settlements in Low Elevation Coastal Zones," *Environment and Urbanization* 19 (2007): 17–37; Warner et al., *In Search of Shelter*, 13.

It is projected that in the future one out of every ten Vietnamese may face displacement by sea-level rise in the Mekong Delta.[109]

The Nile Delta in Egypt—a 31-mile-wide strip along the coast that is less than 6.5 feet above sea level and is also the most productive zone of the country, though it covers only 3 percent of the total land area—will also be particularly at risk from sea-level rise. The Nile Delta supported a population of 40.2 million in 2000, of whom 10.7 million lived in areas that would be inundated by a 6.5-foot sea-level rise. It is feared that the approximately 3-foot sea-level rise predicted for the twenty-first century will force 16 million Egyptians to leave their homes.[110]

Small island states are also particularly vulnerable to sea-level rise, with many of the island communities facing the specter of permanent displacement. For nearly forty small island states—the Maldives, Kiribati, Tuvalu, the Marshalls, plus dozens of states in the Caribbean—sea-level rise could submerge entire parts of sovereign territories. Consider here just two cases, namely, Tuvalu and Maldives. As one of the smallest and most remote low-lying atoll countries on Earth, Tuvalu's existence is threatened by sea-level rise. Its low elevation—no point on Tuvalu is 16.5 feet above high tide—makes the country highly vulnerable to sea-level rise, storm surges, high tides, and other climatic events that affect the entire population. Tuvalu is expected to become uninhabitable by 2050 or so, and migration or relocation to other states will be the only realistic option. Currently, about three thousand Tuvaluans have already migrated to Auckland, New Zealand.[111]

The Maldives, made up of twelve hundred islands, is considered the lowest-lying country in the world. The island nation's highest point is 7.5 feet above sea level, while the average elevation of land is just around 3 feet, with 80 percent of the country's land mass lying under it. Consequently, a sea-level rise of 3.3 feet would inundate most of the country's infrastructure and threaten living areas. In fact, most of the Maldives' population of nearly 300,000, more than one-third

---

[109] S. Dasgupta et al., *The Impact of Sea Level Rise on Developing Countries: A Comparative Analysis.* World Bank Policy Research Working Paper 4136 (Washington, DC: World Bank, 2007); Warner et al., *In Search of Shelter*, 15.

[110] Warner et al., *In Search of Shelter*, 17; Oxfam, *Suffering the Science*, 46.

[111] Warner et al., *In Search of Shelter*, 19; Vikram Odedra Kolmannskog, *Future Floods of Refugees: A Comment on Climate Change, Conflict, and Forced Migration* (Oslo: Norwegian Refugee Council, 2008), 27.

of whom live in the capital city of Male, is condemned to inevitable displacement in the future.[112]

As Vikram Odedra Kolmannskog notes, "What must be a rather seldom phenomenon, however, is the complete extinction of a state without there being any successor state. Several difficult questions arise regarding the rights of the affected population and who would be responsible for protecting them."[113] The people forcibly displaced from the small island nations because of sea-level rise will not be able to return, unlike political refugees or other migrants. Ecological migration in this regard will be a totally new challenge for international law and community.

As evident in the analysis of the drivers leading to ecological migration, the various manifestations of the contemporary ecological crisis are already contributing significantly to forced displacement of communities in different parts of the world. As the 2012 *World Disasters Report* warns, the human cost of forced migration will be "destroyed livelihoods, increased vulnerability especially of women and children, lost homelands and histories, fractured households and disempowered communities, and the destruction of the common bonds and shared values of humanity."[114] Ecological migration is closely linked to and can further exacerbate human vulnerability in other basic areas like food security and health.

Ecological migration, like food insecurity and health insecurity, will hit the poor hardest. People in the least-developed countries and island states will be affected first and worst. The displacement caused by the various ecological factors can be temporary or permanent and will take place largely within vulnerable countries and regions rather than across international borders as most displaced individuals do not possess the financial resources to migrate far. As Clark L. Gray and Valerie Mueller pointed out in a 2012 study, for most rural populations affected by natural hazards, long-distance migration is very difficult. Their study disproves the myth that climate-related natural hazards are a catalyst to significant population movements toward the countries of the global North, as often hyped in the media.[115] On

---

[112] Warner et al., *In Search of Shelter*, 19.

[113] Kolmannskog, *Future Floods of Refugees*, 28.

[114] International Federation of Red Cross and Red Crescent Societies, *World Disasters Report*, 9.

[115] Clark L. Gray and Valerie Mueller, "Natural Disasters and Population Mobility in Bangladesh," *Proceedings of the National Academy of Sciences* 109 (2012): 6000–6005. See also Allan M. Findlay, "Flooding and the Scale of Migration," *Nature Climate Change* 2 (2012): 401.

the contrary, as is already the case with political refugees, it is likely that the burden of providing for ecological migrants will be borne by the poorest countries—those least responsible for greenhouse gas emissions and for causing the crisis in the first place, as Oli Brown of the International Organization for Migration has pointed out.[116] At the same time, the poorer countries are also poorly equipped to meet the challenges of forced displacement on a massive scale. Vulnerable groups like women and children, nomads, indigenous communities, and others will suffer disproportionately. Women and children, for example, account for a large proportion of displaced persons following natural disasters and are the most susceptible to its adverse health effects.[117]

Ecological migration is already a reality, destroying livelihoods, communities, and the social and cultural identities of people. The specter of forced migration in the context of the contemporary ecological crisis calls for a radical rethinking of the concept of migration, moving out of the straitjacket of conceiving migration in terms of political refugees, and beginning to discuss it on a planetary scale. A radical overhauling of the rights of such migrants—individuals, communities, and in some cases entire nations, in the context of small island nations—will have to be carried out by the international lawmakers and concerned institutions.

Humanity Moving Toward the "Perfect Storm"

In the context of the unprecedented challenges thrown up by the contemporary ecological crisis in basic areas of human welfare like food security, health, and shelter, it is no exaggeration to say that the makings of a "perfect storm" are in place. These challenges are a clarion call for societies and institutions to wake up to the contemporary ecological crisis, which hits the poor and vulnerable most. The disproportionate impacts of the contemporary ecological crisis on the most vulnerable sections of the members of our common household, and more precisely the fundamental questions of justice, equity, and solidarity they give rise to, are discussed in Chapter 8.

---

[116] Brown, *Migration and Climate Change*, 9.
[117] Lina Nerlander, *Climate Change and Health* (Stockholm: Commission on Climate Change and Development, 2009), 9.

8

A Moral Crisis

In our description of the ecological crisis as a cry of the poor, we have so far dealt with its deleterious impacts on basic areas of human welfare like food security, health, and shelter. At a still deeper level the ecological crisis is more than just a humanitarian crisis. The ecological crisis is a profoundly "moral" crisis as Pope John Paul II noted in 1990.[1] It is this ethical dimension of the contemporary ecological crisis that is the topic of this chapter. In order to understand the contemporary ecological crisis, we need to complement the physical description of the problem with ethical considerations. As John Houghton points out, our current ecological predicament—climate change in particular—raises deeper "considerations of morality, equity (both international and intergenerational), justice, attitudes and motivation—qualities that make up the *moral climate* [and] that need to be put alongside the physics, chemistry, biology and dynamics that govern the equations describing the *physical climate*."[2] The ecological crisis is thus inextricably linked to social justice. The cry of the earth is also the cry of the poor.

On the one hand, the analysis of the ecological footprint of the consumption of natural resources and the carbon footprint of nations and individuals—both of which are empirically measurable—confirms that the rich world has contributed most to create the contemporary ecological crisis. On the other hand, it is becoming increasingly clear that the most devastating effects of the crisis, ranging from extreme weather calamities to malnutrition and diseases, will fall mainly on the poor, who have contributed least to the precarious situation of

---

[1] Pope John Paul II, "Peace with God the Creator, Peace with All of Creation," Message for the Celebration of the World Day of Peace (January 1, 1990), nos. 7–8, 15.

[2] John Houghton, "Foreword," in *A Moral Climate: The Ethics of Global Warming*, ed. Michael S. Northcott (London: Darton, Longman, and Todd, 2007), vii.

our common home. Such a realization necessitates that the ecological crisis be looked at from a moral angle.

We begin this chapter by describing the ecological crisis in terms of inequality and injustice. The central argument of the chapter is that the ecological crisis calls for eco-justice at the planetary level. As we all live in the common home of Earth, where each person has equal rights to the common ecological space and to the common atmosphere, values like justice and equality are nonnegotiable in offering a moral response to the crisis. An ethical response to the ecological crisis needs to be erected on the solid pillars of justice, equity, and solidarity.

We begin by reflecting on some of the profound situations of injustice and inequality that lie at the root of the contemporary ecological crisis.

The Ecological Crisis in Terms of Injustice and Inequality

The contemporary ecological crisis is unjust because it is caused largely by the rich but disproportionately affects the poor and vulnerable. As the impacts of the crisis on human communities become increasingly evident, it is also becoming clear how "disparities in the distribution of damages between rich and poor nations mount."[3] Rich countries like the United States, Canada, those in Western Europe, Japan, and Australia contribute many times the greenhouse gas emissions per capita as poor countries, but they will face much less of the fallout—from pollution, to increased exposure to droughts, floods, storms, and sea-level rise.[4]

The carbon footprint of the world's poorest 1 billion people is about 3 percent of the world's total carbon footprint.[5] Yet, these populations will be most affected by the contemporary ecological crisis. While the ecological crisis affects our common home and its common household, its deleterious impacts will fall mainly on the poor and the most vulnerable sections of our society. The debate over climate change is often dominated by technical issues of carbon credits and emissions targets. But it is important to put people at the center

---

[3] U. Thara Srinivasan et al., "The Debt of Nations and the Distribution of Ecological Impacts from Human Activities," *Proceedings of the National Academy of Sciences* 105 (2008): 1768.

[4] Julie Sze and Jonathan K. London, "Environmental Justice at the Crossroads," *Sociology Compass* 2 (2008): 1342–43.

[5] UNDP, "Human Development Report 2007/2008: Facing Climate Change: Human Solidarity in a Divided World" (New York: Macmillan, 2007), 43.

while talking about the ecological crisis, precisely the poor who are most affected by it.

According to the "Human Development Report 2007/2008," "millions of the world's poorest people are already being forced to cope with the impacts of climate change."[6] As Caritas Internationalis points out, "The effects of climate change are already a daily reality for many people, particularly for the world's poorest and most vulnerable."[7] The unfortunate tales of poor communities grappling with the consequences of changing weather patterns, natural calamities like droughts and floods, land degradation and increasing desertification, and other manifestations of the contemporary ecological crisis abound all over the globe.

"The poor live in the most polluted places, in proximity to industrial areas, close to transport lines, in neighborhoods poorly serviced in water supply or garbage collection."[8] Some of the most concrete and widespread manifestations of the contemporary ecological crisis like pollution and poor sanitation will take a heavier toll on the lives of poor people. According to the "Human Development Report 2011":

> The disease burden arising from indoor and outdoor air pollution, dirty water and unimproved sanitation is greatest for people in poor countries, especially for deprived groups. Indoor air pollution kills 11 times more people living in low HDI [Human Development Index] countries than people elsewhere. . . . In low HDI countries more than 6 people in 10 lack ready access to improved water, while nearly 4 in 10 lack sanitary toilets, contributing to both disease and malnourishment.[9]

As we saw in the previous chapter, the impacts of the ecological crisis in the basic areas of nutrition, health, and shelter will hit poor people first. In the wake of natural calamities, poor people are exposed to a higher incidence of diseases that have been all but eradicated in most developed countries (measles, tuberculosis, malaria). Natural catastrophes—floods, hurricanes, tidal waves—affect the poor, who have fewer means to protect themselves and no insurance for restoration.

---

[6] Ibid., 1.

[7] Caritas Internationalis, *Climate Justice: Seeking a Global Ethic* (Rome: Caritas Internationalis General Secretariat, 2009), 6.

[8] Hervé Kempf, *How the Rich Are Destroying the Earth* (Devon: Green Books, 2008), 41.

[9] UNDP, "Human Development Report 2011: Sustainability and Equity: A Better Future for All" (New York: UNDP, 2011), 6.

Extreme weather events present a greater risk for people living in urban slums and vulnerable areas in poorer countries than for those in the developed world. During the period from 1970 to 2008, over 95 percent of deaths from natural disasters occurred in developing countries.[10] While in rich countries an average of 23 people die in any given natural disaster, in the least-developed countries the number is 1,052.[11] Local case studies of natural disasters—the 1991 Bangladesh cyclone, the 2003 European heat wave, the 2004 Asian tsunami, the 2005 Hurricane Katrina in the United States—have shown the greater vulnerability of the poor. The disparity in the health impacts of the ecological crisis on the poor, who are low consumers of energy and least responsible for the crisis, is striking. For example, it is estimated that loss of healthy years of life attributable to climate change in low-income African countries is five hundred times that of Europe.[12]

The ecological crisis is radically changing the landscape of risks that poor and vulnerable communities are accustomed to, presenting scenarios that go beyond their historical experience. Climate change, for example, can create new health risks such as increased mortality due to heat waves; increased occurrence of diseases, including new ones or migrating infectious diseases to which the local populations are not resistant; greater incidence of malnutrition due to local food insecurity; and injuries due to violent weather.[13]

The injustices brewed by the contemporary ecological crisis are manifest in the case of climate change, the greatest of the ecological challenges facing humanity. There is no dearth of assessments that emphasize the fact that the impacts of climate change are falling first and most heavily on the poor. As Chris J. Cuomo states:

---

[10] IPCC, *Managing the Risks of Extreme Events and Disasters to Advance Climate Change Adaptation: Special Report of the Intergovernmental Panel on Climate Change*, ed. C. B. Field et al. (Cambridge: Cambridge University Press, 2012), 6–7; UNEP, *Global Environment Outlook GEO4: Environment for Development* (Nairobi: UNEP, 2007), 18.

[11] Tanja Schuemer-Cross and Ben Heaven Taylor, *The Right to Survive: The Humanitarian Challenge for the Twenty-First Century* (Oxford: Oxfam Publishing, 2009), 4.

[12] Laura Anderko et al., *Climate Change and Health: Is There a Role for the Health Care Sector?* (Washington, DC: Catholic Health Association of the United States, 2012), 6. See also A. J. McMichael et al., "World Health Assembly 2008: Climate Change and Health," *Lancet* 371 (2008): 1895–96.

[13] Ian Christoplos et al., *The Human Dimension of Climate Adaptation: The Importance of Local and Institutional Issues* (Stockholm: Commission on Climate Change and Development, 2009), 13.

Climate change was manufactured in a crucible of inequality, for it is a product of the industrial and the fossil-fuel eras, historical forces powered by exploitation, colonialism, and nearly limitless instrumental use of "nature." The world's wealthiest nations, and the privileged elite and industry-owning sectors of nearly all nations, have built fortunes and long-term economic stability on decades of unchecked development and energy consumption. By dumping harmful waste into the common atmosphere we have endangered everyone, including those who have contributed little or nothing at all to the industrial greenhouse effect: the "least developed" nations, the natural world, and future generations.[14]

The disproportionate effects of the contemporary ecological crisis, and climate change, in particular, on the poor people is one of the most bitter ironies of our times. As UN Secretary-General Ban Ki-moon told the heads of state and ministers at the high-level intergovernmental negotiations on climate change in Bali, Indonesia, in December 2007: "Climate change affects us all, but it does not affect us all equally. Those who are least able to cope are being hit hardest. Those who have done the least to cause the problem bear the gravest consequences."[15] The nations that made themselves wealthy by burning fossil fuels will, initially, suffer least from the effects of climate change. "In the temperate zones, for instance, rich countries are buffered by their wealth, and here climate change's impacts may result in milder or even beneficial weather conditions for a brief period. It is in the tropics where the bulk of humanity lives—many of them in poverty—that climate change is hitting now and hitting hardest."[16]
Robert Henson expresses the tragic irony of climate change:

If all that global warming did was to make life a bit steamier for the people who consume the most fossil fuels, then there'd be a karmic neatness to it. Alas, climate change doesn't keep its

---

[14] Chris J. Cuomo, "Climate Change, Vulnerability, and Responsibility," *Hypatia* 26 (2011): 693. For some of the major assessments in this regard see IPCC, *Climate Change 2007: Impacts, Adaptation, and Vulnerability. Contribution of Working Group II to the Fourth Assessment Report of the Intergovernmental Panel on Climate Change*, ed. M. L. Parry et al. (Cambridge: Cambridge University Press, 2007); Nicholas Stern, *The Global Deal: Climate Change and the Creation of a New Era of Progress and Prosperity* (New York: Public Affairs, 2009).

[15] Cited in UNICEF, *Climate Change and Children: A Human Security Challenge* (Florence: UNICEF Innocenti Research Centre, 2008), 1.

[16] Oxfam, *Suffering the Science: Climate Change, People, and Poverty*, Oxfam Briefing Paper (July 6, 2009), 6–7.

multitude of effects so nicely focused. A warming planet is liable to produce a cascade of repercussions for millions of people who have never started up a car or taken a cross-country flight.[17]

According to the "Human Development Report 2007/2008," the poor will face the most immediate and severe human costs:

The world's poor will suffer the earliest and most damaging impacts. Rich nations and their citizens account for the over-whelming bulk of the greenhouse gases locked in the earth's atmosphere. But, poor countries and their citizens will pay the highest price for climate change.[18]

As the report points out, "The world's poorest people walk on Earth with a very light carbon footprint," yet "the poorest billion people are highly exposed to climate change threats for which they carry neg-ligible responsibility."[19] This is echoed in the "Human Development Report 2011," which acknowledges that

in many cases the most disadvantaged people bear and will con-tinue to bear the repercussions of environmental deterioration, even if they contribute little to the problem. [Poor countries] have contributed the least to global climate change, but they have experienced the greatest loss in rainfall and the greatest increase in its variability, with implications for agricultural production and livelihoods.[20]

Historically, fossil-fuel energy has contributed to human develop-ment and improved health and survival. However, these benefits have largely been restricted to rich countries, while the adverse effects of the resulting emissions fall mainly on the poor. This situation of global injustice is denounced by Archbishop Desmond Tutu, who writes:

While the citizens of the rich world are protected from harm, the poor, the vulnerable and the hungry are exposed to the harsh reality of climate change in their everyday lives. Put bluntly, the

---

[17] Robert Henson, *The Rough Guide to Climate Change* (London: Rough Guides Ltd., 2006), 139.

[18] UNDP, "Human Development Report 2007/2008," 3.

[19] Ibid., 43.

[20] UNDP, "Human Development Report 2011," 2. See also p. 23.

world's poor are being harmed through a problem that is not of their own making. The footprint of the Malawian farmer or the Haitian slum dweller barely registers in the earth's atmosphere.[21]

The potential human costs of the contemporary ecological crisis are unimaginable, and will be borne overwhelmingly by those least responsible for causing the problem—the world's poor. As Jamie Hosking notes, it is precisely this "mismatch" between the benefits and harms of emissions that renders the contemporary ecological crisis a key global justice issue.[22]

The poor end up becoming the unequal victims of the ecological crisis due to geography and economy. First, the poor are directly dependent on natural resources and are mostly located within the world's most vulnerable and climatically variable zones. Most of the world's 2.7 billion poor people depend directly on natural resources like water, forests, seas, soil, biodiversity, and so on for survival. The ecological crisis has led to the substantial degradation of these resources in many regions. The poor are most vulnerable to the impacts of climate change because their countries are situated in parts of the world already subject to extreme climatic conditions. Poor countries are particularly affected by droughts, sea-level rise, and more frequent storm tides or hurricanes.[23] Accordingly, the poor in developing countries will experience far worse consequences of climate change, pollution, and other manifestations of the ecological crisis than the wealthy populations living mostly in the industrialized North.

The poor also lack the infrastructure to withstand the effects of the ecological crisis and resources needed to invest in adaptation measures. Many of the developing countries on small islands or those with low-lying coastal areas are especially prone to natural disasters because they lack the resources for protective measures such as seawalls and embankments or for extensive insurance arrangements.[24]

---

[21] Quoted in UNDP, "Human Development Report 2007/2008," 166.

[22] Jamie Hosking et al., "Climate Change: The Implications for Child Health in Australasia," *Journal of Pediatrics and Child Health* 47 (2011): 494.

[23] See Wolfgang Sachs et al., eds., *Greening the North: A Post-Industrial Blueprint for Ecology and Equity* (London: Zed Books, 1998), 72; Donald A. Brown et al., "White Paper on the Ethical Dimensions of Climate Change" (Pennsylvania: Rock Ethics Institute, Pennsylvania State University, 2006), 17; Christian Aid, *Community Answers to Climate Chaos: Getting Climate Justice from the UNFCCC* (London: Christian Aid, 2009), 7.

[24] Sujatha Byravan and Sudhir Chella Rajan, "The Ethical Implications of Sea-level Rise Due to Climate Change," *Ethics and International Affairs* 24 (2010): 246.

While the rich nations can afford to, to an extent, "climate proof" their economies and population, the poor nations are woefully underfunded. For example, international funding for adaptation in developing nations in 2008 amounted to US$26 million (£13 million), roughly the same amount that the UK spends on its flood defenses in a week.[25] The "Human Development Report 2007–2008" notes that inequalities in capacity to adapt to climate change are becoming increasingly apparent:

> For one part of the world—the richer part—adaptation is a matter of erecting elaborate climate defense infrastructures, and of building homes that "float on" water. In the other part adaptation means people themselves learning to "float in" flood water. Unlike people living behind the flood defenses of London and Los Angeles, young girls in the Horn of Africa and people in the Ganges Delta do not have a deep carbon footprint.[26]

As Byravan and Rajan note:

> It is a burden that is all the more unfair because the poor played only a minor role, if any, in causing the climate problem, and certainly did not reap the benefits of economic expansion during the past two centuries or so. More than 2 billion people continue to rely on traditional biomass for their energy and suffer greatly in human development terms as a result, while accounting for nearly zero emissions.[27]

The great ethical tragedy about the contemporary ecological crisis is that a large majority of the members of our common household suffer and will suffer due to the greedy actions of a minority. Brazilian Archbishop Hélder Câmara blames the ecological crisis on "greedy or thoughtless people [who] destroy what belongs to all."[28] Seen from the justice perspective, the contemporary ecological crisis clearly reveals the contours of the ecological segregation into which humanity is drifting.

---

[25] UNDP, "Human Development Report 2007/2008," 25.

[26] Ibid., 13.

[27] Byravan and Rajan, "The Ethical Implications of Sea-level Rise due to Climate Change," 246–47.

[28] Helder Camara, *Sister Earth: Creation, Ecology, and the Spirit* (New York: New City Press, 2008), 7.

Ecological Divide

The gross injustices that lie at the root of the contemporary ecological crisis contribute to a sort of ecological segregation between the poor and rich in our globalized world. The injustices leading to a divided world are especially evident in the ecological and carbon footprints of individuals and communities on our common home planet and on its atmosphere. While carbon footprint analysis indicates the huge disparities between nations in the emissions of greenhouse gases that lead to global warming and cause climate change, ecological footprint analysis reveals profound inequalities in the consumption of natural resources. Through a study of these two analyses it is possible to quantify and empirically measure the unjust divide that exists between countries and between individual citizens in the appropriation of our home planet's resources and its common atmosphere.

As we saw in Chapter 3, the greenhouse gases cause global warming and lead to climate change. A carbon footprint can reveal the impact of a particular individual or group on our common atmosphere in terms of the emissions of greenhouse gases, measured in equivalent units of carbon dioxide, the most important among the gases. A carbon footprint can be both primary—greenhouse gas emissions caused directly through the burning of fossil fuels, energy consumption, and transportation—and secondary—indirect emissions through the consumption of goods and services manufactured elsewhere. The carbon footprint offers an estimate of the contribution of individuals, communities, and nations toward global warming through their emissions of greenhouse gases.

The most scandalous aspect about the contemporary ecological crisis is the huge disparity in the carbon footprint of nations and individuals and thus their relative contribution to climate change. The inequalities in the greenhouse gas emissions are glaring indeed. The "Human Development Report 2007–2008" reports that the state of Texas, with a population of 23 million, registers CO_2 emissions of around 700 million tons or 12 percent of total emissions of the United States. That figure is greater than the total CO_2 footprint left by sub-Saharan Africa—a region of 720 million people. In a similar vein, the 19 million people living in New York State have a higher carbon footprint than the 766 million people living in the fifty least developed countries.[29] Further examples—all culled from the same report—drive home the large disparities and inequalities that exist in this regard:

---

[29] UNDP, "Human Development Report 2007/2008," 43.

- The United Kingdom (population 60 million) emits more CO_2 than Egypt, Nigeria, Pakistan, and Viet Nam combined (total population 472 million).
- The Netherlands emits more CO_2 than Bolivia, Colombia, Peru, Uruguay and the seven countries of Central America combined.
- The state of New South Wales in Australia (population 6.9 million) has a carbon footprint of 116 Mt CO_2. This figure is comparable to the combined total for Bangladesh, Cambodia, Ethiopia, Kenya, Morocco, Nepal and Sri Lanka.[30]

Carbon footprint analysis thus reveals very clearly the ecological segregation between the citizens of the rich and poor nations who inhabit the same common planetary home. With just 15 percent of the world's population, rich countries account for 45 percent of the global CO_2 emissions. In contrast, sub-Saharan Africa, with 11 percent of the world population, represents just 2 percent of global emissions.[31] Such emission patterns are totally unsustainable for the carrying capacity of our home planet's atmosphere. If every person living in the developing world had the same carbon footprint as the average person in high-income countries, we would require the atmospheres of six planets. With a global per capita carbon footprint at Australian levels, we would need seven planets, and with a per capita footprint of Canada and the United States, we would require the atmospheres of nine planets![32]

The ecological segregation between the rich and the poor is clearly evident when one considers the affects of the crisis. As a recent bulletin from the World Health Organization points out: "The greenhouse gases that cause climate change originate mainly from developed countries, but the health risks are concentrated in the poorest nations, which have contributed least to the problem."[33] Nearly 99 percent of the current casualties of climate change are in developing countries.[34]

A second mechanism that exposes the scandalous divide between the rich and the poor is the ecological footprint of nations and individuals,

---

[30] Ibid.

[31] Ibid., 42.

[32] Ibid., 48.

[33] Diarmid Campbell-Lendrum et al., "Global Climate Change: Implications for International Public Health Policy," *Bulletin of the World Health Organization* 85 (March 2012): 235.

[34] Oxfam, *Suffering the Science*, 24.

which was discussed in Chapter 6 in relation to depletion of natural resources. The ecological footprint is an indicator of human pressure on the physical world in terms of humanity's consumption of natural resources, use of ecological services, and production of pollution and waste. Ecological footprint analysis reveals clearly that humanity is living beyond available biophysical means. However, the naked truth is that it is not the lifestyle of the whole of humanity that puts our home planet under pressure. Huge disparities exist in the consumption of natural resources across the globe. There is a real divide between the ecological debtors and ecological creditors of the world. In 2008—the last year for which full data are available—while Earth's biocapacity per person was 2.7 global hectare (gha), Qatar, which topped the list, consumed 11.68 gha. At the same time, East Timor had an ecological footprint of just 0.47 gha. There was only about 1 gha for the average person in India and most of Africa.[35] The "Living Planet Report 2012" offers some examples of the discrepancy in the ecological footprint of citizens around the globe:

> If all of humanity lived like an average Indonesian, for example, only two-thirds of the planet's biocapacity would be used; if everyone liked like an average Argentinian, humanity would demand more than half an additional planet; and if everyone lived like an average resident of the USA, a total of four Earths would be required to regenerate humanity's annual demand on nature.[36]

The over-consumption patterns of a small minority of our home planet's common resources imperil our common home, especially the more vulnerable members of our common household. While a country like the United States, with 4 percent of the world's population, consumes almost 25 percent of the world's resources, nearly 1 billion of the members of our common human family live below the poverty line.[37] The disparities in lifestyles between the developed and the developing worlds are scandalous, as well as being unsustainable.

---

[35] See Global Footprint Network et al., "Living Planet Report 2012: Biodiversity, Biocapacity, and Better Choices" (Gland, Switzerland: WWF, 2012), 140–45; United Nations Population Fund, *State of World Population 2011: People and Possibilities in a World of Seven Billion* (New York: UNFPA, 2011), 94. A global hectare per person average is determined by dividing the total productive land and water available by the population.

[36] Global Footprint Network et al., "Living Planet Report 2012," 43.

[37] See in this regard US National Council of Churches, "God's Earth Is Sacred: An Open Letter to Church and Society in the United States" (February 14, 2005).

The huge disparity in consumption of Earth's natural resources and the pressure this places on our common home are often lost sight of or willfully glossed over in the misguided focus on population increase as the sole or main culprit for the depletion of natural resources—and for the contemporary ecological crisis in general. The increase in human population does put pressure on the carrying capacity of our home planet. It took until 1800 for the human family to reach a population of 1 billion. By the end of the twentieth century the world's population had reached 6 billion. The human population is expected to peak at 9.25 billion by the middle of the twenty-first century.

For several decades people considered rising population to be the main challenge facing humanity and the carrying capacity of the earth. Now we realize that the real problem is not so much population but rather the unsustainable over-consumption of our planet's natural resources by the rich minority. As Robert Bailey points out, "The Malthusian instinct to blame resource pressures on growing numbers of poor people misses the point, because people living in poverty contribute little to world demand. Skewed power relations and unequal consumption patterns are the real problem."[38] Population growth does have an impact on our home planet with its finite resources. However, it pales in the face of consumption inequalities. American scientist Jared Diamond notes: "The average rates at which people consume resources like oil and metals, and produce wastes like plastics and greenhouse gases, area about 32 times higher in North America, Western Europe, Japan and Australia than they are in the developing world." According to Diamond, "The estimated 1 billion people who live in developed countries have a relative per capita consumption rate of 32. Most of the world's other 5.5 billion people constitute the developing world, with relative per capita consumption rates below 32, mostly down toward 1."[39]

The excessive demand of the rich populations on Earth's natural resources and on its common atmosphere, not population growth, is the fundamental driver of the contemporary ecological crisis. We may consider here the case of climate change. The "World Population Report 2011" points out: "An extra child born today in the United States would, down the generations, produce an eventual carbon footprint seven times that of an extra child in China, 55 times that of an Indian

---

[38] Robert Bailey et al., *Growing a Better Future: Food Justice in a Resource-Constrained World* (Oxford: Oxfam International, 2011), 14.

[39] Jared Diamond, "What's Your Consumption Factor?" *The New York Times* (January 2, 2008).

child or 86 times that of a Nigerian child."[40] According to the report, in the case of climate change the world's richest half billion people—about 7 percent of the global population—are responsible for about 50 percent of the world's carbon dioxide emissions. Meanwhile, the poorest 50 percent are responsible for just 7 percent of the emissions.[41]

It is estimated that slowing population growth could provide 16–29 percent of the emissions reductions considered necessary by 2050 to avoid dangerous climate change.[42] But the remaining 71–84 percent decrease in emissions—more than two-thirds—needs to come from reducing consumption and other strategies. Significantly, the UNFPA report concludes that "even if zero population growth were achieved, that would barely touch the climate problem—where we would need to cut emissions by 50 percent to 80 percent by mid-century."[43] While it is true that the per capita consumption of natural resources and carbon emissions are rising in developing countries, they are still nowhere close to the rates of the world's 1 billion largest consumers. In the face of existing income inequalities, it is an inescapable conclusion that over-consumption by the rich is the key problem, not overpopulation by the poor.

Our examination of the double mechanisms of the carbon footprint and of the wider ecological footprint reveals how a small proportion of the world's people consume the majority of the world's resources and produce most of the pollution. Our analysis also lays bare the contours of an ecological segregation that humanity is drifting into.

Ecological segregation is a roadblock to greater justice in our common world. It calls for a radical shift in the reigning economic paradigm:

> Seen against the backdrop of a divided world, the excessive use of nature and its resources in the North is a principal roadblock to greater justice in the world. In a finite world, the claim by 20% of the world's population to 80% of the world's resources

---

[40] UNFPA, *State of World Population 2011*, 94. The report draws the conclusion from a study by statisticians at Oregon State University led by Paul Murtaugh.

[41] Ibid. The calculations were provided by Stephen Pacala, director of the Princeton Environment Institute.

[42] Brian C. O'Neill et al., "Global Demographic Trends and Future Carbon Emissions," *Proceedings of the National Academy of Sciences* 107 (2010): 17521–26.

[43] UNFPA, *State of World Population 2011*, 96. The report here cites Fred Pearce, "Consumption Dwarfs Population as Main Environmental Threat," *Yale University: Environment 360* (April 13, 2009).

makes marginalization of the majority world inevitable. A retreat of the rich from over-consumption is thus a necessary first step toward allowing space for improvement of the lives of an increasing number of people. If the affluent really want to become good neighbors, they will have to set out to build economies which weigh much less heavily on the planet and on other nations.[44]

Historical Responsibility and Personal Responsibility

The divide created by the contemporary ecological crisis comes into sharper relief when we look at a problem like climate change—the most important of the multiple manifestations of the crisis—through a double prism: the principle of *historical responsibility* and the principle of *personal responsibility*. We now examine these two principles in the context of the greenhouse gas emissions that drive the current phase of anthropogenic climate change.

The first prism is historical responsibility. A historical perspective is important not only for attributing the cause of the current state of our home planet's climate, but also for assigning responsibility for its mitigation and adaptation. The principle of historical responsibility is based on the recognition that a disproportionately huge amount of the greenhouse gases in the atmosphere has been emitted over time by the affluent industrialized economies. The "Human Development Report 2011" recognizes that the stock of carbon dioxide trapped in the atmosphere is a product of historical emissions mainly from developed countries, especially from the richest countries. "Today's concentrations are largely the accumulation of developed countries' past emissions. With about a sixth of the world's population, very high HDI [Human Development Index] countries emitted almost two-thirds (64 percent) of carbon dioxide emissions between 1850 and 2005."[45] From the historical perspective, the rich and industrialized nations dominate the cumulative emissions account. Historic emissions amount to around 1,100 tons of CO_2 per capita for Britain and America, compared with 66 tons per capita for China and 23 tons per capita for India.[46]

Thus, regarding the historical material causes of climate change, the situation is no secret. Up to the year 2008 the majority of the

---

[44] Sachs et al., *Greening the North*, x.
[45] UNDP, "Human Development Report 2011," 33.
[46] UNDP, "Human Development Report 2007/2008," 41.

historical emissions on the planet came from Europe (30.6 percent) and the United States (27.2 percent)—the largest single national emitter—and the rest of the developed world; altogether these countries have only 20 percent of the world's population.[47] The contribution of the vast majority of humanity has been almost negligible.

Historical emissions are important on several grounds. The first is physical, and early historical emissions count more than later ones:

> *Early emitters* of carbon dioxide have contributed more significantly to temperature increases compared with later emitters. This is because the relationship between carbon dioxide and radiative forcing—the net difference between incoming and outgoing radiation energy—is closer to a logarithmic than linear function such that increased concentrations have a progressively smaller warming effect.[48]

A second reason that earlier historical emissions are significant is that while achieving prosperity for themselves through the emissions of greenhouse gases for their economic development, the industrialized nations have at the same time deprived others of their rightful carbon space. "The carbon sinks of our world are finite: the planet can only absorb a certain amount of our emissions, and the rest contributes to a blanket which heats up the planet."[49] As the "Human Development Report 2007/2008" points out: "The envelope for absorbing future emissions is a residual function of past emissions. In effect, the ecological 'space' available for future emissions is determined by past action."[50] From a historical perspective, the carbon space has been overwhelmingly and disproportionately appropriated by the developed world. Using someone else's share of the carbon sink is as unjust and as harmful as using their water or the resources they need to survive.[51]

As Christian Aid has pointed out, developed countries owe a twofold climate debt for their disporportionate contribution to the causes of climate change.

---

[47] Cuomo, "Climate Change, Vulnerability, and Responsibility," 697; Christian Aid, *Climate Debt and the Call for Justice* (September 2009), 2.

[48] Byravan and Rajan, "The Ethical Implications of Sea-level Rise Due to Climate Change," 245.

[49] James Garvey, *The Ethics of Climate Change: Right and Wrong in a Warming World* (London: Continuum, 2008), 68–69.

[50] UNDP, "Human Development Report 2007/2008," 41.

[51] See Garvey, *The Ethics of Climate Change*, 69.

For over-using and substantially diminishing the Earth's capacity to absorb greenhouse gases—denying it to the developing countries that most need it in the course of their development—the developed countries have run an 'emissions debt' to developing countries. For the adverse effects of these excessive emissions—contributing to the escalating losses, damages and lost development opportunities facing developing countries—the developed countries have run up an 'adaptation debt' to developing countries. The sum of these debts—emissions debt and adaptation debt—constitutes the 'climate debt' of developed countries.[52]

It is estimated that the climate debt of the rich world far exceeds the foreign debt of poorer nations put together. A study on the debt of nations in the context of the climate change concludes: "Indeed, through disproportionate emissions of greenhouse gases alone, the rich group may have imposed climate damages on the poor group greater than the latter's current foreign debt."[53] The sad irony, as Andrew Simms points out, is that many poor countries have to beg for relief from rich countries that themselves carry much bigger and more life threatening, but generally ignored, ecological debts.[54]

It is thus clear from the historical perspective that the "responsibility for climate change sits squarely with rich and industrialized countries who have left behind deeper carbon footprints. These countries have emitted vastly more greenhouse gases than the planet can cope with, especially given their minority share of the global population."[55] And "because the physical mechanism of the industrial greenhouse effect has been known for over a hundred years, it may be difficult to argue that all past ignorance of the harmful effects of greenhouse gases was justified."[56]

Historical responsibility is important when it comes to compensation and assistance for adaptation and mitigation because of climate change. The "Human Development Report 2007/2008" is forthright when it states: "They [the industrialized nations] carry the burden of historic responsibility for the climate change problem. And they have

---

[52] Christian Aid, *Community Answers to Climate Chaos*, 9.

[53] Srinivasan et al., "The Debt of Nations and the Distribution of Ecological Impacts from Human Activities," 1768.

[54] Andrew Simms, *Ecological Debt: The Health of the Planet and the Wealth of Nations* (London: Pluto Press, 2005), viii–ix.

[55] Christian Aid, *Climate Debt and the Call for Justice*, 2.

[56] Cuomo, "Climate Change, Vulnerability, and Responsibility," 697.

the financial resources and technological capabilities to initiate deep and early cuts in emissions."[57]

The second prism through which climate change needs to be seen is that of personal responsibility. While historical responsibility for climate change is derived from the past emissions of greenhouse gases on the part of nations, personal responsibility for climate change is evident in the per capita emissions of individuals. The personal contributions of individuals to climate change is a crucial element that is often glossed over or ignored in climate-change discussions and negotiations. The prevalent tendency in climate-change negotiations is to lay blame on populous countries like China and India for their current total emissions, which are indeed significant given their billion-plus populations. But the logic of considering emissions on a country basis is absurd. It would mean, for example, that a small country like Austria, with only one-tenth of the population of a country like Germany, would have the right to emit ten times more greenhouse gases. And Germany would be considered the worse polluter due to its total emissions. Such logic fails in the face of equity, as we shall see in the coming section. In this vein, it would be ridiculous to blame countries like India and China for their total emissions while their per capita emissions remain a fraction of those of the developed countries. Earth is home to all of the world's citizens. Huge disparities in the per capita footprints of some—which at the same time deprive others of basic amenities for a dignified human existence—go against the basic principles of equality and justice.

It is within such a perspective that we need to consider the personal responsibility of individuals—members of our common household with equal rights.

The per capita emissions of greenhouse gases from individuals show a profoundly unjust and scandalous disparity. As the "Human Development Report 2011" points out: "Very high HDI countries have generated cumulatively more than nine times more carbon dioxide *per capita* than low, medium and high HDI countries combined" (emphasis added).[58] But apart from the historical perspective, profound inequalities continue to exist in the per capita emissions of greenhouse gases even at current levels. People in the rich world are increasingly concerned—to the point of a mass phobia at times—about emissions of greenhouse gases from developing countries. However, as the "Human Development Report 2007/2008" points out, they tend to be less

---

[57] UNDP, "Human Development Report 2007/2008," 5.
[58] UNDP, "Human Development Report 2011," 33.

aware of their own place in the global distribution of CO_2 emissions. The report is very explicit in this regard:

> While China may be about to overtake the United States as the world's largest emitter of CO_2, per capita emissions are just one-fifth of the size. Emissions from India are on a rising trend. Even so, its per capita carbon footprint is less than one-tenth of that in high-income countries. In Ethiopia, the average per capita carbon footprint is 0.1 tons, compared with 20 tons in Canada.[59]

It is true that the carbon emissions of the developing countries have shown a rapid increase in recent years. China's emissions, for example, are rising, but its cumulative and current per capita emissions are still a fraction of the cumulative and per capita emissions of most North Americans and Western Europeans. In recent years several studies have also pointed out that a significant amount of greenhouse gas emissions from developing countries go for the production of goods and services that are then exported to the developed world for the consumption of their citizens. For example, Bin Shui and Robert Harriss estimate that from 1997 to 2003 "about 7%–14% of China's current CO_2 emissions were a result of producing exports for US consumers."[60] Thus, although China as a nation has become the world's largest producer of global warming emissions, some of these emissions have been produced in creating consumer goods for the developed world.

> Most products that are sold in Europe and the United States are no longer made there. Instead they are made thousands of miles away in often miserable working conditions in countries which are prepared to sacrifice air quality, forests, rivers and oceans to toxic pollution in the quest for rapid economic growth. But ironically Western politicians often point to the increases in CO_2 emissions which fuel the factories that now make the products on behalf of Western corporations in countries like China and Brazil as a reason for refusing to reduce their own CO_2 emissions.[61]

---

[59] UNDP, "Human Development Report 2007/2008," 43.

[60] Bin Shui and Robert C. Harriss, "The Role of CO_2 Embodiment in US China-Trade," *Energy Policy* 34 (2006): 4063. See also Glen P. Peters and Edgar G. Hertwitch, "CO_2 Embodied in International Trade with Implications for Global Climate Policy," *Environmental Science and Technology* 42 (2008): 1401–7.

[61] Northcott, *A Moral Climate*, 35.

Hervé Kempf points out that China's pressure on our home planet—and to a lesser degree, India's—while harmful in itself, cannot excuse that of Western countries. It is "because the latter already weigh so heavily on the biosphere that the additional weight of the new powers makes the ecological crisis unbearable. It's not China that poses the problem: it's the fact that it adds to the problems the United States and Europe had already built up."[62] To blame the Chinese for the problem, and to claim that their rapacious appetites render any effort futile, would be hypocritical on the part of the rich world.[63]

The insistence on the personal responsibilities of individual citizens for causing the contemporary ecological crisis is important for yet another reason. Vast differences exist in emission and consumption levels within nations, both rich and poor. With regard to climate change, for example, some developing countries have rich elite who are very high emitters, while in the developed countries there are individuals who are low emitters and desperately poor. The rich who over-consume Earth's resources and pollute its common atmosphere are not limited to the developed world. In India, for example, "the considerably significant carbon footprint of a relatively small wealthy class (1 percent of the population) in the country is camouflaged by the 823 million poor population of the country, who keep the overall per capita emissions below 2 tons of CO_2 per year."[64] The divide between poor and rich is conspicuous in most of the developing countries. The twenty-seven-story sprawling house of billionaire Mukesh Ambani in the city of Mumbai, the financial captial of India, sits uncomfortably alongside Asia's largest slum, Dharavi, with open sewers and crammed huts, home to more than 1 million people. Ultimately, the responsibility for the ecological crisis comes down to communities, households, and individuals who constitute human society. In the case of climate change, for example, the problem is basically caused by the high emission rates of approximately 1 billion high emitters of our common household. Significantly, a recent scientific study led by Shoibal Chakravarty of Princeton University has shown how global projected emissions can be drastically reduced by engaging the 1.13 billion high emitters.[65]

---

[62] Kempf, *How the Rich Are Destroying the Earth*, 14.

[63] George Monbiot, *Heat: How to Stop the Planet Burning* (London: Allen Lane, 2006), xiii.

[64] Greenpeace India Society, *Hiding Behind the Poor: A Report by Greenpeace on Climate Injustice* (Bangladore: Greenpeace, 2009), 2.

[65] See Shoibal Chakravarty et al., "Sharing Global CO_2 Emission Reductions Among One Billion High Emitters," *Proceedings of the National Academy of Sciences* 106 (2009): 11884–88.

We are accustomed to describing the contemporary ecological crisis and the current phase of global warming as *anthropogenic* in character, the term used in scientific parlance. However, this is misleading. The underlying truth is that the crisis is caused by a small minority who over-consume most of the planet's natural resources and are responsible—in terms of both historical and per capita emissions—for most of the greenhouse gases in our common atmosphere. Chris J. Cuomo states:

> The implication that humans as a species have caused climate change is also misleading. Particular people and particular cultures, nations, industries, and economic systems have caused and contributed to the pollution that created the industrial greenhouse effect, and we need not take those actors to be representative of the entire human species. Attributing blame to humans *simpliciter* diverts attention from the real sources of the problem and reproduces the narrow view that there is a universal greedy human nature that inevitably leads toward planetary destruction.[66]

The contemporary ecological crisis is caused by the rich minority. Its disproportionate and unjust victims are the vast majority of the poor and vulnerable people. Our analysis of the mechanisms of carbon footprint and the wider ecological footprint has revealed that such a situation is contributing to the formation of a divide in our world. Further, our examination of climate change through the double prism of historical responsibility and personal responsibility has helped to bring into sharper relief the unequal and unjust divide between the members of our common household. All this makes the contemporary ecological crisis a profound moral crisis of our times, one of the greatest ethical dilemmas of our age.

The Triple Pillars of Justice, Equity, and Solidarity

The present state of our home planet is unsustainable, not only physically for the common biotic community of the earth, but also socially for our common human family. The ecological crisis threatens not only the physical foundations of our common home, but also tears apart the social bonds that unite us. Given the deeply moral character of the ecological crisis, a true and effective response to it will have

---

[66] Cuomo, "Climate Change, Vulnerability, and Responsibility," 697.

to be distinctly ethical; a physical response alone will not suffice. In order to rebuild our common home and reintegrate all the members of our common household, especially the most poor and vulnerable among us, we stand in need of an ethical vision capable of rendering eco-justice. A moral response to the contemporary ecological crisis needs to be built on the triple pillars of justice, equity, and solidarity.

Justice

The first and central pillar of a moral response to the ecological crisis is justice. The contemporary ecological crisis reveals a profound situation of injustice in which the lifestyles of affluent societies are threatening the livelihoods of more vulnerable populations. The ecological crisis is primarily about justice, or rather, eco-justice. The process of creating eco-justice requires a two-tiered approach. First, it will have to be guided by the twin principles of responsibility and capabilities of nations and individuals. Second, the process needs to guarantee human dignity by recognizing the rights of poor countries to develop.

The burden of responding to the ecological crisis needs "to be shared in accordance with the responsibility and capacity of the countries of the world."[67] It is evident that those most responsible for causing climate change and who have the greatest capacity to provide the solutions must take on the lion's share of responding. The principle of responsibility is an application of the commonly accepted norm that the polluter should pay. The polluter-pays principle suggests "that those who created the need to adapt should pay for it. It is crucial that these payments be considered obligatory restitution for damages done, and not treated as optional or charity."[68] Here it is clearly a question of justice, or rather, a redressing of injustice. In the case of climate change, developed countries need to acknowledge their role as historical polluters and commit themselves to providing assistance to alleviate the impact that climate change is having in the poorest countries. "Basic justice and fairness imply that those who amassed wealth and other benefits through the nearly unrestricted extraction and use of petroleum, coal, and chemicals bear ethical responsibility for addressing the harms produced by the industrial greenhouse

---

[67] Byravan and Rajan, "The Ethical Implications of Sea-level Rise due to Climate Change," 257.

[68] K. Richardson et al., "Synthesis Report from Climate Change: Global Risks, Challenges, and Decisions," Copenhagen, March 10–12, 2009 (Copenhagen: University of Copenhagen, 2009), 23.

effect."[69] It is evident that the initial overuse of the global atmosphere, though unintentional in the early phase, has resulted in harm accruing disproportionately on one group, while another group has benefited disproportionately. Consequently, the major polluters, who were the major beneficiaries, have the duty to make amends.[70]

Justice also demands repayment of debts incurred. As Caritas Internationalis points out, the developed world has "borrowed" from the development potential of poorer countries and these "loans" must be repaid.[71] In effect, nations that have grown rich in part by polluting without facing the costs of doing so—a subsidy, one might say—must now repay their carbon debt. They have the moral responsibility to aid those whose rights have been violated by dangerous climate change. In concrete terms such an exigency requires assistance for mitigation and adaptation as well as compensation to communities and nations affected. In the context of the contemporary ecological crisis we need is not philanthropy but justice for the poor.

Historic responsibility is not the only key issue. The vast difference in capabilities of different countries is also important. In responding to climate change, for example, while all countries need to contribute, their real economic capabilities must be taken into account. We cannot ask poor people to pay to solve a problem created by the wealthy, at least until they, too, have the ability to pay. The solution to climate change must be a progressive one—with rich countries contributing at a level that is commensurate with their wealth. Shouldering the impacts of the crisis cannot be laid on poor countries that are least responsible for it.

Eco-justice also demands that the rights of the poor countries and their populations to reach a minimum level of economic development be respected. Eco-justice demands that the right to development and poverty alleviation be placed at the heart of a true moral response to the contemporary ecological crisis. It is morally unacceptable to constrain these nations' right to development by imposing upon them reductions of greenhouse gas emissions, while hundreds of millions of their citizens remain poor. It is important in this regard to distinguish between luxury emissions and survival emissions, as Anil Agarwal and others have pointed out.[72] While all greenhouse gas emissions

---

[69] Cuomo, "Climate Change, Vulnerability, and Responsibility," 697–98.

[70] Byravan and Rajan, "The Ethical Implications of Sea-level Rise due to Climate Change," 247–48.

[71] Caritas Internationalis, *Climate Justice*, 4.

[72] See Anil Agarwal et al., *Green Politics* (New Delhi: Centre for Science and Environment, 1999). See also Henry Shue, "Subsistence Emissions and Luxury

cause climate change, irrespective of where they come from, they do not have the same ethical standing. Poverty eradication and the guaranteeing of dignified life standards for all members of our common household form an essential part of a moral response to the crisis of our common home.

> In a world with 2.4 billion people without secure supplies of fuel for cooking or heating, and 1.6 billion people without access to electricity, we also need to respect the primacy of poverty eradication. People who have to deal with the day to day reality of crushing poverty cannot be expected to focus their efforts on climate change. Countries with significant populations of poor people must have poverty eradication as their top priority.[73]

The industrialized North has already captured a substantial portion of the earth's available carbon budget; the poorer South, where the bulk of humanity lives, thus has been deprived of its rightful ecological space. So, it is morally obvious that the remaining carbon budget should be divided "fairly" for future economic development, especially of the poorer communities.[74] It is unethical to ask poor countries to reduce their greenhouse gas emissions, which are themselves only a fraction of those of the developed countries and almost insignificant from the historical point of view.

The emissions arising from living in large, inefficient houses, flying for frivolous reasons, and driving inefficient vehicles are qualitatively distinct from those associated with poor households using wood-burning stoves for cooking their frugal meals and kerosene for lighting.[75] We must differentiate between emissions from profligate individuals or societies, whose wasteful lifestyle choices lead to high energy use, and those associated with energy uses for subsistence living. In this regard, "the methane emissions produced by an Indian subsistence farmer growing rice are not comparable with CO_2 discharges by the

---

Emissions," *Law and Policy* 15 (1993): 39–60.

[73] Christian Aid, *Climate Debt and the Call for Justice*, 2.

[74] Byravan and Rajan, "The Ethical Implications of Sea-level Rise due to Climate Change," 246. See also Henry Shue, "Global Environmental and International Inequality," *International Affairs* 75 (1999): 531–45; Stephen Gardiner, "Ethics and Global Climate Change," *Ethics* 114 (2004): 555–600; Steve Vanderheiden, *Atmospheric Justice: A Political Theory of Climate Change* (New York: Oxford University Press, 2008).

[75] Byravan and Rajan, "The Ethical Implications of Sea-level Rise due to Climate Change," 244.

German owner of a big limousine. The former are 'survival emissions,' the latter 'luxury emissions.'"[76] In a similar vein, "the emissions resulting from the efforts of a farmer in Africa as he attempts to feed his family are not on a par with the emissions resulting from the efforts of an American dermatologist as he attempts to get to Vegas for a weekend of gambling."[77] A clear distinction between luxury emissions and survival emissions is vitally important.

The rights of the poor to survival emissions are nonnegotiable:

> If it turns out that there should be some sort of planetary limit on emissions, then you might think that everyone ought to be entitled to emit enough greenhouse gases as required for subsistence. Maybe those emissions are not negotiable. If subsistence emissions fall under the planetary limit, and we still have reductions to make, then we can only discuss reductions to luxury emissions.[78]

The imperative of poverty alleviation and the task of providing poorer populations with basic amenities like electricity and cooking gas cannot be put off in the name of mitigating climate change. While developing countries need to be assisted not to follow the disastrous development path of the rich world, it would be unfair to deny them the minimum fruits of economic development. Energy is central to human development, yet as the "Human Development Report 2011" points out, some 1.5 billion people worldwide—more than one in five—lack electricity.[79] The unjust differences in access to basic energy services have to be considered alongside rising concerns over the rise in CO_2 emissions from developing countries. For example, emissions of CO_2 from India may have become a matter of global concern for climate security. However, approximately 500 million people in India live without access to modern electricity—more than the total population of the enlarged European Union.[80] It would be unethical to require these people and others elsewhere in the world—whose per capita emission rates hardly register in the global emission charts—to forgo basic amenities so that the rich and affluent can carry on with their extravagant lives.

---

[76] Sachs et al., *Greening the North*, 72.
[77] Garvey, *The Ethics of Climate Change*, 81.
[78] Ibid.
[79] UNDP, "Human Development Report 2011," 8.
[80] UNDP, "Human Development Report 2007/2008," 44.

It is estimated that providing basic modern energy services for everyone in the world would increase CO_2 emissions by only 0.8 percent. The projected annual investment to achieve universal access to modern sources of energy is less than one-eighth of annual subsidies for fossil fuels, one of the principal sources of greenhouse gases in the first place.[81] While people remain poor, it is unacceptable and unrealistic to expect them to focus their valuable resources on the climate-change crisis. Others who are wealthier and have enjoyed higher levels of emissions must take on their due share of the burden. For this, we need a fair and adequate global way of sharing that burden that explicitly safeguards the right to development of poor populations. We should not sacrifice the rights of millions for a life of dignity on the altar of luxury and affluence for the minority rich and powerful.

A just and fair climate-change approach at the global level will have to take into account the principles of responsibility and capability. However, the current state of climate-change negotiations—too often marked by intransigency and stagnation—is a far cry from eco-justice. The rich countries, who have the historic responsibility for climate change and have vastly greater capacity and far smaller burden of poverty, are reluctant to tread the path of eco-justice. "Not only are they largely failing to deliver on their commitments," but they are also now bringing forward "proposals that would shift the burden of acting on to developing countries."[82] Richer nations are increasingly citing cost to their economies as an excuse for their unwillingness to take action to reduce their emissions. However, "cost is not an ethically acceptable excuse for failing to take actions to reduce harmful levels of pollution below the emitting party's fair share of global emissions, particularly when that pollution threatens basic human rights to life, health and security."[83] Cost considerations are appropriate only when it comes to efforts to find cost-effective strategies to reduce harmful levels of emissions. Some nations cite the inaction from other major polluters as an excuse for their inaction. Such posturing clearly fails ethical scrutiny, "because no nation or person has a right to continue destructive behavior on the basis that others who are contributing to the damage have not ceased their destructive behavior."[84] Yet another common argument is that people in the developed world should not

---

[81] UNDP, Human Development Report 2011," 9–10.

[82] Christian Aid, *Climate Debt and the Call for Justice* (September 2009), 3.

[83] Brown et al., "White Paper on the Ethical Dimensions of Climate Change," 14.

[84] Ibid., 33.

be asked to sacrifice the high standards of living to which they have long been accustomed. However, when the lifestyles of the rich minority threaten the lives and livelihoods of poor communities around the world—as in the case of the impacts of climate change—it is unethical to carry on with such unsustainable living standards.

Equity

A second pillar on which the edifice of an ethical response to the ecological crisis needs to be built is the principle of equity. Equity is a precondition for justice. The principle of equity is based on the foundational values of human equality and dignity, namely, that that all persons are born equal and have equal rights to the resources of our home planet, including its common atmosphere. Living in our common home and being members of our common human family confer on each human person the right to equal ecological space. In the case of climate change, such a right means that "the Earth's atmosphere is a common resource without borders,"[85] to which all have equal rights, precisely in being members of the common household. As the earth's ability to absorb greenhouse gases is a "global common," it is vital this global common should be shared equally.[86]

The importance of the principle of equity is often lost sight of or consciously ignored in international climate-change negotiations, in spite of being enshrined in global conventions. The 1992 United Nations Framework Convention on Climate Change explicitly states that the nations "should protect the climate system for the benefit of present and future generations of humankind, on the basis of equity" (art. 3.1). The basic principle of equity is fundamental in assigning per capita emissions to countries and blocs, while at the same time taking into consideration other relevant factors like historical responsibilities and capabilities of nations and communities, and even other aspects like geography. For example, very cold countries need greater energy consumption to keep warm, and some countries are rich in renewable energy sources while others are not.[87] However, such considerations

---

[85] UNDP, "Human Development Report 2007/2008," 39.

[86] Anil Agarwal and Sunita Narain, *Global Warming in An Unequal World: A Case of Environmental Colonialism* (New Delhi: Centre for Science and Environment, 1991), 13.

[87] See Eric Neumayer, "National Carbon Dioxide Emissions: Geography Matters," *Area* 36 (2004): 33–40; idem, "Can Natural Factors Explain Any Cross-Country Differences in Carbon Dioxide Emissions," *Energy Policy* 30 (2002): 7–12.

fall strictly within the overall framework of equity, which remains crucial because it is founded on the fundamental values of human dignity and basic human equality.

Human equality lies at the basis of respect for human rights and the rejection of every form of discrimination. Equity is to be applied, also, when it comes to emission rights in the context of climate change. People in the developing countries are entitled for per capita emissions rights on an equal footing with the people of the developed world. As Dale Jamieson writes: "Every person has a right to the same level of GHG emissions as every other person. It is hard to see why being American or Australian gives someone a right to more emissions, or why being Brazilian or Chinese gives someone less of a right."[88] So every person has equal rights when it comes to the ecological and climate space of our common home. To argue to the contrary uses the discriminatory logic that lies at the root of practices like racial, caste, or other forms of segregation, all of which go against the principle of basic human equality.

It is important to safeguard the principle of equity in global treaties on climate-change mitigation. As the "White Paper on the Ethical Dimensions of Climate Change" points out: "Emissions levels from human activity vary greatly around the world and therefore the huge emissions reductions that will be needed to prevent dangerous climate change will fall disproportionately on some if equity is not taken seriously."[89]

> According to relevant principles of justice, those who claim entitlement to use the atmosphere or other natural systems as a sink for their GHG emissions at levels proportionately greater than others have the burden of demonstrating that their claim for entitlement to unequal levels of emissions is based upon morally relevant criteria.[90]

To mitigate dangerous climate change, the world has to cut emissions drastically and rapidly. All countries, developed and developing, need to limit their greenhouse gas emissions. However, such limits have to be worked out within a framework solidly founded on the

---

[88] Dale Jamieson, "Adaptation, Mitigation, and Justice," in *Perspectives on Climate Change: Science, Economics, Politics, Ethics*, ed. Walter Sinnott-Armstrong and Richard B. Howarth (Amsterdam: Elsevier, 2005), 231.

[89] Brown et al., "White Paper on the Ethical Dimensions of Climate Change," 10.

[90] Ibid., 14.

foundational and nonnegotiable principle of equity. Equity thus becomes a precondition for sustainability. As the "Human Development Report 2011" recognizes: "Sustainability is inextricably linked to basic questions of equity—that is, of fairness and social justice and of greater access to a better quality of life."[91]

Solidarity

A third foundational pillar of an ethical response to the contemporary ecological crisis is solidarity. The contemporary ecological crisis reveals how divided our common household is, and solidarity appears to be the sole solution to heal such wounds. Solidarity is more than responsibility. It is co-responsibility for our common home and for all the members of our common household, especially the poor and most vulnerable. Solidarity springs from the profound conviction, as Pope John Paul II wrote in 1987 in his social encyclical *Sollicitudo rei socialis,* that "we are *all* really responsible for *all*" (no. 38). In 2009, in *Caritas in veritate,* Pope Benedict XVI defined solidarity as "first and foremost a sense of responsibility on the part of everyone with regard to everyone" (no. 38). Solidarity gives expression to the underlying interdependence among individuals, the wider human community, and all creation.[92]

In the context of the contemporary ecological crisis, solidarity is based on the truth of "global commons," namely, that our home planet and its common atmosphere, ecosystems, and natural resources are common goods that belong to all. As Pope Paul VI wrote in 1967 in *Populorum progressio*: "God intended the Earth and everything in it for the use of all human beings and peoples. . . . Created goods should flow fairly to all" (no. 22). To desire the common good and strive toward it, according to Pope Benedict XVI, "is a requirement of justice and charity" (CV, no. 7).[93] Solidarity means working to ensure the welfare of all, especially those who are unjustly denied access to the common goods of our planetary home.

On the basis of the principle of solidarity the developed world has an obligation to ensure that the poorest and weakest sections of society have access to the common goods of our planetary home. The "Human Development Report 2011" states: "We have a collective responsibility toward the least privileged among us today and in the

---

[91] UNDP, "Human Development Report 2011," iv.

[92] *The Cry of the Earth: A Pastoral Reflection on Climate Change by the Irish Catholic Bishops' Conference* (2009), 21.

[93] See also Caritas Internationalis, *Climate Justice,* 4.

future around the world—and a moral imperative to ensure that the present is not the enemy of the future."[94] Such an obligation becomes pressing in the context of the contemporary ecological crisis, especially climate change. A document from the World Council of Churches affirms this: "Climate change aggravates the social and economic injustice prevailing between industrialized and developing countries. Through climate change, solidarity acquires a new dimension."[95] Today about 1.7 billion poor people are on the frontline of climate change through no fault of their own. It is imperative for those who are responsible and capable to act first and fast. The developed world needs to act not only because of its responsibility based on justice and equity, as we have shown previously, but also because of solidarity as well as its greater capacities. James Harvey writes:

> Not only do wealthy nations have more room to cut back on emissions and a greater ability to pay for the necessary changes than poorer countries, they also have much more besides. Compared to the poor, the people who live in wealthy countries are formally educated for longer, the technological options available to them are greater, their countries' infrastructures are better, their capacities to produce and store food are more impressive, their access to quality healthcare is easier, their housing is better, and so on. In short, developed countries have the resources to do rather a lot when it comes to dealing with climate change. They are presently best placed for action by just about any measure you like. To garble Kant, sometimes, can implies ought.[96]

In 1961, Pope John XXIII, in his encyclical *Mater et magistra*, called for solidarity within the common family of humanity in the context of the increasing discrepancies between the poor and the rich. According to him, it is "impossible for wealthy nations to look with indifference upon the hunger, misery and poverty of other nations whose citizens are unable to enjoy even elementary human rights. . . . [It is] nothing less than an outrage of justice and humanity to destroy or to squander goods that other people need for their very lives" (nos. 157, 161).[97]

---

[94] UNDP, "Human Development Report 2011," v.

[95] World Council of Churches, *Solidarity with the Victims of Climate Change: Reflections on the World Council of Churches' Response to Climate Change* (January 2002), 12.

[96] Garvey, *The Ethics of Climate Change*, 83.

[97] See also Cahal B. Daly, *The Minding of Planet Earth* (Dublin: Veritas, 2004), 171.

These words were prophetic. The need for solidarity is all the more urgent in our days in the context of the contemporary ecological crisis.

The contemporary ecological crisis, which is not only a physical problem but a profoundly moral predicament, calls for a global ethical response based on the fundamental principles of justice, equity, and solidarity.

A Common Yet Differentiated Responsibility

In the context of the current ecological crisis all of humanity needs to work together to avert the crisis; as it is the common home that is in peril. While all have a *common* responsibility toward the current state of the planet and need to work together to save it, at the same time, that responsiblity is also *differentiated* in terms of past and present responsibilities and current financial and technical capabilities, all within the framework of justice, equity, and solidarity.

Thus, while the whole of humanity has a common responsibility to respond to the contemporary ecological crisis—climate change in particular—such a response entails differentiated responsibilities. The United Nations Framework Convention on Climate Change begins by acknowledging that in tackling climate change countries should respond according to their "common but differentiated responsibilities and respective capabilities and their social and economic conditions." In the case of climate change a responsibility-capacity index subtitled "The Greenhouse Development Rights Framework" has been worked out by some leading nongovernmental organizations.[98] According to this framework—which quantifies each country's responsibility, capacity, and right to development in order to define the level of action that every state should undertake—the industrialized countries need to shoulder more than three-quarters of the cost of current global action. One-third of the burden of dealing globally with climate change falls on the shoulders of the United States, and one-quarter on the European Union. The United States, which has the world's largest share of cumulative emissions since 1990 (responsibility) and has an exceptionally large share of the global population of people with high incomes (capacity), will have to shoulder 33.1 percent of the global action to reduce emissions. The European Union follows with a 25.7

---

[98] See Paul Baer et al., "The Right to Development in a Climate Constrained World: The Greenhouse Development Rights Framework," rev. 2nd ed. (Berlin: Heinrich Böll Foundation; Christian Aid; Ecoequity; Stockholm Environment Institute, 2008).

percent share; China has a 5.5 percent share; and India, also large but much poorer, has a mere 0.5 percent share of the global burden.[99] As countries' economies and carbon emissions grow, the allotment of burden will change and will increasingly shift to developing countries. For example, China's share in the responsibility-capacity index is expected to double to 10.4 percent of the global share by 2020 and triple to 15.3 percent by 2030.[100] However, the majority of the burden will remain with developed countries for decades to come because of their vastly greater capacity and responsibility.

The poorest nations should focus their efforts on achieving sustainable development goals. This does not mean that the countries in which poor people live are not required to cut their emissions, but rather that the global consuming class—the elites both within these countries and in the industrialized countries—are the ones who must pay. The developing nations, of course, are held responsible for mitigation efforts such as reducing reforestation and pursuing sustainable development paths, but they should be granted less stringent emission targets so they might still achieve a baseline of economic and technological development while following more sustainable and less-carbon intensive development paths.[101]

The contemporary ecological crisis is a profoundly moral crisis, one of the greatest ethical dilemmas of our time, due to the stark injustice and inequity masked by it. At the same time, the "silver lining" is that acting against it in the spirit of solidarity, humanity has also a precious opportunity to create a more equitable and just world. It is up to our generation to rise to the occasion and respond to this unique challenge.

The ecological crisis is a global crisis. It is not only Mother Earth that is groaning under the weight of the ecological crisis, it is also the poor who are wailing with her. The gods are groaning too, as we shall see in Part IV.

---

[99] Ibid., 18.

[100] For the table for countries and groups, see ibid., 19.

[101] Cuomo, "Climate Change, Vulnerability, and Responsibility," 698; Byravan and Rajan, "The Ethical Implications of Sea-level Rise Due to Climate Change," 246.

PART IV

THE CRY OF THE GODS

The Dongria Kondh is a small, marginalized tribe that has lived for thousands of years in the remote Niyamgiri hills in the state of Orissa in eastern India. They call themselves Jharnia, meaning "protector of streams." The lush hills where they dwell are blessed with abundant water due to the copious presence of bauxite, the base material for aluminum. The life-giving rivers that rise within the dense forests of the mountains have nurtured a rich ecosystem marked with prolific biodiversity and unusually rich wildlife, providing the local population sustenance and livelihood. These hills are also sacred to them, as the abode of their tribal god, Niyam Raja, who they believe has protected them over the millennia.

The peaceful and harmonious life of the Dongria tribes suffered a rude shock in 2005 when the village of a neighboring tribe in the Niyamgiri foothills was bulldozed to make way for an aluminum refinery, set up by the London-based multinational Vedanta INC, one of the world's biggest mining companies. In connivance with the local government, the company managed, through its Indian subsidiary, to obtain a license for an open-pit mine on the Niyamgiri hills. The company wanted the abundant supply of bauxite ore to feed the furnaces of its aluminum refinery.

The eight thousand members of the indigenous community, nearly all of them illiterate, resisted with all their strength the might of the US$8 billion multinational company. It was tiny David pitted against the mighty Goliath. The Dongria vehemently opposed ceding their lands for the bauxite mine that would destroy their forests, disrupt the rivers, and spell the end of the Dongria Kondha as a distinct people. They knew that once displaced from their homelands, they risked the extinction of their distinctive culture, language, livelihood, and identity, like many other indigenous communities around the world. What they feared most was that the proposed mine would destroy the sacred abode of their indigenous god, Niyam Raja. In fact, at the center of their struggle is the sanctity of the sacred mountain to which their own identity as a people is indissolubly linked.

The tussle between the profit-oriented multinational company and the tiny indigenous tribe resisting eviction from its homeland is indeed a clash of perceptions. To the Dongria, the top of the Niyamgiri hill is the seat of their god, Niyam Raja, and as such the land is sacred to them. To Vedanta, the hill is a US$2 billion deposit of bauxite.

The rare determination and resilience of the Dongria against a powerful multinational company with an array of lobbyists and backed by unlimited money and muscle power garnered the support of some NGOs, civil society, and organizations like Survival International, committed to the defense and welfare of indigenous communities around the globe.[1] Soon the campaign attracted worldwide attention. A high point was when the UK government condemned Vedanta's treatment of the Dongria in 2009, and some of the shareholders of the company, prominently the Anglican Church, chose to disinvest in protest. In August 2010, India's then environmental minister, Shri Jairam Ramesh, refused to grant final clearance for Vedanta's mine, choosing to place the tribal group's rights above the company's balance sheet. As expected, the company refused to abide by the decision of the government and took the fight to the courts.

The battle for Niyamgiri shifted to the Supreme Court of India. In August 2013, the court ordered unprecedented consultations with Dongria Kondh villages surrounding the mine site, dubbed the country's first-ever "environmental referendum." All twelve Dongria villages involved in the consultation courageously rejected Vedanta's mining project, which would have turned their sacred mountain into an industrial wasteland. In January 2014, the Indian authorities finally quashed the company's plans to mine the Dongria Kondh tribe's sacred hills. The struggle and determination of the Dongria people to protect their land, their children, their culture, their identity, and above all, their god, was crowned with an extraordinary victory.

The struggle of the Dongria tribe, and of all who have sustained them in their fight, reveals yet another dimension of the contemporary ecological crisis. The ecological crisis is not only about the collapse of the planet's ecosystems and biochemical cycles with a profound impact on human populations, especially on the poor. The ecological crisis is also a deeply spiritual and religious crisis.

The contemporary ecological crisis points to the forgetfulness of a deeper truth; namely, the physical world is above all God's creation

---

[1] For a brief presentation of the indigenous Dongria Kondh community and its struggle, see the survivalinternational.org website. See also *Mine—Story of a Sacred Mountain* (2009), an acclaimed documentary that depicts the struggle of the Dongria against the multinational company, also available online.

and is permeated with the divine presence. The struggle of a tiny indigenous tribe in a remote valley of the Indian subcontinent reminds the great religious traditions of humanity—Christianity in the industrialized West, Buddhism in high-tech Japan; Islam in the rich metropolis of the Middle East built with petroleum dollars, Taoism and Hinduism in the emerging economies of China and India, and other faith traditions elsewhere—of a profound truth that they appear to have lost sight of, namely, that the physical world is fundamentally God's creation, entrusted to humanity, which is called to be its responsible guardian.

The contemporary ecological crisis, besides being a cry of the earth and of the poor who dwell therein, can also be defined in a symbolic way as a cry of the gods. Modern humans appear to have alienated not only the Earth and the poor of the Earth, but also the gods who dwell therein. The gods are groaning too. This is, in fact, a deeper dimension to the contemporary ecological crisis, one that is not a physical problem and a moral predicament, but also a profoundly spiritual crisis. The crisis is only an externalization of a deeper inner malaise. As Seyyed Hossein Nasr noted decades ago, "The blight wrought upon the environment is in reality an externalization of the destitution of the inner state of the soul of that humanity whose actions are responsible for the ecological crisis."[2] In a similar vein, Pope Benedict XVI pointed out, with a ring of prophecy, in the homily at the inaugural mass of his pontificate in 2005 that "the external deserts in the world are growing, because the internal deserts have become so vast." The ecological crisis is symptomatic of a deeper spiritual and religious crisis.[3]

The spiritual dimension of the contemporary ecological crisis is still to be recognized in an adequate manner by the religions and faith communities. Churches and religions have lagged far behind in acknowledging the underlying spiritual dimension of the crisis. It is true that religious leaders and groups have in recent years increasingly intervened on ecological questions. Pope John Paul's important message for the World Day of Peace in 1990, "Peace with God the Creator, Peace with All of Creation," was the first major intervention from the Catholic Church on ecological questions. In the same year

---

[2] Seyyed Hossein Nasr, *Man and Nature: The Spiritual Crisis of Modern Man* (London: Unwin Paperbacks, 1990), 3.

[3] See Andrea Cohen-Kiener, *Claiming Earth as a Common Ground: The Ecological Crisis Through the Lens of Faith* (Woodstock, VT: Skylight Paths Publishing, 2009), 2; Dave Bookless, *Planet Wise: Dare to Care for God's World* (Nottingham: Inter-Varsity Press, 2008), 41.

the World Council of Churches published a very important document, "Justice, Peace, and the Integrity of Creation." The ecumenical head of the Greek Orthodox Church, Bartholomew of Constantinople, hailed as the Green Patriarch, has constantly spoken about the ecological crisis. Most Catholic bishops' conferences and other national church bodies have issued documents on ecological questions in recent years. There have also been interfaith communiques about the safeguarding of creation, like "The Assisi Declarations: A Call—Buddhist, Christian, Hindu, Jewish and Moslem Statements on Nature," issued at Assisi in September 1986. However, a common drawback to interventions, with the notable exception of individual leaders like Bartholomew, is that they do not measure up to the gravity of the challenge facing our common home. For most faiths and religious groups the ecological crisis still appears as a host of environmental problems, not the crisis of our common home, where God dwells with humanity. It appears that the religions and churches are still to wake up to the magnitude of the contemporary ecological crisis, which is ultimately a crisis facing God's very creation.

A spiritual perspective in understanding the crisis facing our common household and the involvement of faith communities in dealing with the crisis is vitally important. The indispensable role of the religions in this regard has been highlighted by some members of the scientific community and civil society. Carl Sagan, noted astronomer and spokesman of science, led the organization of the Global Forum of Spiritual and Parliamentary Leaders on Human Survival, held in Moscow in January 1990. The gathering, which attracted more than one thousand religious, political, and scientific leaders from eighty-three nations, produced a joint religious-scientific declaration from twenty-four distinguished scientists, including Sagan, Nobel laureate Hans Bethe, physicist Freeman J. Dyson, and biologist Stephen Jay Gould. It was a joint appeal to the world's spiritual leaders to join the scientific community in protecting and conserving an endangered global ecosystem. According to the signatories, "We are close to committing—many would argue we are already committing—what in religious language is sometimes called crimes against creation."[4]

According to the scientists:

Problems of such magnitude . . . must be recognized from the outset as having a religious as well as a scientific dimension.

---

[4] Carl Sagan, "Preserving and Cherishing the Earth—An Appeal for Joint Commitment in Science and Religion," *American Journal of Physics* 58 (1990): 615.

> Mindful of our common responsibility, we scientists—many of us long engaged in combating the environmental crisis—urgently appeal to the world religious community to commit in word and deed, and as boldly as required, to preserve the environment of the Earth.[5]

The fundamental reason the scientists wanted religious leaders and faith communities to collaborate with them in safeguarding our home planet was the realization that "what is regarded as sacred is more likely to be treated with care and respect" and that "efforts to safeguard and cherish the environment need to be infused with a vision of the sacred."[6]

In 2006, noted Harvard biologist Edward O. Wilson renewed the call to faith communities to recognize the contemporary ecological crisis as a crisis of God's creation and appealed for their help to protect planet's dwindling biodiversity. In *Creation: An Appeal to Save Life on Earth*, Wilson writes: "We need your help. The Creation—living Nature—is in deep trouble. . . . Prudence alone dictates that we act quickly to prevent the extinction of species and, with it, the pauperization of Earth's ecosystems—hence of the Creation."[7]

Wilson is perplexed at the lack of engagement by the major religious traditions on such an important theme as the safeguarding of creation, and he even points an accusing finger at them:

> I am puzzled that so many religious leaders, who spiritually represent a large majority of people around the world, have hesitated to make protection of the Creation an important part of their magisterium. . . .
>
> Most troubling of all, our leaders, including those of the great religions, have done little to protect the living world in the midst of its sharp decline. They have ignored the command of the Abrahamic God on the fourth day of the world's birth to "let the waters teem with countless living creatures, and let birds fly over the land across the vault of heaven."[8]

It is time to perceive our ecological predicament as a spiritual and religious crisis at the deepest level. The physical understanding of the

---

[5] Ibid.

[6] Ibid.

[7] Edward O. Wilson, *The Creation: An Appeal to Save Life on Earth* (New York: W. W. Norton, 2006), 4–5.

[8] Ibid., 5, 10.

crisis is well established, thanks to the tireless efforts of the scientific community in the last few decades. There is no dearth of studies and publications on the physical aspects of the contemporary ecological crisis. The last few decades have also witnessed a steady increase in public awareness of the moral dimension of the ecological crisis, as greater attention has been paid to the plight of the poor, the early and disproportionate victims of problems like climate change. The fast-growing field of eco-justice activism and literature is certainly an encouraging sign in this regard. But as for the spiritual and religious dimension of the crisis, there have only been timid openings so far. While there have been pronouncements from religious leaders—usually coinciding with events like the annual Earth Day or important international summits and soon fading into oblivion thereafter—the safeguarding our common home, which is also God's creation, has not become a priority concern for religions and faith communities around the globe. Religious traditions and churches have failed, on the whole, to draw adequately from the rich repertoires of their own scriptures and millennial traditions or to rearticulate their respective theologies of creation, in the face of the current ecological crisis. However, it is becoming increasingly clear that "the ecological crisis cannot be solved without paying particular attention to the spiritual dimension of the problem."[9] As a declaration of The National Council of Churches in the United States affirmed in 2005: "In this most critical moment in Earth's history, we are convinced that *the central moral imperative* of our time is the care for Earth as God's creation."[10] But this urgency is hardly palpable in the mainstream churches and religious traditions. At the same time, it is important to link the spiritual dimension of the crisis directly to the physical and moral dimensions. The three cries of the Earth, of the poor, and of the gods need to be viewed together in order to arrive at a more complete understanding of the contemporary ecological crisis.

In this final part I attempt to offer a theological understanding of the contemporary ecological crisis without losing sight altogether of the scientific and moral perspectives that we have developed in the

---

[9] Nasr, *Man and Nature*, 7.

[10] National Council of Churches, "God's Earth Is Sacred: An Open Letter to Church and Society in the United States" (February 14, 2005). The statement goes on to affirm: "We firmly believe that addressing the degradation of God's sacred Earth is *the* moral assignment of our time comparable to the Civil Rights struggles of the 1960s, the worldwide movement to achieve equality for women, or ongoing efforts to control weapons of mass destruction in a post-Hiroshima world" (ibid.).

preceding three parts. We will see that the ecological crisis, which is markedly anthropogenic in character, results from a double failure. First, the ecological crisis is the outcome of our incapacity to look at the physical world as God's creation, as God's own home *(oikos)*, and therefore to respect its sanctity and integrity. The crisis is the result of our failure to recognize the physical world as God's primary revelation, as an icon and sacrament of God's being and presence in creation. Second, the crisis is the result of irresponsible stewardship of our common home, entrusted by the Lord to humanity. The ecological crisis reveals how we have failed in our original mandate to care for God's creation. Such irresponsible stewardship can be termed ecological sin, understood in a wider and relational sense of rupturing bonds of fellowship with the Creator, with fellow human beings, and with fellow creatures and the rest of creation.

The contemporary ecological crisis reveals, from a theological point of view, deeper and more intricate layers of our failure to respect the sanctity of creation, which is also God's home, and of our inability to be loving and responsible stewards of it.

9

Creation as God's Home

Our common home is also God's home, created in love and blessed with God's abiding presence. While God is present to the entire created universe, Earth has been further sanctified in the supreme event of the incarnation. It is our home planet. John has so beautifully expressed in the Fourth Gospel: "God pitched his tent" (Jn 1:14). From a theological perspective the contemporary ecological crisis results ultimately from our failure to look at the physical world as God's creation and abode, and to treat God's home with the due reverence.

This chapter begins with a reflection on the world as God's creation, the very first article of the Christian credo. We then examine how God is constantly present to creation. The physical world is God's primary revelation, a true icon and living symbol that points beyond itself to God's being and nature. Creation is also a sacrament of God, because created realities have the capacity to make God's presence more tangible in time and space, as with the material objects of sacraments. It is particularly true of the earthly elements of bread and wine in the Eucharist, which, once transformed in the power of the Spirit, become the Lord's body and blood. The contemporary ecological crisis points out that we have lost the capacity to look at and respect the physical world as God's primordial self-revelation, as a divine symbol and sacrament. We conclude by showing how the contemporary ecological crisis stems from our refusal to respect the ultimate destiny *(telos)* of all creation to enter into God's rest (Sabbath). We appear to have lost sight of the fundamental truth that all created reality is preordained to be recapitulated in God, its original source and ultimate destiny, as the cosmos moves toward its eschatological fulfillment.

Our Incapacity to See the World as Creation

The ecological crisis points to our forgetfulness of the fundamental truth about the physical world as creation. For believers, the material world is not just a surrounding "environment" or even just "nature," as in the physical sciences.[1] For them, the world is, above all, God's marvelous handiwork. It is creation. It is the result of God's free creative act, an outpouring of God's self-giving and self-revealing love. As such creation has an intrinsic goodness, beauty, and integrity independent of human perception and utility.

In almost all religious traditions the physical universe is perceived as created by God. The first words of the first book of the Bible, which Jews and Christians share, opens with this majestic expression: "In the beginning, God created the heavens and the earth" (Gn 1:1). The term *creation* is pregnant with deep theological significance, inasmuch as it implies that the material world was created by God, who brought all things from non-being into being, and that humanity is not its absolute ruler.[2]

The Genesis account of creation stands in stark contrast to the cosmological myths of the times and of the surrounding peoples. The cosmogenic myths of Babylonian and other ancient cultures had their own stories of creation, but none had the concept of creation out of nothing. They spoke of a Demiurge or craftsman who fashioned the world from preexisting material.

> The dominant creation myth of the ancient Near East was the *Enuma Elish*, one of several Babylonian creation stories. In its polytheistic view of many gods in a chaotic universe, Marduk, the hero god, slays the monster goddess Tiamat and the servant monsters she has created. The earth is formed from Tiamat's dismembered body. . . . But Marduk himself is no real creator, only a craftsman making a tool for his own use. The cosmos itself, in *Enuma Elish*, existed before the gods and they are but products of it.[3]

---

[1] As Steven Bouma-Prediger points out, the distinction is important: "For many the term nature implies a God-less universe, a cosmos for which there is no maker, whereas the term creation implies a Creator, a claim at the very heart of Christian faith." Steven Bouma-Prediger, *For the Beauty of the Earth: A Christian Vision for Creation Care* (Grand Rapids, MI: Baker Academic, 2001), 17.

[2] Ecumenical Patriarch Bartholomew, "Message, September 1, 2007," in *Cosmic Grace, Humble Prayer: The Ecological Vision of the Green Patriarch Bartholomew*, ed. John Chryssavgis (Grand Rapids, MI: Eerdmans, 2009), 65.

[3] Fred G. Van Dyke, "Ecology and the Christian Mind: Christians and the Environment in a New Decade," *Perspectives on Science and Christian Faith* 43 (September 1991): 174ff.

Genesis instead speaks of creation from nothing *(creatio ex nihilo)*, a concept that was totally alien to the ancients. God's creative act (the Hebrew verb *bara* in the Priestly account of creation is also the term used to refer to creation in the Qur'an) is radically different from all other activities by either humans or animals. Yahweh does not use any pre-existent matter or fashion the world out of the divine Being itself, as in many ancient creation myths. Yahweh creates *ex nihilo*. The concept of creation in this sense emphasizes the absolute power and transcendence of God the Creator and the absolute dependence of creation on the Creator. It is God who confers existence on every created being, as only the Creator can call a being into existence. Creation is also sustained by God in every moment, in every act, as Thomas Aquinas pointed out. According to Aquinas, the world is totally dependent on God for its continuance in being. The fundamental divine providence is that God sustains each creature at every moment. As Denis Edwards writes, basing himself on Karl Rahner: "All creaturely existence is contingent upon God's continuing creation. Things exist only because God conserves them in their being and in their action. All creatures owe their existence at every moment to the ongoing creative activity of God."[4]

Creation is an act of God's love, realized in total freedom. Our physical universe is not an accident or a fluke event, as it is sometimes presumed in secular thought and culture. The whole of creation and every creature is a sign of God's outpouring love. "In contrast to the violent beginning motifs of pagan cosmogonies, the Bible depicts creation as the tender loving act of a gracious God."[5] Every creature is brought into existence out of love and with a definite purpose. God's self-sharing love is what animates every creature. The age-old philosophical question, Why is there something rather than nothing? finds a response here. God creates to let creatures share in God's bountiful goodness and in the joy of existence.[6] Every bit of creation and every creature is precious precisely because God loves all of creation. As the medieval mystic Hildegard of Bingen has so beautifully expressed, the entire creation has been embraced by God's loving kiss:

---

[4] Denis Edwards, "For Your Immortal Spirit Is in All Things," in *Earth Revealing—Earth Healing: Ecology and Christian Theology*, ed. Denis Edwards (Collegeville, MN: The Liturgical Press, 2001), 50.

[5] Richard A. Young, *Healing the Earth: A Theocentric Perspective on Environmental Problems and Other Solutions* (Nashville, TN: Broadman and Holman Publishers, 1994), 85.

[6] See ibid., 89–90.

> As the Creator loves His creation
> so Creation loves the Creator.
> Creation, of course, was fashioned
> to be adorned, to be showered,
> to be gifted with the love of the Creator.
> The entire world has been embraced by this kiss.[7]

Earth, our home planet, is the gift of a loving God, clasped intimately in the Creator's loving embrace. "God so loved the world" (Jn 3:16), says Jesus in the Gospel of John. Here, "world" is *cosmos* in the Greek original, not just humanity—but the entire world. Earth is particularly beloved of the Creator and central to God's purposes. Samuel Rayan writes:

> Think of the infinite care with which God watched over the evolution of the earth and accompanied the endless process of its unfolding into myriad forms of life and movement and color and shape and scent. The earth is central to God's purposes. It is significantly placed at the heart of the prayer Jesus bequeathed to his disciples.[8]

It is the fundamental truth of having been created by God in love that renders creation, including Earth, our home planet, intrinsically good. The biblical word "good," *tob* in Hebrew, has different layers of meaning. The word can mean good, beautiful, joyous, pleasing, desirable, usable, suitable, lovely, friendly, kind, and so on. We focus here on the two common meanings attributed to the word *tob* in biblical interpretation: "good" and "beautiful."

Creation has an original goodness about it. It carries an original blessing. As Mathew Fox has pointed out, we have stressed so much the original sin, while we hardly speak of the original blessing about the fundamental goodness of creation and of every created reality. In the Priestly account of creation, we find this repeated expression after each day of God's creative labor of bringing things and living beings into existence: "and God found it good" (Gn 1:4, 10, 12, 18, 21, 25). On the sixth day, it is expressed even more emphatically by the Creator after the creation of everything: "God saw everything that

---

[7] Gabriele Uhlein, trans., *Meditations with Hildegard of Bingen* (Santa Fe, NM: Bear, 1982), 56, 65.

[8] Samuel Rayan, "The Earth Is the Lord's," in *Ecotheology: Voices from South and North*, ed. David G. Hallman (Maryknoll, NY: Orbis Books, 1994), 130–31.

he had made, and indeed, it was very good" (Gn 1:31). The Creator delights here in creation. Creation is good in the Creator's eyes, even before humans appear on the scene, late on the sixth day of creation. And God confers the appellative of being "very good" to the whole of creation, considered in its entirety, and not just humanity alone. Some of the early fathers of the church like Justin, Theophilus of Antioch, and Tatian, in opposition to the prevailing Gnostic dualism that depicted the created world as radically evil, emphatically affirmed the goodness of creation.[9]

For a believer, it is the basic goodness of creation in God's view that constitutes the intrinsic worth of every created reality. From a theocentric perspective the physical world has intrinsic value, because it has been created by God in love, and God recognized it to be good. God created the world; thus, the world and everything in it, including all forms of animate and inanimate matter, must have value. The intrinsic value of all creation, not just of humanity, is reinforced in the cosmic covenant that God stipulates with the whole of creation after the universal flood (Gn 9). The covenant is between God and all living things (a phrase repeated six times in eleven verses), not just with Noah and his family, or even God and humanity, but with "every living creature that is with you, for all future generations . . . the covenant that I have established between me and all flesh that is on the earth" (Gn 9:12, 17). It was a cosmic covenant that included not only humans but living things of every kind. Jesus' own parting words to his disciples were to "go into all the world and proclaim the good news to the whole of creation" (Mk 16:15). The animals, plants, rivers, and soil have significance to God independent of their value to humanity.[10] "God loves creation for its own sake."[11] The physical world is not merely a neutral object for human use; the natural world has value in itself and should not be valued merely for its usefulness to humanity. As Pope Benedict XVI reminds us in *Sacramentum caritas*: "The world is not something indifferent, raw material to be utilized as we see fit. Rather, it is part of God's good plan" (no. 92).

Creation is also beautiful. The beauty of creation goes beyond the mere considerations of utility. As Ecumenical Patriarch Bartholomew

---

[9] See Sean McDonagh, *The Greening of the Church* (Maryknoll, NY: Orbis Books, 1990), 165.

[10] Shannon Jung, *We Are Home: A Spirituality of the Environment* (Mahwah, NJ: Paulist Press, 1993), 68.

[11] Catholic Bishops' Conference of England and Wales, *The Call of Creation: God's Invitation and the Human Response* (2002), 4.

reminds us, creation's beauty is "first and foremost, the beauty of divine sacredness . . . For everything that lives and breathes is sacred and beautiful in the eyes of God."[12] Creation's beauty originates also from its stupendous order *(cosmos)* and interrelatedness, which can evoke sentiments of wonder and praise. Creation is indeed "clothed with beauty," to borrow a phrase from St. John of the Cross, one of the greatest of Christian mystics. Here is how St. John speaks of creatures who have been visited by their Creator, God, in his *Spiritual Canticle*:

> Scattering a thousand graces
> He passed through these groves in haste,
> And, looking upon them as he went,
> Left them by his glance alone
> Clothed with beauty.[13]

Thus, God's creation is both good and beautiful; it is to be loved and cherished. To love God is to love what God loves. In fact, we cannot be in spiritual communion with God if we destroy and mistreat what God cherishes. To reduce nature to an object for manipulation—or even theologically to a mere witness to God's existence and character—is to miss the fundamental truth about the physical world as God's creation.[14]

The contemporary ecological crisis, it appears, arises precisely from our inability to perceive the physical world as God's creation, to love it as the Creator does, to respect its integrity, and to appreciate its intrinsic goodness and beauty, moving beyond mere considerations of utility and consumption. The human activities that contribute to the ecological crisis are indeed "crimes against creation," to use an expression found in the 1990 joint appeal of the scientific community.[15] The degradation of our home planet is a destruction of God's creation, and constitutes nothing less than disrespect toward the Creator. Ecumenical Patriarch Bartholomew speaks in this regard:

---

[12] Ecumenical Patriarch Bartholomew, "Homily at the Fiftieth Anniversary Dedication of St. Barbara Greek Orthodox Church in Santa Barbara, California, November 8, 1997," in Chryssavgis, *Cosmic Grace, Humble Prayer*, 185.

[13] *The Complete Works of St. John of the Cross*, trans. and ed. E. Allison Peers (Westminster, MD: Newman Press, 1953), 2:26.

[14] Young, *Healing the Earth*, 95.

[15] Carl Sagan, "Preserving and Cherishing the Earth—An Appeal for Joint Commitment in Science and Religion," *American Journal of Physics* 58 (1990): 615.

Our destructive management of creation, besides having a practical impact on the quality of life, assumes a critical, moral dimension that constitutes a profound disrespect toward the Creator.[16]

All that was created "good" by the All Good Creator participates in His sacredness. Conversely, disrespect toward nature is disrespect toward the Creator, just as the arrogant destruction of a work of art is an insult to the artist who created it.[17]

Thus the contemporary ecological crisis—and each of its individual manifestations—is nothing less than an affront from the part of humans toward God's creation, and ultimately to the very Creator. The pastoral statement of the United States Conference of Catholic Bishops on climate change states: "The atmosphere that supports life on earth is a God-given gift, one we must respect and protect. . . . If we harm the atmosphere, we dishonor our Creator and the gift of creation."[18] In a similar vein the statement on water adopted by the World Council of Churches affirms: "Indifference toward the vitality of water constitutes both a blasphemy to God the Creator and a crime against humanity."[19] To pollute our common home not only defaces the beauty of creation but also insults the Creator.[20] Similarly, the current mass extinction of species due to human activities amounts to annihilation of life and existence, gifts that have been originally conferred on them in God's wise plan for the flourishing of life on our physical world.

Our current ecological predicament has resulted precisely from our refusal to perceive the physical world as God's creation and to love and cherish it, moving beyond mere considerations of utility and consumption.

---

[16] Ecumenical Patriarch Bartholomew, "Environment and Communication: Greeting at the Third Summer Seminar on Halki, July 1, 1996," in Chryssavgis, *Cosmic Grace, Humble Prayer*, 160.

[17] Ecumenical Patriarch Bartholomew, "Homily at the Fiftieth Anniversary Dedication of St. Barbara Greek Orthodox Church in Santa Barbara, California, November 8, 1997," 214.

[18] USCCB (United States Conference of Catholic Bishops), *Global Climate Change: A Plea for Dialogue, Prudence, and the Common Good* (Washington, DC: USCCB, 2001), 17.

[19] World Council of Churches, "Water of Life" (Geneva: WCC, 2006), 31.

[20] Young, *Healing the Earth*, 85.

Our Disregard for the Sacredness of God's Home

Another root cause of the contemporary ecological crisis is our failure to recognize God's in-dwelling presence in creation, a presence that renders it God's own home. God is not only transcendent to creation but is also deeply immanent in it. The intimate presence of God in creation is eminently clear in the Christian understanding of creation as a trinitarian event. The enduring presence of God in creation becomes all the more real in the event of the incarnation, in which God assumes matter and sanctifies it. It is precisely God's abiding presence in creation that makes our physical world ultimately sacred.

The belief in the abiding presence of God in creation is shared by almost all religious traditions. United Nations Secretary-General Boutros Boutros-Ghali, speaking at the Earth Summit in Rio de Janeiro in June 1992, recalled: "To the Ancients, nature was the dwelling place of the gods."[21] Ancient peoples lived in a world permeated by the spirits. Such belief continues to permeate the indigenous religious traditions, in which the gods are believed to dwell in particular localities and natural phenomena. It is the belief in the presence of the Divine in the physical world that accounts, even today, for the keeping and flourishing of sacred groves—exceptionally rich in vegetation and biodiversity—in those geographical areas where indigenous and tribal religious traditions, or popular strands of nature-oriented religions like Hinduism, are predominant. For example, we saw in the Introduction to Part IV how the indigenous Dongria tribal community in the remote hill areas of eastern India is struggling to protect its sacred mountain—the abode of its protective deity—from the economic interests of a powerful mining company.

From a theological point of view, God is present throughout creation. The Qur'anic verse goes, "Whithersoever you turn, there is the Face of God" (II:115). As Hans Urs Von Balthasar says, "Creation as a whole has become a monstrance of God's real presence."[22] The truth of God's abiding presence in creation is at the core of almost all religions and is overwhelmingly attested in their scriptures and traditions. God's enduring presence in creation is especially evident in Christianity. Christian theology considers creation as a trinitarian act;

---

[21] Quoted in Fritz Hull, ed., *Earth and Spirit: The Spiritual Dimension of the Environmental Crisis* (New York: Continuum, 1993), 8.

[22] Hans Urs Von Balthasar, *The Glory of the Lord: A Theological Aesthetics*, vol. 1: *Seeing the Form*, trans. Erasmo Leva-Merikakis (San Francisco: Ignatius Press, 1982), 420.

the Father creates through the Son in the Holy Spirit. As the *Catechism of the Catholic Church* recognizes, "Creation is the common work of the Holy Trinity."[23]

The First Person of the Trinity, the Father, is the Source and Origin of creation. One of the early fathers of the church, Athanasius, specifies that in the one act of creation, the First Person is the "beginning" and the "fountain" of creation, while the Word is the one "through" whom things are created, and the Spirit is the one "in" whom things are made.[24] The Father is the eternal source of the outpouring love of the triune God, of which creation is a tangible expression. The Genesis account offers a glimpse of the creative activity of God in this regard. It is the image of a God who lovingly molds the physical universe, not standing aloof from it but actively involved in it. It is a God who works on soil and cultivates the garden, molds the clay (as evident in the fashioning of living creatures, and human beings, on the sixth day of creation), who gets his hands dirty. The Creator of the Book of Genesis is markedly different from many pagan gods of antiquity who belonged to the pure realm of the spirits and considered matter intrinsically evil and judiciously kept away from it. The closeness of the Creator to the creatures is clearly evident in the poetical description in the second chapter of Genesis, where the Creator strolls in the garden in the cool of the evening, walking with Adam and Eve in the garden of our common home. The presence and closeness of God toward creation is all the more evident on the day of Sabbath, the final day of God's creative work, when God rests along with the rest of creation and lovingly contemplates it. As Jürgen Moltmann reminds us, God lets creation exist in coexistence with God, before God's face. "So the world is not merely created by God; it also exists *before* God and lives *with* God."[25] Clearly, God is present to creation, dwells with creation, right from the beginning.

God's presence in creation is above all in the Spirit. The creative process is realized in the power and agency of the Spirit. As we read in one of the earliest verses of the Priestly account of creation, the Spirit of God hovered over the primordial waters: "a wind *(ruach)* from God swept over the face of the waters" (Gn 1:2), the same creative Spirit that overshadowed Mary at the annunciation to herald the dawn of

---

[23] *Catechism of the Catholic Church* (Vatican City: Libreria Editrice Vaticana, 1996), no. 292.

[24] *Letters to Serapion*, I, 28, in *The Letters of Saint Athanasius Concerning the Holy Spirit*, trans. C. R. B. Shapland (London: Epworth Press, 1951), 134–35.

[25] Jürgen Moltmann, *God in Creation: A New Theology of Creation and the Spirit of God* (San Francisco: Harper and Row, 1985), 279.

the new creation (Lk 1:35). In the hovering of the Spirit over creation, the earth was "God betrothed" at the very beginning of creation. It is because of the brooding of the Spirit of God at the primordial waters in creation that, as the English poet Gerard Manley Hopkins reminds us in his poem "God's Grandeur,"

> there lives the dearest freshness deep down
> things, . . .
> Because the Holy Ghost over the bent
> World broods with warm breast and with ah!
> bright wings.

Creation takes place by the power of the Spirit, the very breath of the triune God. The triune God unremittingly breathes the Spirit into creation, calling every created being into existence. As Psalm 104, a poetic celebration of God's wonderful creation, so succinctly states: "When thou send forth your spirit, they are created" (Ps 104:30). All created things are formed from the continual inflow of the divine Spirit: "You sent forth your spirit and it formed them" (Jdt 16:14). The Spirit is poured out on everything that exists. "Your immortal spirit is in all things," proclaims the Book of Wisdom (Wis 12:1). Creation is the differentiated presence of the life-giving breath of God, the presence of the One in the infinite diversity of created things.[26]

> In human speech, though the words and utterances are distinct and different, they are imparted with the same breath. Likewise we can say figuratively that God "speaks" through the individual creatures, or as a beautiful English hymn puts it, "God breathes through the whole creation." The integrity of creation and the community of creatures is sustained by the breath of the Spirit of God.[27]

In the language of the Bible, the Spirit breathes life into all things of flesh: "If he should take back his spirit to himself, and gather to himself his breath, all flesh would perish together, and all mortals return to dust" (Jb 34:14–15).[28] It is for this that the Nicene-Constantinopolitan creed calls the Holy Spirit "the giver of life." If the Holy

---

[26] Ibid., 14.

[27] Jürgen Moltmann, "Reconciliation with Nature," *Word and World* 11 (1991): 120.

[28] See Denis Edwards, "Final Fulfillment: The Deification of Creation," *SEDOS Bulletin* 41 (2009): 191.

Spirit is poured out on created beings, in virtue of them being called into existence by the power of the same Spirit, then this fountain of life is present in everything that exists and is alive. "Everything that is, and lives, manifests the presence of this divine wellspring."[29] It is also in the power of the life-giving Spirit that God continually renews the face of the earth (Ps 104:30). In all this process "the Spirit is creatively present to every creature, dwelling in each, surrounding it with love, holding it in a community of creation and accompanying it in its life and in its death."[30]

The triune God is immanent and in-dwells in all things in the Spirit. The Spirit of God fills the whole Earth *(Spiritus Domini replevet orbem terrarum)* as a constant and accompanying presence (Wis 1:7). The Creator Spirit is the divine presence deep in all things, the intimate presence that enables creatures to exist. As Denis Edwards writes: "The Creator Spirit is present in every flower, bird, and human being, in every quasar and in every atomic particle, closer to them than they are to themselves, enabling them to be and to become."[31] The Spirit is the intimate nearness of God in creation, the "unspeakable closeness of God," as "God's love has been poured into our hearts through the Holy Spirit" (Rom 5:5).[32] In this way God is truly the *Antarayamin* (the in-dwelling Spirit) of creation, present everywhere and in everything, as the Hindu scripture Bhagavad Gita proclaims (13:16).

If God is immanent to creation as the in-dwelling Spirit that animates every being, the incarnation reveals how God "co-dwells" with humanity and the rest of creation. In the supreme event of incarnation the Word, in whom and for whom all things were created (Col 1:16), enters into the material home that God had created. Creation in this sense can be seen as a prelude to incarnation. Creation, which is God's self-donating act, reaches its culmination in the self-emptying kenotic event of the incarnation (Phil 2:1–5), when God humbly becomes part of that same creation.

It is significant that God's incarnation takes place on Planet Earth. Among the billions and billions of celestial bodies in the universe, God chose to "pitch his tent" (Jn 1:14) on this tiny planet. Earth has been rendered unique for the singular capacity to host life and let it evolve

---

[29] Moltmann, *God in Creation*, 11.
[30] Edwards, "Final Fulfillment," 191.
[31] Edwards, "For Your Immortal Spirit Is in All Things," 56–57.
[32] See Denis Edwards, *Ecology at the Heart of Faith: The Change of Heart That Leads to a New Way of Living on Earth* (Maryknoll, NY: Orbis Books, 2006), 45–47; Jürgen Moltmann, *The Spirit of Life: A Universal Affirmation* (Minneapolis: Fortress Press, 1992), 65.

into complex life forms, unlike anywhere else in the vast universe. In the incarnation, in entering into the womb of the humble Virgin of Nazareth, the Creator enters into the womb of the earth, into the womb of our home planet's biosphere, already teeming with life. It is indeed a stupendous moment. Earth, which had become a home for life through a process running into billions of years, becomes a home for life in abundance (Jn 10:10) in the person of God-become-human being, Jesus Christ.

The incarnation is the most visible expression of God's presence in creation. God became "flesh of her flesh," as the Virgin confesses in the Christmas play that Jean-Paul Sartre wrote for his mates while in prison.[33] Incarnation affirms the ultimate value of flesh, of this world, and thus counters all forms of dualisms—both ancient and modern—that devalue the flesh and the material world. "The flesh of Jesus is part of the whole creaturely pattern of life on Earth. When the Word is made flesh, God embraces the long, interconnected history of life in all its complexity and diversity. The incarnation is God-with-us in the 'very tissue' of biological life."[34] For this reason there is no better or greater testimony to the in-dwelling presence of God in creation than the incarnation. As Irenaeus of Lyons noted, incarnation is the bridge between the Creator and the created universe. Incarnation is God's presence made tangible in created matter.

One may speak of a "double sanctification" of creation with the event of the incarnation. Creation, which is already hallowed by the abiding presence of God's Spirit from the initial moment of creation, becomes further sanctified by the physical presence of the incarnate Word. Teilhard de Chardin writes: "Because the Word is made flesh, no part of the physical universe is untouched. All matter is the place of God. All is being divinized. . . . Through your own incarnation my God, all matter is henceforth incarnate."[35] With the incarnation, every inch, every corner of Earth becomes "holy land," sanctified by the presence of the Word-become-flesh. Earth is thus the place of saving encounter with God for the whole of creation.

The intrinsic sanctity of God's creation ultimately derives from the fact that it is infused with the divine presence and is inhabited

---

[33] The play was entitled "Barjona, Jeu scénique en six tableaux" and was written in a Nazi prison camp in the autumn of 1940. It was not published during Sartre's life.

[34] Edwards, *Ecology at the Heart of Faith*, 60.

[35] Teilhard de Chardin, "The Mass on the World," in *Hymn of the Universe* (London: Collins, 1965), 24.

by God: by the in-dwelling Spirit of God and the co-dwelling of the incarnate Word. Our creation is thus holy ground. "Our feet are on holy ground—ground so holy that Moses took off his shoes."[36] The recognition of God's presence in creation is in no way worship of creation. Orthodox theology draws a line between pantheism (equating nature with God) and incarnational spirituality (finding God's presence in all creation). St. John of Damascus, an eighth-century writer, expresses this distinction:

> I do not worship matter. I worship the Creator of matter who became matter for my sake, who willed to take [God's] abode in matter; who worked out my salvation through matter. Never will I cease honoring the matter which wrought my salvation! I honor it, but not as God. . . . Because of this I salute all remaining matter with reverence.[37]

God's presence in creation renders it sacred and reveals how the entire physical universe, and our home planet in particular, where the supreme event of incarnation took place, is not simply a "work of God's hands." It is God's own house.

The contemporary ecological crisis lays bare precisely our incapacity to perceive the physical world as impregnated with the Divine. We have swapped the lofty vision of the physical world as God's own abode, sanctified by the incarnation of the Son of God, with the one-dimensional mechanistic outlook of Modernity. Accordingly, the physical world is reduced to a mere storehouse of resources for human consumption, just real estate for market speculation. It is such a reductivist perception of the physical world that has enabled both materialistic and neoliberal economic systems, aided by modern technology, to ravage our home planet. The current state of the earth shows that we have betrayed the spiritual and religious perception of the physical world as sacred, as permeated by the Divine. For most people, "nature does not radiate a Presence; it provides us with the raw materials to be converted into artefacts that we desire."[38] We have desacralized creation. Through pollution of the planet's land, air, and waters, we have degraded God's

---

[36] James Parks Morton, "Environment and Religion: The Evolution of a New Vision," in Hull, *Earth and Spirit*, 125.

[37] St. John of Damascus, *Apologia Against Those Who Decry Holy Images*, I:16. As quoted in Myroslaw Tataryn, "The Eastern Tradition and the Cosmos," *Sobornost* 11 (1989): 49.

[38] Sam Keen, *Apology for Wonder* (New York: Harper and Row, 1969), 112.

home. We are polluting the earth, reducing it mostly to merchandise, and profligately wasting away its precious resources. The Book of Numbers tells us: "You shall not defile the land in which you live, in which I also dwell" (Nm 35:34).[39] If creation is sacred in virtue of God's abiding presence and cohabitation, "it follows that no part of the creation can be thought of as outside God's grace and there is nowhere called 'away' where things can be thrown."[40] Our present profligate lifestyles demonstrate that we have lost the awareness of Earth as holy ground. Ultimately, "if we are guilty of relentless waste, it is because we have lost the spirit of worship. We are no longer respectful pilgrims on this earth; we are reduced to mere tourists."[41]

As René Dubos has pointed out, what we need most today is a revived sense of the holiness of creation.[42]

Creation as a Symbol and Sacrament of God

Our physical world—the sacred home where God in-dwells and co-dwells with humanity and the rest of creation—is also God's primary revelation. Creation is, as the early fathers loved to call it, God's "book of works" that reveals the divine nature and character. Creation is, in this regard, a living symbol and a true icon of God. Created objects are sacraments that render God's invisible presence in creation tangible in time and space. The contemporary ecological crisis points to our profound spiritual blindness to this great book of God's creation and to our incapacity to look at and respect the physical world as a divine symbol and sacrament.

As John Scotus Eriugena points out, "[Creation] in all its wonderful diversity is a living theophany."[43] We can discern the hand of God in creation, just as we see the hand of Rembrandt in his paintings.

---

[39] See Lewis G. Regenstein, *Replenish the Earth: A History of Organized Religion's Treatment of Animals and Nature—Including the Bible's Message of Conservation and Kindness to Animals* (London: SCM Press, 1991), 20.

[40] Church of England, *Sharing God's Planet: A Christian Vision for a Sustainable Future: A Report from the Mission and Public Affairs Council* (London: Church House Publishing, 2005), 20.

[41] Chryssavgis, *Cosmic Grace, Humble Prayer*, 25.

[42] René Dubos, "Foreword," in Christopher Derrick, *The Delicate Creation: Toward a Theology of the Environment*, Christopher Derrick (London: Tom Stacey Ltd., 1972), v.

[43] John Scotus of Eriugena, *Periphyseon* 681A. See also 446C–D; and Eriugena's *Commentaire sur l'Evangile de Jean*, ed. and trans. Edouard Jeauneau, *Sources Chrétiennes* (Paris: Editions du Cerf, 1972), 124 (PL 122, 302A–B).

God has, in fact, deliberately left clues about God's self in creation. As we read in the Letter to the Romans: "Ever since the creation of the world his eternal power and divine nature, invisible though they are, have been understood and seen through the things he has made" (Rom 1:20). "[God] has not left himself without a witness in doing good—giving you rains from heaven and fruitful seasons, and filling you with food and your hearts with joy" (Acts 14:17). These are God's accredited witnesses—the primal testimony God gives of himself.[44] Creation thus becomes "a gospel which speaks to us of God."[45]

> The heavens are telling the glory of God;
>   and the firmament proclaims his handiwork.
> Day to day pours forth speech,
>   and night to night declares knowledge.
> (Ps 19:1–2)

Creation is, indeed, the very first epiphany of God. Some of the early fathers of the church, like John Chrysostom, spoke of the two books of God: the book of works and the book of words, the book of the creatures and the book of the scriptures. The book of works is the creation, the entire physical universe. God's book of works is even more Planet Earth, with its unique and rich biosphere and infinite diversity of life forms. The book of works has been God's first and primordial revelation, and it has not been canceled by the second book, the book of words. Instead, the two books need to be read together to have a complete understanding of God. As John Scotus Eriugena says: "Christ wears 'two shoes' in the world: Scripture and nature. Both are necessary to understand the Lord, and at no stage can creation be seen as a separation of things from God."[46]

The perception of the physical world as the self-revelation of God is deeply rooted in Christian tradition. St. Augustine is very clear in this regard:

---

[44] Rayan, "The Earth Is the Lord's," 132.

[45] Pope John Paul II, General Audience, January 26, 2000.

[46] J. Matthew Sleeth, "Teachings on Creation Through the Ages," in *The Green Bible* (London: Harper Collins, 2008), 101. See also John Scotus of Eriugena, Periphyseon (PL 122, col. 723D), where Eriugena compares *creatura* and *scriptura* as the two vestments of Christ at his transfiguration. See also Donald F. Duclow, "Nature as Speech and Book in John Scotus Eriugena," *Mediaevalia* 3 (1977): 131–40. On the importance of reading together both books about God—creation and the Bible—see Edward Brown, *Our Father's World: Mobilizing the Church to Care for Creation* (South Hadley, MA: Doorlight Publications, 2006), 98,

Some people, in order to discover God, read books. But there is a great book: the very appearance of created things. Look above you! Look below you! Read it. God, whom you want to discover, never wrote that book with ink. Instead, He set before your eyes the things that He had made. Can you ask for a louder voice than that?[47]

The tradition of looking at the physical world as God's book of works and a visible manifestation of the bountiful Creator carried into the medieval period. Bonaventure spoke of the physical universe as "a book reflecting, representing and describing its Maker, the Trinity."[48] God's infinite love and providential care were sensed, especially by contemplative monks and nuns, as flowing throughout the whole of creation, much of the way the sun's radiance pours down upon Earth. David Toolan writes: "The Christian culture of the medieval period, following Augustine of Hippo, likened nature to a book, a semiotic system, a set of signs signifying and transmitting the energies of what Aristotle called the *nous poetikos*, the prime Poet-Maker of the cosmos."[49]

The belief of creation as the primordial revelation of God was not lost even in the Reformation traditions, in spite of their emphasis on the written scriptures. As the oft-quoted saying commonly attributed to Martin Luther goes, "God writes the Gospel not in the Bible alone, but also on trees, and in the flowers and clouds and stars."[50] And John Calvin adds: "The creation is quite like a spacious and splendid house, provided and filled with the most exquisite and the most abundant furnishings. Everything in it tells us of God."[51] The limpidity of the perception of the physical world as God's book of works, capable of uplifting the hearts of the believers to the Creator, is evident in the following passage from Thérèse of Lisieux:

Jesus set before me the book of nature. I understood how all the flowers He has created are beautiful, how the splendor of the rose and whiteness of the lily do not take away the perfume of the little violet or the delightful simplicity of the daisy.

---

[47] Augustine, *De Civitate Dei*, Book 16.

[48] Bonaventure, *Breviloquium* 2.11–12.

[49] David Toolan, *At Home in the Cosmos* (Maryknoll, NY: Orbis Books, 2001), 33.

[50] As quoted in Sleeth, "Teachings on Creation Through the Ages," 103.

[51] John Calvin, *Institutes* 1:14. Cited in Sleeth, "Teachings on Creation Through the Ages," 103.

With enraptured gaze we beheld the white moon rising quietly behind the tall trees, the silvery rays it was casting upon sleeping nature, the bright stars twinkling in the deep skies, the light breath of the evening breeze making the snowy clouds float easily along; all this raised our souls to heaven.[52]

Creation is thus the primordial and privileged way to God, accessible to all. The physical world possesses an in-built ability to act as a sign toward the Creator. "Nature is like a mirror, itself beautiful while reflecting an even greater beauty of God. Something of the torrent of God's beauty can thus be known in the rivulets of the beauty of creation."[53] For this reason, it is possible by way of analogy to arrive at the Creator, departing from the very created goods, the attributes of God.

In its capacity to point to the Creator, creation and all created realities perform a symbolic function. As the Greek etymology of the word goes, a "symbol" attempts to place together *(sum + ballein)* various fragments for a more profound understanding of reality. Creation as a symbol brings together the finite and the infinite, the natural and the supernatural. Creation's value lies precisely in its symbolism, in its capacity to link the finite with the Infinite. From a theological perspective, every created reality is a symbol, a sign post, that points beyond itself to the Creator. Bonaventure writes:

All the creatures of the sense world lead the mind of the contemplative and wise man to the eternal God. For these creatures are shadows, echoes and pictures of that first, most powerful, most wise and most perfect Principle, of that eternal Source, Light and Fullness, of that efficient, exemplary and ordering Art. They are vestiges, representations, spectacles proposed to us and signs divinely given so that we can see God.[54]

Creation symbolically represents the Creator, often in silence, which is the cherished language of symbols. The earth speaks in the eloquent silence of hills and trees. The Bhagavad Gita celebrates the "silence

---

[52] John Clarke, OCD, trans., *Story of a Soul: The Autobiography of St. Thérèse of Lisieux*, prepared by Mark Foley (Washington, DC: Institute of Carmelite Studies Publications, 2005), xxiii, 159.

[53] Alister McGrath, *The Reenchantment of Nature: The Denial of Religion and the Ecological Crisis* (New York: Doubleday, 2002), 16.

[54] Bonaventure, *The Soul's Journey into God*, trans. Ewart Cousins (New York: Paulist Press, 1978), 75–76.

of hidden realities" that point to the Divine (x.38). And the Psalmist reminds us:

> There is no speech, nor are there words;
>> their voice is not heard;
> yet their voice goes out through all the earth,
>> and their words to the end of the world. (Ps 19:3–4)

As symbols of God, created realities are *vestigia Dei*, signs and traces of God's presence in creation. Such was the profound awareness that permeated medieval Christian world view and cosmology. For the medieval society, "every living form of plant, bird or animal, the sun, moon and stars, the waters and the mountains, were seen as signs of things sacred *(signa rei sacrae)*, expressions of a divine cosmology, symbols linking the visible and the invisible, earth and heaven."[55] For medieval mystic Meister Eckhart, "Every creature is a book about God," and "full of God is every creature."[56] As St. John of the Cross says, "The creatures are, as it were, a trace of the passing of God, whereby are revealed His greatness, power, wisdom, and other Divine virtues."[57]

The Qur'an too speaks of the physical world as filled with signs *(ayah)* of God.[58] In the Qur'an every creature is referred to as *ayah* of God *(ayat allah)*. The Arabic word *ayat* means a sign, token, or mark by which a person or thing is known or can be perceived. In fact, the term *ayah* is used almost four hundred times in the Qur'an.[59] As Seyyed Hossein Nasr notes, sages were able to read the great book of the "cosmic Qur'an":

> They saw upon the face of every creature letters and words from the pages of the cosmic Qur'an which only the sage can read. They remained aware of the fact that the Qur'an refers to

---

[55] Philip Sherrard, *The Rape of Man and Nature: An Enquiry into the Origins and Consequences of Modern Science* (Suffolk: Golgonooza Press, 1987), 64.

[56] Meister Eckhart, *Sermons.*

[57] *The Complete Works of St. John of the Cross*, trans. and ed. E. Allison Peers (Westminster, MD: Newman Press, 1953), 2:48.

[58] See, for example, 2:164; 3:190; 13:2–4; 16:10–13; 27:86; 29:44; 30:20–25; 41:37; 45:3–6. See Jose Abraham, "An Ecological Reading of the Qur'anic Understanding of Creation," *Bangalore Theological Forum* 33 (2011): 168.

[59] Abraham, "An Ecological Reading of the Qur'anic Understanding of Creation," 168; Sachiko Murata and William C. Chittick, *The Vision of Islam* (New York: Daragon Home, 1994), 52, 54.

the phenomena of nature and events within the soul of man as *ayat* (literally signs or symbols), a term that is also used for the verses of the Qur'an. They read the cosmic book, its chapters and verses, and saw the phenomena of nature as "signs" of the Author of the book of nature. For them the forms of nature were literally *ayat Allah, vestigia Dei*.[60]

When created things become *vestigia Dei*, creation becomes a true act of communication. Each created reality in this regard is a *logos*, an intelligible word from the Creator revealing God's inner self and character. "As Maximus the Confessor says, each existent reality is itself a *logos*—a word, an intelligible structure—which carries in its own specific, unique way the universal *logos* within it. This implies that each thing communicates the character of God, by virtue of the eternal Word."[61]

As in every act of communication, no single word or expression is sufficient to communicate reality. This is also true of God's communication in creation. "No one creature, not even the human, can image God by itself. Only the rich diversity of life—huge soaring trees, the community of ants, the flashing colors of the parrot, the beauty of a wildflower along with the humans—can give expression to the radical diversity of otherness of the triune God."[62] According to Bonaventure, as "the one stream of light breaks up into different colors as it flows through a stained-glass window, so the Creator is reflected in the different creatures we see around us. Each and every creature reflects a different aspect of the Creator."[63] The exuberance of creation thus represents the infinite fecundity of God. This point was masterfully brought home by the thirteenth-century medieval theologian Thomas Aquinas, who argued that the diversity of the creatures roaming the earth reveals the richness of the nature of God:

> For God brought many things into being in order that his goodness might be communicated to creatures and represented in them; and because this goodness could not be adequately represented by one creature alone, God produced many and diverse creatures, so that what was wanting to one in the representation

---

[60] Seyyed Hossein Nasr, "Islam and the Environmental Crisis," in *Spirit and Nature: Why the Environment Is a Religious Issue*, ed. Steven C. Rockfeller and John C. Elder (Boston: Beacon Press, 1992), 88.

[61] Quoted in Church of England, *Sharing God's Planet*, vii.

[62] Edwards, *Ecology at the Heart of Faith*, 77–78.

[63] Bonaventure, *Hexameron* 13.14.

of divine goodness might be supplied by another. For goodness which in God is simple and uniform, in creatures is manifold and diverse. Hence the whole universe together participates in the divine goodness more perfectly, and represents it better than any single creature whatever.[64]

The truth of created realities as symbols of God, as *vestigia Dei*, is most clearly expressed in the doctrine of icons in Orthodox thought and spirituality. In Orthodox theology, an icon is something that reveals a thing's eternal dimension. John Chryssavgis writes:

> The icon aspires to reveal the inner vision of all, the world as created and as intended by God. . . . The icon does away with any objective distance between this world and the next, between the material and the spiritual, between body and soul, between time and eternity, between creation and divinity. The icon reminds us that there is no double vision, no double order in creation.[65]

The icon converts beholders from a restricted, limited point of view to a fuller, spiritual vision by which they see everything as reconciled and as united in a single reality. Significantly, in Orthodox theology "it is not just humanity that is likened to an icon. The entire world is an icon, a door, a window, a point of entry, opening up to a new reality. Everything in this world is a sign, a seed."[66] In the Orthodox tradition creation itself is likened to an icon in the same way the human person is created "in the image [or icon] of God" (Gn 1:26). According to seventh-century Eastern theologian John of Damascus, "The whole earth is a living icon of the face of God."[67] Ecumenical Patriarch Bartholomew has repeatedly invited believers to "rediscover this iconic dimension of creation," and to contemplate the Creator God through the icon of the created world.[68] According to this perspective, created realities are truly icons—finite material objects that disclose the light and beauty of the Infinite and Divine.

---

[64] Thomas Aquinas, *Summa Theologica* 1.47.1. Cited from *Summa Theologica*, trans. Fathers of the English Dominican Province (New York: Cosimo Books, 2007), 246. See also the *Summa Contra Gentiles* 2.45.2.

[65] Chryssavgis, *Cosmic Grace, Humble Prayer*, 22.

[66] Ibid., 24.

[67] John of Damascus, *Treatise*.

[68] Ecumenical Patriarch Bartholomew, "Homily at the Fiftieth Anniversary Dedication of St. Barbara Greek Orthodox Church in Santa Barbara, California, November 8, 1997," 186.

In all religious traditions there have been innumerable sages and holy people who were able to see God in the mirror of creation and who were able to perceive creation and created realities as living symbols of God. In the Catholic tradition, for example, St. Francis of Assisi is probably the most illuminating. For the Poverello of Assisi, every flower, every bird spoke of the Creator, of God. Francis's biographer, St. Bonaventure, noted that Francis began his spiritual quest with a contemplation of the world and all its fullness and that it was his wonder at the splendor of creation that directed him to God.[69] In his own treatise, *The Soul's Journey into God*, Bonaventure speaks of a similar contemplation of the world and all the creatures within it:

> Whoever, therefore, is not enlightened
> by such splendor of created things
> is blind. . . .
> For every creature is by its nature
> a kind of effigy and likeness of the eternal Wisdom.[70]

Finally, more than being just symbols of God, created realities are also sacraments, making real God's invisible presence tangible in time and space. It is the capacity of created objects to become a vehicle of communion with God, a means of grace, that renders the whole physical world sacramental. "Ordinary, everyday things can alert to the deeper reality of God's presence among us. Bread, wine, oil, water, human bodies—all speak of a greater mystery that shines through, and is encountered in, life."[71]

The truth of the sacramental power of created realities to become means of communion with God is best expressed in the Christian praxis and theology of the sacraments, where fruits of the earth can signify God's presence and become channels of God's presence and blessings. They thus become means of God's salvific action in time and space, here and now. The archetype of all sacramental activity is Christ's incarnation, the Logos becoming flesh, of the intimate meeting and inextricable intertwining of the spiritual and the material.[72] For Hans Urs Von Balthasar, "The Incarnation expressed in a concentrated

---

[69] Discussed in Ian Bradley, *God Is Green: Ecology for Christians* (New York: Doubleday, 1990), 98.

[70] Bonaventure, *The Soul's Journey into God*, 67, 77.

[71] Christine E. Burke, "Globalization and Ecology," in *Earth Revealing—Earth Healing: Ecology and Christian Theology*, ed. Denis Edwards (Collegeville, MN: The Liturgical Press, 2001), 40.

[72] Sherrard, *The Rape of Man and Nature*, 92.

form the sacramental worldview of the Christian tradition in which creation is the very medium through which God is revealed."[73] It is because of the mystery of the incarnation, in which God entered and embraced the whole of creation, and sanctified every created reality thereby, that "the Church does not hesitate to bless and make generous use of the earth's materials in liturgical celebrations and sacraments."[74]

In this way water in baptism becomes the source of divine life and birth into a new life, just as water is the fount of life in our physical world. It is also true of other natural elements like oil, fire, bread and wine, and so forth. It is in the Eucharist that the sacramental dimension of created realities is most directly and most solemnly expressed. At the eucharistic table the earthly elements of bread and wine "become a means of grace for human beings and also themselves receive new meaning and status as they are offered to God."[75] When Christians gather for Eucharist, they bring the earth and all its creatures, and in some way the whole universe, to the table.[76] Ian Bradley expresses well the marriage of the natural and the supernatural in the celebration of the Eucharist, itself founded on the mystery of incarnation.

> At one level the material elements of bread and wine are offered to God. At another and deeper level these physical elements represent the body and blood of Christ. Physical matter was the vehicle that God used to express his own being to us. In sharing the elements and celebrating the Eucharist we are linking ourselves to the mysterious sacrifice that Christ made for the entire world. We are also offering the whole realm of nature up to God.[77]

In this sense "the whole world is a sacrament" according to the Ecumenical Patriarch Bartholomew. "The entire created cosmos is a burning bush of God's uncreated energies."[78]

---

[73] Matthew T. Eggemeier, "A Sacramental Vision: Environmental Degradation and the Aesthetics of Creation," *Modern Theology* 29 (2013): 352; see Balthasar, *The Glory of the Lord*, 29.

[74] Canadian Conference of Catholic Bishops, "You Love All That Exists . . . All Things Are Yours, God, Lover of Life . . ." Pastoral Letter on the Christian Ecological Imperative from the Social Affairs Commission (October 4, 2003), no. 7.

[75] Church of England, *Sharing God's Planet*, 24.

[76] Denis Edwards, "Eucharist and Ecology," *SEDOS Bulletin* 41 (2009): 169.

[77] Bradley, *God Is Green*, 105.

[78] Ecumenical Patriarch Bartholomew, "Homily at the Fiftieth Anniversary Dedication of St. Barbara Greek Orthodox Church in Santa Barbara, California, November 8, 1997," 185.

The contemporary ecological crisis is, at a deeper level, a consequence of our blindness to God's self-revelation in creation, of our inability to perceive the physical world as a symbol, icon, and sacrament of the Creator. Our generation, it may be said, is characterized by "autism" toward the natural world, an inability to communicate with the beyond. "We have broken the sacred covenant, the symbolic connection between ourselves and our world. By disconnecting this world from heaven, we have in fact desacralized both."[79] The ecological crisis arises precisely from the lack of a unified vision of the natural world as a living symbol of the Creator: Charles Upton writes:

> We destroy nature because we don't really see it. We don't see it because we don't know what it really is. . . . This is because our culture possesses no unified vision of the nature of what we call 'nature.' We see it as a collection of obstacles; as a mass of exploitable resources; as a set of interlocking mechanical processes—or, alternatively, as a setting for leisure, an opportunity for aesthetic enjoyment, a magic world of subtle energies, or a Great Goddess with her retinue of spiritual forces. All of these visions have a degree of truth to them, some much more than others. But the one vision we find hardest to maintain is the truly unified one—that of the natural world as a living symbol of its Creator . . . as the primordial symbol of God.[80]

The danger today is not so much falling into pantheism; that is, equating creation and created entities with God. The risk appears to be just the opposite: a lack of respect for matter.[81] Consequently, creation is no longer a symbol for us of the divine Creator. Instead, our consumerist culture has erected the idols of materialism, while reducing the physical world to a heap of material resources and products to be consumed and thrown away.

The various manifestations of the ecological crisis also point to how we are diminishing the capacity of created goods to be limpid and eloquent symbols of God's presence in creation. In a polluted world created things are no longer symbols of God. The polluted skies and streams cannot speak eloquently of the glory of God; they now fail to reveal God's infinite goodness. The current spasm of extinction of species amounts to nothing less than tearing away pages from God's

---

[79] Chryssavgis, *Cosmic Grace, Humble Prayer*, 22.
[80] Charles Upton, *Who Is the Earth? How to See God in the Natural World* (San Rafael, CA: Sophia Perennis, 2008), 3.
[81] See Derrick, *The Delicate Creation*, 88.

great book of works, which is the physical world. It is also a direct violation of God's plans for the diversity and abundance of life. "When we extinguish species we destroy forever the possibilities those species had for representing in a unique way the mystery of God."[82] Many species are being forced into extinction, and at alarming rates too. "This can only be an affront to a God who delights in creatures in all their diversity and specificity."[83] At a deeper level, as Thomas Berry says, when we destroy the living forms of this planet, "the first consequence is that we destroy modes of the divine presence."[84] When we allow creation to be degraded and damaged, we lose our sense of God's very self.[85] Denis Edwards writes:

> If the sun is hazy or blocked by smog, if the water is unclean, the air poisonous, the wind full of dust and smoke, the soil eroded or desiccated, and biological diversity consumed by the fires burning up the rain forests, the sacramental "light" of nature grows dim. To degrade the earth is to interfere with the message of its Creator.[86]

The contemporary ecological crisis is thus a deeply theological crisis. Instead of letting the physical world be a symbol of the revelation of God's grandeur and goodness, our diabolic lifestyles, which devastate our home planet, appear to create a wedge of separation between creation and the Creator.

The Ecological Crisis and the Disrespect for the *Telos* of Creation

As we have seen so far, the ecological crisis results from our incapacity to perceive the physical world as God's creation and sacred abode, God's primary revelation of God's abiding presence. The contemporary ecological crisis is the result of our disrespect for the supernatural *telos* of God's creation. We may speak of two fundamental

---

[82] Seán McDonagh, *To Care for the Earth: A Call to a New Theology* (London: Geoffrey Chapman, 1986), 47.

[83] Edwards, *Ecology at the Heart of Faith*, 76.

[84] Thomas Berry, *Dream of the Earth* (San Francisco: Sierra Club, 1988), 11.

[85] Catholic Bishops' Conference of England and Wales, *The Call of Creation*, 4.

[86] Toolan, *At Home in the Cosmos*, 37.

teloi in this regard, both of which reveal the profoundly eschatological character of creation, and the denial of which appears to lie at the root of the contemporary ecological crisis. The crisis is, first of all, the consequence of our denial of Sabbath—divine rest—to which the entire creation is not only invited but is also entitled to, as evident in the Genesis creation narrative and in the biblical tradition. Second, the crisis results from our inability to look at the natural world in the light of its final destiny to be recapitulated in Christ, and thus to treat it with due reverence.

The first *telos* of the physical universe, right from the dawn of creation, is to enter ultimately into God's Sabbath. The creation saga as narrated in the Book of Genesis does not end with the creation of the human being on the sixth day. It ends on the seventh day, when God, together with all of the created realities, including humanity, enters into Sabbath, the divine rest. Sabbath is the supernatural destiny of all creation. As Pope Benedict XVI reminds us, "All of creation, in the end, is conceived of to create the place of encounter between God and his creature, a place where the history of love between God and his creature can develop."[87]

The concept of Sabbath is fundamental if we are to understand, respect, and cherish the physical world as God's creation, the sacred home in which God has placed us. Today, it appears we have forgotten that creation's ultimate destiny is God's Sabbath. As Jürgen Moltmann points out, we have reduced creation to the first six days of the Genesis narrative, overlooking the seventh day, the completion and climax of the entire creation narrative. Perhaps, under the impulse of the modern utilitarian world view and a mentality centered on productivity, we have overlooked the supreme moment of Sabbath that alone crowns creation. Moltmann writes:

> Curiously enough, in the Christian traditions, and especially the traditions of the Western church, creation is generally only presented as 'the six days' work'. The 'completion' of creation through 'the seventh day' is much neglected, or even overlooked altogether. . . . The God who 'rests' on the Sabbath, the blessing and rejoicing God, the God who delights in his creation, and in his exultation sanctifies it, recedes behind this different concept. So for men and women too, the meaning of their lives is identified

---

[87] Pope Benedict XVI, address at the opening of the 12th Ordinary General Assembly of the Synod of Bishops (October 6, 2008).

with work and busy activity; and rest, the feast, and their joy in existence are pushed away, relegated to insignificance because they are non-utilitarian.[88]

Yet, it is the Sabbath that completes and crowns creation. It is only through the Sabbath that God completed creation.[89] The Sabbath is not a casual day of rest following six working days, like our modern weekends. "On the contrary: the whole work of creation was performed *for the sake of the Sabbath*."[90] As the *Catechism of the Catholic Church* teaches, "Creation was fashioned with a view to the Sabbath and therefore for the worship and adoration of God. Worship is inscribed in the order of creation."[91] The Sabbath is not just a day of creation; it is the Lord's day, the hallowed day, the holy *kairos* for the entire creation to enter into God's eternal rest and worship of the Divine. The Sabbath is, as Franz Rosenzweig has pointed out, "the feast of creation," the final destiny of creation, creation's own meaning and goal.[92] According to Moltmann, it was "for the sake of this feast-day of the eternal God that heaven and earth were created, with everything that exists in them and lives."[93]

The Sabbath is not only the completion of creation, but represents creation's redemption, namely, participation in God's manifested, eternal presence. On the Sabbath the redemption of the world is celebrated in anticipation.[94] The Sabbath opens creation to its true future—to rest in God, to be with God. All creation is destined for Sabbath. As the ultimate *telos* of creation, the Sabbath is the hope and future of every created being. Creation can find its true existence and ultimate rest only in the very Creator. Moltmann writes:

> Everything that is made has been called by the Creator from non-being into being. Everything that exists is menaced by non-being, for it can again be made a nothingness. That is why everything that *is*, is restless and on the search for a place where this menace cannot reach it—for a 'resting place'. It is not merely the human heart which is 'restless until it finds rest in Thee', as Augustine

---

[88] Moltmann, *God in Creation*, 276–77.

[89] See ibid., 6, 276.

[90] Ibid., 277.

[91] *Catechism of the Catholic Church*, no. 347.

[92] F. Rosenzweig, *Der Stern der Erlösung*, Pt. III, Book 1 (Heidelberg, 1959), 65, 69. Cited in Moltmann, *God in Creation*, 277.

[93] Moltmann, *God in Creation*, 277.

[94] Ibid., 276.

said. The whole creation is filled with this same unrest, and transcends itself in the search for the rest in which it can abide. . . .

. . . In the resting, and hence direct, unmediated presence of God, all created beings find their dwelling. In the resting presence of God all creatures find their sustaining foundation. The sabbath preserves created things from obliteration, and fills their restless existence with the happiness of the presence of the eternal God. On the sabbath all creatures find their own place in the God who is wholly present.[95]

The Sabbath also points to the eternal dimension of all creation. It is itself the presence of eternity in time. Significantly, it is possible to say, echoing a saying attributed to one of the ancient fathers of the church, St. Athanasius, that although the creation story tells us that each day was followed by a night, God's Sabbath knows no night but becomes the "feast without end."[96] The Sabbath is an anticipation and a prefiguration of the world to come. Because of the Sabbath, creation is aligned toward its redemption already from the very beginning. Creation is thus teleologically oriented, from a theological perspective, toward the peace *(shalom)* of God's own Sabbath.

The teleological destiny of all creation to enter into God's peace, however, is to be realized in time. The eternal, eschatological dimension of Sabbath is to be accomplished in the temporal order, spanning the rhythm of the days of the week, the cycle of seven years, and the great Jubilee cycle of forty-nine years, as the institution of Sabbath went on to assume definite contours in the history of the people of God. It is also important to note that observance of the Sabbath is structured at a triple level, involving God, fellow humans, and the whole of creation, with all these levels interlinked.

To celebrate Sabbath is, first of all, to be at peace with God. The Sabbath is the day of worship of the Creator par excellence. It is the hallowed day to contemplate God in the beauty and goodness of creation, to partake in God's delight in creation, and to bow in adoration before the Creator. In the hallowed light of the Sabbath all creation acquires a loveliness of its own. "Questions about the possibility of 'producing' something, or about utility, are forgotten in the face of the beauty of all created things, which have their meaning simply in their very selves."[97] The Sabbath is to be lived in a spirit of thanksgiving, in

---

[95] Ibid., 282.
[96] See ibid., 277.
[97] Ibid., 286.

gratitude toward the Creator for the very gift of existence conferred on every created being. "Just as the Sabbath is sanctified by God's resting presence, so men and women also sanctify the Sabbath through their recollection of their existence, and their grateful expression of that existence."[98]

To celebrate Sabbath is also to be at peace with fellow humans, especially the poor, the *anawim* of Yahweh; with the whole of creation, including animals, both domestic and wild; and with the land itself. The commandment that deals with the observance of the Sabbath "requires not only *your* rest, but the rest of all of your household, including everyone who works for you and all of your animals—and the land itself. It demands that we not push to the limits our ecological systems or the people who work for us."[99] The observance of Sabbath assumes very concrete and down-to-earth implications in the Old Testament as evident in the Sabbath commandment given in the Book of Exodus, where respect for Yahweh's sovereignty, care for the earth, concern for the poor, sensitivity to the needs of both wild and farm animals, are all intricately woven together.[100] God commands the people to set aside one day in seven as a day of rest for people and for animals:

> Six days you shall do your work, but on the seventh day you shall rest, so that your ox and your donkey may have relief, and your homeborn slave and the resident alien may be refreshed. (Ex 23:12)

Nothing in all creation must be relentlessly pressed. The Sabbath year is given to protect the land from relentless exploitation, to help it rejuvenate, to give it a time of rest and restoration, and to guarantee sustenance for the poor of the land and for wild animals. In both Exodus and Leviticus it is clearly stated that the land also must have its time of rest.[101]

> For six years you shall sow your land and gather in its yield; but the seventh year you shall let it rest and lie fallow, so that

---

[98] Ibid., 285.

[99] Andrea Cohen-Kiener, *Claiming Earth as a Common Ground: The Ecological Crisis Through the Lens of Faith* (Woodstock, VT: Skylight Paths Publishing, 2009), 38.

[100] See McDonagh, *The Greening of the Church*, 127.

[101] See Calvin B. DeWitt, "Reading the Bible Through a Green Lens," in *The Green Bible* (London: Harper Collins, 2008), 30–31.

the poor of your people may eat; and what they leave the wild animals may eat. You shall do the same with your vineyard, and with your olive orchard. (Ex 23:10–11)

In the seventh year there shall be a sabbath of complete rest for the land, a sabbath for the Lord; you shall not sow your field or prune your vineyard. You shall not reap the aftergrowth of your harvest or gather the grapes of your unpruned vine: it shall be a year of complete rest for the land. (Lv 25:4–5)

In the context of the observance of Sabbath, which allows the land to recuperate and the poor to recover, the concept of the Jubilee Year is of particular significance. According to Leviticus 25:8–55, after seven Sabbath years, on the Day of Atonement, the trumpets were to sound throughout the land, to proclaim the fiftieth year as God's year of release. The liberation associated with the Jubilee Year consisted in the restoration of the original harmony of human communities and of creation. It was the time to wipe out debt, to set free slaves, and to restore liberty to every member of God's chosen people as well to foreigners. The land was also to find rest in the Jubilee Year so that it too could recuperate and celebrate. The Jubilee commandment (Lv 25; Dt 19:14; Prov 23:10–11; Mic 2:1–5) clearly links care for the land and care for people.[102] In leaving the land fallow and in forgiving the debts of the poor there is an integration of the social and ecological concerns, intended to recreate the original peace and harmony associated with the Sabbath of creation. "There is release for the ground, that is given a year of recovery from farming. There is release from the buildup of capital only in the hands of the few, and every jubilee it reverts to its original owner. . . . There is the release of hired laborers from their servitude, because, they, too, belong to the Lord."[103]

The Sabbath laws were God's ecological strategy to preserve the land and protect its inhabitants. As Moltmann notes, the Sabbath year of the land makes it clear the Sabbath is not merely a feast for humans alone. It is the feast of the whole creation, "of a future in which God's creation and his revelation will be one. That is redemption. . . . When

---

[102] Jung, *We Are Home*, 64.

[103] See David Atkinson, *Renewing the Face of the Earth: A Theological and Pastoral Response to Climate Change* (Norwich: Canterbury Press, 2008), 83. The Sabbath, as Walter Brueggemann notes, "is a theological affirmation of Yahweh's ownership of the land." Walter Brueggemann, *The Land: Place as Gift, Promise, and Challenge in Biblical Faith* (Philadelphia: Fortress Press, 1977), 154.

'the whole Earth will be full of his glory' (Isa. 6.3), when God is 'all in all' (1 Cor. 15.28) and when God 'dwells' in his whole creation (Rev 21.3), then creation and revelation are truly one."[104]

The Sabbath is a prefiguration of the ultimate destiny awaiting all creation, namely, its final consummation in God. The celebration of the Sabbath in time and space points beyond itself to the future of the messianic era, to the final redemption of the physical universe, to creation's definitive return to the *shalom* of the primordial Sabbath. This messianic Sabbath will be the Sabbath without end, fulfilling the primordial Sabbath of creation.

For Christians, creation's final destiny is to be recapitulated in the mystery of the life, death, and resurrection of Jesus Christ. From the perspective of Christian faith the entire creation has an essentially christological dimension, as all things have been created in him and in him all things hold together. The mystery of Christ is the ontological glue that holds together the whole of creation. Christ is the Alpha of creation, the firstborn of all creation.

> In the prologue of John's gospel, the birth and life of Jesus is framed within the widest context of cosmic history. He is active in bringing forth creation; through him the universe, the earth and all life was created (Jn 1:3–5). All the rich unfolding of the universe, from the first moment of the fireball, through the formation of the stars, the molding of planet Earth, the birth and flowering of life on Earth and the emergence of human beings, is centered on Christ. Hence all of these crucial moments in the emergence of the universe have a Christological dimension.[105]

Christ is also the Omega, the final end of creation. The mystery of Christ, in his passion, death, and resurrection, reveals the final destiny of all creation. Christ's death on the cross reconciled all creation to God (Col 1:20).

> Through his Son, God bore the full cost of the evil and selfishness that have been unleashed throughout history and across all creation. The Creator became the crucified, in order to bring the

---

[104] Moltmann, *God in Creation*, 288.

[105] Sean McDonagh, "A Theology of Creation," in Operation Noah, *Between the Flood and the Rainbow: Climate Change and the Church's Social Teaching—A Study Guide* (London: Operation Noah, 2008), 22.

whole creation, made and sustained in love, back into restored relationship with himself.[106]

It is the resurrection of Christ that is the true revelation of the final transformation of the whole of creation. In Christ's resurrection, incarnated matter, a part of our material universe that contained traits of the evolutionary history of life stretching into billions of years, was transformed and glorified. For this reason it is precisely Christ's bodily resurrection—the writers of the New Testament take pains to affirm the visible, bodily nature of Christ's resurrection, insisting that he rose in the flesh (Mt 28:1–8; Mk 16:1–8; Lk 24:1–10; Jn 20:1–10)—that is the beginning of the transformation of the whole creation in Christ. "Through the reality of Christ's resurrection all visible created reality is touched, given a new significance and transformed."[107] As Karl Rahner says, this resurrection of Jesus is not only the *promise* but the *beginning* of the glorification and divinization of the whole of reality.[108] The resurrection of Christ is indeed the beginning of the new creation (2 Cor 5:17). The resurrection is the ultimate guarantee that the whole created order, set free from its bondage to decay, will be transformed and renewed.[109] The whole creation, as Paul portrays it, eagerly awaits its full transformation (Rom 8:22). Christ's resurrection is thus a symbol of our own resurrection and of the restoration of all creation.

According to Christian faith, the risen Christ is the final end, the ultimate *telos* of all creation, including humanity. Christ will reunite (*anakephaloiosis*), recapitulate all creation in himself in the end of times. St. Paul has expressed this profound truth in the hymn contained in the Letter to the Colossians.

He is the image of the invisible God, the firstborn of all creation; for in him all things in heaven and on earth were created, things visible and invisible, whether thrones or dominions or rulers or powers—all things have been created through him and for him. He himself is before all things, and in him all things hold together.

---

[106] Dave Bookless, *Planet Wise: Dare to Care for God's World* (Nottingham: Inter-Varsity Press, 2008), 71.

[107] McDonagh, *The Greening of the Church*, 163.

[108] Karl Rahner, "Dogmatic Questions on Easter," in *Theological Investigations* (New York: Seabury Press, 1974), 4:129.

[109] Bookless, *Planet Wise*, 72, 76.

He is the head of the body, the church; he is the beginning, the firstborn from the dead, so that he might come to have first place in everything. For in him all the fullness of God was pleased to dwell, and through him God was pleased to reconcile to himself all things, whether on earth or in heaven, by making peace through the blood of his cross. (Col 1:15–20)

The hymn from Colossians puts the earthly life of Jesus into a perspective that is both cosmic and eternal. St. Paul tells us that Christ is the center of all creation, since it was God's will to reconcile to himself all things in Christ. Everything in heaven and earth comes together in him. The Father "has made known to us the mystery of his will, according to his good pleasure that he set forth in Christ, as a plan for the fullness of time, to gather up all things in him, things in heaven and things on earth" (Eph 1:9–10). So all things (literally, *ta panta*, "of all") will be recapitulated in Christ, the eternal *Logos* through whom the universe, Earth and all life were created (Jn 1:3–5). All things are destined to be redeemed in Christ, who will recapitulate the whole of creation. The hope for cosmic redemption is profoundly rooted in scripture (Is 11:6–9; 65:17, 25), especially in the writings of St. Paul (Col 1:14–20; 1 Cor 15:28; Eph 1:10; Rom 8:19–22). Every creature is destined for resurrected glory, and Jesus' Resurrection is the pledge of that universal salvation.[110]

It is important to remember that it is the whole of creation, the entire physical universe, and not just humanity alone that is destined to be redeemed and transformed in Christ. The belief in the redemption of all creation in Christ prevailed in the early church and was articulated by theologians like Irenaeus, Athanasius, and Augustine. In much of the Patristic literature Christ is portrayed as the ruler of all *(pantocrator)* and the ruler of the universe *(cosmocrator)*. St. Irenaeus of Lyons, for example, spoke eloquently of the recapitulation of all creation in Christ. However, the concept of cosmic redemption was gradually undermined, partly because of the incorporation of Platonic depreciations of nature into Christian thought. After the Patristic period, cosmic redemption was not featured significantly, if at all, in Western Christian thought.[111]

---

[110] James A. Nash, *Loving Nature: Ecological Integrity and Christian Responsibility* (Nashville, TN: Abingdon Press, 1991), 125. See also Allan D. Galloway, *The Cosmic Christ* (New York: Harper, 1951), x.

[111] Nash, *Loving Nature*, 125.

Today, the profound truth about the supernatural *telos* of the whole of creation appears to have been lost sight of in much of Christian faith and praxis, with direct implications for the state of our home planet and for the common household of its biosphere. Modern theology has limited redemption mostly to individual salvation and appears to have disregarded the redemption of the whole of creation. "Somehow the sense of *all* creation—the whole Earth, the universe, transfigured and made new in Christ—was lost."[112] James Nash states:

> The prominent characteristic of Western theological traditions, Roman Catholic and Protestant, has been the absence of the hope for the consummation of creation. Heaven is exclusively for humans. . . . This exclusivistic belief has served as a major justification for depreciating the value of creation and destroying its allegedly valueless components. Humans can neglect or abuse what is not redeemable. Since the nonhuman creation is ultimately meaningless or useless, it has no intrinsic value for God, and, therefore, no intrinsic value that should be respected by others. It can be treated as an instrumental value, if it has utility for humans, and without hindrance if it does not.[113]

Instead, the profound truth about the universal redemption of all things in Christ, which is the ultimate *telos* of all creation, places created goods in the eschatological light. It is such a vision that gives ultimate meaning and worth to the physical world. "If the natural world as a whole will participate in God's redemption, then all things must be treated with respect in accordance with divine valuations, and all living creatures must be treated as ends in themselves—not simply as means to human ends."[114]

The contemporary ecological crisis is evidently a result of our neglect of the supernatural destiny of creation to share in God's Sabbath and to be recapitulated in Christ. The crisis has resulted, first of all, from our denial of Sabbath to God's creation. Our society has forgotten a vital aspect of God's creation: the need for Sabbath. We deny Sabbath to the very Creator—the giver of all gifts, including our very existence—by not sanctifying time and setting apart time and space to worship God. Modern hectic lifestyles have largely pushed the Creator

---

[112] Morton, "Environment and Religion," 123.
[113] Nash, *Loving Nature*, 124.
[114] Ibid., 133.

God out and created a new pantheon of the false gods of profit and consumerism, as evident, for example, in the sprawling shopping marts and malls, open day and night, every day of the week.

We have denied Sabbath also to the poor of the land. We exploit our fellow human beings, as evident in the increasing prevalence of cheap labor, factory supply chains, and call centers where people work around the clock to increase the profits of a minority. Modern society appears to have understood rest only in terms of entertainment. While the very rich live lavishly, holidaying in exotic places, millions of men and women toil day and night to eke out a living. Nearly 1 billion go to bed with empty stomachs, in spite of all the growth churned out by an economic system that does not respect the Sabbath rhythms of creation and of fellow human beings.

We deny the Sabbath rest to God's creation as well. Sabbath rest is about rediscovering the rhythms of creation conferred by God. It is vitally important to respect these rhythms, "if we are to live at the pace of the planet, living as part of a healthy creation rather than separate."[115] We deny the Sabbath rest to the land and to our planet's life-sustaining ecosystems, as evident in the increasing degradation of the land and in the fast depletion of natural resources. The exploitation of the land is clear in modern intensive agriculture, which has led to land degradation and even to desertification in some parts of the world.

The results of the negation of the Sabbath to God, to the poor, and to creation are before our very eyes in the form of the contemporary ecological crisis. The contemporary ecological crisis is, indeed, God's judgment on a generation deaf to the cry of the land and the poor of the land.

The contemporary ecological crisis also reveals that we have not respected the ultimate *telos* of all creation to be recapitulated in Christ. As Ecumenical Patriarch Bartholomew reminds us, "The final purpose of creation is not its use or abuse for humankind's individual pleasure, but something far more sublime and sacred."[116] We appear to be incapable of a long-term view of God's creation, namely, the eschatological perspective, which enables us to perceive creation in the light of eternity and to dwell on Earth, mindful of the ultimate destiny of all creation to be consummated in God. The ecological

---

[115] Bookless, *Planet Wise*, 109.

[116] Ecumenical Patriarch Bartholomew, "Greeting During the Symposium at Holy Trinity Monastery, Halki, June 1, 1992," in Chryssavgis, *Cosmic Grace, Humble Prayer*, 84.

crisis results ultimately from our forgetfulness of the eschatological dimension of the physical universe, including our home planet, which is sacred not only because of God's presence and as a symbol and icon of God's revelation, but also for its supernatural destiny to be recapitulated in God. Creation is not a heap of material objects for unbridled consumption and wanton destruction. Creation's true destiny is to be transformed and renewed in the risen Christ. "I am making all things new" (Rev 21:5) is the promise of God in the Book of Revelation.

Rediscovering the Physical World as God's Creation

In the context of the contemporary ecological crisis it is vitally important to recover our awareness of the physical world as God's creation, not just something for human exploitation. As Pope Benedict reminds us: "Our faith in creation is the ultimate basis of our responsibility for the earth. The earth is not simply our property, which we can exploit according to our interests and desires. Rather, it is a gift of the Creator."[117] Jürgen Moltmann writes:

> For centuries, men and women have tried to understand God's creation as *nature*, so that they can exploit it in accordance with the laws science has discovered. Today the essential point is to understand this knowable, controllable and usable nature as *God's creation*, and to learn to respect it as such. The limited sphere of reality which we call 'nature' must be lifted into the totality of being which is termed 'God's creation'.[118]

The ecological crisis is "about the future of God's creation"[119] as much as about the future of our common home and household. We will be able to save our common home only when we will begin to see it, love it, and cherish it as God's creation.

---

[117] Pope Benedict XVI, Address to the Members of the Roman Curia (December 22, 2008), no. 1. See also *Caritas in veritate*, no. 48.

[118] Moltmann, *God in Creation*, 21.

[119] USCCB, *Global Climate Change*, 1.

10

The Ecological Sin
of Irresponsible Stewardship

In the present chapter we reflect on how, in practice, we have failed to be responsible stewards of God's creation and betrayed the divine mandate to care for our common home. We begin by reflecting on the primary human vocation to be stewards of our common home, to be "co-carers" with God of the physical world. The irresponsible stewardship of our home planet—as evident in the contemporary ecological crisis—does merit the appellative of ecological sin, understood in a wider relational sense of rupturing bonds of fellowship with the Creator, with fellow human beings, and with the rest of creation. We then examine how the repercussions of our sinful conduct fall on the creation, as evident in the mounting devastation of our home planet and its life-sustaining ecosystems. At a deeper level the ecological crisis stems from human *hubris*, namely, from our refusal to accept our proper identity as creatures and acknowledge our radical dependence on the Creator and our interdependence on the rest of creation. We conclude by referring to the need for a profound ecological conversion from the part of humanity, so as to become once again responsible and loving stewards of God's creation, and reestablish peace with the Creator and the rest of creation.

The Human Vocation for the Stewardship of Creation

The stewardship of creation is the first and primary task entrusted to Adam, the first human being, as we read in the creation narratives contained in the opening chapters of the Bible. It is the first commandment given to humanity. In the Yahwistic account of creation in the Book of Genesis, which predates the Priestly account by a few hundred years, the creation of Adam out of dust from the ground and the task of cultivating the garden where he lives are intimately connected:

When no plant of the field was yet in the earth and no herb of the field had yet sprung up—for the LORD God had not caused it to rain upon the earth, *and there was no one to till the ground*. . . . Then the LORD God formed man from the dust of the ground, and breathed into his nostrils the breath of life; and the man became a living being. And the LORD God planted a garden in Eden, in the east; and there he put the man whom he had formed. Out of the ground the LORD God made to grow every tree that is pleasant to the sight and good for food, the tree of life also in the midst of the garden, and the tree of the knowledge of good and evil. . . . The LORD God *took the man and put him in the garden of Eden to till it and keep it.* (Gn 2:5, 7–9, 15, emphasis added)

From this passage it is clear that the creation of Adam is closely associated with the task of taking care of the garden. Adam is created from *adamah* (dust), and hence there is an intimate relationship between him and the earth that gives him existence and meaning. The earthly garden is prepared by Yahweh, and the first human being, formed from the dust, is placed there to cultivate it and guard it (Gn 2:15). His responsibility is then extended to a proper management of the animal world (Gn 2:19).

The garden of God is what we would today call an ecosystem; different species of organisms, from the smallest to humans, coexist in a state of symbiosis, fulfilling God's plan and the purpose for which they were created.[1] In a wider sense, the garden entrusted to humanity is the *oikos* of the planet Earth, a veritable garden in the vast cosmic expanses, which was gradually prepared for life to flourish. It is the care of this common home, lovingly prepared by God as an abode for humanity and the rest of creation, with which humanity is entrusted.

A number of significant characteristics emerge from the accounts of stewardship contained in the first chapters of the Book of Genesis that have direct implications for the care of our planetary home, especially in light of the contemporary ecological crisis.

Caring for Creation with God

The first characteristic is that humans are called to care for creation along with God. God is already caring for creation; humans need only

---

[1] Renthy Keitzar, "Creation and Restoration: Three Biblical Reflections," in *Ecotheology: Voices from South and North*, ed. David G. Hallman (Maryknoll, NY: Orbis Books, 1994), 56.

to assist God. Adam's task is to serve and preserve the garden already prepared and cared for by God. "Wherever humans will touch the soil, God's footmarks and fingerprints are already there."[2] The human vocation is garden with God, to partake in God's loving tending of creation. God is the chief gardener; humans are God's assistants. Here the Genesis command of stewardship is in sharp contrast with other cosmogenic creation myths.

In many popular pagan myths of creation, where manual labor was disparaged, the human beings are called in as slave laborers in order to maintain creation for the gods. The best example in this regard is the Mesopotamian epic *Atrakhasis* (1800–1600 BCE). The story is about two groups of gods: the greater and the lesser. The greater gods assign the more numerous lesser (labor) gods the heavy work of digging irrigation channels on Earth to provide food and drink for them. After forty years of long and oppressive labor, the lesser gods rebel, setting their tools on fire. The greater gods meet to discuss the problem and work out a solution. The craft god, Ea, comes up with a brilliant idea. The proposal is to create humans who will perform the slave labor in place of the gods, so that the gods can rest forever. The plan is accepted, and the birth goddess, Mami, is assigned to create humans. It is thus that the humans are born into the world, namely, to do slave labor for the gods.[3] There is no dignity for humans in this and similar creation narratives. "I will establish a savage," says Marduk in the *Enuma elish*, "'man' shall be his name. He shall be charged with the service of the gods that they might be at ease."[4] Such a pessimistic concept of the identity of human beings as mere slave laborers is common to many creation myths in antiquity, including Greek mythology.

In this regard the biblical concept of stewardship is unique and radically different from both the ancient creation myths and the survivalist mentality inherent in many a modern environmental and

---

[2] Charles Upton, *Who Is the Earth? How to See God in the Natural World* (San Rafael, CA: Sophia Perennis, 2008), 55. See also Theodore Hiebert, *The Yahwist Landscape: Nature and Religion in Early Israel* (New York: Oxford University Press, 1996), 66–67.

[3] See Joan O'Brien and Wilfred Major, *In the Beginning: Creation Myths from Ancient Mesopotamia, Israel, and Greece* (Chico, CA: Scholars Press, 1982), 70–84; Fred H. Van Dyke et al., *Redeeming Creation: The Biblical Basis for Environmental Stewardship* (Downers Grove, IL: InterVarsity Press, 1996), 29ff.; Brigitte Kahl, "Fratricide and Ecocide: Rereading Genesis 2—4," in *Earth Habitat: Eco-Injustice and the Church's Response*, ed. Dieter Hessel and Larry Rasmussen (Minneapolis: Fortress Press, 2001), 55.

[4] O'Brien and Major, *In the Beginning*, 25; Fred H. Van Dyke et al., *Redeeming Creation*, 28.

conservation movement. The biblical understanding of stewardship is essentially an invitation to become part of God's loving and providential care for the whole of creation, which is itself a fruit of God's outpouring love. The work of cultivating the garden, manual labor, is not a menial job, as in other ancient creation myths. In fact, we find a God who works with the soil, who gets his hands dirty, first in fashioning Adam out of the dirt *(adama)*—the Hebrew word describes a potter working with clay—and later in planting and tending the garden, where the first human being will live.[5] It is not so much an air of compulsion about the task of stewardship entrusted to humanity, but rather one of intimacy and trust. Significantly, Adam and Eve are to take care of the very garden where God used to stroll in the cool of the day, and God relished their presence along with that of the rest of creation. The original primordial spirit that reigned in the garden of Eden was one of close intimacy and harmony between the Creator and the rest of creation. It is of this garden, and of the original harmony of creation, that humans were invited to be co-responsible. In fact, cultivating and keeping the garden were to take place under the loving and watchful eye of God.

There is thus a great element of dignity about the task of stewardship entrusted to humanity. Humans are called to partake in God's stewardship of the world. As Ecumenical Patriarch Bartholomew reminds us: " God has not allowed humanity to be a mere *spectator* or an irresponsible *consumer* of the world and of all that is in the world. Indeed, humanity has been called to assume the task of being primarily a *partaker* and a *sharer in the responsibility* for everything in the created world."[6] In other words, humanity is called to serve as God's representative or steward in the created order. It is a stewardship that comes close to being the representative of God, on Earth and for earth.[7]

Reflecting God

In being "co-carers" of God's creation, humans are to imitate and reflect God's own tender and loving way of caring for the physical world. Reflecting God in caring for creation is fundamental to what

---

[5] Upton, *Who Is the Earth?*, 55.

[6] Ecumenical Patriarch Bartholomew, "Message for September 1, 1992." in *Cosmic Grace, Humble Prayer: The Ecological Vision of the Green Patriarch Bartholomew*, ed. John Chryssavgis (Grand Rapids, MI: Eerdmans, 2009), 142.

[7] See Robert Murray, *The Cosmic Covenant: Biblical Themes of Justice, Peace and the Integrity of Creation* (London: Sheed and Ward, 1992).

we are. It is our clear job description, stated in the Bible.[8] It is in this role that humans reveal their specific identity of being created in the image of God *(imago Dei)*. Fashioned in the image and likeness of God, the human being is expected to tend creation with the same care and compassion of God. As former Archbishop of Canterbury Rowan Williams points out: "Genesis tells us that when we are called to relationship with our creator, we are in the same moment summoned to responsibility for the non-human world. That's how we express our relationship with the creator, our reality as made in God's image."[9]

Since humans are called to mirror God's own concern for creation, stewardship can never mean humanity's absolute dominion over the physical world. Stewardship has nothing to do with ruthless rule over creation, on the part of humanity, as it was at times understood in past—and is claimed in some quarters even today. Lynn White, for example, sought to trace the historical roots of the ecological crisis within the Judeo-Christian scriptures, basing his view on the particular verse contained in the Priestly account of creation that apparently grants humans dominion over creation (Gn 1:28).[10] However, as Lewis G. Regenstein, notes, probably no passage in the Bible has been so misunderstood and misinterpreted as this verse: "This has often been mistakenly interpreted as a synonym for superiority, giving humans the right to treat nature and animals as they see fit. However, the Bible makes it clear that this dominion consists of *stewardship* over the natural world. This duty carries the responsibility not to mistreat the earth and to protect it from abuse."[11] Many modern biblical scholars insist that the verse cannot be interpreted as a license for humans to change and transform the natural world according to any human whim. According to Ted F. Peters, originally the commission was, in fact, a challenge to human beings to imitate God's loving kindness and faithfulness and to act as his viceroy in relationship with the nonhuman component of the earth. This, he argues, is the original meaning of the Hebrew word *radah* used in the text. Like viceroys of the king,

---

[8] Dave Bookless, *Planet Wise: Dare to Care for God's World* (Nottingham, UK: Inter-Varsity Press, 2008), 90.

[9] Rowan Williams, "The Ark and the Covenant," *The Tablet* (October 24, 2009).

[10] Lynn White, "The Historical Roots of Our Ecological Crisis," *Science* 155 (1967): 1203–7.

[11] Lewis G. Regenstein, *Replenish the Earth: A History of Organized Religion's Treatment of Animals and Nature—Including the Bible's Message of Conservation and Kindness to Animals* (London: SCM Press, 1991), 26–27.

men and women are expected to be just and honest and to render real service. They are forbidden to exploit the people or the earth.[12]

Human stewardship of the rest of creation can never be ruthless; it is to be exercised imitating God's own care for creation. Pope John Paul II clearly states in *Sollicitudo rei:* "The dominion granted to man by the Creator is not an absolute power, nor can one speak of a freedom to 'use and misuse,' or to dispose of things as one pleases" (no. 34). Pope Benedict XVI in a General Audience on August 26, 2009, added, "We cannot consider ourselves creation's absolute master. We are called, rather, to exercise responsible stewardship of creation."

A clear understanding of stewardship, as opposed to ruthless dominion over creation, is vitally important in the context of the contemporary ecological crisis. It has been the latter interpretation that has dominated in the last few centuries in many parts of the world, and that has contributed significantly to the current state of our home planet. In this context the Catholic Bishops' Conference of England and Wales teaches in its 1996 document *The Common Good* that "we have to reject some of the easy assumptions of an earlier stage of industrialization, such as that the human race, because God had given it dominion over the world, had an unlimited freedom to despoil the natural environment for its own purposes" (no. 106). As custodians and stewards of God's creation, our task is to restore the physical world, so far as possible, to its paradisal condition, imitating God's own tender care for creation.

Responsible Stewardship

Human stewardship of creation is meant to be responsible. Along with the unique privilege of being "co-carers" of God's creation, mirroring God's own goodness by being *imago Dei*, comes accountability for what has been entrusted to us. Our stewardship of the planet will one day be judged. Like in the parables in the Gospels, we will be called to account by the Creator for what has been entrusted to us. It is God's world, and God will ask us to give account of our stewardship of its resources. As Pope John Paul II reminds us in *Evangelium vitae*, "As one called to till and look after the garden of the world (cf. Gen 2:15), man has a specific responsibility towards the environment in which he lives, towards the creation which God has put at the serice of his personal dignity, of his life, not only for the present but also for future generations" (no. 42). As stewards, will be called by the

---

[12] Ted F. Peters, *The Cry of the Environment* (Santa Fe, NM: Bear, 1984), 415–16.

Owner to give an account of how we have used or abused what has been entrusted to our care.

We are only stewards, subordinate to God and never masters of creation. Humanity does not own the land or have the right to exploit. The earth belongs to God (Ps 24:1), not to us, and our place is as leaseholders or tenants, living on God's property and answerable to God. Creation belongs to God, and to God alone. "Thus, although we can talk about 'my land' or 'our country,' and people may buy and sell land, human landownership is always secondary to God's. Human beings can only ever be lease-holders or managers of God's land."[13] As the Church of England's document *Sharing God's Planet* asserts: "A Christian understanding of the environment has to start with this fundamental premise. The creation belongs to God, not to humans. The human role is defined as a steward of creation, exercising dominion under God, whose rule is sovereign."[14]

As stewards, God's representatives, we are responsible for the whole of creation. *Ktisis* ("creation") in the Bible includes not only humans but all created things. Paradigmatic in this regard is God's concern to save not only Noah and his family but also representatives from the rest of the animal world from the Great Flood that threatened the extinction of all life on Earth. By taking the various animals on board and caring for them throughout the days of the flood till the ark touched dry ground, Noah and his family proved to be responsible stewards of God for the whole of creation. As Williams remarks: Noah was "made responsible for the continuation of what we would call an ecosystem."[15] As responsible stewards of God's creation, humanity's task is to ensure that nothing is lost, because all *(ta panta)* of creation, is destined to be recapitulated in God in the eschatological fullness (Col 1:19–20).

The Greek word *oikos* signifies "home." Stewardship is about responsible housekeeping; it is about dwelling on Earth, our common home. Stewardship—and any talk of "dominion" over creation—is possible only within the overall context of dwelling in the common home along with the rest of creation and under the watchful eye of God. It appears that we have forgotten that *dominion* has its root in *dominus*, "dweller in the house" or "caretaker," the Latin equivalent

---

[13] Bookless, *Planet Wise*, 48.

[14] Church of England, *Sharing God's Planet: A Christian Vision for a Sustainable Future: A Report from the Mission and Public Affairs Council* (London: Church House Publishing, 2005), 16.

[15] Williams, "The Ark and the Covenant," 10.

of *oikos* in ecology.[16] We have reduced stewardship only to ourselves, forgetting about the *oikos*. Ecumenical Patriarch Bartholomew writes:

> How unfortunate and indeed how selfish it is, however, that we have restricted the application of this word to ourselves. This world is indeed our home. Yet it is also the home of everyone, as it is the home of every animal creature, as well as of every form of life created by God. It is a sign of arrogance to presume that we human beings alone inhabit this world. Indeed, it is also a sign of arrogance to imagine that only the present generation inhabits this earth.[17]

Jesus tells several stories about being good stewards or managers. Often these parables are seen as being about money, but actually they are about managing all that God has made and entrusted to our care.

The concept of stewardship is particularly strong in Islam, where the human being is a *khalifa*, a representative of God for creation. A *khalifa* is a person appointed by the supreme ruler to have responsibility over a given area in an empire. The word *khalifa* and its plurals occur nine times in the Qur'an. As *khalifa*, representative and steward of God, the human is not a proprietor or owner of creation. Humanity's role needs to be interpreted in relation to the sovereignty of God, not independently. Human beings should use their authority within the limit of the servants of God.[18] "Nothing is more dangerous for the natural environment than the practice of the power of vice-gerency by a humanity which no longer accepts its place as God's servant, obedient to His commands and laws."[19]

In Buddhism compassion *(karuna)* toward all living entities is the very characteristic of "buddhahood." The fundamental concept of *ahimsa* (nonviolence not only toward fellow human beings but toward all living beings), which is central to religions like Jainism, Buddhism,

---

[16] James Parks Morton, "Environment and Religion: The Evolution of a New Vision," in *Earth and Spirit: The Spiritual Dimension of the Environmental Crisis*, ed. Fritz Hull (New York: Continuum, 1993), 124.

[17] Ecumenical Patriarch Bartholomew, "Message for Caretakers International Youth Summit, June 2–9, 2005," in Chryssavgis, *Cosmic Grace, Humble Prayer*, 310.

[18] Jose Abraham, "An Ecological Reading of the Qur'anic Understanding of Creation," *Bangalore Theological Forum* 33 (2011): 171. *Note:* Abraham uses *vice-gerency* from the word *gerent* ("one who rules).

[19] Seyyed Hossein Nasr, "Islam and the Environmental Crisis," in *Spirit and Nature: Why the Environment Is a Religious Issue*, ed. Steven C. Rockefeller and John C. Elder (Boston: Beacon Press, 1992), 92.

and Hinduism, is also intimately linked to the stewardship of the earth along with its biosphere.

The current state of our home planet reveals how miserably we have failed in responsible stewardship of our common home entrusted to us by God. As Pope John Paul II and Ecumenical Patriarch Bartholomew jointly declared: "If we examine carefully the social and environmental crisis which the world community is facing, we must conclude that we are still betraying the mandate God has given us: to be stewards called to collaborate with God in watching over creation in holiness and wisdom."[20] As John Paul II pointed out in a General Audience on January 19, 1990: "Man is no longer the Creator's 'steward' but an autonomous despot, who is finally beginning to understand that he must stop at the edge of the abyss." Our present generation, more than any other in the geological history of our home planet, has failed in responsibly stewarding the gift of creation entrusted to our care. "As we look at the state of the planet today, with an uncertain future due to climate change, over-exploited resources, and species rapidly heading toward extinction, we can see how far we have fallen from the job entrusted to us in Genesis I."[21]

The contemporary ecological crisis is not only a colossal failure in our stewardship of the earth, but it is also a betrayal of our identity as *imago Dei*, as icons of God, of our duty to mirror God's love and care for creation:

As human beings we have dismally failed to reflect God's image in caring for creation. When we fail to care for the earth in a godly way, we fail to reflect God's image. If we neglect the planet, we become less truly human and God's image in us begins to fade away. . . . As the human species, our destructive relationships with God, one another, and the rest of creation have badly blurred and damaged God's image. We no longer reflect it, and desperately need help in modelling what it means to be truly the image of God in human skin.[22]

As the prayer of confession in the Anglican communion service says, "We have wounded your love and marred your image in us."[23] The

---

[20] Pope John Paul II and Ecumenical Patriarch Bartholomew, "Common Declaration on the Environment" (June 10, 2002).

[21] Bookless, *Planet Wise*, 90.

[22] Ibid.

[23] Church of England, *Order for the Celebration of Holy Communion* (London: Church House Publishing, 2000), 165.

contemporary ecological crisis evidences our failure to be responsible stewards, "co-carers" with God of His wonderful creation.

Irresponsible Stewardship as Sin

In the context of the contemporary ecological crisis we need to widen radically our understanding of the concept of sin. Traditionally, sin has been apprehended in an individual sense—as something limited to the personal sphere, concerning one's relationship with God. In recent times there has been greater critical awareness of the societal structures of sin and a condemnation of them in the teachings of the churches, including the papal magisterium.[24] Today, we need to broaden our understanding of sin within a planetary perspective. In fact, the ecological crisis and the host of actions contributing to it are best understood in the context of sin conceived within a broader planetary perspective. Churches and religions are called today, in the context of the contemporary ecological crisis, to widen their understanding of sin. John Zizioulas, the Metropolitan of Pergamon, writes:

> The protection of the natural environment is a fundamental religious obligation demanded from humankind by God himself. This means that the Church will have to revise radically her concept of sin, which traditionally has been limited to the social and anthropological level, and start speaking of *sin against nature* as a matter of primary religious significance.[25]

Accordingly, any human action that damages our common home and endangers the life and survival of our common household becomes a sin. On a collective level ecological sin is irresponsible stewardship of our home planet and its biosphere. The various manifestations of the ecological crisis are not mere natural disasters, as they are still largely seen by the general public. The current ecological crisis is a consequence of our own values, beliefs, and conscious choices—and of our sinful behavior.

---

[24] See, for example, Jürgen Moltmann, *The Spirit of Life: A Universal Affirmation* (London: SCM Press, 1992), 126–28. For a critique of the structures of sin, see also John Macquarrie, *Principles of Christian Theology*, rev. ed. (London: SCM Press, 1977), 262. For an overview of Moltmann, Macquarrie, and others in this regard, see Paula Clifford, *All Creation Groaning: A Theological Approach to Climate Change and Development* (London: Christian Aid, 2007), 11.

[25] Zizioulas, "Foreword," in Chryssavgis, *Cosmic Grace, Humble Prayer*, viii.

It is only within a relational view of reality, where everything is interrelated and interdependent, that the concept of ecological sin makes sense. Nothing in creation exists in isolation. There exists a physical and spiritual connectedness among all of creation. Sin is the distortion of this underlying and all-embracing relational unity. Sin is the rupture of relationships and of communion among created realities and with the Creator. As Ecumenical Patriarch Bartholomew reminds us: "Our original sin with regard to the natural environment lies, not in any legalistic transgression, but precisely in our refusal to accept the world as a sacrament of communion with God and neighbor."[26] The root of humanity's original sin is "not a transgression against some invisible 'principle,' but the rupture of the primal connection between ourselves, our world, and our God." Unfortunately, we have reduced the concept of sin to individual guilt "while overlooking the social and cosmological implications of sin, whereby division and brokenness are introduced into the world, barring us from discerning God in all things and all things in God."[27]

Ecological sin is a valid religious category to understand the contemporary ecological crisis. To disfigure God's creation and to fail in stewardship of the common home of the earth entrusted to human care amounts to nothing less than a moral failure, and therefore a sin against the Creator and one's fellow beings. Ecumenical Patriarch Bartholomew has spoken extensively of ecological sin. For him, "Each human act that contributes to the destruction of the natural environment must be regarded as a very serious sin."[28] Accordingly, every harm to the creation of the almighty God, "even out of negligence, constitutes not simply an evil, but a grave sin."[29]

Ecological sin is not only an offense against the Creator but against our fellow humans and the very creation. The patriarch affirms very clearly that to devastate the natural world, as in the case of the

---

[26] Ecumenical Patriarch Bartholomew, "Address During the Official Sophie Prize Presentation Ceremony, June 12, 2002," in Chryssavgis, *Cosmic Grace, Humble Prayer*, 284.

[27] John Chryssavgis, "Foreword," in *The Sermon of All Creation: Christians on Nature*, ed. Judith Fitzgerald and Michael Oren Fitzgerald (Bloomington, IN: World Wisdom, 2005), vii.

[28] Ecumenical Patriarch Bartholomew, "Greeting During the Symposium at Holy Trinity Monastery, Halki, June 1, 1992," in Chryssavgis, *Cosmic Grace, Humble Prayer*, 84.

[29] Ecumenical Patriarch Bartholomew, "Message of the Synaxis of Hierarchs of the Ecumenical Patriarchate, September 1, 1998," in Chryssavgis, *Cosmic Grace, Humble Prayer*, 201.

human-induced contemporary ecological crisis, is a sin against God, humanity, and the world:

> It follows that to commit a crime against the natural world is a sin. For human beings to cause species to become extinct and to destroy the biological diversity of God's creation; for human beings to degrade the integrity of the earth by causing changes in its climate, by stripping the earth of its natural forests, or by destroying its wetlands; for human beings to injure other human beings with disease; for human beings to contaminate the earth's waters, its land, its air, and its life, with poisonous substances—all of these are sins before God, humanity and the world.[30]

The Catholic bishops of England and Wales also come close to labeling human-induced ecological crisis a sin by declaring it contrary to the vision of the Gospel. The bishops write: "A way of life that disregards and damages God's creation, forces the poor into greater poverty, and threatens the right of future generations to a healthy environment and to their fair share of the earth's wealth and resources, is contrary to the vision of the Gospel."[31] On a similar note is the document from the Catholic Bishops of the Philippines, which states: "As we reflect on what is happening in the light of the Gospel we are convinced that this assault on Creation is sinful and contrary to the teachings of our faith."[32]

Ecological sin ruptures the relational fabric of reality at all levels. It is sin not only against God but also against our human and cosmic fellowship. Such a holistic triangular perspective in the understanding of ecological sin is also in keeping with the overarching theme of the present book, which understands the contemporary ecological crisis as a triple cry of the earth, the poor, and the gods.

---

[30] Ecumenical Patriarch Bartholomew, "Address During the Environmental Symposium in Santa Barbara, November 8, 1997," in Chryssavgis, *Cosmic Grace, Humble Prayer*, 190. See also Ecumenical Patriarch Bartholomew, "The Orthodox Church and the Environment—An Interview Published by the Divinity School of Yale University, June 2007," in Chryssavgis, *Cosmic Grace, Humble Prayer*, 359–60.

[31] Catholic Bishops' Conference of England and Wales, *The Call of Creation: God's Invitation and the Human Response* (2002), 1.

[32] Catholic Bishops of the Philippines, *What Is Happening to Our Beautiful Land?* (Manila, January 1988).

A Sin Against God

The ecological crisis is, first and above all, a sin against God, the Creator, to whom the disfiguring of creation is an affront. Any abuse of creation is a willful rebellion against God's project for creation and against the ingrained natural and supernatural *telos* conferred on created realities by the Creator. Sin is the rupturing of the most important of all relationships, namely, the bond with the Creator. This truth is supremely evident in the original sin of Adam and Eve. The failure of Adam and Eve, while dwelling in the garden lovingly created for them, to respect a limit imposed on them regarding a tree in the same garden, shattered their relationship with the Creator.

The original sin is indeed a tragic story of broken relationships. Adam and Eve had originally walked with God in the garden, enjoying God's friendship and the goodness of creation. With sin, a profound alienation between God and humanity creeps in. "When they heard God walking in the garden, they hid among the trees. The God whose purpose in creating was to enter into and facilitate loving relationships was rejected by the creatures chosen to bear his image."[33] The ecological crisis—our refusal to accept and respect the natural order of things—is a sin against the Creator—a longing to be "like God," to take God's place. The sin is to regard humanity and the world as autonomous and without the need of God.

Ecological sin is the opposite of cherishing God's creation. Creating lunar landscapes of pollution and destruction, veiling the sun with industrial smoke, and filling the heavens with CFCs are offenses to the Creator, whose glory the created firmaments are ordained to proclaim. It is for this reason, as Ecumenical Patriarch Bartholomew writes, that "the thoughtless and abusive treatment of even the smallest material and living creation of God must be considered as a mortal sin. An insult toward the natural creation is seen as—and in fact actually is—an unforgivable insult to the uncreated God."[34] The patriarch also points out that "every destruction of the natural environment caused by humanity constitutes an offense against the Creator Himself and arouses a sense of sorrow. In relation to the degree to which people are responsible for their actions, *metanoia*—a radical change of course—is

---

[33] Bookless, *Planet Wise*, 36.

[34] Ecumenical Patriarch Bartholomew, "Christmas Encyclical Message, 1994," in Chryssavgis, *Cosmic Grace, Humble Prayer*, 127.

demanded of us all."[35] It is certainly God's forgiveness that we must ask for causing harm to God's creation.[36]

A Sin Against Fellow Humans

In the second place, the ecological crisis is a sin against our own fellow human beings, against those of our own flesh. The ecological crisis is a profound injustice especially toward the poor and vulnerable sections of society." The crisis ruptures the bonds of human fellowship. In this regard, to pollute the land, water and atmosphere and to endanger the health of fellow citizens is clearly a sin. In the case of anthropogenic climate change, excessive emissions of greenhouse gases, especially by the rich countries—which have direct consequences on poorer and vulnerable communities elsewhere—is clearly a sin. Causing climate change that can in turn exacerbate the already precarious situation of food security in the world, endanger health security for poor communities, or cause forced mass migration is clearly a sin.

The ecological crisis reveals, above all, how we have betrayed the eucharistic vocation of human communities, namely, to share the gifts of creation with all the members of our common household in a spirit of communion *(koinonia)*, like the one bread broken and shared at the table of the Lord. As Samuel Rayan reminds us, quoting from the prophet Isaiah: "Earth is the Lord's table, laid with care for God's daughters and sons, 'a feast of rich food, a feast of well-aged wines' (Is 25:6), a table God lays with flowers every morning."[37] The earth is indeed humankind's common table laid by God. Around that table we gather, in a spirit of conviviality, not in competitive scramble but in joyful fellowship, nurturing and sheltering one another.

The unequal distribution and consumption of our home planet's life-essential resources and the tragic fact that nearly one in seven of our fellow humans go to bed hungry every night are grave sins against the eucharistic nature of human communities. A statement from the Catholic Bishops' Conference of New Zealand asks:

---

[35] Ecumenical Patriarch Bartholomew, "Greeting During the Symposium at Holy Trinity Monastery," 84.

[36] Ecumenical Patriarch Bartholomew, "Address During the Environmental Symposium in Santa Barbara," 190.

[37] Samuel Rayan, "The Earth Is the Lord's," in *Ecotheology: Voices from South and North*, ed. David G. Hallman (Maryknoll, NY: Orbis Books, 1994), 133.

What does the commandment "Thou shall not kill" mean when 20 percent of the world's population consumes resources at a rate that robs poorer nations and future generations of what they need to survive? What does it mean to respect life when 30,000 people die each day from poverty? What does it mean to be stewards of the earth when up to half of all living species are expected to become extinct in the next 200 years?[38]

The contemporary ecological crisis reveals the sin of injustice in our world today. The ecological crisis is thus closely linked to the theme of social justice. The sinful character of the contemporary ecological crisis is evident in an inequity that is both intergenerational and international—that each person in the world has equal right to global environmental space and to the earth's resources. A key principle of Catholic social teaching is universal destination of material goods. As St. Ambrose wrote, citing the Gospel of Luke: "The fruits of the earth were given to feed all without distinction and nobody can claim any particular rights. Instead, we have lost the sense of the communion of goods, rushing to turn these goods into private property."[39] As clearly evident in the case of the ecological footprint analysis mechanism, human greediness and accumulation of wealth in the hands of a few nations, communities, and individuals are depriving large numbers of our common household of their rightful share in the resources of our planet. This is clearly a sin. In 1990, Pope John Paul II denounced in his message for World Peace Day this situation as contrary to the very order of creation:

The earth is ultimately *a common heritage, the fruits of which are for the benefit of all.* In the words of the Second Vatican Council, "God destined the earth and all it contains for the use of every individual and all peoples" (*Gaudium et Spes*, 69). . . . It is manifestly unjust that a privileged few should continue to accumulate excess goods, squandering available resources, while masses of people are living in conditions of misery at the very lowest level of subsistence. Today, the dramatic threat of

---

[38] Catholic Bishops' Conference of New Zealand, "Our World Is Facing an Ecological Crisis" (September 2006).

[39] St. Ambrose, *On the Gospel of St. Luke*, 7, 124ff. As quoted in *Drinking from the Hidden Fountain: A Patristic Breviary: Ancient Wisdom for Today's World*, ed. Tomáš Špidlik (Michigan: Alban Books Ltd., 1994), 155.

ecological breakdown is teaching us the extent to which greed and selfishness—both individual and collective—are contrary to the order of creation, an order which is characterized by mutual interdependence (no. 8).[40]

The multiple manifestations of the human-induced ecological crisis are grave moral sins against our very fellow human beings. Actions that cause and exacerbate the ecological crisis are indeed—especially when the lives of millions of our poor brothers and sisters in our common home are at stake—crimes against our fellow humans. In this context ecocide is also homicide, and as such is a grave sin.

The contemporary ecological crisis reveals how we are also sinning against future generations by leaving them a home with polluted land, water, and atmosphere, a planet scarce in resources because we consumed renewable natural resources at an unsustainable rate, and a climate that is fast turning awry. In the case of climate change, for example, we are letting the sins of the parents fall on their children and children's children, as the impacts of current anthropogenic global warming will last for thousands of years into the future.

A Sin Against Creation

In the third place, ecological sin is, from a theological perspective, an offense against God's creation. When we devastate our home planet, it is sin, inasmuch as it constitutes disobedience to the divine command to care for creation. Adam's naming the creatures at the command of God in the Book of Genesis (Gn 2:19) can be interpreted as an expression of the personal care and concern that humanity is expected to practice with regard to nonhuman creation. While the first commandment given to humanity was the stewardship of God's creation, the sin of Adam and Eve consisted in their refusal to serve *(abad)* and keep *(shamar)* the garden where they dwelled in fellowship with the rest of God's creation. When we act like the owner of creation, with absolute property rights, rather than like responsible and humble stewards of creation, we sin against the natural world.

The multiple manifestations of the ecological crisis—from pollution and profligate consumption to biodiversity loss and climate change—are all expressions of humanity's sinful conduct toward God's creation. There are both sins of omission and commission in this regard. "Our actions destroy the ozone layer; our inaction allows the

---

[40] John Paul II, "Peace with God the Creator, Peace with All of Creation," Message for the Celebration of the World Day of Peace (January 1, 1990).

destruction of biodiversity around us—both are equally sinful acts."[41]
In a similar way, the consumer-driven lifestyle that is fast depleting
our home planet's finite natural resources is a symptom of sin. "So
is the poisoned air that comes from a factory whose owners have
neglected to install appropriate filters. And so is war of every kind,
with the loss of life to humans and the devastation of God's creation
that inevitably results."[42] Human-induced biodiversity loss is also
sinful. We have usurped the ecological space of other species, failed
to protect a number of species, or denied the conditions necessary for
their perpetuation and ongoing evolution. We have even driven some
species into extinction.

Ultimately, the greatest sin of our present generation against creation is undoubtedly human-induced climate change. Climate change,
as we saw earlier, affects practically the whole biosphere on our home
planet. A document from the World Council of Churches states: "It
constitutes a threat for animals and plants, and disturbs the subtle
equilibrium on which the present civilization is built in nature. To
contribute to this deterioration is not only sin against the weak and
unprotected but also the earth—God's gift of life."[43]

The various manifestations of the ecological crisis are indeed offenses against our common home and against the survival and flourishing
of the human and nonhuman members of our common household,
both of which are entrusted to our responsible stewardship by the
Creator. The contemporary ecological crisis thus amounts to sin, in
the widest sense possible, as it ruptures the bonds of divine, human,
and cosmic fellowship.

Ecological Crisis Resulting from Our *Hubris*

In the previous sections we have examined the various layers of
ecological sin as an offense against the Creator, one's fellow beings,
and the rest of creation. There is a still deeper level of ecological sin
that has implications for the rest of creation. It is a sin against ourselves, namely, our refusal to accept that we are creatures. It is the sin

---

[41] Frederick Quinn, *To Heal the Earth: A Theology of Ecology* (Nashville, TN: Upper Room Books, 1994), 25.

[42] Edward Brown, *Our Father's World: Mobilizing the Church to Care for Creation* (South Hadley, MA: Doorlight Publications, 2006), 57.

[43] World Council of Churches, *Solidarity with Victims of Climate Change: Reflections on the World Council of Churches' Response to Climate Change* (Geneva: WCC, 2002), 12.

of human *hubris* that lies at the root of our irresponsible stewardship of God's creation and of our common household. As Michael S.
Northcott notes:

> At the heart of the pathology of ecological crisis is the refusal
> of modern humans to see themselves as creatures, contingently
> embedded in networks of relationships with other creatures, and
> with the Creator. This refusal is the quintessential root of what
> theologians call sin. And like the sin of Adam, it has moral and
> spiritual as well as ecological consequences.[44]

Such a refusal constitutes a twofold denial: first of all, a refusal to
acknowledge our radical dependence on the Creator, and second, a
disavowal of our fundamental interdependence on the rest of creation.

Refusal to Accept Our Nature as Creatures

First of all, from a theological point of view the ecological sin consists in the "refusal to accept limits placed upon humanity on account
of its creaturely status."[45] Our current ecological predicament results
from our stubborn refusal to accept any limit whatsoever—whether
those regarding the carrying capacity of the earth in the case of the
ecological footprint of individuals, communities, and nations, or in the
case of the carbon footprint directly linked to climate change. Such a
refusal is a rebellion against the very natural order of creation conferred on it by God, and a revolt ultimately against the very Creator.
In fact, the refusal to accept any limit that arises from our creaturely
status was the original sin of humanity, as we read in the third chapter
of the Book of Genesis. Such arrogant posturing also masks the unbridled human desire to have dominion over all of creation, overruling
the exclusive lordship of God over creation.

The sin of Adam and Eve was a sin of disobedience, a sort of "theo-
cide," an attempt to live without God, to be free from God's norms
regarding dwelling in the garden of Eden, to substitute their own free
will for God's project of creation. Northcott notes: "Adam's sin is
a prideful refusal of the dependence of the creature on the Creator.

---

[44] Michael S. Northcott, *A Moral Climate: The Ethics of Global Warming*
(London: Darton, Longman, Todd, 2007), 14; see also 5, 16.

[45] Alister McGrath, *The Reenchantment of Nature: The Denial of Religion
and the Ecological Crisis* (New York: Doubleday, 2002), 79.

And this refusal has the consequence of destroying interdependence and solidarity not only between humanity and God, but between Adam and Eve, and between them and other creatures."[46] Euripides described *hubris* as "the desire to become greater than the gods."[47] The human defiance of God's lordship over creation and the human urge to usurp the power and privileges of the Creator is also evident in the narrative about the building of the tower of Babel (Gn 11:1ff.). As Alister McGrath points out: "It is a powerful symbol of the human refusal to accept limits—whether natural or ordained—and to quest for domination and transformation. It is in the birth of this mind-set that the true roots of our ecological crisis lie."[48] The refusal to accept divinely ordained limits is equally evident in the violation of the Sabbath rest for the land (Ex 23:10–11)—a theme that runs throughout the Old Testament.

The contemporary ecological crisis reveals the unbridled human desire to be the arbitrary dictator of the whole of creation, leaving out any reference whatsoever to God, the Creator. From a theological point of view, the roots of the ecological crisis lie in modern anthropocentrism, which makes the human being the measure of all things, with no accountability to any higher Being. Modern anthropocentrism, along with the *hubris* associated with it, appears to have replaced the traditional theocentrism of the Christian scriptures and of other religious traditions of humanity. From a theological viewpoint, all creation proceeds from God and is destined to return to God. Creation's Alpha and Omega is God, and God alone!

The human being certainly possesses a certain uniqueness among creatures, in being *imago Dei*, created in the very image and likeness of God. Such a uniqueness is to be interpreted, as we have seen previously, in the distinctive capacity and responsibility that humans are endowed with by the Creator to reflect the goodness and concern of the Creator toward the rest of the created order, and not to lord their authority over the rest of creation as its despots. Our kingly role over creation, conferred on us in total gratuity in spite of our absolute insignificance, according to Psalms, cannot be exercised "on our own but only in dependence on our Lord, the Creator, Sustainer, Savior God."[49]

---

[46] Northcott, *A Moral Climate*, 153.

[47] Cited in Ecumenical Patriarch Bartholomew, "Address During the Official Sophie Prize Presentation Ceremony, June 12, 2002," 282.

[48] McGrath, *The Reenchantment of Nature*, 79.

[49] Bookless, *Planet Wise*, 95.

We are *imago Dei*, and not our own images. Modern anthropocentrism, it appears, has disowned our true identity as God's images and our absolute dependence on God, the Creator. As Pope Benedict XVI wrote in 2011: "The first step toward a correct relationship with the world around us is the recognition by humans of their status as created beings. Man is not God; he is His image."[50]

The contemporary ecological crisis reveals how we have displaced the Creator's lordship over creation with human despotism and denied our fundamental dependence on God. We have refused to comply with all the moral implications that derive from the acknowledgment of God's centrality with regard to all created realities. As Ecumenical Patriarch Bartholomew points out: "The arrogant apostasy of humanity from its relationship with our divine Creator's creation is the deeper reason behind the presumptuous and improper exploitation of the ecological environment."[51]

Refusal to Accept Our Interdependence with Creation

Second, the contemporary ecological crisis reveals that we have denied our creaturely identity as created like every other creature from the dust of the earth—from stardust, as modern cosmology has revealed—and our consequent interdependence on the rest of creation.

Our creaturely identity and our intimate fellowship and consequent interdependence with the rest of creation are clearly evident from the first verses of the Bible, especially in the older Yahwist narrative of creation. For the Yahwist author, human life and identity emerge out of arable soil. In fact, both humans and animals are made from the earth's soil. In Genesis 2:7 we read that God formed the first human being from the "dust of the ground." Like the animals to come, humanity is made out of Adam's substance: dust from the earth. We are basically "earthlings," creatures of the earth, with feet of clay.[52] It is precisely our earthly origin that underlies our fundamental kinship and fellowship with the rest of creation.

Thus, before the Creator all living beings (*nepes hayya*, Gen 2:7, 19) are interrelated as creatures. "Just as God is a relational God,

---

[50] Pope Benedict XVI, Message to Archbishop Geraldo Lyrio Rocha of Mariana (president of the National Conference of Bishiops of Brazil) (Vatican Information Service, March 9, 2011).

[51] Ecumenical Patriarch Bartholomew, "Greeting on Arrival at Novorossisk for the Second International Symposium, September 22, 1997," in Chryssavgis, *Cosmic Grace, Humble Prayer*, 169.

[52] Bookless, *Planet Wise*, 31–32.

so he has made us relational beings, tied to the earth by our dusty origins."[53] But we often forget that we are an integral part of creation, interrelated with a world of creatures "good" for their own sake, the "whole" of which was declared by the Creator as "very good." The interrelatedness of all creation means that unity is primary. The ark on which we travel carries all of God's creatures. So any talk of human uniqueness needs to be placed within the wider relational frame of unity.

The interrelatedness of all creation implies the interdependence of all creatures, including humanity. "We are all connected to one another, our very existence is interdependent, *we need each other to survive*."[54] As Archbishop Desmond Tutu says, "The first law of our being is that we are set in a delicate network of interdependence with our fellow human beings and with the rest of God's creation."[55]

The interdependence of all creation is especially evident in the case of biodiversity, which is fundamental to the existence and flourishing of life on Earth. Like a spider's web, each strand supports the whole. Within such a framework of interdependence among all creatures, the paradox is that a higher form of life, like humans, needs the lower forms, while the lower ones can survive without humans, as was the case for millions of years on Earth. While the simpler forms can generally survive the elimination of the more complex forms, the more complex forms will not be able to survive without the simpler forms. Thus, for example, if the plankton in the sea, which produce most of our oxygen, were to die out, the survival of a multitude of living beings on the planet would be threatened. So also with the bacteria in the soil and the worms and insects that perform immensely important roles in the web of life.[56]

Modern biology clearly shows that human beings are not only interrelated with their fellow creatures but are also fundamentally interdependent on them. Human beings can only exist as part of the total web of life. The very late arrival of human beings on our home planet—only after biodiversity had transformed Earth into a "home for life"—signifies precisely this, namely that they need the creatures that have preceded them and cannot exist without them. From a

---

[53] Ibid., 50.

[54] Morton, "Environment and Religion," 128.

[55] Desmond Tutu, *God Has a Dream: A Vision of Hope for Our Times* (London: Random House, 2011), 25.

[56] Thomas Berry, "The Emerging Ecozoic Period," in *Thomas Berry, Dreamer of the Earth: The Spiritual Ecology of the Father of Environmentalism*, ed. Ervin Laszlo and Allan Combs (Rochester, VT: Inner Traditions, 2011), 13.

theological point of view, while the entire physical world can be seen as a preparation for the arrival of humans, they are at the same time completely dependent on those that have preceded them and cannot exist apart from them.[57]

Significantly, most spiritual traditions have a rich heritage in recognizing and appreciating human fellowship with the rest of creation and human dependence on them. The trend existed strongly in Christianity, at least up to modern times. One cannot but remember here the Franciscan fellowship with all creation, beautifully expressed in St. Francis of Assisi's "Canticle of Creatures." The medieval saint and mystic Hildegard of Bingen echoed the same perception of interdependence when she wrote: "God has made all things in the world in consideration of everything else."[58] As Pope John Paul II reminds us, the order of creation is characterized by mutual interdependence.[59]

The contemporary ecological crisis reveals how humans are committing the sin of denying their interdependence on the rest of creation. We do not really feel that we belong with the rest of creation.[60] This is a folly that threatens our very survival. We need to acknowledge that we are earthlings, that we are born out of the earth, that we have no future except within the earth community.[61] We need to rediscover our self-identity as *imago mundi*, created from the dust of the earth. Only the honest recognition of our origin from the *humus* ("soil") of the earth will enable us to stand with humility (from the Latin *humilis,* "on the ground") before the Creator and in fellowship with the rest of creation. We need to recover this profound sense of humility in order to see ourselves in perspective. Such creaturely humility will be a sure antidote for the *hubris* of modern anthropocentrism, in which lie some of the roots of our contemporary ecological crisis.

Ecological sin is the denial of the fundamental truth of creaturely dependence on the Creator and our radical interdependence of the rest of the common web of life. James A. Nash asserts:

Ecologically, sin is the refusal to act in the image of God, as responsible representatives who value and love the host of

---

[57] See Jürgen Moltmann, *God in Creation: A New Theology of Creation and the Spirit of God* (San Francisco: Harper and Row, 1985), 187.

[58] Gabriel Uhlein, *Meditations with Hildegard of Bingen* (Rochester, VT: Bear and Company, 1983), 9.

[59] John Paul II, "Peace with God the Creator, Peace with All of Creation,"no. 8.

[60] See Daniel Martin, "The Joining of Human, Earth, and Spirit," in Hull, *Earth and Spirit*, 43.

[61] Berry, "The Emerging Ecozoic Period," 15.

interdependent creatures in their ecosystems, which the Creator values and loves. . . . It is breaking the bonds with God and our comrades in creation. It is acting like the owner of creation with absolute property rights. Ecological sin is expressed as the arrogant denial of the creaturely limitations imposed on human ingenuity and technology, a defiant disrespect or a deficient respect for the interdependent relationships of all creatures and their environments established in the covenant of creation.[62]

Repercussions of Sin on Creation

From a theological point of view, a significant link exists between human sin and the state of the physical world. Sin defiles the land. In the faith traditions of humanity, and in the biblical tradition in particular, the land acts as a spiritual barometer of the moral lives of its inhabitants. In the great biblical drama the land is not just scenery or backdrop but an active character.[63] A fundamental principle in the Bible and in life is that sin has consequences. "God created us to live in harmony with him, and in a comfortable web of relationships within his creation. Any break in those relationships—sin—results in consequences."[64] Failure to keep God's ways inevitably has a negative effect on creation as well as on our relationship with God as creatures. This fundamental truth is evident from the earliest chapters of the Book of Genesis. In fact, the first two chapters of Genesis, which speak about the grandeur and goodness of creation, are immediately followed by the tragic events of human sin with its conspicuous effects on the rest of creation. As we read in the third and fourth chapters, both the sin against God—the disobedience of Adam and Eve and Cain's assassination of Abel—lead to negative repercussions for the land. The pattern is tragically repeated throughout the Old Testament and still in our own days, as evident in the contemporary ecological crisis.

Sin Against the Creator

First of all, the sin against the Creator is bound to affect creation. As Pope John Paul II pointed out in "Peace with God the Creator,

---

[62] James A. Nash, *Loving Nature: Ecological Integrity and Christian Responsibility* (Nashville, TN: Abingdon Press, 1991), 119.

[63] Bookless, *Planet Wise*, 55.

[64] Brown, *Our Father's World*, 58.

Peace with All of Creation," if humanity is not at peace with God, then Earth itself cannot be at peace:

> When man turns his back on the Creator's plan, he provokes a disorder which has inevitable repercussions on the rest of the created order. If man is not at peace with God, then earth itself cannot be at peace: "Therefore the land mourns and all who dwell in it languish, and also the beasts of the field and the birds of the air and even the fish of the sea are taken away (Hos 4:3)." (no. 5)

Humanity's rebellion against the Creator and its repercussions on the rest of creation are evident in the narration of original sin in the third chapter of the Book of Genesis. The original sin, in fact, shatters the harmony not only between human beings and their Creator but also between humans and the rest of creation. As Pope John Paul II and Ecumenical Patriarch Bartholomew write in their 2002 "Common Declaration on the Environment": "At the beginning of history, man and woman sinned by disobeying God and rejecting His design for creation. Among the results of this first sin was the destruction of the original harmony of creation." The disharmony created by original sin casts a gloomy shadow over the whole of creation. In "Peace with God the Creator, Peace with All of Creation," Pope John Paul II writes:

> Made in the image and likeness of god, Adam and Eve were to have exercised their dominion over the earth (Gn 1:28) with wisdom and love. Instead, they destroyed the existing harmony by deliberately going against the Creator's plan, that is, by choosing to sin. This resulted not only in man's alienation from himself, in death and fratricide, but also in the earth's "rebellion" against him. (no. 3)

The fallout of original sin ripples through various layers of human relationships: with the Creator, among ourselves, and with the rest of creation. Obedience gives way to rebellion, and the primary relationship of intimacy between the Creator and humanity is broken. Responsible living gives way to guilt and shame; the original blessing conferred on humanity to increase and multiply turns into the original curse to toil hard on the land by the sweat of our brow. There is also disharmony within the first human community, as mutual intimacy gives way to conflict and sexual complementarity is relegated to domination and subordination. The disharmony with the Creator ultimately falls on the very creation. Humans were originally created to live in harmony with the rest of creation, a harmony that depended on an ongoing relationship with the Creator. Once the relationship was broken, disharmony—disease, thorns, thistles—followed.[65] Because of the original sin humanity is not only alienated from God and from its own members, but the land, the rest of creation, also suffers the consequences of sin. According to the Book of Genesis:

> Cursed is the ground because of you;
> in toil you shall eat of it all the days of your life;
> thorns and thistles it shall bring forth to you;
> and you shall eat the plants of the field.
> By the sweat of your face
> you shall eat bread
> until you return to the ground,
> for out of it you were taken;
> you are dust,
> and to dust you shall return. (Gn 3:17b–19)

The repercussions of humanity's rebellion against God on creation are striking. *Adamah*, the source of life—the very ground from which Adam and all living creatures were formed (Gn 2:7, 19)—is cursed because of Adam's disrespect of the tree, and it will start to bring forth thorns and thistles. Life-giving, natural fertility will become difficult for the land, for *adamah*.[66] The original sin ruptured humanity's relationship with their home-garden. It was no longer the bountiful and fruitful garden (Gn 2:9), but a place that became antagonistic and inhospitable.[67]

It is significant that the Yahwist account continues the story of early humanity with the spread of evil to Cain and his descendants. Like a rock flung into a still pool, original sin sends ripples out in all direction. Sin begets sin. The lowest point comes when "the Lord was sorry that he had made humankind on the earth, and it grieved him to his heart" (Gn 6:6). The death-dealing curse on land and on living things closely follow upon human sin—just as shadows follow light—as evident in the Great Flood, which led to the obliteration of all life on Earth except for Noah and his family and the creatures that found shelter in the ark. As sin multiplied on Earth the waters in which,

---

[65] See David Atkinson, *Renewing the Face of the Earth: A Theological and Pastoral Response to Climate Change* (Norwich: Canterbury Press, 2008), 125; Brown, *Our Father's World*, 55–56.

[66] Upton, *Who Is the Earth?*, 57; Kahl, "Fratricide and Ecocide," 57.

[67] McDonagh, *The Greening of the Church*, 122.

according to God's original project, living creatures were called to swarm and multiply (Gn 1:20–22) ended up kissing them with death. "And all flesh died that moved on the earth, birds, domestic animals, wild animals, all swarming creatures that swarm on the earth, and all human beings; everything on dry land in whose nostrils was the breath of life died. . . . Only Noah was left, and those that were with him in the ark" (Gn 7:21–22, 23b).[68] The Noah story is paradigmatic of how the defilement of creation through human sin has repercussions also on the rest of creation, with even innocent animals caught up in the punishment inflicted on guilty humans.

The intimate connection between human sin and ecological disaster so graphically portrayed in Genesis is repeated throughout the Bible (Lv 18:25; Dt 29:22–25; Am 4:7; Rv 8:10–11). There are many examples in the scriptures of how sin against the Creator leads to the devastation of creation. In Isaiah we read about how infidelity to God's commands and statutes leads to the devastation of the land (Is 24:5–6), while the prophet Jeremiah speaks of how infidelity toward God leads to the withholding of rain (Jer 3:5).

The biblical principle here is that failure to keep God's ways inevitably has a negative effect on the land.[69] What underpins this truth is the Israelite understanding of the land as a sacred gift from God.

> With this gift comes a set of obligations—to the Lord, and to other members of the community (Dt 12:1). If the people obey God, he promises them blessings: health, peace, fertility and fruitfulness for them and their land (Dt 28:1–14). If they are disobedient these promises will fail; instead both they and the land will be cursed (vv.15–44).[70]

Sin creates disharmony with the divine intent, and its repercussions reverberate on creation. This is because the Jews perceived the land and the people as a single entity, extending the corporate identity to all creation. As the prophets of the Old Testament testify, human sin is reflected in the earth's suffering.[71] In Isaiah we read:

---

[68] See ibid., 123.

[69] Bookless, *Planet Wise*, 57.

[70] Hilary Marlow, "Justice for All the Earth: Society, Ecology, and the Biblical Prophets," in *Creation in Crisis: Christian Perspectives on Sustainability*, ed. Robert S. White (London: SPCK, 2009), 201.

[71] Catholic Bishops' Conference of England and Wales, *The Call of Creation*, 4–5.

> The earth dries up and withers,
>> the world languishes and withers;
>> the heavens languish together with the earth.
> The earth lies polluted
>> under its inhabitants;
> for they have transgressed laws,
>> violated the statutes,
>> broken the everlasting covenant.
> Therefore a curse devours the earth. (Is 24:4–6)

From a theological point of view, it is plausible to interpret the current state of our home planet as a consequence of humanity not respecting God's norms regarding its stewardship. The repercussions of human sin will be on the very inhabitants of the land and on the land itself.

Sin Against Fellow Human Beings

In a similar vein, sins against one's fellow beings also have negative repercussions for the land, and for creation as a whole. Fratricide can lead to ecocide, as tragically illustrated in the story of Cain and Abel. As in every sin, Cain's anger against his brother is also a revolt against God. This is clearly evident in the biblical narrative:

> In the course of time Cain brought to the Lord an offering of the fruit of the ground, and Abel for his part brought of the firstlings of his flock, their fat portions. And the Lord had regard for Abel and his offering, but for Cain and his offering he had no regard. So Cain was very angry, and his countenance fell. The Lord said to Cain, "Why are you angry, and why has your countenance fallen? If you do well, will you not be accepted? And if you do not do well, sin is lurking at the door; its desire is for you, but you must master it." (Gn 4:3–7)

Cain's "fall" occurs when "his countenance fell" before God, closing him away both from God and from his brother, Abel.[72] Cain refuses to accept both God's supremacy and his coexistence with his brother. The stage is thus set for the first fratricide in biblical history:

---

[72] Kahl, "Fratricide and Ecocide," 61.

Cain said to his brother Abel, "Let us go out to the field." And when they were in the field, Cain rose up against his brother Abel, and killed him. (Gn 4:8)

Cain's doing away with his brother is completed in his staunch refusal of any stewardship whatsoever of his younger sibling. To the Lord's query, "Where is your brother Abel?"—echoing "Where are you?" to Adam in the garden (Gn 3:9)—Cain replies with indifference couched in arrogance, "I do not know; am I my brother's keeper?" (Gn 4:9). He disowns his brother by refusing to care for him. Just as Adam refused to "keep" the garden through his disobedience, Cain too refuses to be a "keeper" of his own brother. He refuses any positive relationship of watching, protecting, and taking care of his younger brother. In fact, "the Hebrew word for *keeping* used here is exactly the same that originally had described Adam's task with regard to the garden: taking care, preserving next to serving."[73]

The fratricide has direct repercussions on the land, as we read in the verses that immediately follow. The field, the ground, exactly where bushes and plants were to grow (Gn 2:5), the garden entrusted to humanity to "till it and keep it" (Gn 2:15), is now soaked with the innocent blood of Abel, which cries out to the Creator. As a consequence of sin, the land becomes barren. The very land out of which "God made to grow every tree that is pleasant to the sight and good for food" (Gn 2:9), basking in God's original blessing of creation, is now cursed along with the sinner and loses its natural fertility.

And now you are cursed from the ground, which has opened its mouth to receive your brother's blood from your hand. When you till the ground, it will no longer yield to you its strength; you will be a fugitive and a wanderer on the earth. (Gn 4:11–12)

The earth cannot live with a murderer, one who has rebelled against God and has killed his own brother. Instead of life-giving water and seeds from Cain's hand, the first farmer in the Bible, the land received blood—and its fertility ceased.

As a result, the communication between the two is irreversibly destroyed and Cain is driven away from the *face of the earth* (2:14). She expels him, she refused him her strength and fertility, she spits him out. Abel's blood crying to God from the *mouth* of

---

73 Ibid., 62.

Adama has made her cursed, barren, and resistant to Cain. The first death in human history is not a peaceful receiving of dust returning to dust, but a desperate rearing up of the blood-soaked earth on behalf of the slain victim.[74]

Defiled by sin, the land will no longer yield, and humans will be condemned to wander on it and not to dwell on it, as God originally planned. It is no wonder that Cain ends up *wandering*. He is no more a servant of the *Adama*, and we anticipate the desert growing again.[75] Fratricide results in eco-cide.

The Bible contains several instances of the impact of human sin on creation, often with graphic descriptions of the devastation of the land. Human beings' sins against fellow beings, especially in the form of social injustice and the oppression of the poor and weak—the *anawim* of Yahweh—cause the land to turn dry and barren. This theme is particularly evident in the prophets. According to prophet Hosea

> There is no faithfulness or kindness
>   and no knowledge of God in the land.
> Swearing, lying, and murder
>   and stealing and adultery break out;
>   bloodshed follows bloodshed.
> Therefore the land mourns. (Hos 4:1–3)

A clear link between cause and effect is evident here. "Lying, stealing, murdering and immorality not only have an effect on the relationships with other people and with God. They also affect the natural world."[76] In Amos 4 we find a list of calamities, among them those that affect the well-being of the land. Crops have been afflicted by drought, blight, and pests (vv. 6–9) that the Lord inflicted upon the unrepentant people of Israel in a vain attempt to convert them. Amos repeats the message. Marlow writes, "Devastation in the natural world—both failure of crops and wider cosmic disruption—are the result of the people's shortcomings, both in their worship and in their inability to practice justice and righteousness (5:4–15; 8:4–12)."[77] The prophet sees a close link not only between worship of God and relationships toward other people, but also between how society operates and the fruitfulness of the wider world.

---

[74] Ibid., 63.
[75] Ibid., 64.
[76] Bookless, *Planet Wise*, 42.
[77] Marlow, "Justice for All the Earth," 199.

In these and similar passages it is clear that the land becomes a spiritual barometer—reacting to the moral disobedience of God's people by "mourning" and wasting away. Wildlife and natural systems are all affected. As in Hosea, the cause is not simply poor steward-ship or ecological mismanagement. It is moral failure that has a direct impact on the land and ecosystems. Elsewhere, sins such as idolatry (Jer 3:6–10; 16:18), bloodshed (Nm 35:33–34), and broken promises (Is 24:5–6) all have an effect on the land.[78]

The contemporary ecological crisis reveals how human sin has concrete repercussions on the rest of creation. Ecological problems are ultimately sin problems. What we are seeing in the world today is ample evidence of this. "We cannot disobey with impunity. There are limits to how far we can push our rebellion against God when it comes to his creation. After too much abuse, the land will refuse to produce crops. The ocean will stop yielding fish. Wells will dry up. Rules matter. Sin has consequences."[79] This truth is founded on the relational character of all reality. which is also, from a theological point of view, a moral order.

"The wages of sin is death," wrote St. Paul in the Letter to the Romans (Rom 6:23). This is clearly evident in the contemporary ecological crisis. Our continued sin, our persistent sinful behavior, is preventing the healing of the land.

Ecological Conversion in Response to Ecological Sin

The only valid response to ecological sin—the rupturing of the bonds of fellowship with the Creator, with our fellow human beings, and with the rest of creation—is repentance and reconciliation. Since the root cause of the contemporary ecological crisis is human sin and human selfishness, what we need, in the first place, is deep repentance *(metanoia)*. Ecumenical Patriarch Bartholomew writes:

The root cause of our environmental sin lies in our self-cen-teredness and in the mistaken order of values that we inherit and accept without any critical evaluation. We need a new way of thinking about our own selves, about our relationship with the world and with God. Without this revolutionary "change of mind," all our conservation projects, however well intentioned,

---

[78] Bookless, *Planet Wise*, 56.
[79] Brown, *Our Father's World*, 59.

will remain ultimately ineffective. For we shall be dealing only with the symptoms, not with their cause. Lectures and international conferences may help to awaken our conscience, but what is truly required is a baptism of tears.[80]

In the face of the contemporary ecological crisis it is becoming increasingly clear that we need a change of heart—a true *metanoia*—and a new sense of humility. We need what John Paul II in a January 17, 2001, General Audience called an "ecological conversion" if we are to manage to "finally stop before the abyss."[81] He wrote in *Peace with God the Creator, Peace with All Creation* that the needed "genuine conversion in ways of thought and behavior" (no. 13) is about learning to co-dwell in our common home of the earth with God the Creator and with our fellow creatures, including humans. In the same document he pointed out that the ecological conversion is precisely about establishing peace with the Creator and the rest of creation. It is about this conversion toward the Creator and the rest of creation that we offer a few reflections.

Return to the Creator

First of all, ecological conversion calls for a return to the Creator. The ecological crisis is, at the deepest level, "a rebellion against God as source and mystery of all created life, and our willful misuse of God's creation."[82] In this context Seyyed Hossein Nasr noted nearly half a century ago: "It is hopeless to expect to live in harmony with that grand theophany which is virgin nature, while remaining oblivious and indifferent to the Source of that theophany both beyond nature and at the center of man's being."[83] This profound realization is an ancient truth contained in the various religious traditions of humanity. Faith traditions have always emphasized that in order to have peace and harmony with the natural world, we must be in harmony and equilibrium with heaven, and ultimately with the Source and Origin of all things.[84] Human beings cannot expect to live in harmony with

---

[80] Ecumenical Patriarch Bartholomew, "Closing Address During the Concluding Ceremony for the Fourth International and Interreligious Symposium on the Adriatic Sea, June 10, 2002," in Chryssavgis, *Cosmic Grace, Humble Prayer*, 276.

[81] Pope John Paul II, General Audience Address (January 17, 2001).

[82] Quinn, *To Heal the Earth*, 26.

[83] Seyyed Hossein Nasr, *Man and Nature: The Spiritual Crisis of Modern Man* (London: Unwin, 1990), 9; originally published in 1968.

[84] See ibid., 136.

creation if they are not at peace with the Creator. Pope Benedict XVI speaks poignantly in this regard:

> The brutal consumption of creation begins where God is missing, where matter has become simply material for us, where we ourselves are the ultimate measure, where everything is simply our property. . . . The waste of creation begins where we no longer recognize any claim beyond ourselves, seeing only ourselves.[85]

> Is it not true that an irresponsible use of creation begins precisely where God is marginalized or even denied? If the relationship between human creatures and the Creator is forgotten, matter is reduced to a selfish possession, man becomes the "last word," and the purpose of human existence is reduced to a scramble for the maximum number of possessions possible.[86]

The ecological crisis reveals how the modern "gods" have displaced faith in a divine Creator and sacred respect for the order of creation. As Northcott writes: "The excess greenhouse gases produced by industrial capitalism are the fruits of the modern devotion to the gods of secular reason, technological power and monetary accumulation, and the sidelining of traditional understandings of community, justice and the sacred."[87] In the face of the contemporary ecological crisis, we require a genuine *metanoia*. In this vein, Pope John Paul II and Ecumenical Patriarch Bartholomew wrote in their "Common Declaration on the Environment" in 2002: "What is required is an act of repentance on our part and a renewed attempt to view ourselves, one another, and the world around us with the perspective of the divine design for creation."

Just as the consequences of human sin fall on the land, so too will the repentance of the people of God lead to the healing of the land. This is a profound ecological truth that we find in the scriptures. When people return to God and keep God's covenant, God will heal the land: "If my people who are called by my name humble themselves, pray, seek my face, and turn from their wicked ways, then I will hear from heaven, and will forgive their sin and heal their land" (2 Chr 7:14).

---

[85] Pope Benedict XVI, Meeting with Priests, Deacons, and Seminarians of the Diocese of Bolzano-Bressanone (August 6, 2008).

[86] Pope Benedict XVI, General Audience (August 26, 2009).

[87] Northcott, *A Moral Climate*, 14.

What is so significant is that healing the environment comes about not primarily by recycling, down-sizing or resource management, but by repentance and returning to God. The land can only be healed when its inhabitants recognize whose land it is, and repair their broken relationship with God and each other. If the ecological crisis is ultimately a spiritual crisis, then the cure is also a spiritual one.[88]

The conversion to the Creator in a humble and genuine spirit of repentance is fundamental, if we are to survive the contemporary ecological crisis and heal our land and ourselves. A theocentric focus is vital to the well-being of creation.[89]

A Turning to Creation

Ecological conversion calls for a turning *(metanoia)* to creation itself. This means recreating communion with all the members of our common household, both human and nonhuman, and with the rest of creation.

Ecological conversion is about turning back to our fellow humans, especially to the poor and most vulnerable members of our common family. As we have seen earlier, most of the manifestations of the ecological crisis like climate change and depletion of natural resources are caused primarily by rich communities and nations whose victims are poor and vulnerable communities. The crisis is caused mainly by our unsustainable lifestyles, dictated solely by the values of modern consumerism, which take a heavy toll on the bodies of the poor and of the planet's ecosystems. Therefore, a starting point of any genuine ecological conversion must be a profound change in our lifestyles.

If we wish to see our land healed and our poor brothers and sisters reinstated with equal rights into our common household, we need to change radically our lifestyles and our use of Earth's resources. As Pope John Paul II and Ecumenical Patriarch Bartholomew affirm in the "Common Declaration on the Environment," a solution to the ecological crisis "can be found only if we undergo, in the most radical way, an inner change of heart, which can lead to a change in lifestyle and a change of unsustainable patterns of consumption and production."

An ecological conversion is one ultimately to the Earth itself, the *adamah*, the *humus* from which humans originated. In the face of

---

[88] Bookless, *Planet Wise*, 58.

[89] Shannon Jung, *We Are Home: A Spirituality of the Environment* (Mahwah, NJ: Paulist Press, 1993), 60.

the contemporary ecological crisis—as it was in the aftermath of the original sin of our first parents—the Creator's command to humanity is to return to the earth and to till the ground from which they originally came.

> By the sweat of your face
>   you shall eat bread
> until you return to the ground,
>   for out of it you were taken;
> you are dust,
>   and to dust you shall return. . . .
> therefore the Lord God sent him forth from the gar-
>   den of Eden, to till the ground from which he
>   was taken. (Gn 3:19, 23)

Ecological conversion is about humanity's penitent return to the earth. In the context of the contemporary ecological crisis, it is obvious that the salvation of the earth is intimately tied to our humble return to it. Scripture scholar Brigitte Kahl writes:

> *Until you return to the earth. For from her you were taken.* Throughout the centuries, the "back to earth" of Gen. 3:19 has been almost exclusively remembered at the tombs of the dead. Its challenge to Christian life practices was seldom heard. But the text very explicitly talks about a change of direction, for the Hebrew word for *return* implies also the theological dimension of repentance, turning back to God. Taking the fruit of the forbidden tree has damaged the relationship not only between God and Adam, but also between Adam and Adama, as the *thorns and thistles* demonstrate. When Adam is sent out from the garden, his task to serve the earth is repeated by God.[90]

So a return to the earth is at the core of a genuine ecological conversion. It is also important to recall here that Jesus' own final commission to his disciples was to "go into all the world and proclaim the good news to the whole creation" (Mk 16:15). Our mission, our God-given great commission, includes the whole of creation, not just people. So today, in the context of the contemporary ecological crisis, we need to ask ourselves, What is the good news that we proclaim to the whole of creation?

---

[90] Kahl, "Fratricide and Ecocide," 57.

What is the good news for a rainforest that is being chopped down to feed our meat-hungry lifestyles? What is the good news for those who face the spread of deserts and failing crops as a result? What is the good news for creatures that God lovingly made but are now driven toward extinction? What is the good news for the world's climate systems as they become thrown off course by our polluting lifestyles?[91]

The *metanoia* of a genuine ecological conversion thus requires a return to the Creator, to our fellow humans—especially the poor and vulnerable—and to the *adamah*, the earth itself. The ecological crisis that we have described as a triple cry of the earth, of the poor, and of the gods requires nothing short of a triple conversion on the part of humanity.

---

[91] Bookless, *Planet Wise*, 135.

Conclusion

Responding to a Creation in Crisis

We began our journey by taking stock of the marvelous way in which Earth, the third planet from the sun, became a home for life, including human life, during a process that spanned billions of years. The contemporary ecological crisis is about the crisis of our common home, which we share not only with our fellow brothers and sisters, but also with millions of other forms of life in an intricate web of interrelationship and interdependence. The crisis, as I have sought to underline throughout the book, is markedly anthropogenic; it is caused by human activities. Our arrival in the common home of the earth has been very recent. For over 99.9 percent of Earth's history, humans were not around. And for 99.9 percent of human beings' relatively brief sojourn on Earth, our impact on Earth's ecosystems and natural cycles was barely evident. However, in the last few centuries—in a mere fraction of geological time termed the Anthropocene era, that is, the era of the humans—we have begun to jeopardize the capacity of the earth to be a home for humanity and for the rest of the biotic community. The ecological crisis is about the alarming state of our common home.

The rest of our journey—the second, third, and fourth parts of the book—was dedicated to understanding the contemporary ecological crisis. I described the crisis, in a symbolic way, as a triple cry of the earth, of the poor, and of the gods. The three aspects of the cry dealt with the physical, moral, and theological aspects of the crisis, respectively.

Part II, "The Cry of the Earth," offered a physical description of the contemporary ecological crisis based on authoritative studies from the scientific community. Part II dealt primarily with the problem of climate change, the most important of the multiple manifestations of the current ecological crisis. After a physical description of the phenomenon of global warming and associated climate change, we discussed on some of the major impacts of climate change: extreme meteorological events, droughts and desertification, melting of glaciers, sea-level rise, ocean acidification, and biodiversity loss. In addition to climate change, we also discussed other problems like species extinction. The present rate of biodiversity loss, unprecedented in the recent history of our planet, is a cause for serious alarm. It is feared that human activities are currently driving Earth toward a sixth mass extinction of species. We then examined some other major ecological challenges like pollution, waste, and depletion of natural resources. We are not only polluting our common home—its atmosphere, land, and waters—but also fast depleting its finite natural resources, including fresh water, so fundamental for life on Earth. The ecological crisis is a global crisis because it is about the whole of our common home and affects all of our common household, both human and nonhuman communities. The crisis also rings bells of alarm because, as in the case of climate change and of biodiversity loss, we are dangerously close to crucial tipping points.

Part III, "The Cry of the Poor," offered a moral perspective on the ecological crisis, examining the deleterious impacts of the crisis on some of the most basic areas of human life like nutrition, health, and shelter. In each of these areas, especially food security, the challenges raised by the crisis are formidable. The ecological crisis, in this regard, impinges on the fundamental human right to a dignified life. The tragic realization that the crisis will affect most the poor and the most vulnerable—those who have contributed least to causing the crisis—makes the contemporary ecological crisis one of the greatest ethical dilemmas of our age. The existing economic disparities and social inequalities are further exacerbated by the impacts of the ecological crisis. Our ecological predicament becomes a moral crisis, which in turn raises some profound questions regarding equity and justice. The ecological crisis is a clarion call for eco-justice.

Part IV, "The Cry of the Gods," sought to deepen our understanding of the contemporary ecological crisis. From a theological point of view our current ecological predicament is a spiritual and religious problem. The ecological crisis results primarily from our inability to look at the physical world as God's creation, as God's own home with humanity, as the supreme event of the incarnation. We appear to have become increasingly blind to the symbolic and sacramental dimension of creation, the primordial revelation of God's goodness and glory. The ecological crisis also results from our *hubris*, a refusal to accept our self-identity as creatures and our disobedience to the very first commandment given to humanity, namely, to be responsible stewards of God's creation (Gn 2:5). Our irresponsible stewardship of creation can rightly be called ecological sin and has negative repercussions for the rest of creation. In the final analysis, the ecological crisis results from our incapacity to respect the *telos* of God's creation, both here and now, as in the historical institution of Sabbath, and all the more in the eschatological sense of the final destiny of the entire creation to be recapitulated in Christ (Eph 1:9–10; Col 1:19–20). The spiritual dimension of the ecological crisis reveals how humanity stands in need of a profound ecological conversion.

As this book emphasizes throughout, it is important to look at the contemporary ecological scene from a triple perspective—physical, moral, and theological—in order to gain a more complete understanding of the crisis. Only such a holistic perspective can offer a total view of our ecological predicament, commensurate with the magnitude of the challenges ahead of us.

The contemporary ecological crisis is the greatest challenge that we have faced since our arrival on Earth. In the last few millennia human communities have had to grapple with local and regional ecological challenges. Examples abound in this regard. However, these past historical instances pale in comparison with the unique and unprecedented challenge thrown up by the contemporary ecological crisis. For the first time since modern humans spread around and occupied our common home, humanity is up against a truly global challenge. We are playing a reckless gamble with our common home and ultimately with our own survival.

The contemporary ecological crisis points to how humans have become a global geophysical force. Human activities today have the power to alter and disrupt stable climatic conditions as well as the fundamental biological and geochemical systems of our home planet, as evident in the present crisis. The destiny of the planet appears to be conditioned more than ever by the activities by one dominant species. Brian Swimme and Thomas Berry write:

> By now the human has taken over such extensive control of the life systems of the Earth that the future will be dependent on human decision to an extent never dreamed of in previous times. We are deciding what species will live or perish, we are determining the chemical structure of the soil and the air and the water, we are mapping out the areas of wilderness that will be allowed to function in their own natural modalities.[1]

---

[1] Brian Swimme and Thomas Berry, *The Universe Story: From the Primordial Flaring Forth to the Ecozoic Era: A Celebration of the Unfolding of the Cosmos* (New York: Penguin, 1992), 4.

No other generation has had to accept responsibility for the state of our home planet. "No generation has faced a challenge with the complexity, scale, and urgency of the one that we face."[2] Our actions today will determine the future not only of the present generations but also of future generations for millennia. As Sean McDonagh points out, "If this generation does not act, no future generation will be able to undo the damage that this generation has caused to the planet."[3] A 2011 report warns:

> This is a unique time in history—humanity is facing a future that is very different from the past. Decisions made now and over the next few decades will disproportionately influence the future. . . .
>
> Human activities have now become a dominant driver of the Earth system; decisions made now to mitigate their detrimental effects will have a very great influence on the environment experienced by future generations, as well as the diversity of plant and animal species with which they will share the planet.[4]

We live in a unique moment. It appears that humans now have to make the fundamental choice between life and death, not only for themselves, but also for their fellow creatures: "I call heaven and earth to witness against you today that I have set before you life and death, blessings and curses. Choose life so that you and your descendants may live" (Dt 30:19). As David W. Orr points out, no generation before our own could feel the full, global, and permanent weight of these words, but we can. "We are the generation that will choose between life and death, but now on a planetary scale and for all that will be born or could have been born."[5]

Truly, the ecological crisis places humanity at a crossroads with regard to its own future.

The response to the contemporary ecological crisis, which we have described as a triple cry of the earth, of the poor, and of the gods, is our generation's unique responsibility and opportunity. The magnitude of

---

[2] Lester Brown, *World on the Edge: How to Prevent Environmental and Economic Collapse* (London: Earthscan, 2011), xi.

[3] Sean McDonagh, *The Death of Life: The Horror of Extinction* (Dublin: Columba Press, 2004), 151.

[4] The Government Office for Science, *Foresight: The Future of Food and Farming: Final Project Report* (London: The Government Office for Science, 2011), 50.

[5] David W. Orr, "Foreword," in Nancy Roth, *Grounded in Love: Ecology, Faith, and Action* (Portland, OR: Ken Arnold Books, 2008), xv.

the ecological crisis is compounded by the urgency to act in order to stave off the worst consequences of the crisis. In the case of climate change, for example, a growing number of analyses indicate that the costs of both adapting to and mitigating climate change will escalate if action is postponed.[6] If we keep on delaying action, it will be too late. We have little time left to respond to the contemporary ecological crisis.

However, the tragic irony is that we are becoming increasingly deaf to the triple cry of the earth, of the poor, and of the gods. We continue to remain largely insensitive to the groaning of the planet, to the wailing of the millions of our poor brothers and sisters, and to the defilement of God's beautiful creation. Today, the triple cry of the earth, of the poor, and of the gods is unfortunately drowned in the cacophony of our times, ranging from the lulling but hallow promises of modern consumerism and neoliberal market economy, which are rapidly polluting the earth and depleting its finite resources, to the petty tribal wars fought in the name of religious fundamentalism, nationalist ideology, and cultural chauvinism. Saving our common home for ourselves, for future generations, and for our fellow species appears nowhere near the top of humanity's current list of priorities.

Humanity's failure to respond to the crisis reveals the human tendency for self-destruction. It is nothing less than a schizophrenic behavior for the humans to mutilate the womb of life that brought them into being, tear down the web of existence that sustains them, and devastate the planet that is home to them. Human civilization, unfortunately, appears to be marching down such a suicidal path, as revealed by the contemporary ecological crisis. Bertolt Brecht expresses in a very touching manner the folly of humanity in destroying planetary home.

> They sawed away the branches on which they sat,
> and exchanged their experiences in a loud voice,
> as to how to saw even more quickly,
> while some crashed to the ground,
> others shook their heads,
> and continued to saw away.[7]

---

[6] K. Richardson et al., "Synthesis Report from Climate Change: Global Risks, Challenges, and Decisions," Copenhagen, March 10–12, 2009 (Copenhagen: University of Copenhagen, 2009), 18.

[7] Bertolt Brecht, Exil III, in *Gedichte* V (Frankfurt am Main: Suhrkamp Verlag, 1964), 62.

When it comes to responding to the contemporary ecological crisis, we are at the most only making gestures in terms of half-hearted and piecemeal solutions. We live under the blissful illusion that a bit of recycling, signing an occasional treaty, and drawing up grandiose future projects for geo-engineering are all it will take to ward off the crisis. When it comes to responding to the global ecological crisis, international political leadership has fallen miserably short. Political initiative in this regard is largely reduced to routine high-level meetings that often end up with only pompous but practically futile summits and statements. In the case of climate change, for example, none of the recent summits has been able to produce mutually binding agreements among concerned parties. In response to the suffering of the poor caused by climate change and other manifestations of the ecological crisis, even the more socially sensitive individuals and communities largely end up soothing their conscience through a dose of public philanthropy and development aid—often attached to strings of self-interest—without addressing the more basic questions about justice and equality. Even the religious communities are still to wake up to the magnitude of the crisis that has fallen on God's creation, which is entrusted to human stewardship. As Thomas Berry observed in a speech in 1982, "Church authorities, religious orders, the Catholic universities and seminaries, priests and people have shown an amazing insensitivity to this most urgent of all issues confronting the human community. My question is: After we burn our lifeboat, how will we stay afloat?"[8]

Humanity's present awareness of and response to the ecological crisis hardly match the magnitude of the challenge. The stewarding of our home planet, on the proper conditions of which human life and all human endeavors inevitably and ultimately depend, is yet to become a major concern for us. Zeal for our common home is yet to inflame us. The coming years will be crucial, as we have little time left to pool our resources and energies to protect and heal our common planetary home.

There is, however, a silver lining in the dark clouds. The hopeful element with regard to the contemporary ecological crisis is that there is no dearth of resources to respond effectively to the triple cry of the earth, of the poor, and of the gods. We have valuable and abundant resources in the little and great wisdom traditions of humanity both in terms of practice and theory. The scriptural texts and faith traditions

---

[8] Quoted in Albert J. LaChance and John E. Carroll, eds., *Embracing Earth: Catholic Approaches to Ecology* (Maryknoll, NY: Orbis Books, 1994), x.

of the world's religions, for example, are a veritable repertoire in this regard. We also have concrete examples not only of outstanding historical figures like Henry David Thoreau and Mahatma Gandhi—just to cite two well-known protagonists—but also of thousands of grassroots level communities and movements all over the globe, especially among women and young people. The resources are there. We only need to look for them.

In looking for resources and inspiration to respond to the triple cry of the earth, of the poor, and of the gods, one example stands out—Francis of Assisi, the Poverello of Assisi. Francis of Assisi is at times reduced to an idealized nature mystic, in whom many modern eco-warriors find inspiration. Obviously, this is simplistic. The conversion of young Francis was indeed a triple conversion: to the whole of creation, to the poor, and ultimately to the very Creator. It was thus a total conversion. Francis's life—simple, compassionate, and saintly—was a real response to the triple cry of the earth, of the poor, and of the gods. In 1979 Pope John Paul II proclaimed Francis of Assisi the heavenly patron of ecology.[9] Later, in 1990, he stated:

> [Francis] offers Christians an example of genuine and deep respect for the integrity of creation. As a friend of the poor who was loved by God's creatures, Saint Francis invited all of creation—animals, plants, natural forces, even Brother Sun and Sister Moon—to give honor and praise to the Lord. The poor man of Assisi gives us striking witness that when we are at peace with God we are better able to devote ourselves to building up that peace with all creation which is inseparable from peace among all peoples.[10]

Francis of Assisi—significantly evoked by Pope Francis as a model for the guardianship of creation in the homily of the inaugural mass of his pontificate—was indeed one who listened to the triple cry of the earth, of the poor, and of the gods, and responded to each aspect. Like St. Francis, we too need to listen to the cry of the earth. We need to rediscover and love the earth as our home. For this, we need to look at the earth in a new way. "Francis did not look at the natural world from a utilitarian perspective. He did not see it as merely providing food, clothing and shelter for humans. Rather, his response to the gift

---

[9] John Paul II, Apostolic Letter, *Inter Sanctos*, AAS 71 (1979), 1509.
[10] John Paul II, "Peace with God the Creator, Peace with All of Creation," Message for the World Day of Peace (January 1, 1990), no. 16.

of creation was joy, wonder, praise and gratitude."[11] Today, we need to rediscover a joyful and grateful mode of existence in our marvelous common home. We also need to embrace the poor with the same love shown by Francis. We need to "re-member" the poor, gathering once again the fragments of the vulnerable and marginalized that the mighty and powerful have contemptuously flung to the peripheries of our society. We need to break together the miraculously multiplying loaf of bread that is the earth and share it with all of God's children. To embrace the poor, we also need to adopt a lifestyle that is sober and frugal, remembering the words of Jesus that it is only the meek who will inherit the earth (Mt 5:8). Above all, we need to return to the Creator, the original source and ultimate destiny of all creation. in "Peace with God the Creator, Peace with All of Creation," Pope John Paul II teaches that "if man is not at peace with God, then earth itself cannot be at peace" (no. 5). Today, as Ecumenical Patriarch Bartholomew points out, we need "a Copernican revolution of the spirit that will free the inner universe to no longer gravitate around the ego, be it individual or collective, but around the divine light itself."[12] In order to steward creation, we need to respect the divine design imprinted in creation and acknowledge the supremacy of the Creator rather than trying to usurp God's place for ourselves.

In order to respond to the triple cry of the earth, of the poor, and of the gods, we stand in need of a triple conversion as exemplified by the life of St. Francis of Assisi. In the wake of the contemporary ecological crisis we stand in need of a vision and a lifestyle that embrace all three sides of the relational triangle of reality. We do *not* need, as Peter-Hans Kolvenbach points out, "an anthropocentrism independent of God and the environment, a theocentrism that pretends to ignore creatures and all created things, a biocentrism that would ignore the Creator and the call to collaborate with him in relationship with the environment."[13] We need, rather, to weave together the cosmic, human, and divine strands of reality into a seamless fabric. We are called to dwell in the common home of the earth with all our fellow

---

[11] *The Cry of the Earth: A Pastoral Reflection on Climate Change by the Irish Catholic Bishops' Conference* (2009), 26.

[12] Ecumenical Patriarch Bartholomew, "Closing Remarks at the Conference on Peace and Tolerance in Istanbul, Turkey, February 9, 1994," in *Cosmic Grace, Humble Prayer: The Ecological Vision of the Green Patriarch Bartholomew*, ed. John Chryssavgis (Grand Rapids, MI: Eerdmans, 2009), 113.

[13] Peter-Hans Kolvenbach, "Our Responsibility for God's Creation," Address at the Opening of Arrupe College, Jesuit School of Philosophy and Humanities, Harare, Zimbabwe (August 22, 1998).

creatures in cosmic fellowship, in harmony with our fellow human beings in fraternal solidarity, and in harmony with God, the Creator, in creaturely dependence.

It is significant that the original etymological meaning of the word *crisis* in Greek does not have the negative connotation it has in English and other modern languages. It meant a propitious "opportunity" in the wake of a serious obstacle, a chance to pause and look back at the journey in order to give it a radically new direction. In fact, only a crisis brings real change. In this vein the contemporary ecological *crisis*, with all its grim prospects, holds a beacon of hope for humanity to enter into a new *kairos*. The crisis may offer at the same time a historical opportunity for change, provided we are willing to "under-stand" (humbly stand under) the crisis and be willing to undergo, like Francis of Assisi, a profound *metanoia*—the triple conversion to the earth, to the poor, and to the Creator. We owe such a conversion to ourselves, especially the poorest and weakest among us, to other forms of life on Earth that face the specter of extinction, and to future generations.

The task of responding to the triple cry of the earth, of the poor, and of the gods is urgent. We do not have much time left. Christians speak of God as our common Father in heaven. In the face of the ecological crisis we probably need to speak also of Mother Earth, just as St. Francis of Assisi did, looking at our home planet as the mother that sustains and nourishes us. Such spiritual paternity and earthly maternity are vital if we are to live in true solidarity with all the members, human and nonhuman, of the common household of our planetary home.

Index

www.ingramcontent.com/pod-product-compliance
Lightning Source LLC
Chambersburg PA
CBHW021845020426
42334CB00013B/190